DEVELOPMENTS IN ENGLISH HISTORICAL MORPHO-SYNTAX

CURRENT ISSUES IN LINGUISTIC THEORY

AMSTERDAM STUDIES IN THE THEORY AND HISTORY
OF LINGUISTIC SCIENCE – Series IV
ISSN 0304-0763

Current Issues in Linguistic Theory (CILT) is a theory-oriented series which welcomes contributions from scholars who have significant proposals that advance our understanding of language, its structure, its function and especially its historical development. CILT offers an outlet for meaningful contributions to current linguistic debate.
A complete list of titles in this series can be found on *http://benjamins.com/catalog/cilt*

Volume 346

Claudia Claridge and Birte Bös (eds.)

Developments in English Historical Morpho-Syntax

DEVELOPMENTS IN ENGLISH HISTORICAL MORPHO-SYNTAX

Edited by

CLAUDIA CLARIDGE
University of Augsburg

BIRTE BÖS
University of Duisburg-Essen

JOHN BENJAMINS PUBLISHING COMPANY
AMSTERDAM & PHILADELPHIA

The paper used in this publication meets the minimum requirements of the American National Standard for Information Sciences – Permanence of Paper for Printed Library Materials, ANSI Z39.48-1984.

DOI 10.1075/cilt.346

Cataloging-in-Publication Data available from Library of Congress:
LCCN 2019003730 (PRINT) / 2019018915 (E-BOOK)

ISBN 978 90 272 0323 6 (HB)
ISBN 978 90 272 6247 9 (E-BOOK)

John Benjamins Publishing Company · https://benjamins.com

Table of contents

Introduction

Claudia Claridge and Birte Bös

1. Survey

English has a long and rich history. It started out as a small Germanic language in the North Sea area and has meanwhile become a wide-spread, highly diverse world language. In linguistic form English has also moved on from its typically (West) Germanic beginnings, dropping considerable morphological baggage as well as acquiring syntactic rules and constructions that led to a wide-ranging (typological) restructuring (e.g. Hawkins, 2012: 624–625). The first point above is not a major aspect of this volume, but nevertheless four chapters link to it, one highlighting the North-Sea family relationships by comparing Old English and Old Frisian (Colleran) and three others either focussing completely on the major modern post-colonial variety, American English (Schützler; Schwarz), or comparing it with British English (Vosberg & Rohdenburg). All papers are concerned with the second aspect mentioned above, with four taking a morphophonological fact as their anchor (Adamczyk; Middeke; Nykiel; Rohdenburg) and the remainder dealing with syntactic constructions and word order.

Due to a mix of factors like phonological attrition, already far-reaching syncretism, and language contact, morphological change since Old English has involved mostly loss or reduction, in line with Sapir's (1921, 160–182) drift towards the "invariable word" and the change towards a more analytic language. As English still retains some synthetic elements, we are often not dealing with simple loss, but with intricate restructuring of the inflectional system, the dynamics of which can be and is here described in more detail for the Old English nominal system (Adamczyk). Loss can be a fairly protracted affair and deaths proclaimed somewhat prematurely, however. The decline of the English subjunctive, for example, has not led to its death, but to an interesting history of waning, reviving, and surviving in niches (cf. Leech et al., 2009: Chapter 3). Similarly, the half-dead Old English instrumental might have been somewhat less ailing than usually claimed (Middeke). In contrast to cases of loss, even a language on the road to analyticity may give some morphemes/morphological processes a new lease of life. An instance of such a success story is *-ing*, a formal-functional conflation of various morphemes with

https://doi.org/10.1075/cilt.346.01cla

multiple uses and high frequency in modern English (De Smet & Heyvaert, 2011; Fonteyn & Van De Pol, 2016). Another instance is originally adjectival *-ly*, given the new and now highly productive task of forming adverbs, but making its way through the system only slowly (Rohdenburg). At the borderline of morphology, cliticization can at any time also create new complex unified forms in the language, which may have specific characteristics without being either integrated into a coherent system or long-lasting (Nykiel).

In the syntactic area, the developments in English have prominently involved word order changes and the evolution of various periphrastic constructions. Some, such as word order, may be seen as a consequence of morphological change, but by no means all. While the tendency of English to have a multi-word item do the work that a single unit might do (e.g. in another language) is an analytic tendency, many or most of these combinations do not replace earlier synthetic forms. It is such constructions and the auxiliaries they include that are the focus of the chapters dealing with the verbal area, namely modal (Wischer; Bemposta-Rivas; Colleran), aspectual/perfect (Huber; Calvo Cortes) and passive (Schwarz) constructions. They can be seen as instances of grammaticalization, as most of the authors here do, or as constructionalizations (e.g. Traugott & Trousdale, 2013). They also fall under Leisi and Mair's (2008, 94–111) concept of *Wortverband*, i.e. more or less fixed word bundles with a specific meaning or function. In the case of lexically filled bundles, such as phrasal verbs, one may rather speak of lexicalized items. The chunk *far from* (Vosberg & Rohdenburg) in a downtoning function may be developing in this direction.

As just indicated, the contributions of this volume are grouped under three headings to be introduced in the following sections: I. nominal constructions, II. verbal constructions, and III. adverbs and adverbials.

2. Nominal constructions

The three papers in **Section I** focus on Old and Middle English nominal phenomena. Nominal inflections have been the target of reduction and analogical restructuring processes since Old English (and even before). The interplay of the factors frequency and salience for such processes in Old English is highlighted in Elzbieta **Adamczyk**'s contribution. Frequency, both in relative and absolute terms, may exert its influence on four different levels, namely frequency of a specific paradigm form, lemma token frequency, paradigm type frequency and the ratio of singular to plural. The morphophonological salience of inflectional suffixes in a paradigm, both replaced and replacing ones, interacts with frequency to produce "local" analogical changes within paradigms first, leading to more extensive changes later.

Other factors, such as crucially the overlap between paradigms, are also shown to play a relevant role.

In contrast, the contribution by Kirsten **Middeke** is concerned with a case of at least temporary resilience against morphological reduction processes. The Old English instrumental, often considered a minor relic, is shown to be a functionally distinct and productive case. According to Middeke's analysis, the instrumental can still be clearly separated from the dative by its specialisation for adverbials of time, place, and manner, which is a logical result of its syncretistic origins as a conflation of ablative, instrumental and locative. Further, there are indications that its occurrences are not due to fossilisation or fixed collocations, but at least partly caused by ongoing productivity driven by semantic principles, as indicated by a collexeme analysis.

The final paper here, by Jerzy **Nykiel**, deals not with inflection, but with cliticization and phonological processes within noun phrases as well as their consequences for the latter's syntactic behaviour. The superficially similar-looking forms *thother, thone,* and *tother, tone* behave differently, as the *th*-forms are never preceded by the definite article *the*, whereas the *t*-forms are variably accompanied by it. This can be explained by the former including reduced and cliticized forms of the article and thus themselves being analysable as determiner plus noun structure and therefore excluding the presence of another article. The *t*-forms, in contrast, show variant determiner because of two potential rival analyses of the forms, either as cliticized instances or as syllabic mis-segmentations of, e.g., *that* + *other*. While clitics may turn into or develop out of inflectional material, here we find a fairly short-lived instance without lasting influence in the system.

3. Verbal constructions

The interest in periphrastic constructions involving auxiliaries has certainly not abated since their treatment took up more than half the space of Denison's (1993) historical treatment of verbal constructions. The six contributions in **Section II**, the largest of this volume, also attest to this. Unsurprisingly, grammaticalization also looms large in most papers.

The more theory-oriented chapter by Rebecca **Colleran** uses grammaticalization as a methodological tool for finding evidence for or against three competing explanatory scenarios of attestable Old English and Old Frisian similarities, namely drift, contact (with resultant borrowing), or common inheritance. Two case studies, one on the auxiliarisation of the preterite-present verb *agan* and one on the participle as verb complement, are shown to be marked by such wide-ranging similarity with regard to semantic, combinatorial and phonological features as to call them globally shared grammaticalizations. This, together with the diagnostic of attesting the presence of (the same) intermediate steps of the grammaticalization process in both Old English and Old Frisian, makes Colleran decide for inheritance as the most likely of the three scenarios.

The following two contributions fall into the field marked by *agan* above, namely preterite-present and later auxiliary verbs. Ilse **Wischer**'s chapter focuses on the Old English uses of *wolde* and *sceolde*, which were formally past tense but functionally already more diverse than their form suggested. She shows, on the basis of a verse corpus, that their auxiliarisation was already prevalent in Old English, that they already specialized to a great extent in dynamic (*wolde*) and deontic (*sceolde*) modality, but that nuclei of later temporal uses are also present. Her analysis nicely highlights the connection between inflectional syncretism (here past indicative and subjunctive), contextual semantics, and syntax in this instance of grammaticalization.

Sofia **Bemposta-Rivas** moves on to the post-Old English history of such verbs and sets out to disentangle the complex web of the uses of three of them, *dare, tharf* and *need,* in Middle and Early Modern English. The confusion between these verbs attestable in her corpus data is due to a mix of orthographical as well as phonological similarity, and semantic and syntactic conflation centring on the meaning 'necessity'. This state of affairs leads both to the ultimate demise (in Middle English) of *tharf* and to *dare* exhibiting more lexical features instead of the expected auxiliary/modal ones. It is in this respect that *dare* may be called a counterexample to the posited unidirectionality in grammaticalization – and thus different from Wischer's *would* and *should.*

The next two chapters deal with the long-standing, but meanwhile defunct, variation between the auxiliaries *be* and *have* in perfect(–like) constructions. Judith **Huber** puts differing accounts of this BE/HAVE 'rivalry' to the test in her study of Middle English motion verbs. The choice of *be* or *have* with past participle is shown to depend on three major factors, namely, counterfactuality in an almost categorical manner, followed by *aktionsart*, and finally by the form of the auxiliary. Controlling for various factors and using logistic regression analysis allows her to both confirm parts of earlier accounts (e.g. with regard to *aktionsart*), but to also add new insights, such as the importance of counterfactuality.

Focusing on the same kind of variational context, Nuria **Calvo Cortes**' contribution on Jane Austen's usage of *be* and *have* in the Late Modern English period adds other, partly extra-systemic aspects. It combines a socio-stylistic approach, comparing private letters with novels, with a cognitive-semantic one, using the figure-ground semantic construal as a parameter of choice. With regard to the first aspect, greater use of *be* in letters versus *have* in the novels is interpreted as conservativeness on the part of Austen and as a potential effect of prescriptive grammar. The second aspect is shown to be at most a lexical, not a general, effect.

The final contribution in this section focuses on a late-comer in the realm of voice. The study by Sarah **Schwarz** on *get*-passives in American English from 1870 to 1990 attests to the ongoing grammaticalization of this construction. Indicators of this process are found in an increasing frequency of inanimate subjects, a greater range of past participial types and fewer high frequency ones, and a spread to non-conclusive situation types like activity and momentary act. The latter is noticeable in the fiction genre, which generally leads in the rise of the *get*-passive, while other genres illustrate the delayed acceptance of such informal changes in (formal) written registers.

4. Adverbs and adverbials

The chapters in **Section III** fall into two groups, the first dealing with the sentence level and the second with the phrase level. The first two contributions thus share a concern with constituent order and information structure. The study by Susanne **Chrambach** shows how word order change, information structure principles and other discourse factors intersect to bring about a shift in the default preference of adverbial sequencing within the clause. The fixing of verb position favours adverbials following verbs and thus locative adverbials as the more likely obligatory element in first position. Simultaneously, the shift from short deictic to longer referential time adverbials puts time adverbials last, in line with new after given information. Late Middle English is identified as the crucial period for this shift to the sequence place-before-time adverbial as opposed to vice versa in all earlier periods.

Ole **Schützler**'s chapter focuses on the positions of adverbial clauses, headed by the concessive conjunctions *although, though* and *even though,* relative to their matrix clause in late 19th and late 20th century American English. Among the variables: subordinator choice, semantic type of clause, syntactic type, length of concessive clause in syllables, genre and period, it is the conjunction as well as the semantic and syntactic clause type that show the clearest effects. *Even though* tends most strongly towards final position and also towards heading longer clauses. All three conjunctions increasingly prefer finite clauses, which in turn prefer final position. With both *although* and *though,* content and epistemic concessive are more often sentence-initial, whereas speech-act concessives are more likely in final position.

The final two chapters share a focus on degree-marking adverbials with rivalling variant forms. The contribution by Günter **Rohdenburg** charts a systematic roadmap for the increasing morphological marking of intensifiers (e.g. *mighty* > *mightily*) during early and late modern English. His proposed verbality cline, predicting greater proportions of *-ly* forms with more verb-like structures (e.g. past participles vs. present participle/adjective, predicative vs. attributive uses) is shown to have wide-reaching explanatory force, leaving only manner adverbs and prepositional phrases in further need of more detailed investigation. Methodologically, the study shows the value of combining several large databases of various kinds and of looking both at pooled category data and at individual forms. It thus highlights the systematic nature of change, on the one hand, and the idiosyncratic behaviour of some lexemes, on the other hand.

The co-occurrence of quasi-downtoning *far from* with either copular *being* or with zero is the topic of the paper by Uwe **Vosberg** and Günter **Rohdenburg**. The competition of the two variants, which can be traced back to the 17th century, is shown by extensive analysis, involving a wide range of sources, to be sensitive to linguistic complexity and to regional variety. In line with the Complexity Principle, more complex predicative items, such as morphologically complex adjectives and syntactically complex noun phrases, induce the use of *far from being* as the more explicit variant and thus the one easier to process. The less explicit zero variant is installed in suitable contexts earlier and more frequently in British English, with American English lagging behind, while the latter more recently surpasses British English in its use of zero forms. Thus, the form under investigation is an instance of Hundt's (2009) lag-and-overtake scenario.

This last contribution takes us to the recent state of English, whereas the first contribution concerned Old English. The foci of the present volume are indeed the first and the most recent periods in the history of English, with four papers on Old English and five on (Late) Modern English. It is this latter focus, in particular, that highlights the recent interest in Late Modern English as a period in its own right (e.g. Tieken-Boon van Ostade, 2009) and generally in changes from the 18th century onwards and ongoing. Equally the present interest in the historical depth of (newer) English varieties is emphasized by three contributions focusing on American English. Besides this shift in focus, this volume provides a nuanced approach to many core phenomena and issues in the morphosyntactic history of English, shedding new light on them with the help of more or innovatively combined data, by applying new methods to data, or by taking a fresh theoretical perspective.

References

Denison, David (1993). *English Historical Syntax*. London: Longman.

Fonteyn, Lauren, & Van De Pol, Nikki (2016). Divide and conquer: the formation and functional dynamics of the Modern English *ing*-clause network. *English Language and Linguistics*, 20(2), 185–219. https://doi.org/10.1017/S1360674315000258

Hawkins, John A. (2012). The drift of English toward invariable word order from a typological and Germanic perspective. In Elizabeth Closs Traugott, & Terttu Nevalainen (Eds.), *The Oxford Handbook of the History of English* (622–632). Oxford: Oxford University Pres.

Hundt, Marianne (2009). Colonial lag, colonial innovation or simply language change? In Günter Rohdenburg, & Julia Schlüter (Eds.), *One Language, Two Grammars? Differences between British and American English* (13–37). Cambridge: Cambridge University Press. https://doi.org/10.1017/CBO9780511551970.002

Leech, Geoffrey, Hundt, Marianne, Mair, Christian, & Smith, Nicholas (2009). *Change in Contemporary English. A Grammatical Study*. Cambridge: Cambridge University Press. https://doi.org/10.1017/CBO9780511642210

Leisi, Ernst, & Mair, Christian (2008). *Das heutige Englisch: Wesenszüge und Probleme*. 9th edition. Heidelberg: Winter.

Sapir, Edward (1921). *Language: An introduction to the study of speech*, New York: Harcourt, Brace & World.

De Smet, Hendrik, & Heyvaert, Liesbet. (2011). The meaning of the English present participle. *English Language and Linguistics*, 15(3), 473–498. https://doi.org/10.1017/S136067431100013X

Tieken-Boon van Ostade, Ingrid (2009). *An Introduction to Late Modern English*. Edinburgh: Edinburgh University Press.

Traugott, Elizabeth Closs, & Trousdale, Graeme (2013). *Constructionalization and Constructional Changes*. Oxford: Oxford University Press. https://doi.org/10.1093/acprof:oso/9780199679898.001.0001

The dynamics of changes in the early English inflection

Evidence from the Old English nominal system

Elżbieta Adamczyk

This study examines the mechanisms of the reorganisation of the Old English nominal morphology, which embraced a range of phonological and analogical developments conditioned by a variety of factors deriving from different domains. The immediate consequences of these changes are most prominent in the minor (unproductive) declensional classes, whose inflection tended to be remodelled on the patterns of the major (productive) paradigms. The focus of the study is primarily on three factors which had a major impact on the restructuring patterns of the Old English nominal morphology: frequency of occurrence, morpho-phonological salience of inflectional exponents and the formal inflectional overlap across paradigms. Interacting mostly in a synergetic way, they largely determined the shape of the nominal system as it is known now in modern English. The analysed material demonstrates as well that the dynamics of the changes in the nominal system worked towards retaining or enhancing the functionality of the system.

Keywords: Old English, nominal morphology, frequency of occurrence, morpho-phonological salience

1. Introduction

The present paper discusses the transformation of the early English nominal system, concentrating on the patterns of reorganisation of nominal paradigms and the mechanisms involved in this process. The Old English nominal system formed a complex structure, organised into a range of declensional classes with distinct inflectional profiles, originally depending on the stem type. The system was characterised by an increasing number of syncretisms within and across paradigms, which contributed to the instability of many declensional classes. The focus of the present study is on analogical developments which led to a gradual demise of the original stem type distinctions and thus to a decline in the declensional class

https://doi.org/10.1075/cilt.346.02ada

diversity. The changes in the shape of the nominal paradigms, triggered primarily by phonological developments, are evinced in the gradual infiltration of analogical inflections from the productive paradigms (*a*-stems, *ō*-stems and *n*-stems) into the unproductive ones. The resulting fluctuation between the inherited and analogical inflections is most prominently attested in the following declensional types (minor classes): *i*-stems, *u*-stems, root nouns, *r*-stems, *s*-stems, *nd*-stems and dental stems (*þ*-stems). With the increasing amount of analogical inflection in their paradigms, these classes tended to lose their integrity and the status of independent declensional types. The minor paradigms shared a number of characteristics which had a bearing on the patterns of inflectional restructuring. These included: (a) the lack of productivity (as defined by Wurzel, 1989: 149), (b) the presence of morphophonemic alternations in the paradigms as exponents of case and number, i.e. *i*-mutation and consonantal alternations (*r*-formative and *þ*-formative) in the NOM./ACC.PL., GEN.SG. and DAT.SG., and (c) a specific quantitative profile, with low type frequency and high token frequency (e.g. *mann, sunu, fæder, burg*). All these minor paradigms attest to traces of analogical inflections from the productive patterns, which tended to increasingly oust the inherited inflectional endings. The ultimate shape of these minor paradigms and the degree to which they succumbed to the external analogical pressures of other declensional types depended upon some further class-specific properties, including the phonological structure, frequency and semantic profiles.

The question of the reorganisation of nominal paradigms in early English, although recognised in the existing research on early Germanic nominal morphology, has not been subjected to a systematic investigation of a quantitative nature. In the standard grammars of Old English (e.g. Brunner, 1965; Campbell, 1977; Hogg & Fulk, 2011), the restructuring tendencies involving analogical reshufflings in the declensional classes are qualitatively observed and briefly discussed; none of them, however, provides an exhaustive description of these developments. Some observations about this phenomenon have been made in a number of individual studies on morphological developments in Old English (e.g. Bertacca, 2009; Hogg, 1997; Lass, 1997; Kastovsky, 1995, 1997; Krygier, 1998, 2002, 2004), where especially the question of a taxonomic classification of Old English nouns has been addressed. An early systematic study where a fruitful attempt was made at a quantitative framing of the changes in the nominal system of Early Old English was Dahl's (1938) investigation, which focuses on the vocalic stems, including the productive classes of the *a*-stems and *ō*-stems. None of these studies, however, have explicitly addressed the question of the mechanisms involved in the restructuring of the nominal inflectional system in Old English. The aim of the present study is to discuss these mechanisms by identifying the factors involved in this process, and the interactions between them. The focus of this investigation will be in particular on three conditioning factors that played a major role in the process, namely the frequency of occurrence (use), the salience of inflectional exponents and the formal overlap between productive and unproductive paradigms. The interplay between these factors turns out to account for most of the restructuring patterns identified in the Old English material. On the conceptual plane, the study follows the usage-based theoretical paradigm, where language is conceived of as a dynamic system conditioned by a complex interplay of competing factors, which strives to achieve a balance and to increase its functionality, and linguistic structure is shaped by or emerges from language use (e.g. Langacker, 1988; Bybee, 1985, 1995, 2001).

The paper is organised in the following way: The major tendencies and patterns that can be identified in the gradual analogical remodelling of the minor stem paradigms, both qualitative and quantitative, will be outlined in Section 2. The subsequent Section 3 discusses the factors conditioning the changes in the nominal inflection (Section 3.1, 3.2, 3.3, 3.4) and their interactions (Section 3.5). The correlations between the patterns of change in the paradigms and individual factors are illustrated by the data from selected minor declensions. Section 4 summarises the major findings of the study and their implications for the mechanisms of the restructuring of the Old English inflection.

2. Restructuring of the Old English nominal inflection: Major tendencies

The process of the reorganisation of the Old English nominal inflection and paradigms was a cumulative effect of *inter*paradigmatic and *intra*paradigmatic analogical developments. The latter refer to the elimination or reduction of the allomorphy originally present in the paradigms, in particular the loss of *i*-mutated vowels and their replacement by unmutated vowels from other paradigm forms (especially in the NOM./ACC.PL. of the *s*-stems, and in the DAT.SG. of root nouns and monosyllabic *nd*-stems), as well as the loss of consonantal alternations (from the paradigms of the *s*-stems, root nouns and dental stems). The levelling of morphophonemic alternations, instigated by the working of *intra*paradigmatic analogy, interacted with the external pressure from other paradigms and classes (*inter*paradigmatic analogy), potentially facilitating the extension of new inflectional markers (Adamczyk, 2018: 121–126). These *inter*paradigmatic developments, involving the analogical shifts of nouns between declensional classes, are the primary focus of the quantitative part of this study.

The process of the reorganisation of the nominal inflection in English was an early development, dating back before the time of the first written attestations. In formal terms, two stages of the restructuring of the declensional system can be distinguished: (1) the early, pre-Old English transfers of nouns to productive declensions and (2) the later, historical transfers, attested in the Old English period. Importantly, such a division has a purely practical rationale, and it is not to be interpreted in absolute terms but rather as an abstraction: the process of inflectional transformation was a dynamic and continuous development that began at the prehistoric stage and continued into the historical period. The prehistoric dating of the process is manifested, for instance, in the Old English forms of the GEN.PL. (*-a*) and DAT.PL. (*-um*), which in many minor paradigms cannot be a continuation of the etymological forms, but must be interpreted as the effects of analogical remodelling on the pattern furnished by the expanding *a*-stems and *ō*-stems (but cf. incidental, relic GEN.PL. *i*-stem *winiġa*; e.g. Campbell, 1977: 241, 258; Boutkan, 1995: 262, 268, 275). Another category where the early influence of the productive inflections is identifiable is the GEN.SG. in masculine nouns, which surfaced predominantly with the expansive *a*-stem marker *-es* (e.g. *u*-stem *flōres* 'floor', root noun *fōtes* 'foot', *s*-stem *cealfes* 'calf', *nd*-stem *frēondes* 'friend' instead of the historical *flōra, fēt, calfur, frēond*). The second stage of the restructuring process, which can be captured with all its complexity, belongs to the attested Old English period. The discussion in the present paper concentrates on this second stage, relying largely on the findings from a comprehensive, quantitative study of the reorganisation of the nominal inflection in Old English (Adamczyk, 2018). The investigation of the Old English material was conducted on the complete collection of the Old English texts from the *Dictionary of Old English Electronic Corpus* (Healey et al., 2009). The analysis involved identifying all inflectional forms belonging to nouns affiliated with the relevant minor declensions and interpreting them as *archaic* (i.e. etymological) or *innovative* (i.e. analogical). The focus of the quantitative analysis was on the relation between the incidence of archaic and analogical inflections in the paradigms. The scale of the dissemination of the analogical inflections in the paradigms was an index of their level of innovation, reflecting how far a given paradigm departed from its etymological inflectional shape.[1]

Table 1 presents the competing inflections in two selected minor stem paradigms, the monosyllabic *nd*-stems (*frēond* 'friend') and dental stems (*hæleð* 'hero') (Adamczyk, 2018: 215, 222; cf. Campbell, 1977: 257; 259–260; Hogg & Fulk, 2011: 61–63). It must be emphasised that the restructuring of inflections hardly ever involved entire paradigms; instead, it is rather individual paradigm forms that were analogically remodelled on the template provided by the productive declensions.

The phonological profile of the paradigms greatly affected the shape of the nominal inflection, constituting the trigger for analogical reshufflings between classes. Two phonological tendencies had a profound influence on the dynamics of the restructuring process in Old English, namely, the more or less consistent presence of *i*-mutation in certain minor classes (root nouns, monosyllabic *nd*-stems)

1. Due to the limitation of space, the details concerning the procedure applied in the quantitative analysis as well as exact figures for all investigated paradigms are not included. More detailed information can be found in Adamczyk, 2018: 68–76 and 137–140.

Table 1. The competing inflections in the Old English *nd*-stem and dental stem paradigms*

	monosyllabic *nd*-stems				dental stems			
	archaic		innovative		archaic		innovative	
	SG.	PL.	SG.	PL.	SG.	PL.	SG.	PL.
NOM.	*frēond*	frīend, frȳnd	*frēond*	frēond**as**	*hæle*	hæleð	*hæle(ð)*	hæleð**as**
GEN.	frīend, frēond	*frēonda*	frēond**es**	*frēonda*	hæleð	*hæleða*	hæleð**es**	*hæleða*
DAT.	frīend, frȳnd	*frēondum*	frēond**e**	*frēondum*	hæleð	*hæleðum*	hæleð**e**	*hæleðum*
ACC.	*frēond*	frīend, frȳnd	*frēond*	frēond**as**	*hæle*	hæleð	*hæle(ð)*	hæleð**as**

* The endings marked in bold are analogical inflections from the productive classes, which provide information on the level of innovation in the paradigms. The forms marked in italics are those in which no synchronic alternation could be captured on account of their overlap with the forms of the productive declensional types (*neutral* forms).

and the progressive process of attrition of vowels in unaccented syllables, with its wider scope in Late Old English. A direct consequence of the latter development was the emergence of syncretisms across declensional paradigms, which opened the way for interparadigmatic analogical interactions.

One of the overarching patterns identified in the examined material concerns the directions of the interdeclensional transitions of nouns. They are summarised in Table 2 for the individual declensional classes, including gender and (where relevant) stem-type distinctions (cf. Adamczyk, 2018: 299).

The analogical transitions of nouns affiliated originally with minor classes turn out to be almost entirely polarised by two dominant classes, the masculine *a*-stems and feminine *ō*-stems, the former increasingly prevailing with the gradual loss of stability of the gender system at the beginning of the Middle English

Table 2. Directions of interdeclensional transfers of minor stems in Old English

	historical declensional class	new declensional class
masculine stems	*i*-stems	= > *a*-stems
	u-stems	= > *a*-stems
	root nouns	= > *a*-stems
	r-stems	= > *a*-stems
	monosyllabic *nd*-stems	= > *a*-stems
	disyllabic *nd*-stems	= > *a*-stems, adjectival infl.
	þ-stems	= > *a*-stems
neuter stems	*i*-stems	= > *a*-stems
	s-stems	= > *a*-stems (m, n)
feminine stems	*i*-stems	= > *ō*-stems
	u-stems	= > *ō*-stems
	root nouns	= > *ō*-stems
	r-stems	= > *ō*-stems, *a*-stems

period. The trend is a continuation of the analogical developments present already in Proto-Germanic, where the gradual dissemination of the *a*-stem and *ō*-stem inflections began. Another potential attractor of minor stems, the *n*-stem inflection, does not display extensive traces of productivity at this early stage; weak inflections appear occasionally, for instance, in the GEN.PL. (*-ena*, *-ana*, e.g., *æpplena* 'of apples' *wudana* 'of forests') and NOM./ACC.PL. (*-an*, e.g. *nosan* 'noses', *feldæn* 'fields'), but this tendency is clearly a marginal phenomenon. They tend to be more frequent in the feminine nouns and, in terms of the distribution across declensional classes, in the *u*-stem paradigms. Altogether, the influence of the *n*-stem inflection is very limited, especially when seen from the perspective of the Middle English period, where this inflectional pattern was much more widespread, especially in the southern dialects (Wełna, 1996: 88–90; cf. Hogg & Fulk, 2011: 124–129).

Another characteristic of the restructuring process is the nearly consistent preservation of gender alongside the change of declension class affiliation, with the masculine and neuter nouns following the *a*-stem inflection, and the feminine nouns following the *ō*-stems (cf. Carstairs-McCarthy, 1994). As becomes apparent on a closer examination, this gender consistency is to some extent distorted, and consequently the influence of the masculine *a*-stem inflection in the paradigms of feminine nouns can be observed. This refers in particular to the two most stable inflectional exponents, i.e. the GEN.SG. *-es* and the NOM./ACC.PL. *-as*, which can be found in the feminine *u*-stems and root nouns, especially in Late Old English (e.g. *cuus* 'cow', *fures* 'fir', *nihtes* 'night', *mōdres* 'mother' (*r*-stem); *ācas* 'oaks', *bōcas* 'books', *burgas* 'towns', *flōras* 'floors'). Admittedly, their dissemination did not necessarily entail a change in gender affiliation, but testifies rather to the pervasiveness of these two remarkably stable inflectional exponents.

Table 3 presents the distribution of analogical inflections (referred to as *innovative*) in the individual minor classes, including the incidence with respect to number, but irrespective of case or stem-type distinction. Importantly, the *total* figures represent aggregated values and do not capture many details of the distributions in the individual classes and paradigms. One of the tendencies to be observed in the data is the demonstrably divergent pattern of inflectional restructuring in the singular and plural across all minor declensional classes.

Taking the figures at face value, it must be concluded that the class of *s*-stems and the residual class of dental stems (*þ*-stems) were the most innovative types, where the level of innovation reached more than 60%. The root nouns, *i*-stems and *r*-stems turn out to have been in general the least conducive to analogical pressures from the productive *a*- and *ō*-stems, but at the same time they show strikingly divergent levels of innovation in the singular and plural. The low level of innovation in the *i*-stems is partly a result of this bias as well, but primarily a consequence of the fact that only several subclasses of the *i*-stems could be included in the investigation, i.e. those which attested to fluctuations between archaic and

Table 3. Distribution of innovative inflections in the OE minor stems with respect to number (cf. Adamczyk, 2018: 227–228)*

declension type	% innov. SG.	% innov. PL.	% total innov.
i-stems	10% (n = 1563)	80% (n = 410)	28%
u-stems	40% (n = 2948)	71% (n = 617)	45%
root nouns	27% (n = 2208)	6% (n = 1344)	21%
r-stems	9% (n = 2057)	82% (n = 1184)	36%
s-stems	90% (n = 238)	42% (n = 205)	69%
monosyll. *nd*-stems	75% (n = 309)	9% (n = 1110)	53%
disyll. *nd*-stems	93% (n = 893)	74% (n = 270)	
þ-stems	77% (n = 574)	38% (n = 278)	64%

* The figures in brackets refer to a total number of singular and plural tokens (n), excluding the tokens which were *neutral*, i.e. overlapping with the forms of the productive types and thus not informative about the restructuring process.

innovative inflections. In the other subtypes of the *i*-stems the restructuring process occurred at the prehistoric stage and thus could not be captured in the analysis. Different stages of inflectional development are found in the two types of *nd*-stems, mono- and disyllabic ones, the former largely preserving the archaic inflection in the plural, the latter being substantially more innovative. In most minor classes the paradigm of the singular tended to be more easily and earlier remodelled on the pattern of the productive classes than the plural. The high amount of innovation in the singular is to be ascribed predominantly to the category of the GEN.SG., which, irrespective of the class, was very susceptible to analogical influence. This analogical pressure came primarily from the *a*-stem masculine marker *-es*, which emerges as a very stable and salient inflectional exponent, whose spread began prior to the first written attestations of English. The classes where the pattern of restructuring is clearly reversed are the root nouns, monosyllabic *nd*-stems and dental stems; in all these paradigms, the plural turned out to be much more conservative than the singular. In order to account for these largely divergent distributions of analogical forms across the minor declensional classes, a number of factors needs to be examined and their share in the restructuring process evaluated.[2]

2. It should be noted that the figures for the plural are based on the two more frequent cases, i.e. the NOM. and ACC. (PL.), whereas the figures for the singular predominantly on the GEN. and DAT. (SG.), which are essentially the less frequent cases and are thus more prone to analogical modification. This contrast is a result of the fact that only forms that did not overlap with the forms of the productive declensions could be informative about the restructuring process (cf. Table 1). This does not hold for the light-syllable vocalic stems (*i*-stems and *u*-stems), where the NOM./ACC.SG. were included in the counting as they attested to synchronic alternation between archaic and innovative inflections, too (e.g. *i*-stem *mete* vs. *mett* 'food', *u*-stem *sidu* vs. *sida* 'custom').

3. Factors affecting the dynamics of changes in the nominal paradigms

The attested diverse levels of innovation in the paradigms of individual minor classes can be attributed to a range of interrelated factors, whose interaction could have enhancing or neutralising effects on the restructuring patterns. The major factors which directly affected the dynamics of the reorganisation of the minor paradigms included: (1) the frequency of occurrence/use, (2) the salience of inflectional exponents (both of the etymological and the analogical ones) and (3) the percentage of *neutral* forms, i.e. forms overlapping with those from the productive paradigms. These factors could work towards retention or innovation of inflectional patterns. More specifically, high (token) frequency and salience of the *archaic* marker tended to have a conserving effect, reflecting the entrenchment of the inherited inflections, whereas salience of the *innovative* marker and the presence of neutral forms in the paradigms facilitated analogical levelling, thus contributing to higher levels of innovation in the paradigms. These factors emerge as the most significant determinants of the attested patterns and seem to explain most of the inflectional variation present in the Old English paradigms. A closer examination of these factors and especially the interaction between them allows us to gain some insight in and a better understanding of the mechanisms involved in inflectional restructuring. It must be observed, at the same time, that a number of other determinants, both language-internal and external, such as semantics, syllable structure (stem weight), functionality of the system, play a role in the mechanism of the restructuring. Due to the limitation of space, they will not be discussed as independent factors, but their relevance will be occasionally addressed in the context of the interaction with the main agents. The following subsections will first present the general effects that the individual factors may have on language structure and change, and then their pertinence for the specific developments in the early English nominal inflection will be demonstrated and discussed.

3.1 Frequency of occurrence (use)

The factor which turned out to be the major determinant of the restructuring of the nominal inflection is frequency of use, operating on the level of lemma, morphosyntactic category and paradigm/class. The significance of frequency in language structure and language change has been recognised in many studies, which emphasise a tight correlation between frequency of items/lemmas and their rate of change (e.g. Greenberg, 1966; Bybee, 1985, 2003, 2007, 2010; Diessel, 2004; Haspelmath & Sims, 2010). The effects of frequency are expressed on various linguistic levels and are clearly opposite when manifested in the phonological vs. morphological structure. In phonology, high (token) frequency of occurrence leads to reduction through routinization (e.g. phonetic reduction, coalescence or assimilation), i.e. items used more frequently tend to be more susceptible to change and the development of new forms. In contrast, in morphology, token frequency can have a distinctly conserving effect, rendering lexical items, structures or expressions resistant to the working of analogical processes (Bybee, 1985: 75; Bybee, 2007). In other words, lexical items and paradigms which are characterised by high frequency of occurrence tend to preserve the inherited morphological patterns longer, whereas those used infrequently tend to submerge to analogical pressure of new, dominant patterns. These frequency effects are manifested on a few distinct planes which include (cf. Adamczyk 2018: 47):

a. frequency of the paradigm form (i.e. morphosyntactic category) (e.g. NOM./ACC.SG. vs. GEN./DAT.SG.)
b. relative frequency (e.g. the singular/plural proportion)
c. lemma frequency (word-form) (token frequency)
d. frequency of the paradigm/scheme (pattern) (type frequency)

The frequency of case/number form (paradigm form), defined by extra-linguistic factors in combination with how the linguistic system functions, turns out to be the most significant factor in the mechanism of the restructuring process. The high frequency of occurrence of paradigmatic forms worked as a conserving factor, rendering them more resistant to analogical pressures. This assumption involves the feature hierarchy, i.e. the hierarchy of individual grammatical categories, as specified by Greenberg (1966), which are tightly linked to frequency of use. With regard to case marking, the hierarchy involves the following order: nominative > accusative > dative > genitive (Hawkins, 2004: 64–68). Accordingly, the lower positions on the feature hierarchy will tend to collapse distinctions before higher positions, being thus more susceptible to change. Consequently, the NOM.SG., which is the most frequent morphosyntactic category, tends to remain unaffected by the analogical influence from other declensional types, while low frequency categories such as the GEN.PL. and DAT.PL. show considerable susceptibility to analogical pressures.[3] For instance, the *i*-mutated vowel tends to be preserved in the NOM.PL. and ACC.PL., which are more frequent categories than the DAT.SG. (and GEN.SG.), where it tends

3. Additionally, the attested pattern of distribution of analogical inflections testifies to the impact of the reducing effects of frequency of occurrence, visible on the phonological level. Phonological erosion, which affects the most frequent categories, items or forms, leads to a situation where the most frequent morphosyntactic categories are characterised by the simplest inflectional markers (often zero markers). Therefore, high frequency categories, such as the NOM.SG. tend to be endingless in many classes, while low frequency categories, such as the GEN.PL. and DAT.PL. tend to be explicitly marked.

to be eliminated. This can be illustrated by the paradigm of monosyllabic *nd*-stems, where the amount of innovative inflection in the DAT.SG., characterised originally by *i*-mutation, reaches 38% (n = 100), while in the NOM.PL. and ACC.PL., consistently marked by *i*-mutation, 7% (n = 600) and 11% (n = 510), respectively. Likewise, the GEN.SG., being one of the categories affected earliest by analogical pressure, shows the innovative marker *-es* across many declensional classes. The correlation with frequency on the level of morphosyntactic category can also be found in the *u*-stems, which show a clear bias resulting from different frequencies of individual paradigmatic forms. The class comprised nouns referring to natural environment, describing certain topographical features (e.g. *wudu, wi(o)du* 'wood, *feld* 'field', *ford* 'ford', *weald* (Anglian *wald*) 'wood, forest'), which were very often used in the DAT.SG. – a category which is otherwise characterised by moderate frequency. The high frequency of the *u*-stems in the DAT.SG. led to a conservation of the archaic inflection in this category, which is not found in any other minor declension (cf. 43% of innovative forms in the DAT.SG. vs. 87% in the GEN.SG.).

A closer inspection of the distribution of analogical infections in the plural paradigms reveals the significance of the relative frequency of occurrence in the inflectional restructuring (i.e. the number of plural tokens as a proportion of all tokens). Table 4 illustrates the correlation between the plural proportion and the overall level of innovation in the plural paradigms of individual minor classes (cf. Adamczyk 2018: 231.

Table 4. The correlation between the level of innovation in the plural (NOM./ACC. PL.) and the plural proportion (r = 0.84)

class	% PL. innovation	plural proportion
nd-stems (dis.)	74%	11%
r-stems	82%	18%
i-stems	80%	20%
u-stems	71%	40%
s-stems	42%	41%
þ-stems	38%	41%
root nouns	6%	42%
nd-stems (mon.)	9%	65%

The correlation between the level of innovation in the paradigm and the relative plural proportion holds for almost all the examined declensional classes. A low percentage of plural forms is largely responsible for the instability of the inherited plural inflection. Accordingly, the disyllabic *nd*-stems, *r*-stems and *i*-stems, which are less frequent in the plural, tend to exhibit a high level of innovation in their plural paradigms (≥ 70%). In contrast, the monosyllabic *nd*-stems (*fēond, frēond*), much more frequent in the plural, attest to hardly any traces of analogical inflection in the plural paradigms. In the other minor classes, where the plural proportion reaches around 40%, the level of innovation is limited, varying from very low in the archaic root nouns to relatively high in the *u*-stems. The divergent patterns found in these stems must be ascribed to the fact that the frequency factor is not the sole determinant of the attested distribution, but is accompanied by the activity of other factors, in particular the salience of inflectional marking (see § 3.2).

Some further insight into the relevance of relative frequency in the reorganisation of inflection can be gained by analysing the distribution of analogical forms in the *r*-stems. The correlation between the spread of the analogical inflections in the plural and the plural proportion becomes even more explicit when the distribution of forms in individual lemmas is taken into account, as illustrated in Table 5 (cf. Adamczyk 2018: 196).

Table 5. Distribution of innovative inflections in the plural and the proportion of plural inflection in individual *r*-stems

r-stems	% innovative PL.	% plural
mōdor	100%	2% (n = 1246)
fæder	97%	16% (n = 2507)
sweostor	69%	19% (n = 382)
brōþor	61%	32% (n = 2083)
dohtor	38%	26% (n = 801)

The data indicate that the innovation level is the highest in those lemmas which have the lowest plural proportion. Both *mōdor* and *fæder*, on account of their semantics, are very infrequent in the plural and there the analogical features are found in almost 100 percent of forms. In contrast, in *sweostor* and *brōþor*, which tend to be used more often in the plural than *mōdor* and *fæder*, the innovation level is lower. *Dohtor* shows a lower level of innovation in the plural, but the figures comply with the general tendency. The attested distribution corroborates the assumption that high (relative) token frequency has a conserving effect on morphological patterns, and implies that despite the fact that the plural inflection of the *r*-stems was not marked by any salient exponent, it could survive (for some time) on account of the mere frequency of use.[4]

The correlation in the paradigms of the *r*-stems reveals an important characteristic of frequency as a factor determining the dynamics of the restructuring

4. The *r*-stems tended to retain the inherited inflection relatively long. For instance, the inherited endingless form of the GEN.SG. is preserved in *brother* until 1600 (e.g. Scots *brother son* (nephew), *broder bairn*); likewise PDE expressions of the type *mother tongue* or *mother wit* can be viewed as relics of the original endingless form (OED, s.v. *brother, mother tongue, mother wit*).

process, namely its reliance on semantics. The frequency profiles of individual lemmas are defined by their semantics and the frequency profiles of individual classes are defined by the semantics of the nouns affiliated with them. The fact that a given lemma was more commonly used in the plural than in the singular, or in a given morphosyntactic category is entirely dependent on its meaning. In the *r*-stems, comprising nouns of relationship, the nouns *mother* and *father* were found more often in the singular, while the other terms (*sisters, brothers*) tended to be more frequent in the plural. A similar example comes from the root nouns, many of which denoted small animals, which due to their semantic properties, are used more often in the plural. The high token frequency in the plural allowed forms such as *lice* and *mice* (in contrast to *goats*) to preserve their (synchronically) irregular plural forms until present-day English. Likewise, the nouns denoting body parts, such as *feet, teeth, hands*, tended to be more frequent in the plural than in the singular, and they consistently show greater resistance to analogical pressures in the plural (though PDE *hands* not any longer). In the same way, the frequency of morphosyntactic categories is determined by semantics. The aforementioned *u*-stems denoting natural environment (e.g. *eard* 'earth', *wudu* 'wood') tended to be more frequently attested in prepositional phrases, typically in the DAT.SG. In contrast, the *r*-stems or *nd*-stems, referring to people (agents), are attested more often in the NOM.SG./PL. These frequencies affect their patterns of restructuring in that the frequently used forms tend to be more resistant to analogical pressure. In all these cases, it is eventually the frequency of occurrence that determines the susceptibility of paradigms to analogy, but frequency itself is tightly dependent on semantics. In this sense, semantics affects the dynamics of the restructuring process in a significant but indirect way: it translates into the frequency profiles of lemmas, paradigms and classes.[5]

The other two planes involving frequency, namely the lemma level and frequency of the scheme, reveal the relevance of absolute rather than relative frequency. The former refers especially to instances where the frequency of individual lemmas triggers patterns of restructuring significantly different from the expected pattern. An example here is the OE *u*-stem *sunu*, whose very high frequency

5. Significantly, the semantic profile of the declensional classes did not turn out to have had much influence on the pattern of restructuring. Admittedly, the overall profile of semantically-coherent classes, such as the *r*-stems turned out to be fairly archaic, but this archaism is to be ascribed rather to the relatively high (token) frequency of individual lemmas than to the class-semantics. Likewise, the conservatism of the plural paradigm of the *s*-stems, which comprised agrarian vocabulary, including animal names, is determined by the salience of inflectional marker (*r*-formative), combined with the need to retain a functional contrast between the singular and the plural, and the high proportion of plural tokens in many of these lemmas rather than the semantics of this class.

allowed it to retain the inherited inflection in 94% of forms, while the level of innovation in the rest of the class of *u*-stems reached 45% (Adamczyk, 2010: 79–380; cf. Krygier 2004). Another instance where the lemma frequency plays a role is the level of phrase, involving specific collocations. An example is the extension of the masculine GEN.SG. marker *-es* to the feminine root noun *neaht* by analogy to the *a*-stem *dæg* in the frequently attested phrase *dæges & neahtes*, found as early as in *Vespasian Psalter* (9th c.) (cf. Gothic DAT.PL. *dagam jah nahtam* in place of the expected **nahtim*; Wright, 1910: 103).

The frequency of scheme involves specifically *type* frequency and its significance is manifested in the productive classes, being an important factor facilitating their spread. Both *a*-stems and *ō*-stems were classes comprising many lemmas (of low token frequency), and were thus characterised by high *type* frequency, which ensured that their inflections were used frequently and could be productive. In compliance with the claim: "(...) the greater the number of types in a construction, the more bases there are for the item-based analogy that creates novel instances of the construction" (Bybee, 2013: 62), the high type frequency of these patterns was the major determinant of their morphological productivity.

3.2 Morpho-phonological salience of inflectional exponents

Morpho-phonological salience is a relative concept, which in broad terms can be associated with prominence or conspicuousness. Two aspects of salience are relevant in the context of the restructuring of nominal paradigms: (a) phonological salience and (b) morphological complexity. Phonological salience can be defined in terms of acoustic weight: a zero ending is considered to be less salient than a vowel, which in turn is less salient than a VC-ending (Goldschneider & DeKeyser, 2001: 22–23). It involves perceptual salience, which depends on three factors, including (a) the number of phones in the functor, i.e. morpheme (phonetic substance), (b) the presence/absence of a vowel in the surface form (syllabicity), and (c) the total relative sonority of the functor. On the sonority hierarchy (e.g. Laver 1994: 504), each level of the hierarchy is assigned a value, with (low) vowels being the most sonorous and stops being the least sonorous.[6] In the context of the present investigation, the major assumption made with respect to salience is that the more salient inflectional markers will tend to be more resistant to analogical pressure. In most general terms, overt marking can be expected to be preferred

6. The following assumptions are involved: (a) the more phones in a functor, the more perceptually salient it should be; (b) functors containing a vowel in the surface form should be more perceptually salient than those without a vowel; (c) functors that are more sonorous should be more salient (Laver, 1994: 504).

over zero marking, across all declensional classes. In other words, it is the phonological shape of the inflectional exponents that determines their proneness (or resistance) to analogical developments. The preference for the type of marker between these two extremes, i.e. the zero marker and overt marker, can be expressed on a scale, which involves the concept of morphological complexity, understood here as the complexity of formal marking, i.e. of inflectional exponents. With respect to the quantitative measurement of complexity, a form which consists of more allomorphs will be more complex. As far as the qualitative aspect is concerned, the morphological complexity can be presented on a scale which can be referred to as a complexity hierarchy of morphological marking (here of case/number exponency) (Wurzel, 1990: 139; cf. Corbett et al., 2001: 212–214; Dammel & Kürschner, 2008: 248–256). The aspects which were considered relevant for defining complexity include: (1) stem involvement, (2) redundant marking, (3) zero expression, (4) subtractive expression, (5) allomorphy, (6) fusion of number and case expression. The present study, employing the hierarchies discussed above, combines the perceptual salience and complexity of the different types of inflectional marking techniques to create a ranking which will be referred to in general as *salience scale*. Two of the original complexity criteria turned out applicable to the present ranking, namely stem involvement and zero marking. The status of the zero marking was modified in that it was not considered to be a separate marking technique, but part of the phonological salience scale, where it occupies the lowest position. Accordingly, the strength/salience of the inflectional exponents extends over the following continuum (Adamczyk 2018: 56):

NON-SALIENT → SALIENT

zero marking | suffixation (V) | suffixation (V+C) | cons. stem modulation | vocalic stem modulation

Figure 1. The combined salience and complexity scale of inflectional marking

The type of suffix is ordered according to the discussed sonority scale, e.g. vowels (V) will tend to be less salient than vowels plus consonants (VC). As regards vocalic stem modulation, only qualitative modulation is relevant here (i.e. *i*-mutation), since contrasts in vowel length emerge only in Middle English, i.e. after the operation of Open Syllable Lengthening. For consonantal stem modulation, a distinction needs to be made between the alternations which are synchronically transparent and those which are obsolete and constitute only a part of the inflectional suffix. This refers to the consonantal alternation in the *s*-stems and dental stems, where the markers -*(e)r* and -*eþ* (as in OE *lomb*: *lombor* and OE *hæle*: *hæleþ*) are historical stem formatives, but in the Old English period can be considered part of the inflectional suffix (inflectional ending). These consonantal alternations differ from the 'genuine' consonant stem modulation, as in OE *bōc* /k/: *bēċ* /tʃ/ (in the DAT.SG. and NOM./ACC.PL.), which are, however, rare in Old English and have no independent morphological function.

The findings of the present investigation demonstrate that the correlation between the amount of innovative inflection in the paradigm and the salience of inflectional markers is very strong. The paradigms characterised by the presence of morphophonemic alternations, in particular the root nouns, show a very low level of innovation both in the singular and plural. The vocalic stems (*i*-stems and *u*-stems), where the relevant categories in the singular and plural are marked with a back vowel (–*u* or -*a*) or a zero ending, attest to a much higher amount of analogical inflection, especially in the plural. In the other consonantal minor classes, the plural tends to remain altogether more conservative, except in the *r*-stems, where the pattern is entirely opposite (cf. Table 3 and the discussion in Section 3.1). The correlation between the salience of inflectional exponents and the level of innovation is very straightforward in the plural paradigm, as presented in Table 6. The type of plural marker is juxtaposed with the percentage of analogical inflections in the plural paradigm in the individual declensional classes. The plural refers to the NOM./ACC.PL., except in the class of *s*-stems, where the forms of the oblique cases were also taken into consideration (on account of the *r*-formative potentially present in these categories, e.g. GEN.PL. *lambra* vs. *lamba*, DAT.PL. *lambrum* vs. *lambum*).

Table 6. The correlation between the salience of inflectional marker and the innovation level in the plural paradigms of the OE minor stems (r = 0.95)

stem class	inherited infl. marker(s)	% innovation PL.
r-stems	Ø marker	82%
disyll. *nd*-stems	Ø marker	74%
i-stems (light-syllable)	vocalic ending -*e*, –*i*	76%
u-stems	vocalic ending -*a*	71%
s-stems	*r*-formative	42%
þ-stems	*þ*-formative	38%
monosyll. *nd*-stems	Ø + *i*-mutated vowel	9%
root nouns	Ø + *i*-mutated vowel	6%

The data indicate that the less salient the (inherited) inflectional exponent, the more extensive the spread of analogical inflections in the paradigm. The presence of *i*-mutation as a distinctive case/number exponent turns out to have been a major factor which impeded the activity of analogical processes, enhancing the retention of the inherited inflection. This is demonstrated in the class of root nouns, as well as the monosyllabic *nd*-stems, which turn out to be remarkably archaic in the plural (6% and 9%, respectively; e.g. *bēc* 'books', *cȳ* 'cows', *tēþ* 'teeth', *tyrf* 'turves'). This contrast becomes even more conspicuous when one compares the monosyllabic *nd*-stems, marked by the *i*-mutated vowel (*frȳnd* 'friends', *fȳnd* 'enemies'), and the disyllabic *nd*-stems (e.g. *wigend* 'warrior', *wealdend* 'master'), without *i*-mutation, where the level of innovation is very high (74%). Another relatively salient marker of plurality is the *r*-formative, present in the *s*-stems (e.g. *lambru* 'lambs'), which turns out to have a conserving effect as well (42% of innovation). This conserving effect of the consonantal stem alternation is evident also in the dental stems, which, characterised by a distinctive dental marker (–*þ*), show a relatively low level of innovation (38%).[7] In contrast, the class of *r*-stems and disyllabic *nd*-stems, where the plural is marked by a zero ending, turn out to be the two most innovative plural paradigms. A high percentage of analogical features is found also in the *i*-stems, where the plural is characterised by the inflectional ending -*e*, with a very low acoustic salience (e.g. *hyse* ~ *hyssas* 'warrior', *mete* ~ *met(t)as* 'food'). The other vocalic class, the *u*-stems, emerges as only slightly more conservative, with the vocalic marker -*a* in the NOM./ACC.PL., attesting to some more resistance to the pressure of analogical inflections (e.g. *felda* ~ *feldas* 'fields', *æppla* ~ *æpplas* 'apples').

The significance of the salience of inflectional exponents is evident also in the restructuring of the singular, as manifested, for instance, in the DAT.SG. of the root nouns, characterised originally by an *i*-mutated vowel. The relatively low percentage of innovation in the DAT.SG. (25% vs. 83% in the GEN.SG.) can be ascribed to both the consistent presence of the *i*-mutated root vowel and the exceptionally high frequency of occurrence of certain forms in this category (e.g. in *neaht* 'night' 42% and in *burg* 'town' 48% of all tokens). The role of *i*-mutation in the preservation of the inherited morphological patterns becomes conspicuous when the paradigms of root nouns with and without the *i*-mutated vowel are compared. For instance, both *neaht* and *meolc* 'milk' show a remarkably high level of innovation in the DAT.SG. (51% and 95% respectively), which especially for *neaht*, frequently attested in this category, is not the expected outcome. The morpho-phonological shape of these nouns, namely the lack of the *i*-mutation alternation in the paradigm, seems to account for the attested pattern. In the case of *meolc* the reason for the absence of this morphophonemic alternation is purely phonological: the root vowel was not subject to *i*-mutation; in the case of *neaht*, the situation is more complex as the vowel was mutated in the DAT.SG., but the paradigm was subject to internal analogical pressures. Consequently, alongside the form *neaht*, the *i*-mutated *niht*, originally pertinent only to the oblique cases, is frequently attested also in the NOM.SG. The

7. The marker is eventually extended to the other cases in the paradigm of dental stems, losing thus its original functional strength.

identical shape of the root vowel in the NOM.SG. and in the oblique cases facilitated analogical developments in the paradigm, rendering it highly innovative. Such *intra*paradigmatic levelling, entailing the spread of the *i*-mutated forms throughout the paradigm, was a more general phenomenon, attested also in the paradigms of some other lemmas, such as *āc* 'oak' (ACC.SG. *ǣc*), *burg* 'town' (*byrig*), and at a later stage *brōc* 'breech', in which the *i*-mutated variant became eventually the basic paradigm form (PDE *breech*) (cf. local markedness, Tiersma, 1982). Consequently, in all these lemmas *i*-mutation was no longer distinctive and did not provide any protection from *inter*paradigmatic analogical levelling.[8]

Apart from the salience of the inherited inflectional markers, the salience of the new, analogical markers from the productive classes turned out to have played a role in the restructuring process, too. The importance of this factor becomes evident when examining the divergent patterns of restructuring in the masculine and feminine stems, where the salience of inflectional exponents considerably differed. More specifically, the innovative masculine *a*-stem GEN.SG. marker *-es* and the NOM./ACC.PL. marker *-as*, in compliance with the presented salience scale, are more salient than the respective feminine *ō*-stem markers, i.e. *-e* and *-a*. Accordingly, the level of innovation in the minor paradigms can be expected to correlate with the salience of these analogical exponents as well. A closer look at the distribution of forms in three selected classes, *r*-stems, root nouns and *u*-stems, sheds some more light on this correlation (Table 7).

Table 7. The type of inflectional markers and innovation levels in the GEN. SG. and NOM./ACC. PL. in masculine and feminine minor stems

		root nouns	***r*-stems**	***u*-stems**	
				light	**heavy**
INNOVATIVE GEN. SG.					
masculine	-es	95%	23%	62%	96%
feminine	-e	82%	5%	13%	62%
INNOVATIVE NOM./ACC.PL.					
masculine	-as	*3%*	73%	90%	72%
feminine	-a	*8%*	64%	44%	19%

8. A parallel pattern can be found also in the *s*-stems and dental stems, where the *r*-formative and the dental element (*-þ-*), respectively, were inflectional exponents ranked relatively high on the salience scale, and as such they had the potential to resist analogical pressure of the productive inflections. However, with the extension of the *r*- and the dental element to the NOM.SG. (e.g. *hrīðer* 'rind', *hæleþ* 'hero'; cf. Table 1), resulting from *intra*paradigmatic analogy, their distinctive function was lost, despite their high ranking on the salience scale.

In nearly all classes, the levels of innovation in the masculine paradigms turn out to be higher than in the feminine paradigms. The attested distribution of forms corroborates the assumption that the salience of analogical exponents had a bearing on the pattern of restructuring of the paradigms. At the same time, the data demonstrate that the reorganisation of nominal inflection cannot be explained by the activity of one single factor, but the varying contrasts between individual classes are rather an effect of a complex interaction of several determinants. This is evident especially in the contrast between the levels of innovation in the plural, which was clearly dependent on the salience of the *etymological* inflectional marker (in root nouns, where *i*-mutation blocked nearly any innovation, and in *r*-stems where a zero ending facilitated the innovation).

3.3 Neutral forms and analogical pressure

An aspect closely related to salience of inflectional marking, being its mirror image in the restructuring process, is the presence of *neutral* forms in the paradigms, i.e. forms which are indistinctive in that they overlap with those of the productive declensions. The existence of cross-paradigmatic similarities has been considered to be the major factor triggering analogical reshufflings between paradigms (Blevins, 2004: 55). The analysed data reveals that the scope and intensity of the analogical pressure in the minor paradigms was at least partly dependent on the percentage of these overlapping forms. The percentage of neutral forms in the paradigm correlates with the level of innovation, being an indicator of how powerful the analogical processes were in the paradigm. The details of this correlation in the individual classes are presented in Table 8.

Table 8. The correlation between the percentage of neutral forms and the level of innovation in the paradigms

	% neutral	**% innovation**
nd-stems (dis.)	74%	88%
i-stems (heavy)	69%	55%
r-stems	59%	36%
nd-stems (mon.)	54%	23%
s-stems	52%	68%
u-stems (heavy)	51%	51%
i-stems (light)	48%	15%
dental stems	42%	64%
root noun	38%	21%
u-stems (light)	28%	30%
correlation with % innovation	r = 0.54	

The correlation between the formal inflectional overlap of the productive and minor paradigms (% neutral) and the level of innovation in the morphosyntactic categories with non-overlapping forms is fairly strong (r = 0.54). The paradigms with high percentage of forms overlapping with the corresponding forms in the productive classes were more easily affected by analogy, showing a high level of innovation (e.g. the disyllabic *nd*-stems, heavy syllable *i*-stems or *s*-stems). Approximately 25%–30% of all the innovation found in the minor paradigms can be explained alone by the formal overlap across the classes and thus this overlap can be considered a reliable measure of analogical attraction. In order to account for the lack of ideal correlation in certain paradigms, the effect of the paradigm overlap on the level of innovation must be combined with other factors, especially token and type frequency. It can be concluded that analogical remodelling of the minor paradigms was induced or facilitated by the presence of overlapping forms, which created a direct interface between the unproductive and productive inflectional types. In particular, the phonological similarity (overlap) of the NOM.SG. across different classes, an "important" (Lahiri & Dresher, 1984) and frequent category, opened the way for the restructuring in the other morphosyntactic categories, eventually leading to the generalisation of declensional class shifts. It was the major trigger, for instance, for the large-scale transition of the OE heavy-syllable *i*-stems to the *a*-stem declension, which began prior to the first attestations of English. This formal overlap was a result of a regular phonological development, whereby the final vowels were lost in heavy-syllable stems in the NOM.SG (e.g. Hogg & Fulk, 2011: 38). A parallel mechanism is visible in the development of the historical neuter *s*-stems, which at the prehistoric stage shifted predominantly to the *i*-stems, and this transition was facilitated by the presence of the *i*-mutated vowel in the NOM./ACC.SG. (e.g. neut. OE *flǣsc* 'flesh' < PGmc **flaiskiz*, light-syll. OE *sige* < PGmc **sigiz* 'victory') (e.g. Bammesberger, 1990: 124, 138–139).

3.4 Interaction between frequency and morpho-phonological salience

Although the correlations between the level of paradigmatic restructuring and frequency of occurrence, the salience of morphological exponents or the amount of overlapping inflection in the paradigms seem fairly straightforward, not all the attested patterns can be accounted for by one factor, as was already observed in the previous section. The present section will concentrate on several aspects of the interplay between frequency and salience, illustrating how it can account for the attested patterns of restructuring. One form of interaction between two independent factors is when both work in a synergetic way, enhancing the effects of their combined activity. Table 9 demonstrates that the effects of the salience of etymological inflectional exponents can be reinforced by the frequency of occurrence, in this case relative frequency, i.e. plural proportion.

Table 9. The interaction between the salience of inflectional exponents and frequency of occurrence

class	plurality marker	% plural proportion	% innovation (PL.)
nd-stems (dis.)	Ø marker	11%	74%
r-stems	Ø marker	18%	82%
i-stems (light syll.)	vocalic marker *-e*/*–i*	20%	76%
u-stems	vocalic marker *-a*	40%	71%
s-stems	*r*-formative	41%	42%
þ-stems	*þ*-formative	41%	38%
root nouns	Ø + *i*-mutation	42%	6%
nd-stems (mon.)	Ø + *i*-mutation	65%	9%

The high level of innovation in the plural paradigms of the disyllabic *nd*-stems, *r*-stems and *i*-stems can be explained by the low proportion of the plural forms combined with the low salience of the inflectional markers (zero marker or the vowel *-e*/*–i*), where the two factors work in a synergetic way. In turn, the relatively high proportion of the plural (NOM./ACC.PL.) in the root nouns and monosyllabic *nd*-stems is enhanced by the salience of their inflectional marker (*i*-mutation), which renders the plural paradigms in these stems very conservative. The overlap of these two factors is responsible for the resistance of the original root nouns to analogical plural formation patterns until present-day English (e.g. *feet*, *teeth*, *mice*). In contrast, in the *u*-stems, *s*-stems and dentals stems, where the levels of plural proportion are nearly the same (ca. 40%), the independent effect of salience of the inherited marker on the innovation levels can be observed. The lower salience of the vocalic marker *-a* in the *u*-stems, compared to that of the consonant markers (*r*-formative and *þ*-formative), renders the paradigms of the *u*-stems more vulnerable to analogical pressure (71%) than those of the *s*-stems (42%) and dental stems (38%).

Another type of interaction between two or more factors involves a situation when the interacting factors work in a neutralising or even contradictory way, moderating the effects of the combined activity. The relevance of the salience of *analogical* ending was discussed in the previous section and, as could be seen, this factor could not satisfactorily account for all the patterns of restructuring. A closer inspection of other inflectional exponents from productive classes and their correlation with innovation levels reveals the complexity of the mechanism involved in the restructuring of inflection. The classes of *r*-stems and root nouns were selected to illustrate this interaction since both historical paradigms are characterised by lack of any explicit inflectional markers in the singular and in the NOM./ACC.PL., which allows us to evaluate the impact of the salience of new inflectional ending. Table 10 presents the correlation between the salience of innovative markers, the levels of innovation in individual categories and frequency as one of the additional factors that can account for the attested patterns.

Table 10. The correlation between innovative markers, frequency and the level of innovation in the *r*-stems and root nouns

frequency (n)	**innovative marker(s)**	**% innovation**
r-stems		
1351	vocalic ending *-e*	2%
97	vocalic ending *-a*	64%
648	VC ending *-es*	23%
526	VC ending *-as*	73%
root nouns		
2120	vocalic ending *-e*	38%
30	vocalic ending *-u*	87%
18	VC ending *-es*	95%

As can be observed, the salience of innovative markers on its own does not account for all the attested patterns. This refers in particular to the class of *r*-stems, where the innovation level found in the category marked by the vocalic ending *-a* (NOM. / ACC.PL.) is higher than could be expected given its placement on the salience scale. This "irregularity" can be explained by the (relative) frequency of these forms (NOM. /ACC.PL. of feminine *r*-stems), which was relatively low (n = 97, Table 5). In turn, the impact of the *a*-stem GEN.SG. ending *-es*, which is evidently lower than could be expected given its salience, can be ascribed to the high frequency of occurrence of the *r*-stem lemmas (especially *fæder*) in the singular, including the GEN. SG. (n = 648). The expected correlation with salience (i.e. when salience can independently explain the attested patterns) is found in the case of the vocalic ending *-e* (GEN. DAT.ACC.SG., FEM.), where the low level of innovation can be attributed to its low salience, and in the ending *-as* (NOM./ACC.PL., MASC.), which as a salient marker had a substantial analogical influence in the paradigm (73%).

In the root nouns, (token) frequency and the salience of the innovative exponent work in the same direction: highly frequent case forms where the innovative marker is not very salient (vocalic ending *-e*) show relatively little innovation, while the less frequent categories (e.g. GEN.SG.) where the innovative marker has a CV-structure (*-es*) are very innovative. The innovation level in the categories marked by the analogical marker *-u* (NOM. ACC.SG., FEM.) is higher than could be expected from salience alone. This can be ascribed to the metrical structure (light syllable feminine stems, e.g. *hnut* 'nut'), which is yet another conditioning factor involved in the mechanism of the restructuring process, remaining beyond the scope of this study.[9]

9. Its significance is manifested also in the divergent innovation levels in the *r*-stems (disyllabic) and root nouns (monosyllabic) in the categories marked by identical markers (*-e* and *-es*), where the disyllabic structure of the former worked as a factor inhibiting the influence of analogical inflections.

4. Conclusions

The process of remodelling of the nominal inflection in Old English emerges as a multifaceted development, which involved analogical forces operating within and across the paradigms. The rearrangement of inflectional exponents and consequently the shifts of nouns across different declensional classes, evident at the earliest attested stage of English, were a reaction to phonological developments. As a result of the activity of extensive reduction processes (*Auslautgesetze*) in the prehistoric period of Germanic, the nominal system of Old English emerged as rather deficient, with a range of non-functional distinctions present in the paradigms. The number of formal exponents by which grammatical categories were expressed (i.e. case, number, and gender) was substantially reduced when compared to the system reconstructed for the Proto-Germanic stage. Such a syncretism and consequently multifunctionality of nominal inflections resulted in a growing lack of transparency of the paradigms, rendering them less and less stable.

The dynamics of the restructuring of the nominal inflection depended on the interplay of several factors, whose range of influence depends on class-specific features, including the phonological and frequency profiles. The morpho-phonological salience of inflectional exponents and the frequency of occurrence, operating on different levels, emerge as the most important determinants in the inflectional restructuring, and can account for most of the patterns attested in the early English material. Additionally, the presence of forms overlapping across different paradigms (*neutral* forms) constituted an important organisational factor in the analogical extension of inflectional patterns.

According to the assumptions of the usage-based approach, the 'natural selection' of forms or structures by language use will favour functional forms or structures over the less functional ones. In the cases where the functionality is at stake, such as the lack of explicit marking of the contrast in number, the deficiency will tend to be repaired by employing equivalent, more functional elements. The less salient and ambiguous inflections of the unproductive classes will tend to be replaced by more salient, unambiguous ones extended from the productive paradigms, where type frequency plays a crucial role. Etymological inflections, even if salient but low in terms of type frequency (e.g. the dental suffix), are not likely to develop into sustainable, functional markers. At the same time, markers with a high token frequency, which serves as a proxy for their entrenchment in the mental lexicon and easy retrieval, will tend to escape analogical pressure, especially when they are salient (e.g. *i*-mutation). In this competition analogy emerges as a functional mechanism and its scope and impact are largely predictable from the factors recognised as relevant for shaping the morphological structure of language. In this sense, the analogical restructuring of the nominal inflection (in early English) can be viewed as an attempt at bringing back the transparency and functionality of the system.

With regard to the mechanism of the morphological change (analogy), it can be observed that analogical developments operated along individual morphosyntactic categories and not along declensional classes or paradigms. Accordingly, individual morphosyntactic categories were affected by analogical pressure to a various extent and at a different pace. The analogical shifts of nouns began with "local" extensions of innovative paradigm forms, and only at the more advanced stage of the process did they involve entire paradigms. However, the abstract concept of paradigm has some relevance in the reorganisation of inflection. Namely, the factor triggering the activity of analogical processes on the paradigm level is the formal similarity between paradigms, manifested in the spontaneous overlap of forms between the productive and unproductive paradigms. In the restructuring process, this formal overlap had certain class effects, in that the declensional classes which were most exposed to analogical pressures were those in which the percentage of overlapping forms was very high.

References

Adamczyk, Elżbieta (2010). Morphological reanalysis and the Old English *u*-declension. *Anglia. Zeitschrift für englische Philologie*, 128(3), 365–390.

Adamczyk, Elżbieta (2018). *Reshaping of the Nominal Inflection in Early Northern West Germanic*. John Benjamins. https://doi.org/10.1075/nss.31

Bammesberger, Alfred (1990). *Morphologie des Urgermanischen Nomens*. Heidelberg: Winter.

Bertacca, Antonio (2009). *Natural Morphology and the Loss of Nominal Inflections in English*. Pisa: Plus-Piza University Press.

Boutkan, Dirk (1995). *The Germanic 'Auslautgesetze'*. Amsterdam/Atlanta, GA: Rodopi.

Blevins, James P. (2004). Inflection Classes and Economy. In Gereon Müller, Lutz Gunkel, & Gisela Zifonun, (Eds.), *Explorations in Nominal Inflection*, 41–85. Berlin: Mouton de Gruyter. https://doi.org/10.1515/9783110197501.51

Brunner, Karl (1965). *Altenglische Grammatik*, 3rd ed, Tübingen: Niemeyer. https://doi.org/10.1515/9783110930894

Bybee, Joan (1985). *Morphology: A Study of the Relation between Meaning and Form*. Amsterdam: John Benjamins. https://doi.org/10.1075/tsl.9

Bybee, Joan (1995). Regular Morphology and the Lexicon. *Language and Cognitive Processes* 10(5), 425–455. https://doi.org/10.1080/01690969508407111

Bybee, Joan (2001). Main clauses are innovative, subordinate clauses are conservative: consequences for the nature of constructions. In Joan Bybee, & Michael Noonan (Eds.), *Complex Sentences in Grammar and Discourse: Essays in Honor of Sandra A. Thompson*, 1–17. Amsterdam: Benjamins.

Bybee, Joan (2003). Mechanisms of Change in Grammaticization: The Role of Frequency. In Brian D. Joseph, & Richard Janda (Eds.), *The Handbook of Historical Linguistics*, 602–623. Oxford: Blackwell. https://doi.org/10.1002/9780470756393.ch19

Bybee, Joan (2007). *Frequency of Use and the Organisation of Language*. Oxford: Oxford University Press. https://doi.org/10.1093/acprof:oso/9780195301571.001.0001

Bybee, Joan (2010). *Language, Usage and Cognition*. Cambridge: Cambridge University Press. https://doi.org/10.1017/CBO9780511750526

Bybee, Joan (2013). Usage-based Theory and Exemplar Representations of Constructions. In Thomas Hoffmann, & Graeme Trousdale (Eds.), *The Oxford Handbook of Construction Grammar*, 49–69. Oxford: Oxford University Press.

Campbell, Alistair (1977). *Old English Grammar*. Oxford: Clarendon Press.

Carstairs-McCarthy, Andrew (1994). Inflection Classes, Gender and the Principle of Contrast. *Language* 70, 737–788. https://doi.org/10.2307/416326

Corbett, Greville, Hippisley, Andrew, Brown, Dunstan, & Marriott, Paul (2001). Frequency, Regularity and the Paradigm: A Perspective from Russian on a Complex Relation. In Joan Bybee, & Paul Hopper (Eds.), *Frequency and the Emergence of Linguistic Structure*, 201–226. Amsterdam: John Benjamins. https://doi.org/10.1075/tsl.45.11cor

Dahl, Ivar (1938). *Substantival Inflexion in Early Old English*. Lund: C.W.K. Gleerup.

Dammel, Antje, & Kürschner, Sebastian (2008). Complexity in Nominal Plural Allomorphy: A Contrastive Survey of ten Germanic Languages. In Matti Miestamo, Kaius Sinnemäki, & Fred Karlsson (Eds.), *Language Complexity: Typology, Contact, Change*, Studies in Language Companion Series 94, 243–262. Amsterdam: John Benjamins Publishers. https://doi.org/10.1075/slcs.94.15dam

Diessel, Holger (2004). *The Acquisition of Complex Sentences*, Cambridge Studies in Linguistics 105. Cambridge: Cambridge University Press. https://doi.org/10.1017/CBO9780511486531

Goldschneider, Jennifer, & DeKeyser, Robert (2001). Explaining the 'Natural Order of L2 Morpheme Acquisition' in English: A Meta-Analysis of Multiple Determinants. *Language Learning* 51, 1–50. https://doi.org/10.1111/1467-9922.00147

Greenberg, Joseph (1966). *Language Universals*. The Hague: Mouton.

Haspelmath, Martin, & Sims, Andrea (2010). *Understanding Morphology*. London/New York: Routledge.

Hawkins, John A. (2004). *Efficiency and Complexity in Grammars*. Oxford: Oxford University Press. https://doi.org/10.1093/acprof:oso/9780199252695.001.0001

Healey, Antonette di Paolo, Holland, Joan, McDougall, David, McDougall, Ian, & Xiang, Xin (Eds.). (2009). *The Dictionary of Old English Corpus in Electronic Form*. Toronto: Toronto University Press.

Hogg, Richard M. (1997). Some Remarks on Case Marking in Old English. *Transactions of the Philological Society* 95. 95–109. https://doi.org/10.1111/1467-968X.00014

Hogg, Richard M., & Fulk, R. D. (2011). *A Grammar of Old English. Volume II: Morphology*. Oxford: Blackwell.

Kastovsky, Dieter (1995). Morphological Reanalysis and Typology: The Case of the German r-Plural and Why English did not Develop it. In Henning Andersen (Ed.), *Historical Linguistics: Selected Papers from the Eleventh International Conference on Historical Linguistics*, Los Angeles, 16–20 August 1993, *Current Issues in Linguistic Theory*, 124, 227–238. Amsterdam: Benjamins.

Kastovsky, Dieter (1997). Morphological Classification in English Historical Linguistics: The Interplay of Diachrony, Synchrony and Morphological Theory. In Terttu Nevalainen, & Leena Kahlas-Tarkka (Eds.), *To Explain the Present: Studies in the Changing English Language in Honour of Matti Rissanen*, Mémoires de la Société Néophilologique de Helsinki 52, 63–75. Helsinki: Société Néophilologique.

Krygier, Marcin (1998). On a Synchronic Approach to Old English Morphology. *Folia Linguistica Historica* 19, 119–128.

Krygier, Marcin (2002). A Re-Classification of Old English Nouns. *Studia Anglica Posnaniensia* 38, 311–319.

Krygier, Marcin (2004). Heargas þēoda: In Search of the *u. In Radosław Dylewski, & Piotr Cap (Eds.), *History and Present-day Pragmatics of the English Language*, 7–13. Łódź: Wyższa Szkoła Humanistyczno-Ekonomiczna w Łodzi.

Lahiri, Aditi, & Dresher, Bezalel Elan (1984). Diachronic and Synchronic Implications of Declension Shifts. *The Linguistic Review* 3, 141–163.

Lass, Roger (1997). Why House is an Old English 'Masculine a-Stem'? In Terttu Nevalainen, & Leena Kahlas-Tarkka (Eds.), *To Explain the Present: Studies in the Changing English Language in Honour of Matti Rissanen*, Mémoires de la Société Néophilologique de Helsinki 52, 101–109. Helsinki: Société Néophilologique.

Langacker, Ronald W. (1988). A Usage-Based Model. In Brygida Rudzka-Ostyn (Ed.), *Topics in Cognitive Linguistics*, Current Issues in Linguistic Theory 50, 127–161. Amsterdam: Benjamins. https://doi.org/10.1075/cilt.50.06lan

Laver, John (1994). *Principles of Phonetics*. Cambridge: Cambridge University Press. https://doi.org/10.1017/CBO9781139166621

Tiersma, Peter (1982). Local and General Markedness. *Language* 59, 832–849. https://doi.org/10.2307/413959

Wełna, Jerzy (1996). *English Historical Morphology*. Warszawa: Wydawnictwo Uniwersytetu Warszawskiego.

Wright, Joseph (1910). *Grammar of the Gothic Language*. Oxford: At the Clarendon Press.

Wurzel, Wolfgang U. (1989). *Inflectional Morphology and Naturalness*. Berlin: Akademie-Verlag.

Wurzel, Wolfgang U. (1990). Morphologisierung – Komplexität – Natürlichkeit. Ein Beitrag zur Begriffsklärung. In Norbert Boretzky, Werner Enninger, & Thomas Stolz (Eds.), *Spielarten der Natürlichkeit – Spielarten der Ökonomie*. Beiträge zum 5. Essener Kolloquium über 'Grammatikalisierung: Natürlichkeit und Systemökonomie' vom 6.10.-8.10.1988 an der Universität Essen, 129–153. Bochum: N. Brockmeyer.

“Subsumed under the dative”?
The status of the Old English instrumental

Kirsten Middeke

Most descriptions of Old English grammar do not count the instrumental as a separate case, since distinctly instrumental forms are not available for all lexical categories that are inflected for case in Old English. Assuming that the instrumental has been completely subsumed under the dative is misleading, however. In actual fact, any definite, quantified or adjective-modified masculine or neuter NP in the singular can be marked either dative or instrumental, and a clear functional difference emerges if we contrast noun phrases containing instrumental forms with those containing exclusively dative forms. Instrumental-case NPs are adverbials of time, manner and place, whereas dative-case NPs usually refer to persons and are often verbal arguments. This paper explores the extent to which the instrumental and the dative can be distinguished in Old English, the functional load of the distinction and the degree of its productivity, drawing on the results of collexeme analyses carried out on data from the *York-Toronto-Helsinki Parsed Corpus of Old English Prose*.

Keywords: case, Old English, noun phrase, productivity, collexeme analysis

1. Introduction

The instrumental is not usually counted as a separate case in descriptions of Old English grammar. Marsden talks of the language having “four main cases […] and the *remnants of a fifth*” (2015: 572; emphasis added), Hogg calls the instrumental “vestigial” (2012: 73) and Baker speaks of “traces” (2012 [2003]: 34). Mitchell (2000 [1985]: 3, § 6) calls the remnants of the instrumental “significant” but declares that any “attempt to distinguish the dative and instrumental on syntactical grounds” is “foredoomed to failure”; he later (2000 [1985]: 565, § 1345) states that the instrumental had been “subsumed under the dative”. Statements such as these, though not wrong, as far as they go, turn out to be only half the story. They should not prevent us from asking questions. To what extent can the instrumental and the dative still

https://doi.org/10.1075/cilt.346.03mid

be distinguished in Old English? How great is the functional load of the distinction? How productive is it?

In pursuit of these questions, this contribution will present the results of collexeme analyses (Stefanowitsch & Gries, 2003; Gries & Stefanowitsch, 2004) carried out on data from the *York-Toronto-Helsinki Parsed Corpus of Old English Prose* (Taylor *et al.*, 2003; henceforth YCOE), demonstrating that although the instrumental has partly merged with the dative formally, a functional difference still exists between the two categories in Old English that merits the postulation of, if not a case in its own right, then definitely independent epicentres in the merged case's semantic network.

2. What is a "vestigial" case?

The designation of the instrumental as only vestigial has formal as well as functional reasons. As far as form is concerned, it is justified by the fact that distinctly instrumental forms are not available for all lexical categories that are inflected for case in Old English. Leaving aside interrogative *hwan* and *hwī*, instrumental forms exist only in the masculine and neuter singular of the determiners *se* 'the' and *þes* 'this', of quantifiers like *eall* 'all' or *sum* 'some' and of strong adjectives, including possessives and the numeral *ān* 'one'. (The distinction between quantifiers and adjectives is fluid; nothing will depend on it.) The forms in question are arranged in Table 1. In all other positions the instrumental is identical with the dative, and these forms are usually analysed as datives.

Since nouns and personal pronouns have no separate instrumental forms, there are no unambiguously instrumental NP heads. The analysis adopted in the tagging of the YCOE consequently assumes that the instrumental exists only on the word level, not on the phrase level. All instrumental-case determiners and adjectives are

Table 1. Distinct instrumental forms in Old English, by part of speech

	instrumental	**dative (M/N SG.)**
determiners *se* 'the'; *þes* 'this'	*þȳ, þon; þys**	*þam, þissum*
quantifiers	*ealle, sume*, etc.	*eallum, sumum*, etc.
other strong adjectives	*ōþre, mīne, ān*, etc.	*ōþrum, mīnum, ānum*, etc.
interrogative *hwā* 'who', *hwæt* 'what'	*hwan, hwī*	*hwam*

* Brunner (1951: 119) notes that *þon*, which originally occurred in prepositional phrases and comparative constructions like *nohte þon leas* 'nonetheless' and goes back to a comparative particle (cf. modern *than*), is confused with dative *þam* in late Old English texts. The results of collexeme analyses indeed strongly suggest that, as anticipated by Taylor (2003a: #instrumental_case), instrumental *þon* is not consistently distinguished from dative *þam*, which is why it has been excluded from the present analysis. *Þys* has likewise been excluded, since it is not consistently distinguished in spelling from nominative *þes*. The analysis presented in Section 3 will thus be restricted to *þȳ*.

considered part of a noun phrase in the dative case, so noun phrases containing instrumentals as well as datives, like *þȳ ilcan dæge* '(on) the same day' in (1), are not distinguished from noun phrases containing only dative forms, like *þære ilcan nihte* '(in) the same night' in (2), on the phrase level.

(1) ***þy ilcan dæge***
[the-INS same-DAT day-DAT]$_{\text{DAT}}$[1]
he forðferde ....
'The same day, he died.' (Bede's History of the English Church, cobede, Bede_5: 20.474.1.4754 – YCOE analysis)[2]

(2) ***þære ilcan nihte***
[the-DAT same-DAT night-DAT]$_{\text{DAT}}$
wes Eadwine dohter acenned
'The same night, a daughter was born to Eadwine.'
(Anglo-Saxon Chronicle E, cochronE, ChronE_[Plummer]: 626.3.292 – YCOE analysis)

This analysis was adopted for purely practical reasons (cf. the disclaimer in Taylor, 2003b, #dative_and_instrumental); it is not necessarily a good interpretation of linguistic reality. As Figure 1 shows, the category we are accustomed to calling the dative represents the merger of four originally distinct cases, the Proto-Indo-European (PIE) ablative, locative, instrumental and dative.

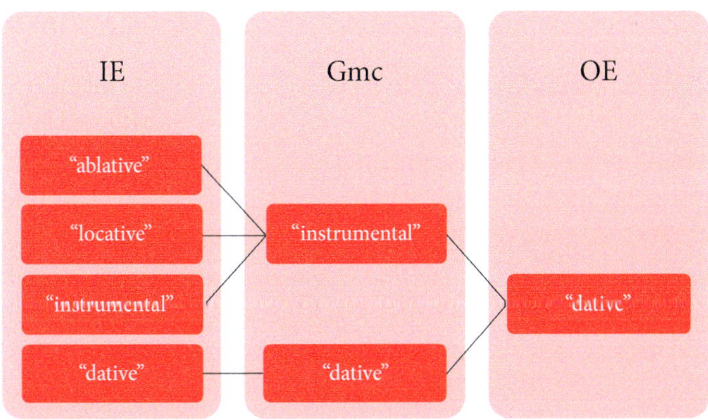

Figure 1. The syncretic nature of the Old English dative (based on Brunner, 1951: 4, 5–6)

1. For the sake of legibility, I omit number and gender information in the glossing (instrumentals are always singular and ambiguous between masculine and neuter) except where it becomes relevant (Examples 3–5).

2. All examples are cited by text and YCOE token ID, which includes the YCOE filename, the *Dictionary of Old English* short title and page or line numbers. All translations are my own.

Table 2 gives the etymologies of Old English dative morphemes on nouns. The masculine/neuter suffix *-e* represents the phonological merger of early OE *-æ* (dative) and early OE *-i* (instrumental<locative). The feminine singular ending *-e* also represents a phonological merger, deriving from both PIE **-ãi* (dative) and PIE **-āí* (instrumental<locative cf. Brunner, 1951: 4, 5–6; Ringe & Taylor, 2014: 114–119, 377–381). The plural ending *-um* derives from Proto-Germanic (PGmc) **-imaz, *-umaz, *-amaz,* (dative) and **-imiz, *-umiz, *-amiz* (instrumental), depending on the thematic vowel (cf. Ringe, 2006: 269–272). Etymologically speaking, then, the dative may just as well be said to have been subsumed under the instrumental as vice versa.

Table 2. Etymologies of Old English dative morphemes on nouns (based on Brunner, 1951: 4, 5–6; Ringe, 2006: 269–272; Ringe & Taylor, 2014: 114–119, 377–381)

	"dative"-case NPs	case morpheme on noun	ancestral forms
M/N SG.	*(þam) dæge*	*-e*	eOE *-æ* (dative) eOE *-i* (instrumental<locative)
F SG.	*(þære) nihte*	*-e*	PIE **-ãi* (dative) PIE **-āí* (instrumental<locative)
PL.	*(þam) dagum*	*-um*	PGmc **-imaz, *-umaz, *-amaz* (dative) PGmc **-imiz, *-umiz, *-amiz* (instrumental)

There is thus no compelling reason to assume that the ambiguous forms are datives rather than instrumentals. In fact, the compilers of the YCOE's sister corpus of poetic texts have opted for a different analysis: in the YCOE-P (Pintzuk & Plug, 2001); there are NPs carrying the extension-tag -INS for "instrumental", and nouns in *-e*, representing the dative-instrumental merger, are analysed as instrumentals in such phrases, i.e. when modified by an unambiguously instrumental determiner or adjective. In Code 1, we see that the phrase *ðy þriddan dæge* '(on) the third day' is analysed as a dative NP in the YCOE, but as an instrumental NP in the YCOE-P, with the head noun *dæge* and the adjective *þriddan* considered instrumentals in the latter, but datives in the former:

```
(NP-DAT-TMP (D^I +dy ADJ^D +triddan) (N^D d+age)[...])
(NP-INS-TMP (D^I +dy ADJ^I +triddan) (N^I d+age))
```

Code 1. Two analyses of *ðy þriddan dæge*: Alexander's Letter to Aristotle, coalex,Alex: 31.9.396 (YCOE); Elene, cocynew,71.181.265 (YCOE-P)

On purely formal grounds, then, we might equally well analyse ostensible dative-case nouns like the ones in Examples 1 and 2 as ambiguous or neutral with respect to the dative-instrumental distinction.

This leads us to functional considerations. What can we say about the use of the two cases where their forms *can* be distinguished?

In noun phrases, the instrumental alternates with the dative wherever it occurs. However, the reverse is not true: the dative does not alternate with the instrumental in all constructions, even where instrumental forms are available. As we will see, the instrumental is strongly preferred over the dative in clearly-defined sets of constructions, most prominently adverbials of time and manner, but rarely encroaches upon the dative in other contexts, e.g. referring to recipients or experiencers, for instance. The merger of the two cases is thus not reciprocal: the dative takes on functions of the instrumental but not vice versa. This entails that – unless we consider all constructions containing instrumental forms as fossilizations, which I will argue against – language users must have been able to discriminate between the two overlapping sets of forms and to make judgements of their respective appropriateness in differing contexts. This indicates that the functions of the two constructions cannot have been identical.

In the following, I will present data on the distributional difference between dative and instrumental in Old English before discussing the implications of these findings for the theoretical status of the instrumental and the Old English case system at large.

3. Distributional analysis: Frequencies and collexemes

3.1 Overview

In the YCOE, as has already been stated, the instrumental is only labelled at the word level. Table 3 gives an overview of how many word forms are tagged for instrumental case in the various parts-of-speech that are inflected for this category.

Table 3. Absolute frequencies of instrumental-case word forms in the YCOE, by part-of-speech tag

POS-tag	n	POS-tag	n	POS-tag	n	POS-tag	n
determiners		*quantifying adjectives*		*other adjectives*		*prns/nouns*	
D-I	6,257	Q-I	1,102	ADJ-I	359	WPRO-I	166
P + D-I	2	NEG + Q-I	39	WADJ-I	15	PRO$-I	33
		NUM-I	39	VBN-I	6	N-I	2
				ADJR-I	4		

Determiners are the largest group, accounting for 78% of all instrumentals in the corpus. Next in line are quantifiers and other strong adjectives, including the numeral *ān* 'one', the negated quantifiers *nān* 'not one, none' and *nænig* 'not any' as well as the interrogatives *hwylc* 'which' and *hweþer* 'which (of two)'. These collectively make up 20% of instrumentals. The interrogative pronouns in the instrumental, *hwan* 'what' and *hwī* 'why', are always part of complex conjunctions (*to/for hwan* 'why', *to/for/mid hwī* 'why'); they are assumed to be lexicalized and will be disregarded, as will the preposition-determiner liaison *efterþon* 'afterwards'. Instrumental-case possessive pronouns are comparatively infrequent, but some do occur in bare-case NPs (see Section 3.3). The two instances of the instrumental-case extension tag on nouns (*[to] nahte* and *[mid...] manþrymme*) are unexpected, since there is no instrumental-dative opposition with nouns in Old English.

In the following I will discuss the use of instrumental determiners and adjectives. Only bare-case noun phrases will be considered, since instrumental forms following prepositions, notably *mid* 'with', are assumed to be conditioned by the preposition rather than by function directly.

3.2 Instrumental-case determiners

Determiners unambiguously marked for instrumental case display a strong bias towards occurring in temporal adverbials. In the YCOE, of all dative-tagged nouns occurring with instrumental determiner *þȳ* (a total of 545), 314 are forms of *gēar* 'year', 161 are forms of *dæg* 'day', seven are compounds ending in *-dæg*, 17 refer to seasons or time periods (*sumer* 'summer', *winter* 'winter', *lencten* 'lent, spring', *lenctenfæsten* 'the fast of lent', *indictio* 'indiction' (a 15-year cycle), *mæssepreosthad* 'priesthood'), six refer to times of day (*morgen* 'morning', *æfen* 'evening', *niht* 'night') and three are *mōnþ* 'month'. Among the items occurring only once in the construction are *sīþ* 'time' (as in 'this time'), and *līf* 'life'. In other words, of all nouns occurring with instrumental *þȳ*, 94% are expressions for time. The noun collocates of *þȳ* are listed in Table 4.

Table 4. Noun collocates of instrumental *þȳ* (YCOE data, span = 0:2). 38 types, 545 tokens. Temporal nouns in bold face

types	tokens	types	tokens
***gēar* 'year'**	**314**	*dōm* 'fate'	1
***dæg* 'day'**	**161**	*fyrd* 'army'	1
***sumer* 'summer'**	**9**	*gehrōr* 'ruin, downfall'	1
weg 'way'	6	***indictio***	**1**
þēaw 'custom, usage'	5	***lencten* 'lent, spring'**	**1**

(*continued*)

Table 4. (*continued*)

types	tokens	types	tokens
Ēasterdæg **'Easter day'**	4	***lenctenfæsten*** **'the fast of lent'**	1
winter **'winter'**	4	*lēoþ* 'song'	1
gemet 'measure, manner'	3	*līchama* 'body'	1
hēafod 'head'	3	***līf*** **'life'**	1
mōnþ **'month'**	3	***mæssepreōsthad*** **'priesthood'**	1
morgen **'morning'**	3	*mōd* 'mind'	1
wīcdæg **'weekday'**	3	*nama* 'name'	1
niht **'night'**	2	*ryht* 'right'	1
ǣfen **'evening'**	1	***sīþ*** **'time'**	1
āna 'one'	1	*slǣp* 'sleep'	1
botl 'abode'	1	*wǣl* 'slaughter'	1
clyf 'cliff'	1	*wæpen* 'weapon'	1
camp 'battle'	1	*weorc* 'work'	1
dēaþ 'death'	1	*wyrd* 'fate'	1
total			545

There is one unexpected item on the list: *niht* 'night' is a feminine noun, but occurs twice with masculine/neuter *þȳ*. Both instances, plus a third that was not retrieved because an intervening adjective is tagged as a participle, are from the C-text of Wæferth's translation of Gregory's *Dialogues*. In this text, *niht* is otherwise (n = 40) consistently used with feminine determiners. Compare Examples 3 and 4:

(3) ***þy*** ***æfterfylgendan*** ***nihte***
the-INS.SG.M/N following-DAT/INS night-DAT/INS
þæt lic læg unbebyrged
'the following night, the body lay unburied...'
(Gregory's Dialogues, cogregdC,GDPref_and_4_[C]: 37.318.5.4763)

(4) ***þære*** ***æfterfylgendan*** ***nihte***
the-DAT.SG.F following-DAT/INS night-DAT/INS
aweox þær [...] mara sweg ...
'the following night, more noise arose...'
(Gregory's Dialogues, cogregdC,GDPref_and_3_[C]: 30.236.11.3302)

Wright & Wright (1914: 198, § 411) note that Old English *niht* also sometimes occurs with masculine genitive-suffix *-es* on analogy with *dæg*. Again, we find an example in Gregory's *Dialogues*:

(5) ***dæges*** ⁊ ***nihtes***
day-GEN.SG.M & night-GEN.SG.M
'by day and by night'.
(Gregory's Dialogues, cogregdC,GD_2_[C]: 38.176.16.2153)

The noun *niht* seems to be coerced into the masculine declension for the sake of morphological parallelism and/or the *-es* suffix had been reinterpreted as a general marker of temporal adverbs and thus become available to feminine nouns as well. The same phenomenon can be witnessed in modern German, where the form *nachts* occurs in masculine, genitive-case NPs functioning as temporal adverbials (cf. *tags und nachts* 'day and night', *des nachts* 'by night' or even *eines Nachts* 'one night'), but never in genitive modifiers (*Königin der Nacht* 'Queen of the Night', not **Königin des Nachts*). The form *nachts* goes back to Old High German times at least (DWB, s.v. *nachts*), so the phenomenon may well be a common West-Germanic one. A similar kind of analogy is perhaps responsible for the unexpected instrumental determiner with Old English *niht* as well. The three instances of *þȳ nihte* are opposed by 155 instances of *þære/þissere nihte* in the corpus, which shows that *niht* has not generally changed grammatical gender, but seems to have occasionally been coerced into the pattern. (One of the three instances of *þȳ nihte* occurs in close vicinity of *þȳ dæge*.) Extension to feminine nouns means that the association of *þȳ* with expressions for time must go beyond word-based collocation, i.e. must be the association of a lexical item (*þȳ*) or a grammatical category (the instrumental case) with nouns from a specific semantic field (time) or with a specific constructional function (adverbial of time).

The association of *þȳ* with nouns referring to time is specific to the instrumental – a countercheck reveals that *gēar* and *dæg* do not rank especially high as collocates of *dative*-case determiners, where words for persons are much more prominent. There are only 337 co-occurrences of dative-case determiners with the set of nouns from Table 4, as opposed to the 545 co-occurrences with instrumental determiners, despite the fact the dative is much more frequent in the corpus generally. (In order for results to be comparable, feminine determiners, for which no instrumental counterparts exist, have been excluded.) If we take only the temporal nouns into consideration (i.e. items in bold face in Table 4, which constitute 94% of instrumental-determiner collocates), the number of occurrences with dative-case determiners goes down to 35. This substantial difference[3] in the distribution of instrumental and dative determiners strongly suggests a transparent functional difference between the two cases. Highest-ranking among the collocates of dative *þam* are *cyning* 'king', *folc* 'people', *bisceop* 'bishop' and *God* 'God', followed by other nouns referring to persons or groups of people (cf. Table 5); no preference

3. Based on the observed 510 co-occurrences of *þȳ* with time-span nouns and the general corpus frequencies of instrumental *þȳ* and dative *þam* in noun phrases (545 and 2,312, respectively), the observed frequency of only 35 temporal NPs with *þam* betrays a significantly non-random distribution ($\chi^2 = 2{,}415$, df = 1, p < 2.2e-16), with the case distinction having a strong effect on the distribution of nouns (Cramer's V = 0.92).

Table 5. Top ten noun collocates of dative *þam* (YCOE data, span = 0:2), by frequency of co-occurrence. 185 types, 1,604 tokens

types	tokens	types	tokens
cyning 'king'	164	*caser* 'caesar'	47
folc 'people'	130	*Gāst* '[holy] Ghost'	39
bisceop 'bishop'	84	*dēofol* 'devil'	30
God 'God'	80	*fæder* 'father'	29
Hǣlend 'Saviour'	75	*abbod* 'abbot'	25
total			1,604

for expressions of time can be made out. Temporal nouns do occur with *þam* as well (*dæg, gēar, mōnþ, ǣfen, morgen*) but collectively make up only some 2% of all noun collocates.

A distinctive collexeme analysis (for this method, see Stefanowitsch & Gries, 2003; Gries & Stefanowitsch, 2004) provides us with a numeric assessment of the strengths of association that hold between the two constructions (i.e. instrumental- and dative-determiner noun phrases) and their collexemes, as well as with measures of statistical significance, based on the frequencies with which each noun occurs in either construction.[4] The output, shown in abbreviated form in Table 6, confirms the trend established so far, in accordance with the functions of the instrumental identified by Mitchell & Robinson (2001 [1964]: § 92): the lexical items most strongly associated with *þȳ* are the temporal nouns *gēar* 'year', *dæg* 'day' and *sumer* 'summer', followed by *weg* 'way' and *þēaw* 'custom, manner', both of which are conventionally used in adverbials of manner ('in this way', 'in this manner' – see below); those most strongly associated with *þam* refer to persons (*folc* 'people', *man* 'man', *bisceop* 'bishop', *god* 'God' and *hǣlend* 'Saviour'), which reflects the central functions of the OE dative case, the designation of recipients and experiencers.

4. The analysis was carried out in R (R Core Team, 2016) with the script collex.dist() from the package 'collostructions' (Flach, 2016). The collex.dist() script calculates a measure of association (in this case the -log(10)-transformed p-value of the Fisher-Yates exact test) for each lexical item on a joined frequency list. The output (see Table 6) shows observed and expected frequencies of occurrence of each noun in construction 1 (with instrumental *þȳ*) and construction 2 (with dative *þam*), the construction each item is more strongly associated with, the strength of this association and the level at which the result is statistically significant.

Table 6. Distinctive collexemes (nouns) of *þȳ* and *þam*. YCOE data, span = 0:2

1	word	O.cxn1	E.cxn1	O.cxn2	E.cxn2	assoc.	coll. str.	sign. level
1	*gēar*	314	82.5	9	240.5	INS	960.55393	*****
2	*dæg*	161	45.2	16	131.8	INS	379.83425	*****
3	*sumer*	9	2.3	0	6.7	INS	24.68931	*****
4	*weg*	6	1.5	0	4.5	INS	16.43465	****
5	*þēaw*	5	1.3	0	3.7	INS	13.68866	***
…	…	…	…	…	…	…	…	…
445	*hǣlend*	0	18.9	74	55.1	DAT	44.52413	*****
446	*god*	0	20.4	80	59.6	DAT	48.21582	*****
447	*bisceop*	0	21.4	84	62.6	DAT	50.68396	*****
448	*man*	0	29.6	116	86.4	DAT	70.63460	*****
449	*folc*	0	33.2	130	96.8	DAT	79.48012	*****

The very strong association of instrumental, but not dative, determiners with expressions for time shows that it was the instrumental rather than the dative or a category comprising both cases that was associated with the function of forming temporal adverbials. The fact that dative-case determiners are also found in this construction, though much less frequently, shows that the forms, but not the function, of the instrumental were falling out of use.

The overwhelming majority of instrumental-case noun phrases, then, are temporal adverbials. What about the rest?

The nouns in the remaining 6% are *weg* 'way' (n = 6), *þēaw* 'custom, usage' (n = 5), *gemete* 'measure, way, manner' (n = 3) and *hēafod* 'head' (n = 3) plus various hapax items as such as *nama* 'name', *ryht* 'right' and *clyf* 'cliff' (see Table 4 above). These do not seem to constitute a coherent semantic field at first glance. However, the close reading of the passages in question reveals two functional groups: adverbials of place, as in Example 6, and adverbials of manner, accompaniment, instrument etc., as in Examples 7 and 8:

(6) *On þære ea ofre stod hreod ⁊ pintreow ⁊ abies þæt treowcyn ungemetlicre gryto ⁊ micelnysse*
þy ***clyfe***
the-INS cliff-DAT/INS
weox ⁊ wridode.
'Above the river, reeds and pinetrees stood, and fir trees of huge size grew and flourished on the cliff.'
(Alexander's Letter to Aristotle, coalex,Alex: 12.11.100–13.103)

(7) *Tealdon hie ⁊ wendon þæt his oþer lichoma*
þy ***þeawe*** ***deadra*** ***manna***
the-INS manner-DAT/INS dead-GEN men-GEN
fornumen wære
'They reported and believed that his other body, by the nature of dead men, had dissolved …'.
(Bede's History of the English Church, cobede,Bede_4: 31.374.20.3742)

(8) … *⁊ hu mon mæg*
þy ***ilcan*** ***weorce***
the-INS same-DAT/INS work-DAT/INS
cweþan þæt netenu send gesælige …
'…and how one can, by the same logic, say that animals are happy …'.
(Boethius' Consolation of Philosophy [chapter headings], coboeth,BoHead: 31.37)

As an interim conclusion, we can note that instrumental-case noun phrases with *þȳ* express place, manner/instrument and time. To see whether these findings are representative of the instrumental at large, we will take a look at the other frequent word class for instrumentals, adjectives, before discussing this combination of functions and its significance for the Old English case system.

3.3 Instrumental-case adjectives

Most instrumental-case adjectives are quantifiers occurring in adverbials of time and manner. (Quantifiers are distinguished from other adjectives by YCOE part-of-speech tag; the categorization is somewhat arbitrary and not of consequence for the issue at hand.) In the YCOE, there are 365 instances of ten different instrumental-case quantifiers occurring in bare-case noun phrases, the most frequent ones being *sum* 'some' (n = 152) and *ælc* 'each' (n = 148). In addition, there are 158 instances of 42 different instrumental-case adjectives not tagged as quantifiers, the most frequent one by far being *ōþer* 'other' (n = 102), which is, in fact, very often used much like a quantifier, meaning 'another' (as in *ōþre naman* 'by another name'). The rest of the types have low frequencies. The use of instrumental-case adjectives is exemplified in (9)–(15) below. Table 7 lists those noun collocates that occur more than once.

Table 7. Noun collocates of instrumental-case adjectives (including quantifiers), by frequency of co-occurrence. 56 types, 602 tokens

types	tokens	types	tokens
dæg 'day'	265	*dǣl* 'part'	5
gēar 'year'	67	*dōm* 'judgement'	4
sīþ 'time'	65	*morgen* 'morning'	4
nama 'name'	32	*sunnandæg* 'Sunday'	4
þing 'thing'	25	*fæc* 'interval'	3
werod 'host, troop'	17	*mōnaþ* 'month'	3
mōd 'mind, spirit'	16	*mūþ* 'mouth'	3
gemet 'measure'	15	*þēaw* 'custom, manner'	3
word 'word'	9	*frigedæg* 'Friday'	2
mægen 'strength'	8	*hlēt* 'lot, fate, fortune'	2
man 'man'	8	*līf* 'life'	2
dēaþ 'death'	6	*weorc* 'work'	2
total			602

(9) *Þa gelamp hit* ***sume dæge,***
there happen-3SG.PST it-NOM some-INS day-DAT/INS
þæt his broðer Gregorius ...
'Then it happened some day that his brother Gregory ...'.
(Gregory's Dialogues, cogregdC,GDPref_and_4_[C]: 9.273.6.3975)

(10) ***Ælce monað,***
every-INS month-DAT/INS
heo yrnð under an ðæra tacna.
'Every month it [the sun] runs under one of the signs [of the zodiac].'
(De Temporibus Anni, cotempo,+ATemp: 4.2.123)

(11) *Forþy we sceoldon* ***ealle mægene***
for we-NOM shall-3PL.PST all-INS strength-DAT/INS
spyrian æfter Gode.
'Because we are supposed to inquire after God with all [our] strength.'
(Boethius' Consolation of Philosophy, coboeth,Bo: 41.147.10.2938)

(12) *Gallie ⁊ Hispanie þam mæstum dælum Europe*
myccle ***fæce*** *ongegen*
great-INS interval-DAT/INS against
'...opposite Gaul and Spain and the greater part of Europe in a great distance ...'.[5]
(Bede's History of the English Church, cobede,Bede_1: 0.24.29.178)

5. *Myccle fæce ongeagen* translates *multo intervallo adversa*, a Latin construction containing a dative/ablative of similar function as *myccle fæce*. The choice of a bare-case NP (as opposed to a PP) may have been prompted by the original; cf. Mitchell, 2000 [1985]: 595, § 1424 for a similar take on the influence of the Latin ablative of duration on the use of temporal instrumentals. With

(13) *ærest on Easter æfen, and*
oþre *siþe* *on candelmæsse æfen*
other-INS time-DAT/INS on Candlemas-DAT evening-DAT
'...first on the night before Easter, and another time on the night before Candlemas ...'. (Canons of Edgar, cocanedgX,WCan_1.1.2_[Fowler]: 54.64)

(14) *Wæs Breotene ealond Romanum uncuð, oððæt Gaius se casere,*
oðre ***naman*** *Iulius,*
other-INS name-DAT/INS Julius-NOM
hit mid ferde gesohte ⁊ geeode syxtygum wintra ær Cristes cyme.
'The island of Britain was unknown to the Romans, until Gaius the caesar, by another name Julius, sought it out and came there with an army sixty years ere the coming of Crist.'
(Bede's History of the English Church, cobede,Bede_1: 4.32.1.248)

(15) *forþon þe hie [...] oþ heora lifes ende,*
untweogende ***mode*** *þurhwunodan*
unwavering-INS mind-DAT/INS continue-3PL.PST
'...because they [...] continued unwavering in mind until the end of their lives.'
(Blicking Homilies: Peter and Paul, coblick,LS_32_[PeterandPaul[BlHom_15]]: 171.5.2159)

The picture that emerges resembles the distribution of the collocates of instrumental-case determiners. *Dæg* and *gēar* again head the list and there is a good deal of overlap between the two sets of nouns. With the collocates of instrumental-case adjectives, nouns used in adverbials of manner have a greater relative share than with the collocates of instrumental-case determiners. This difference in distribution may be due not only to chance but also to the likely semantics of indefinite noun phrases and the quantifiers occurring in them. Temporal adverbials tend to refer back to given information to anchor new information in the sequence of events; they are therefore more likely to contain determiners such as *þȳ*. Adjectives, by contrast, are more likely to introduce the kind of additional information that characterizations or descriptions of manner provide. The slightly different distribution and ranking of the collocates can thus be accounted for with reference to other properties of the different word classes. In sum, the functions of noun phrases containing instrumental-case adjectives match those identified for noun phrases with instrumental-case determiners: the expression of time and of manner.

YCOE data, however, no statistically significant difference in the rate of instrumental use can be made out between texts known to be based on Latin originals and other texts. If anything, texts that are believed to have been composed in Old English tend to contain more instrumental forms. This fits in with Callaway's observation that Latin ablatives of duration are more frequently rendered as accusatives in Old English than as (instrumental) datives (Callaway, 1922; see also Mitchell, 2000 [1985]: 596, § 1423). The grammar of the original was thus not necessarily decisive.

Note that Table 7 contains the noun *man* 'man', which refers not to time or manner, but to a person. There are eight instances of *man* occurring in instrumental-case NPs, all of them verbal arguments, five of which are *nane man* 'no man, nobody' and two *ælce/æghwylce mæn* 'each man, everybody'. Six out of the eight examples are found in Alcuin's *De Virtutibus et Vitiis*; two of them are given in (16) and (17):

(16) *ærest ealre þingen*
æighwylce mæn *is* *to secene*
each-INS man-DAT/INS be-3SG.PRS to seek-INFL.INF
hwæt seo se soðe wisedom.
'Above all, each man should seek to find out what true wisdom is.'
(Alcuin's *De Virtutibus et Vitiis*, coalcuin,Alc_[Warn_35]: 1.3)

(17) *For þan sceal* **ælce mæn** *sceamigen*
for the-INS shall-3SG.PRS each-INS man-DAT/INS shame-INF
þæt he ofermod seo.
'Therefore each man should be ashamed of being proud.'
(Alcuin's *De Virtutibus et Vitiis*,coalcuin, Alc_[Warn_35]: 253.186)

Mitchell (2000 [1985]: 566, § 1345) lists some other examples illustrating the variation between the two cases, including instrumentals and datives juxtaposed within phrases or in parallel constructions and variant readings from different manuscripts of the same text. Only one of his examples, as far as I can see, contains a verbal argument in the instrumental case, i.e. an instrumental clearly intruding into the realm of the dative proper. This is the sentence in (18), in which an addressee/recipient is encoded by an instrumental:

(18) *Gas on middengeord alne*
bodigað god spel **elce gescæfte**
proclaim-IMP.PL gospel-ACC each-INS creature-DAT/INS
'Go into all the world [and] proclaim the gospel to each creature.'
(Gospel of St. Mark, 16,15, Ruthwell glosses, Skeat 1871: 133)

Mitchell unfortunately does not say anything about the frequency of such examples in his data. The sentences in (16) and (17) are the only examples of verbal arguments that the queries for NPs with instrumental-case determiners or adjectives in the YCOE produce. Extending the query to possessive pronouns unearths three additional addressees and even one apparent instrumental in an external possessor construction, reproduced in (19), which is a clear intrusion into the domain of the dative case.

(19) ⁊ *nu leof* ***mine cnihte*** *ða honde*
& now dear my-INS servant-DAT/INS the-NOM hands-NOM
forswælede beoð.
'and now, dear [Lord], my servant's hands are scorched'
(History of the Holy Rood Tree, corood,LS_5_[InventCrossNap]: 168.173)

Such occurrences must be taken into consideration, of course. However, Examples 16 and 17 make up less than 1% of all noun collocates of instrumental-case quantifiers. More importantly, even a total of half a dozen or even a dozen recipients, addressees and experiencers in the instrumental case would represent only a tiny fraction of all the verbal arguments in the dative case in the corpus (more than 17,000). As isolated occurrences, such examples do not, I think, challenge the general observation that instrumentals only very rarely intrude upon the territory of the dative proper. Without wishing to dismiss counter-examples such as the ones in (16)–(19) as scribal or editorial errors, or as necessarily due only to the weakening of unaccented vowels in late texts (*ælce man* vs. *ælcum man*), I argue that they do not change anything about the significant functional difference between dative and instrumental that can be witnessed in Old English if we take collexeme semantics into account.

3.4 Interim synthesis and discussion

That the Old English instrumental should express time, manner and place makes perfect sense given that the case represents the merger of the PIE locative, ablative and instrumental. The concept of place, i.e. location in space, contributed by the locative, would have served as a source domain for location in time, which explains the very strong association of the Old English instrumental with temporal noun phrases. That this metaphor is at work in Old English is immediately obvious in view of such frequent polysemous words as *þā* 'there, then' and *hēr* 'here, now', for instance. Instrumental-case phrases expressing location in space are rare, especially in prose, since this function has largely been transferred to prepositional phrases, but they do exist (see *þȳ clife* 'on the cliff' in Example 6 above), testifying to the semantic origin of the instrumental location-in-time construction. The function of expressing manner, instrument and related senses is contributed by the PIE instrumental.

Can we detect any traces left by the PIE ablative as well? I have come across only two examples of instrumentals potentially expressing spatial origin, one literal, the other metaphorical. They are given in Examples 20 and 21:

(20) *Gif mon gesiðcundne monnan adrife,*
<u>*fordrife*</u> *ðy* ***botle*** *næs* ***þære*** ***setene.***
drive-away-3SG.SBJ the-INS abode-DAT/INS not the.DAT/GEN set.DAT/GEN
'If one expells a tenant, let him be driven from the abode, but not [deprived of] what he has planted.' (The Laws of Ine, colawine,LawIne: 68.175)

(21) *Mid þy heo þa*
þy ***slæpe*** <u>*tobræc,*</u>
the-INS sleep-DAT/INS break-apart-3SG.PST
'When she awoke from sleep, ...'.
(Bede's History of the English Church, cobede,Bede_4: 24.340.13.3410)

Example 20 involves a literal place of origin, *botl* 'the abode', in the instrumental, as well as a conjoined dative- or genitive-case possessum which someone is not to be driven away from (*seten* 'what is set, planted' is feminine, hence no instrumental determiner would have been available). The instrumental in Example 21 can be counted as a metaphorical extension of the origin construction if we accept that states (here: sleep) can be conceptualized as areas (cf. Lakoff & Johnson, 1980: 31) so that they can be talked about in spatial terms. Bosworth and his editors (BT, s.v. *tobregdan*) translate 'break of, start from' and note that Icelandic cognate *bregða* occurs in a parallel construction *bregða svefni* 'awake from sleep'. The association of this verb with the instrumental/dative thus seems to be common to Germanic; perhaps it can be attributed to the ablative part of the syncretic case. In general, however, the function of designating spatial origin is fulfilled by prepositional phrases in Old English, so the instrumental/dative of origin must really be considered a vestige rather than a productive construction.

Having thus established that the Old English instrumental case fulfils functions distinct from those of the dative proper, and that these functions accord well with what we know about the syncretic case's etymology, the question arises how productive this functional differentiation is in Old English.

4. Fixed formulae or productive pattern?

The corpus analysis leads to two somewhat paradoxical conclusions. On the one hand, the instrumental is never obligatory but alternates with the dative in all of its functions; on the other hand, its occurrence is clearly semantically restricted. In other words, speakers/writers knew in which contexts it was appropriate to use an instrumental but did not necessarily use one in all of them, even where the forms would have been available. What does this say about the status of the instrumental as a case? Can we take the strong preference for instrumentals in phrases expressing manner and time as indicative of productive case functions, or are we dealing with fossilizations?

Productivity depends on type frequency. A high token frequency of one particular collocation only strengthens the entrenchment of that particular collocation; it is not until the host class of a construction contains a reasonably large number of different lexical items that speakers abstract away from individual expressions and form categories with more schematic slots (cf. Bybee, 2007, 2013). Particular combinations of instrumental-case modifier and noun, it is true, are very frequent and probably represent strongly entrenched expressions. Table 8 lists the most frequent phrases, how large a percentage of all tokens of the respective construction they represent, and over how many different texts their occurrences are dispersed, as a rough indication of how current they might have been language-wide.

Table 8. The most frequent combinations of instrumental-case determiners/adjectives and nouns (YCOE data)

combination	tk.	cxn	% in cxn	dispersion over corpus texts
þȳ ilcan gēare 'in the same year'	237	[DET-INS + N]	44 (n = 539)	Anglo-Saxon Chronicles (194), Bede (6); 6 other texts
sume dæge 'some day'	117	[Q-INS + N]	32 (n = 365)	Gregory's *Dialogues* (74);15 other texts
ælce dæge 'each day'	79	[Q-INS + N]	22 (n = 365)	28 texts
ōþre sīþe 'another time'	40	[ADJ-INS + N]	23 (n = 172)	21 texts
ōþre naman 'by another name'	32	[ADJ-INS + N]	19 (n = 172)	Orosius (17); Bede (6); Boethius (5); 3 other texts

What Table 8 shows is that some instrumentals occur in relatively fixed expressions with high token frequencies, which could indicate that the instrumental is not used productively in these cases. Thus 237 (44%) of all noun phrases with *þȳ* are *þȳ ilcan gēare* and 117 (32%) of all noun phrases with instrumental-case quantifiers are *sume dæge* (i.e. 19% with respect to adjectives overall). The phrase *ōþre sīþe* '(at) another time' is frequent in narrative and accounts for all 48 instances of *sīþ* in the instrumental.

We cannot attribute *all* occurrences of the instrumental to more or less fixed multi-word expressions, however. The temporal nouns occurring with instrumental-case determiners are a set of 16 different items, seven of which are hapaxes in the construction. With instrumental-case adjectives, there are 56 different nouns on the list. Here, fossilization is even less likely.

While the figures are small, they are large enough to suggest that the association is not a purely lexical one that might be frozen and archaic, but one between a case and a specific semantic function. Note that Latin loan *indictio* occurs with *þȳ* (see Table 4 above). This indicates that the location in time construction with instrumental was extensible to new lexical items at least as late as when Latin computus-related terms entered the language, which must have been in historical times. This is not surprising given its high degree of semantic coherence, which, together with type frequency, determines productivity (cf. Barðdal, 2008: 34).

Productivity is a gradable concept, so the answer to the question of whether instrumental-headed noun phrases are fossilizations will be more complicated than yes or no. The constructions display considerable variation, both in terms of syntactic structure and in terms of host class, so they are not entirely fossilized. If we consider all noun collocates of instrumental modifiers together, about 25% of the temporal nouns and about 75% of the non-temporal nouns are hapax legomena in the construction. Since the noun slots of the constructions are thus filled with a substantial number of different items, they must be semantically, not lexically defined.

I argue that combinations of the types *þȳ (ilcan) gēare*, *sume dæge* and *ōþre sīþe* are best analysed as colligations, i.e. entrenched combinations of grammatical categories with specific (sets of) lexical items (cf. Stubbs, 2001: 65), rather than fossilizations. The type frequencies are, I think, too great to assume fossilizations. Old English instrumental-case noun phrases must therefore be considered at least partly productive, which makes the instrumental an integral part of the Old English case system.

5. What influences the degree to which the instrumental is used?

No straightforward correlation between the proportion of instrumentals in a given text and the time of its production can be made out in the YCOE. In all three temporal slices of the corpus for which there is sufficient data to compare (OE 2, OE 3, OE 4) there are texts with 100% of dative-case temporal adverbials containing instrumental forms as well as texts with 0%. Mean scores vary between 75% and 50% (see Figure 2), but the differences are not statistically significant. In other words, with the amount of data we have, we cannot exclude the possibility that this is random fluctuation.

Nor do the poetic texts included in the YCOE-P display greater relative frequencies of instrumentals in temporal adverbials, despite the fact that Old English poetry is linguistically more conservative than prose. On the contrary, as Figure 3 shows, instrumentals are much more frequent in Old English prose than in poetry, perhaps due to the kinds of genres represented.

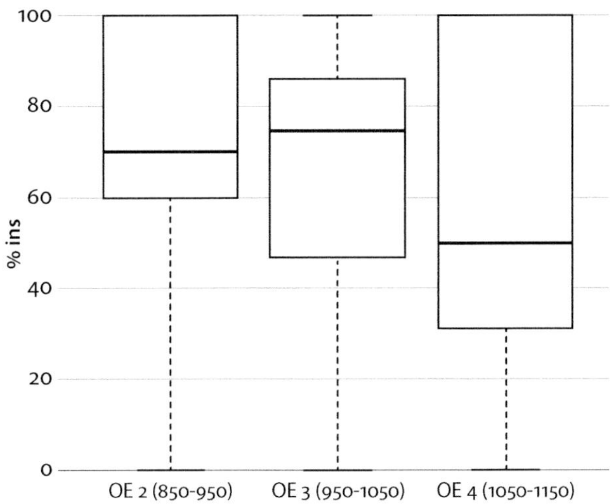

Figure 2. Proportions of dative/instrumental-case temporal NPs that contain instrumental forms, by sub-period; all texts with at least one NP-TMP considered (OE 2: 9 texts; OE 3: 41 texts; OE 4: 21 texts)

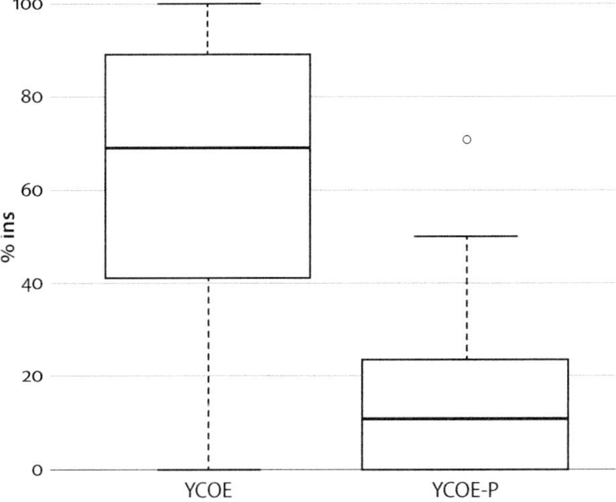

Figure 3. Proportions of dative/instrumental-case temporal NPs that contain instrumental forms in OE prose (YCOE) and OE poetry (YCOE-P); all texts with at least one NP-TMP considered (YCOE: n = 71; YCOE-P: n = 11)

A great proportion of instrumentals is found in relatively fixed phrases that are typical for specific text types (see Table 8 above). The phrase *þȳ ilcan gēare*, for instance, is very frequent in the four Anglo-Saxon Chronicle texts included in the corpus and in Bede's *History of the English Church*, a text closely related to the Chronicles. Chronicles A, C and D are also the texts with the highest relative frequencies of instrumentals in temporal adverbials (99%, 97% and 90%, respectively). This suggests that it may be the genre or format of a text (chronicle or list) rather than its age that correlates with the degree to which instrumentals are used. Set phrases like *þȳ ilcan gēare* are used as text-structuring devices and recur in identical shape in many chronicle entries, which may have induced more consistency in instrumental usage than might otherwise have been produced.

6. Conclusion: The instrumental as "vestigial"

Since, as we have seen, the instrumental is associated with very specific functions, what exactly do we mean when we say that the instrumental is "vestigial"?

The instrumental is not a fully functional case in Old English. The opposition between the instrumental and the dative cannot be made explicit in all cases where it might be relevant. This, however, is to a lesser extent also true of the dative and the genitive, for instance, which are indistinguishable in the feminine. No case in Old English has all unambiguous forms. The difference is one of degree.

Dative forms were encroaching upon even the remaining uses of the instrumental, which effectively transfers their functions to the dative as well and renders the instrumental-dative opposition optional. In this sense, then, the instrumental, or, rather, the opposition between dative and instrumental, is "vestigial".

Going beyond the terminological question of whether we may call the Old English instrumental a separate case, I argue that its most important functions, the expression of location in time and of manner/instrument, are best viewed as independent epicentres of the merged dative case's semantic network. That is, the instrumental contributes senses to the merged case on par with the dative proper, senses that are not semantically derived from or directly related to those of the dative. If we want to understand the Old English case system as a system and the motivations behind it, we should treat the instrumental as a category in its own right.

Acknowledgement

I thank the editors of the present volume and two anonymous reviewers for their very helpful comments on an earlier version of this paper. All remaining errors are my own.

References

Baker, Peter S. (2012) [2003]. *Introduction to Old English.* (3rd ed.). Chichester, West Sussex, Hoboken, N.J.: Wiley-Blackwell.

Barðdal, Johanna (2008). *Productivity. Evidence from Case and Argument Structure in Icelandic.* Amsterdam: John Benjamins. https://doi.org/10.1075/cal.8

BT = Bosworth, Joseph, Northcote Toller, Thomas, Christ, Sean, & Tichý, Ondřej (Eds.). (2012) [1898/1921]. *An Anglo-Saxon Dictionary Online.* Prague: Faculty of Arts, Charles University. Retrieved from http://bosworth.ff.cuni.cz/

Brunner, Karl (1951). *Die englische Sprache. Ihre geschichtliche Entwicklung. Zweiter Band. Die Flexionsformen, ihre Verwendung, das Englische außerhalb Europas.* (Sammlung kurzer Grammatiken germanischer Dialekte). Halle: Niemeyer.

Bybee, Joan L. (2007). *Frequency of use and the organization of language.* Oxford, New York: Oxford University Press. https://doi.org/10.1093/acprof:oso/9780195301571.001.0001

Bybee, Joan L. (2013). Usage-based theory and exemplar representations of constructions. In Thomas Hoffmann, & Graeme Trousdale (Eds.), *The Oxford handbook of construction grammar* (49–69). Oxford, New York: Oxford University Press.

Callaway, M. (1922). The dative of time how long in OE. *Modern Language Notes* 37, 129–141. https://doi.org/10.2307/2914993

DWB = Grimm, Jacob, & Wilhelm Grimm (Eds.). (1854–1961). *Deutsches Wörterbuch.* 16 vols. Leipzig: Hirzel.

Flach, Susanne (2016). *collostructions: An R Implementation for the Family of Collostructional Methods.* Version 0.0.3. Retreived from www.bit.ly/sflach

Freeman, Aaron (2018).[6] Patterns of retention of the instrumental case in Old English. *North-Western European Language Evolution* 71:1, 35–55.

Gries, Stefan, & Stefanowitsch, Anatol (2004). Extending collostructional analysis: A corpus-based perspective on 'alternations'. *International Journal of Corpus Linguistics* 9, 97–129. https://doi.org/10.1075/ijcl.9.1.06gri

Hogg, Richard M. (2012). *An Introduction to Old English.* (Edinburgh Textbooks on the English Language). Edinburgh: Edinburgh University Press.

Lakoff, George, & Johnson, Mark (1980). *Metaphors we live by.* Chicago: University of Chicago Press.

Marsden, Richard (2015). *The Cambridge Old English Reader.* Cambridge: Cambridge University Press. https://doi.org/10.1017/CBO9781107295209

Mitchell, Bruce (2000) [1985]. *Old English Syntax.* Oxford: Oxford University Press.

Mitchell, Bruce, & Robinson, Fred C. (2001) [1964]. *A Guide to Old English.* Oxford: Blackwell.

R Core Team. (2016). *R: A Language and Environment for Statistical Computing.* Vienna.

Ringe, Donald (2006). *From Proto-Indo-European to Proto-Germanic* (A linguistic history of English 1). Oxford: Oxford University Press.

Ringe, Donald, & Taylor, Ann (2014). *The development of Old English* (A linguistic history of English 2). Oxford: Oxford University Press. https://doi.org/10.1093/acprof:oso/9780199207848.001.0001

6. Freeman (2018) could unfortunately not be considered, since the present article was already in press.

Skeat, Walter W. (1871). *The Gospel According to Saint Mark*. Cambridge: Cambridge University Press.

Stefanowitsch, Anatol, & Gries, Stefan (2003). Collostructions: investigating the interaction between words and constructions. *International Journal of Corpus Linguistics* 8, 209–243. https://doi.org/10.1075/ijcl.8.2.03ste

Stubbs, Michael (2001). *Words and phrases: Corpus studies of lexical semantics*. Oxford: Blackwell.

Taylor, Ann (2003a). The York-Toronto-Helsinki Parsed Corpus of Old English Prose. Part-of-speech Reference Manual. Retrieved from http://www-users.york.ac.uk/~lang22/YCOE/doc/annotation/YcoePos.htm

Taylor, Ann (2003b). The York-Toronto-Helsinki Parsed Corpus of Old English Prose. Syntactic Annotation Reference Manual. Retrieved from ftp:/www.ling.upenn.edu/facpapers/tony_kroch/mideng-corpus/ppcme2dir/YCOE/doc/annotation/YcoeRef.htm

Wright, Joseph, & Wright, Elizabeth Mary (1914). *Old English Grammar*. London: Humphrey Milford; Oxford: Oxford University Press.

YCOE = Taylor, Ann, Warner, Anthony, Pintzuk, Susan, & Beths, Frank (2003). *The York-Toronto-Helsinki Parsed Corpus of Old English Prose (YCOE)*. Heslington: Department of Language and Linguistic Science, University of York.

YCOE-P = Pintzuk, Susan, & Plug, Leendert (2001). *The York-Helsinki Parsed Corpus of Old English Poetry (YCOE-P)*. Heslington: Department of Language and Linguistic Science, University of York.

‘Thone vpon thother’

On pronouns *one* and *other* with initial *th*- and *t*- in Middle English

Jerzy Nykiel

A frequent result produced by a search of the digital corpora of Middle English (henceforth ME) for instances of reduced *th*’ is a nominal involving the pronouns *one* or *other* with initial *th*- or *t*- attached. In this study I argue that two different mechanisms, that is reduction of the definite article and misanalysis of the preceding demonstrative, need to be taken into account when scrutinizing the emergence of what turns out to be four different pronouns, namely *thone, thother, tone*, and *tother*. First I flesh out the ways in which these pronouns were used in ME. Then I analyze textual evidence which sheds light on the question when and how these pronouns emerged. Finally I argue that while initial *th*- is always a definite determiner reduced as expected given the DP cycle, initial *t*- can be either a definite determiner or, less likely, part of a lexicalized pronoun.

Keywords: pronoun, determiner, Middle English, definiteness, DP cycle

1. Introduction

This study originates in an investigation of a reduced variant of the definite article in ME and EModE. As shown in Viereck (1995), van Gelderen (2011), Nykiel (2015, 2016), throughout the ME and EModE periods, definite nominals are attested where the definite article has its form reduced to a proclitic realized orthographically as *þ*, *ð* and later as *th* and *th*’.[1] A typical example would be (1a) and (1b) where reduced *th*’ attaches to the host noun *abbotrice* ‘abbey’ and *admyrall* ‘admiral’, as well as (1c) where the host to reduced *th*’ is the attributive adjective *alde* ‘old’. Such examples can be found throughout ME and up until the 18th century.

1. Beginning with the middle of the 16th century reduced *th*’ comes to be spelt with an apostrophe following Hart’s (1569) advice (Salmon, 1999, 30). For reasons of convenience, *th*’ is used is this study when no particular orthographic variant of the reduced definite article is meant.

https://doi.org/10.1075/cilt.346.04nyk

(1) a. ⁊ *begæt Thare priuileges an Of alle þe lands of* ***þabbotrice***
And obtained Their privileges one Of all the lands of the-abbey
"and obtained their privileges, one for all the lands of the abbey,"
?a1160 *Peterb.Chron.*(LdMisc 636) an.1137 (CMEPV)

b. *[they] made grete slaughter of the turkes & of the persans. And*
they made great slaughter of the Turks and of the Persians and
whan ***thadmyrall*** *sawe this,*
when the-admiral saw this
"they slaughtered many Turks and Persians. And when the admiral saw this,"
1489 Caxton *Sonnes of Aymon* (Caxton: Richardson) 504/9 (CMEPV)

c. *Unnderr all* ***þalde*** ***laȝhess*** *fresst/ Wærenn alle þe prestess*
Under all the-old laws first were all the priests
"According to the old laws, all the priests were first".
?c1200 *Orm.* (Jun 1) 481 (CMEPV)

Nykiel (2015) finds pragmatic differences between the use of nominals with the full form of the definite article and the use of nominals with reduced *th'*. Reduced *th'*, when used in an anaphoric nominal, tends to appear with a shorter antecedent distance than the full form, it also tends to appear with discourse topics and it is used if there are no competing references in the preceding discourse. Nykiel (2016) goes beyond anaphorically used nominals with reduced *th'* and reports on a correlation between the choice of reduced *th'* and givenness of information.

Reduced *th'* as such is not a focal point of this study, however. While searching for examples of reduced *th'* nominals in the corpora of ME, a common finding is a variant of the pronouns *one* and *other* with initial *t-* or *th-* such as *tane/tone/toon/thone* and *tother/tothur/tothir/tothyr/thother.*[2] At first sight they seem to be instances of reduced *th'* where the host is a pronoun rather than a noun or an adjective as in Example 1, but such a straightforward account turns out not to be accurate. I argue for a division between the forms with initial *th-* on the one hand, which I will refer to as *thone* and *thother* in this study and the forms with initial *t-* on the other, handled under the umbrella terms *tone* and *tother*. The former two are not noted in the literature apart form a brief entry for *thother* in the *Middle English Dictionary* (henceforth MED). *Tone* and *tother* are mentioned by Barry (1972) and Jones (2002) but are far from central to their discussions and are somewhat dismissed as forms arising from incorrect syllable division. Central to this study is the claim that *thone, thother, tone,* and *tother* are four different pronouns in ME. I present evidence showing that *thother* appears earliest as a product of reduction of

2. Variants with alternative spelling with an initial thorn or eth are not listed here but were common throughout ME.

the definite article. The pronouns with initial *t-* cliticized are only partly attributable to incorrect syllable division, and partly also to reduction of the definite article. In this study I aim to argue that initial *th-* is a more straightforward case of a definite article whose reduction can be accounted for by the operation of the DP cycle. Initial *t-*, on the other hand, is a more complex case. It is a reduced definite article often preceded by a full form of the definite article but it can also be construed as incorporated into the form of the pronoun, having no clear syntactic function.

This paper is structured in the following way. In Section 2 I introduce the notions of the DP cycle and double articulation pertinent to the analysis of *thone, thother, tone,* and *tother.* Then I proceed to an examination of the meaning and functions of the four pronouns in ME in Section 3. Section 4 is concerned with an attempt to trace the origins of *thone, thother, tone,* and *tother.* This section combines insights from the literature, an examination of select early ME texts and data retrieved from the digital corpora of ME. In Section 5, I verify the validity of the idea that reduced *th'*, also realized as initial *t-*, after a period when it cliticized onto nouns and adjectives only, was extended to the pronouns *other* and *one.* A final stage in this study is an attempt at accounting for the development of the pronouns in terms of the DP cycle (Section 6). For reasons of convenience I refer to *one* and *other* as pronouns throughout this study regardless of whether they head the NP or modify the head noun in the NP.

2. Setting the stage – The DP cycle and double articulation of definiteness

From a theoretical standpoint, the development of *tother*/*thother* and *tone*/*thone* intersects with two phenomena, namely the DP cycle and double articulation of definiteness. In this section both are fleshed out.

It has been observed in the literature that cross-linguistic developments affecting definite determiners are common, with definite articles developing from demonstrative pronouns and at a later stage tending to become clitics and affixes (Greenberg, 1978; Diessel, 1999; Lehmann, 2015). As definite articles become clitics or affixes, they may also further grammaticalize into gender markers, case markers or noun class markers, that is, they may lose the definiteness marking function. Such developments are referred to as the DP cycle in Lyons (1999) and van Gelderen (2011). At a stage where a definite article is a clitic/affix it will need a host such as a noun or an adjective in an NP. An often cited case in point is the suffixed definite article in the Scandinavian languages (see e.g. Taraldsen, 1990; Julien, 2005; Lohrmann 2011), as illustrated with a Swedish example in (2).

(2) film-en
film-DEF
"the film". (example taken from Lohrmann, 2011: 112)

Van Gelderen (2011: 201) notes that at this point, that is at the stage of the cycle where a definite article is a clitic/suffix, definiteness can be renewed and reinforced by the use of an additional definiteness marker. This may lead to double articulation of definiteness.

Plank (2003) offers a cross-linguistic typology of NPs which mark (in)definiteness twice, which is the essence of double articulation. Double articulation is most common if an NP contains an attributive adjective and a noun, and it has often been discussed in connection with NPs in the Scandinavian languages by e.g. Julien (2005), Lohrmann (2011), and Schoorlemmer (2012). This is illustrated with an example from Swedish in (3) where apart form the definite article suffix *-en*, there is also a definite article preceding the adjective.

(3) den *rolig-a* *film-en*
DEF funny-w[eak] film-DEF
"the funny film". (example taken from Lohrmann, 2011: 112)

Plank (2003) goes on to note, however, that there are languages where an NP has definiteness marked twice even if the NP is composed of the head noun only.

The DP cycle and double articulation are relevant to this study for two reasons. First, as I argue below that *tother/thother* and *tone/thone* emerge also via reduction of the definite article, this development will be seen as an instantiation of the DP cycle. Secondly, since the pronouns are attested with a preceding definite article, I will regard such NP as cases of double articulation of definiteness. It is to be noted that I will not use the notion of DP in this study apart from recurring references to the DP cycle. DP standardly indicates a determiner phrase where a determiner heads its own functional layer complemented by NP (see Abney, 1987 for the DP hypothesis). Instead I use a more traditional notion of the NP.

3. The pronouns *tone/thone* and *tother/thother* in ME

I begin this section with describing the ways of obtaining data for this study. As a next step I survey the ME uses of *tother/thother* and *tone/thone* based on the instances of the pronouns retrieved through a search of two digital corpora. Finally I proceed to briefly relate those uses to the functions of *other* and *one* in Present-day English.

I have made use of two digital corpora in order to obtain the instances of *tother/thother* and *tone/thone* necessary for this study, namely the *Penn-Helsinki Parsed Corpus of Middle English* (henceforth PPCME2) and the *Corpus of Middle English Prose and Verse* (henceforth CMEPV). The former is a small corpus as it contains around 1.2 million words. Since PPCME2 breaks the ME period down in to four sub-periods, that is M1 (1150–1250), M2 (1250–1350), M3 (1350–1420), M4 (1420–1500), I used this corpus to provide an overview of the use and changing frequency of the pronouns in ME. As PPCME2 contains mostly samples of texts, I did not consider it sufficient when it came to an investigation of the origins of *tother/thother* and *tone/thone.* I carried out such an investigation, as shown in Section 4, with the aid of CMEPV. Even though the information about the exact number of words this corpus contains is not available, it is obviously a much larger corpus than PPCME2. It has the advantage of offering access to the full texts of 146 ME works, including the texts pertinent to the origins of *tother/thother* and *tone/thone.*

The instances of *tother/thother* and *tone/thone* obtained from PPCME2 allow for a number of generalizations. Typically *tother/thother* is used anaphorically with a reference to the second of two entities mentioned earlier in the text. Very often *tother/thother* co-occurs with the pronoun *one* or its variant *tone/thone* where the latter stands for the first of the two entities mentioned. This use is illustrated in Example 4a where *tane* and *toþer* have *body* and *saule* respectively as antecedents.

(4) a. *Force in body and in saule, and hele, if It be þi will, of þe*
force in body and in soul and health if It be thy will of the
tane *and offe þe* ***toþer****.*
the-one and of the the-other
"Strength of the body and soul, and health, if it is your will, of one and the other." CMEDTHOR,39.549 (PPCME2)

b. *Tanne schal þe liȝt Of Crist goo Down fro dwellyng in þis*
then shall the light Of Christ go Down from dwelling in this
world, and schynen in þe ***toþur*** *world by mene Of þe day*
world and shine in the the-other world by means Of the day
of doom.
of doom
"Then the light of Christ will leave this world and will shine in the other world due to the day of doom." CMWYCSER,379.2752 (PPCME2)

c. *Þa hirdess þatt, (...) Haffdenn an hæfedd hird tatt was* Abufenn
those kins that Had one head kin that was Above
alle ***þoþre****,*
all the-others
"Those kins that had a head kin that was above all the others," CMORM,I,17.259 (PPCME2)

d. *þou sall understande fowre þynges. þe fyrst þyng es: what þyng*
you shall understand four things the first thing is what thing
fyles A man. þe ***toþer*** *þyng: what Makys hym clene. þe þyrd:*
defiles A man the the-other thing what Makes him clean the third
what haldes hym in clennes. þe ferþ:...
what holds him in cleanliness the fourth
"You will understand four things. The first thing is what it is that defiles a man. The second thing is what it is that makes him clean. The third thing is what it is that keeps him clean. The fourth …".
CMROLLEP,96.563 (PPCME2)

Optionally, while there is no anaphorical reference, *tother/thother* can still indicate the second of two entities as long as the presence of such two entities is understood. This is the case of Example 4b where the mention of this world implies existence of the other world as part of the Christian doctrine. Yet another possibility has *tother/thother* employed with reference to the remaining members of a set after one or more members of the same set have been first singled out. Example 4c displays *þoþre* 'the others' interpreted as pointing to the remaining kins after the head kin has been selected out of the set of kins. Finally *toþer/thother* appears in the context of enumeration where it is an ordinal numeral indicating a second item on a list. Needless to say, the list of items is not limited to just two, as in (4d).

The pronoun *tone/thone*, as noted earlier in this section, can co-occur with *thother/tother* or *the other* and convey a reference to the first of two entities either present in the earlier discourse, i.e. via anaphora or inferable from the context. Parallel co-occurrence of *one* and *other* goes back to OE, as noted by Mustanoja (1960 [2016]: 216). Example 4a above serves as an illustration of *tone/thone* used anaphorically. *Tone/thone* can obviously occur without *the other/tother/thother* but its application seems limited to contexts where it serves to select the first entity out of a set of two. Both of these aspects are visible in (5) where *tone* without co-occurring *the other/tother/thother* points to one member in a set of two knights. *Tone/thone* does not surface in a context of enumeration where more than two items are listed.

(5) 'A! ' seyde sir Tarquyne, 'thou Arte To me moste welcom of ony
Ah said sir Tarquyne you Are To me most welcome of any
knyght for we shall Never departe Tylle the **tone** of us be dede
knight for we shall Never depart Till the the-one of us be dead
"'Oh!' said sir Turquyne, 'you are the most welcome of all knights to me for we will never depart until one of us is dead.'"
CMMALORY,192.2833 (PPCME2)

It should be also said that *tother*/*thother* and *tone*/*thone* can serve as the head of an NP, as in (4a), as a modifier preceding the head noun, as in (4b) and (4d), or as an element that seems to show some properties of both the NP head and a modifier, as in (4c). *þoþre* 'the others' in (4c) can be interpreted as the head of the NP but it can also be argued to be a modifier with the head noun ellipted. Any further exploration of this issue is however outside the scope of this study.[3] These examples also show that the pronouns frequently admit definite determiners. Even without a definite determiner, however, the pronouns typically convey a reference to a definite entity, which follows from the way these forms of the pronouns *one* and *other* arose, as elaborated on in Section 4.

Most of the uses and features of *tother*/*thother* and *tone*/*thone* presented in this section are compatible with what Quirk *et al.* (1985) and Huddleston and Pullum (2002) say about the use of *one* and *other* in Present-day English. One notable exception is the use of *other* as an ordinal numeral synonymous to 'second' when a list contains more than two items. While Quirk *et al.* (1985: 262) classify *other* as a general ordinal numeral, the OED (s.v. *other*) notes that such an ordinal use of *other* is obsolete with the examples not extending beyond the year 1500.[4] It is at this time that the ordinal numeral *other* seems to be replaced with the numeral *second*, attested since the late 13th century (OED, s.v. *second*).

4. The origins of *tone*/*thone* and *tother*/*thother*

With the ME use of *thone*/*thother*/*tone*/*tother* fleshed out in Section 3, I investigate how and when these pronouns came into being. First, I consult the literature and dictionaries where the pronouns are mentioned or discussed, then I verify this information against evidence from the early ME texts, and finally I elicit instances of the pronouns from the two digital corpora of ME with a view to corroborating the findings. I first look into the origins of the variants of *other* as these variants seem to be older than those of *one*.

3. There is a significant lack of consensus in the literature as to how to approach such cases. A grammar of Present-day English such as Huddleston and Pullum (2002) talks about the head being fused with the modifier. There is a sizable body of literature which argues for an empty category, the head noun being present without taking any form, e.g. Lobeck (1995), Nerbonne and Mullen (1999). There are also those who see such NPs as cases of head noun ellipsis where the information about the head noun is distributed over the NP, e.g. Branco & Costa (2006).

4. A reviewer notes that the last example of the numeral *other* in the OED from 1875 comes from a translation of Virgil and is with much probability intended as archaic usage.

The OED and MED argue that we in fact have two different items. The first one is *thother* with initial *th-* attached, which is argued to be a result of coalescence (OED, s.v. *other*) or contraction (MED, s.v. *thother*) of the definite article. *Thother* never, at least in PPCME2, co-occurs with a definite article, or any determiner, and is an actual case of reduced *th'*. If *other* has initial *t-*, surfacing as *tother*, it is argued to have been a result of misanalysis of the demonstrative pronoun *that* which precedes *other* whereby the final *-t* is misinterpreted as the initial consonant of *other* (MED, s.v. *tother*, OED, s.v. *tother)*. Similar accounts of the emergence of *tother* can also be found in Onions (1966, s.v. *tother*) and Barry (1972), the latter account pointing to incorrect syllable division as the source of misinterpretation. At the same time, however, the MED does not rule out the possibility that *tother* is also a product of the reduction of the definite article, with the reduction leaving only a voiceless plosive attached to *other*. Such a reduction is even more likely given that early ME had a variant of the definite article spelt as *te*, where the consonant was a voiceless plosive. This form occurs first in the Peterborough Chronicle, the same text that exhibits the first attestations of the definite article in English according to van Gelderen (2011: 163). Viereck (1995) and Jones (2002) show that it is typically assimilation to a preceding alveolar plosive /d/ or /t/ that accounts for the form *te* of the definite article. *Tother* is typically preceded by a definite article in PPCME2, as in (6a), but there are also cases where there is no determiner preceding, as in (6b). The presence of the definite article validates the misanalysis hypothesis while the lack of the definite article in front of *tother* lends support to the possibility that *tother* results from reduction of the definite article. I have not found any examples with the demonstrative *that* preceding *tother*, which is another argument in favor of the misanalysis hypothesis.

(6) a. *In þe fyrst degre er men lickend to þe sternes; in the* ***toþer****,*
in the first degree are men likened to the stars in the the-other
till þe mone; in þe thyrd, til *þe sonne.*
to the moon In the third to the sun
"In the first degree men are likened to the stars, in the second to the moon and in the third to the sun." CMROLLEP,107.723 (PPCME2)

b. for *þe mare þat sho est* heȝid Ouir ***toþir****, þe mare aȝh sho*
for the more that she is high Over the-other the more ought she
at Halde þe cumandement of þe reule.
to Hold the commandment of the rule
"for the more she is raised above the rest, the more carefully she should observe the precepts of the rule." CMBENRUL,44.1354 (PPCME2)

By and large the same applies to *one* to the extent that the variants listed at the beginning of this section represent two different items. The pronoun *one* is quite frequent with the initial plosive, where the plosive originally belonged to the preceding demonstrative but was later misanalysed as part of the pronoun (MED, s.v. *ton*; OED, s.v. *tone*). *Tone* is typically preceded by a definite article in ME, as a search of PPCME2 indicates. Still, as the MED cautiously remarks, the option cannot be excluded that *tone* represents a reduced definite article attached to the pronoun for the same reasons as those discussed in connection with *tother*. As for the other of the two items, i.e. *thone*, the pronoun *one* is also attested in ME with initial *th'* attached, despite there being no note to this effect in either the OED or the MED. Needless to say, the form *thone* suggests that the definite article is reduced and attaches to the pronoun *one* as well. Examples of *thone* are rare, however. There are none in PPCME2, but I have been able to find a few in CMEPV, for example (7).

(7) whan *bayarde & braiforde sawe their maisters at the grounde /*
when Bayard and Braiforde saw their masters at the ground
incontynent they went **Thone** *to* **thother** */ and began to byte eche*
immediately they went The-one to the-other and began to bite each
other, & Cast their fete **thone** vpon **thother**
other and Cast their feet the-one upon the-other
"when Bayard and Braiforde saw their masters on the ground, they immediately went at each other, and began to bite each other and kicked at each other".
1489 Caxton *Sonnes of Aymon* (Caxton: Richardson) 267/4 (CMEPV)

The changes whereby the new forms of the pronouns *one* and *other* arose, as indicated in the literature cited in the section above, are summarized in Table 1.

Table 1. The origins of *toþer, þoþer, tane,* and *þane*

Change	**Mechanism held accountable**
þæt oþer > (þe) toþer	misanalysis triggered by incorrect syllable division
te oþer > toþer	reduction of definite article
þe oþer > þoþer	reduction of definite article
þæt ane > (þe) tane	misanalysis triggered by incorrect syllable division
te ane > tane	reduction of definite article
þe ane > þane	reduction of definite article

With a view to obtaining some independent evidence for the speculated origins of *thother/tother* and *tone*, I consider it worthwhile to look into some early ME sources where the forms are attested for the first time. Admittedly, there are no occurrences in the Peterborough Chronicle, a text which I have pointed to elsewhere as the earliest to display reduced *th'* in English (Nykiel, 2015: 110). The earliest examples of any of the pronouns investigated in this study are those of *thother* in the Ormulum, an early 13th century East Midland text whose author is considered to have applied a very meticulous orthography faithfully representing the dialect used by the author (Anderson & Britton, 1999). There are 11 occurrences of *thother* in the Ormulum and no occurrence of *tother* or *thone*/*tone*. Each time *thother* appears in a plural NP where it is never preceded by a definite article, as illustrated in (4c), repeated here as (8a), as well as in (8b). This strongly suggests that the reduction of the definite article is operative in the case of *other*, as it is with NPs headed by nouns (cf. Nykiel, 2015: 111). There is no evidence for misanalysis of the demonstrative in the Ormulum, however, as first, forms of *other*/*one* are not attested with initial *t-*, and secondly, *that* precedes *other* thirty two times and it precedes *one* sixteen times and neither *other* nor *one* take any initial *t-*.

(8) a. *Þa hirdess þatt, (...) Haffdenn an hæfedd hird tatt was* Abufenn
those kins that Had one head kin that was above
alle ***þoþre,***
all the-others
"Those kins that had a head kin that was above all the others,"
CMORM,I,17.259 (PPCME2)
?c 1200 Orm. (Jun 1) 585 (CMEPV)

b. *Þiss lott off all Crisstene follc Iss heȝhesst unnderr Criste, Forr itt iss*
this lot of all Christian folk is highest under Christ For it is
sett her att te ster To sterenn baþe **þoþre.**
set here at the helm To steer both the-other
"This lot of all Christian folk is highest under Christ for it is set here at the helm to govern the other two." ?c 1200 Orm. (Jun 1) 15259 (CMEPV)

Two other early ME texts, namely the Ancrene Riwle and Laȝamon's Brut, confirm the findings based on the Ormulum. A digital edition of the Cotton Cleopatra manuscript of the Ancrene Riwle, available through PPCME2 and estimated to have been composed between 1225 and 1230 (Dobson, 1972, x), reveals seventeen occurrences of *thother*. Much as in the Ormulum none of them take a preceding definite article but unlike the instances in the Ormulum, *thother* in the Ancrene Riwle is not limited to plural NPs. Laȝamon's Brut, whose text is available in CMEPV through two late thirteenth century manuscripts, namely Cotton Caligula and Cotton Otho (McColl Millar, 2000: 120), contains only one instance of *thother* elicited from the Otho manuscript and no relevant instance in the Caligula manuscript. While the three texts testify to the use of *thother* in early ME, it is difficult to pinpoint the earliest instances of *thone*. As was remarked above, a search of PPCME2 turns up no instances and the ones shown in Example 7 can be placed in late ME. The earliest examples of *tone* and *tother* come from 1300 according to the MED (MED, s.v. *ton*, *tother*) and I have not found any attestations prior to that date. The example cited by the MED is shown in (9).

(9) Wanne i ðenke ðinges ðre … **Đe Ton** is dat i sal awei, **ðe**
When I think things three The The-one is that I shall away the
toþer is i ne wot wilk dei, ðe ðridde is mi moste kar
the-other is I not know which day the third is my most care
"When I think of three things, first I must go away, second I don't know when, the third is my greatest worry."
a1300 *Wanne i ðenke ðinges ðre* (Arun 292) 4 (CMEPV)

All in all, a conclusion that an analysis of the early texts and of Examples 8 and 9 permits is that reduction of the definite article affects *other* before misanalysis of the demonstrative and that a definite article preceding *other* is reduced earlier than that preceding *one*.

With the exception of *thother*, the new pronoun forms *tother*, *thone*, and *tone* mentioned in this section so far were extremely infrequent in early ME, with the main thrust of such occurrences attested in the latter half of the 14th century and later. This statement is based on a search of such instances in PPCME2, a corpus that breaks the ME period down into four sub-periods, as noted in Section 3. The number of occurrences of the pronouns in the four sub-periods of ME obtained through a search of the PPCME2 is shown in Table 2. It is to be noted that all the twenty-three instances in M1 are those of *thother*. Six of them come from the Ormulum and seventeen from the Ancrene Riwle. There is no relevant instance in M2. The periods designated as M1 and M2 in the corpus cover the time frame of the early texts analyzed above, and thus the fact that only instances of *thother* are registered at that time is expected. It is in fact in M3 and M4, i.e. after the year 1350, that instances of the other pronouns, that is *tone*, and *tother* in addition to *thother* begin to show up more copiously in the corpus. We can see that at each stage *tother*/*thother* is more frequent than *tone* and there are more instances of both in the last period of ME, i.e. M4, than in M3. That the greater number of instances in M4 reflects an actual rise in frequency is borne out by the graph in Figure 1, which shows the normalized frequencies of both items per 100,000 words in the sub periods of ME. The increase in gross numbers in Table 2 correlates with an increase expressed in normalized form. Both *tone* and *tother*/*thother* undergo a frequency increase toward the end of ME, if this period is compared with the 14th century, and in the early 15th century.

Table 2. Occurrences of *tone*/*thone* and *tother*/*tother* in PPCME2 (gross numbers)

	M1 (1150–1250)	M2 (1250–1350)	M3 (1350–1420)	M4 (1420–1500)
tone/*thone*	0	0	19 (*tone* only)	23 (*tone* only)
tother/*thother*	23 (*thother* only)	0	49 (*thother* and *tother*)	79 (*thother* and *tother*)

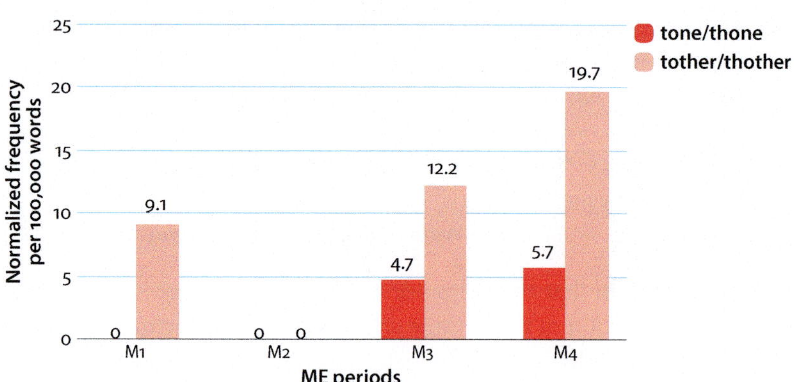

Figure 1. Normalized frequencies of *tone/thone* and *tother/thother* in ME

In this section it has been argued that reduction of the definite article can be held responsible for the formation of *thother* and *thone* as well as some instances of *tother* and *tone*. The evidence elicited from the Ormulum, Ancrene Riwle, and Laȝamon's Brut, points in the direction of reduction of the definite article as a mechanism leading to the earliest instances of the four pronouns. In Section 5, the focus is on whether the formation of the forms of pronouns may have been reinforced by reduction of the definite article with nouns.

5. A correlation between reduced *th'* and development of *tone/thone* and *tother/thother*

As I have noted elsewhere (Nykiel, 2015), reduced *th'* is first attested with nouns in the 12th century and is present throughout the ME period. In this section, I juxtapose the ME lifespans of reduced *th'* and the forms of *tone/thone/tother/thother* triggered by reduction of the definite article. Before such a juxtaposition can be achieved however I compare the frequency of the two structures in PPCME2.

In order to enable comparison in terms of frequency between reduced *th'* and *tone/thone/tother/thother* in ME, I have culled instances of reduced *th'* NPs from PPCME2. The NPs are limited to those that have the definite article attached to a head noun. The results in the form of gross numbers broken down so as to reflect the ME sub-periods follow in Table 3. It can be observed that the instances spread out over each ME sub-period with a peak in M3, unlike in the case of *tone/thone/tother/thother*, as shown in Table 2. That this peak is misleading, however, can be gathered from Figure 2 where the frequency of the reduced *th'* instances is presented in normalized form. The motivation behind this mode of presentation is again feasibility of comparison with the normalized frequencies of *tone/thone/tother/thother* displayed in Figure 1. Figure 2 shows that the use of reduced *th'* begins in early ME, as expected, and then it has a sudden frequency peak in M2, after which its frequency gradually decreases. These results are partially unexpected and skewed, a consequence of PPCME2 containing a relatively small sample of words in comparison with CMEPV. First of all the frequency peak in M2 is more apparent than real, as all the ninety instances of reduced *th'* in this sub-period come from one text only, namely the Earliest Complete English Prose Psalter. What is more, reduced *th'* attaches to one host noun only in this text, namly *erðe* 'earth'. Secondly, there are grounds to say that the very low frequency of reduced *th'* in M4 should be regarded with skepticism for two reasons. The first reason is that despite a small number of instances of reduced *th'* elicited from M4, they spread over as many as seven different texts. Admittedly this is a higher number than in any earlier sub-period. The other reason is that it has been shown in Nykiel (2015) that the use of reduced *th'* continues in EModE until it eventually wanes toward the end of the period. This can be seen in the graph in Figure 3 where the normalized frequency of reduced *th'* in EModE is shown. The frequency in Figure 3 is calculated on the basis of the data adduced in Nykiel (2015: 114) taken from the Penn-Helsinki Parsed Corpus of Early Modern English, which contains over 1.7 million words.

Table 3. Reduced *th'* in PPCME2 (gross numbers)

	M1 (1150–1250)	M2 (1250–1350)	M3 (1350–1420)	M4 (1420–1500)
reduced *th'*	21	90	128	10

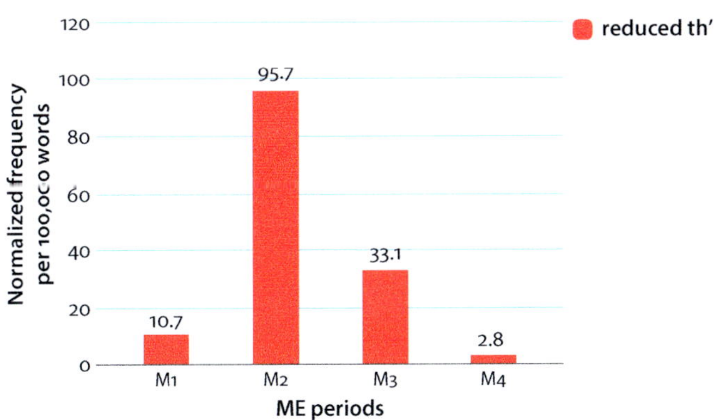

Figure 2. Normalized frequencies of reduced *th'* in PPCME2

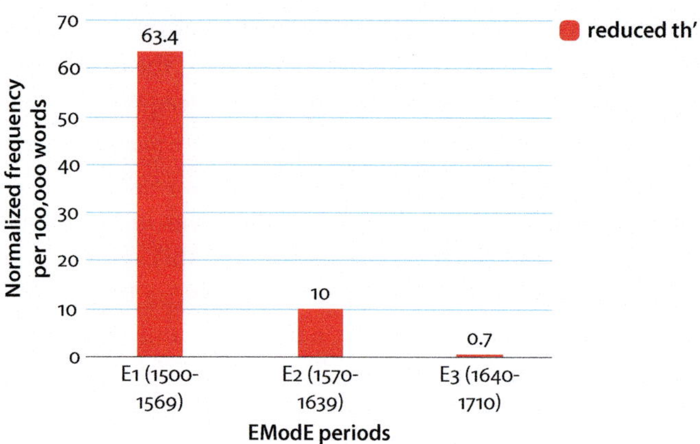

Figure 3. Normalized frequencies of reduced *th'* in EModE

A solid observation that a comparison of the graphs in Figure 2 and Figure 3 yields is that reduced *th'* on the one hand and forms of *thother* on the other hand both arise in early ME, i.e. M1, with reduced *th'* being attested slightly earlier than *thother.* It is also remarkable that in that period *thother* is attested only in those texts that also have reduced *th'*, namely the Ormulum and the Ancrene Riwle. There are grounds to say therefore that once reduced *th'* becomes acceptable with a noun as a host, the range of hosts is extended to the pronoun *other*, and also to *one* in late ME. After 1350, that is from M3 onwards, the use of both reduced *th'* with nouns and with the two pronouns spreads to a greater variety of texts, until in M4 the frequency of *tone/thone/tother/thother* exceeds that of reduced *th'*.

6. Toward an account of *thone/thother* and *tone/tother*

In this section I relate the reduction of the definite article in the case of *tother/thother* and tone/*thone* to the DP cycle and argue that the reduction ultimately leads to double articulation of definiteness.

In a study on reduced *th'* nominals in ME and EModE (Nykiel, 2015) I argue, following van Gelderen (2011: 214), that a reduced definite article, i.e. a phonologically weakened definite article, is an expected stage in the development of the DP cycle in that free standing definite articles are likely to turn into clitics. It seems that the same applies in the case of *thone* and *thother*, that is when we have to do with reduction of the definite article. If *thone/thother* is the head of an NP, as could be seen in Example 7, it is a pronoun that takes a reduced definite article. In this respect ME *one* and *other* behave in a way similar to the pronoun *one* in Present-day English. I follow Déchaine & Wiltschko (2002: 419ff.), who take this pronoun to be what they call a Pro-NP, that is a pronoun of a special type which shares the syntactic features of nouns. *One*, among other things, has no referential content, takes modifying adjectives and accepts definite and indefinite determiners and thus it functions as the head of the NP. ME *one* and *other* at the very least share acceptance of a determiner with Pro-NPs, which merits their construal as NP heads. If *thone/thother* functions as a modifier in an NP, I also interpret it as having a reduced article.

When it comes to *tone* and *tother*, there are more interpretational possibilities. The first point that should be reiterated is that *tone* and *tother*, as noted in Section 3, can either take a definite determiner or occur without it. If *tone/tother* has no determiner preceding, note that the NP is still definite. *Tother* in (10) has a definite interpretation as it refers to the remaining nuns.

(10) *When þe priuresse es ordainde, with mikil reuerence sal sho do þat*
when the prioress is ordained with much reverence shall she do that
tabbesse cumandis hir, ... for Þe mare þat sho est heȝid ouir
the-abbess commands her for the more that she is high over
toþir, *Þe mare aȝh sho at halde þe cumandement of þe reule.*
the-other The more ought she to hold the commandment of the rule
"When the prioress is ordained, she will with great reverence do whatever the abbess commands her to do ... for the more she is raised above the rest, the more carefully she should observe the precepts of the rule."
CMBENRUL,44.1354 (PPCME2)

It can be gathered that initial *t-* contributes a definite interpretation, so that it is a variant of the reduced definite article attached to the pronoun. It would follow then that *tone/tother*, which comes without a preceding definite article but which has a definite reference, results from reduction of the definite article. Admittedly, examples such as (10) are rare in the ME corpora, but the OED adduces more examples taken from the later periods.

It is much more often that *tother* as well as *tone* is preceded by the determiner *the*, as in (11).

(11) *...no mon may serue wel twey Fulle lordys, for oþur he schal hate* ***þe***
no man may serve well two Full lords for either he shall hate the
toon *and loue* ***þe*** ***toþur,***
the-one and love the the-other
"no man can serve two masters well for either he will hate one and love the other,"
CMWYCSER,279.950 (PPCME2)

There are two possibilities of interpretation in this case. The first possibility is that we have two definite articles, namely full *the* and reduced *t-*. This interpretation would make these NPs cases of double articulation of definiteness, that is to say definiteness in these NPs is marked twice. This interpretation also runs parallel to what I have suggested in the case of nouns, such as *emperor* in (12) which has reduced *th* attached and is at the same time preceded by the definite article *the* (Nykiel, 2015).

(12) *The king was moost sory / & Brought* ***Þe Themperour*** *to his chambre,*
The king was most sorry and Brought the The-emperor to his chamber
'the king was very sorry and took the emperor to his chamber,'
1500 *Three Kings' Sons* (Harl 326) 202/23

The difference between the NPs containing *tone* and *tother* as in (11) and the NPs with reduced *th'* cliticizing onto nouns as in (12) is that the former NPs are common in ME and beyond, while the latter are very rare in that there are only two such instances in CMEPV and one in the Penn-Helsinki Parsed Corpus of Early Modern English (see Nykiel, 2015: 133). This makes the pronouns *tone/tother* with a preceding definite article perhaps the clearest examples of double articulation in the history of English. The reduced article turns out to require reinforcement by means of a full article. The weakening of the article following from the development of the DP cycle results in double articulation of definiteness.

The other possibility is that we have to do with lexicalization, that is incorporation of part of the demonstrative into the structure of the pronoun, and definiteness follows from the use of the full form of the definite article. The part of the demonstrative incorporated into the pronoun is fossilized having no contribution to the meaning or function of the pronoun. It could be argued that the misanalysis of the demonstrative pronoun which has final *-t* attached to the pronoun leads to lexicalization following Greenberg (1991: 304–305) and also Brinton & Traugott (2005: 53). This possibility however is much less likely given that there are no attestations of *tone/tother* with an indefinite article.

7. Conclusion

The main argument of this study has been that neither the forms of the pronouns *one* and *other* serving as a host to initial *t-*, nor those taking initial *th-*, as attested in ME, can be thoroughly accounted for in a straightforward way by saying that they result from misanalysis of the preceding demonstrative. Evidence has been presented pointing to reduction of the definite article as responsible for the earliest instances of these pronouns. The development of reduced *th'* attaching to nouns slightly predates the development of *other* with initial *th-*, yet both emerge in early ME and continue unabated throughout the ME period. The use of the pronoun *one* with reduced *th'* is a later development in ME. It has also been noted that the definite article can materialize into initial *t-* attached to *one* and/or *other.*

At the very least four different pronouns should be distinguished, namely *thone, thother, tone,* and *tother*. The former two are clear cases of reduction of the definite article, while the instances of the latter should be split into two groups, i.e. those which were triggered by reduction of the definite article and those caused by misanalysis of the demonstrative. The reduction of the definite article follows from the DP cycle and in the case of *tone* and *tother,* which often display a preceding free-standing definite determiner, results in NPs where definiteness is marked twice.

Sources

Corpus of Middle English Prose and Verse, (CMEPV). (1997–). Developed by the Humanities Text Initiative. https://quod.lib.umich.edu/m/med/ (11 October, 2018).

Kroch, Anthony & Taylor Ann (2000). *The Penn-Helsinki Parsed Corpus of Middle English* (PPCME2). Department of Linguistics, University of Pennsylvania. CD-ROM, second edition, release 4 (http://www.ling.upenn.edu/ppche-release-2016/PPCME2-RELEASE-4)

References

Abney, Stephen P. (1987). *The English noun phrase in its sentential aspect*. Cambridge, MA: MIT dissertation.

Anderson, John, & Britton, Derek (1999). The Orthography and Phonology of the Ormulum. *English Language and Linguistics* 3(2), 299–334. https://doi.org/10.1017/S1360674399000258

Barry, Michael (1972). The Morphemic Distribution of the Definite Article in Contemporary Regional English. In Martyn F. Wakelin (Ed.), *Patterns in the Folkspeech in the British Isles* (164–181). London: Athlone.

Branco, António, & Costa, Francisco (2006). Noun Ellipsis without Empty Categories. In Stefan Müller (Ed.), *Proceedings of the 13th International Conference on Head-Driven Phrase Structure Grammar, Varna* (81–101). Stanford, CA: CSLI Publications.

Brinton, Laurel J., & Traugott, Elizabeth Closs (2005). *Lexicalization and Language Change*. Cambridge: Cambridge University Press. https://doi.org/10.1017/CBO9780511615962

Déchaine Rose-Marie, & Wiltschko, Martina (2002). Decomposing Pronouns. *Linguistic Inquiry* 33(3), 409–442. https://doi.org/10.1162/002438902760168554

Diessel, Holger (1999). *Demonstratives. Form, Function, and Grammaticalization*. Amsterdam: John Benjamins. https://doi.org/10.1075/tsl.42

Dobson, Eric J. (1972). Introduction. In Eric J. Dobson (Ed.), *The English Text of the Ancrene Riwle edited from B.M. Cotton ms. Cleopatra C vi. EETS O.S. 267* (iv clxxiii). London: Oxford University Press.

van Gelderen, Elly (2011). *The Linguistic Cycle: Language Change and the Language Faculty.* Oxford: Oxford University Press. https://doi.org/10.1093/acprof:oso/9780199756056.001.0001

Greenberg, Joseph H. (1978). How Does a Language Acquire Gender Markers? In Joseph H. Greenberg (Ed.), *Universals of Human Language* (Vol. 3, 47–82). Stanford: Stanford University Press.

Greenberg, Joseph H. (1991). The Last Stages of Grammatical Elements: Contractive and Expansive Desemanticization. In Elizabeth Closs Traugott, & Bernd Heine (Eds.), *Approaches to Grammaticalization. Vol* 1 (Vol. I, 301–314). Amsterdam: John Benjamins. https://doi.org/10.1075/tsl.19.1.14gre

Hart, John (1569). *An Orthographie.* London: Seres [EL 209, 1969].

Huddleston, Rodney, & Pullum, Geoffrey K. (2002). *The Cambridge Grammar of the English Language.* Cambridge: Cambridge University Press. https://doi.org/10.1017/9781316423530

Jones, Mark J. (2002). The Origin of Definite Article Reduction in Northern English Dialects: Evidence from Dialect Allomorphy. *English Language and Linguistics* 6, 325–345. https://doi.org/10.1017/S1360674302000266

Julien, Marit (2005). *Nominal Phrases from a Scandinavian Perspective.* Amsterdam: John Benjamins. https://doi.org/10.1075/la.87

Lehmann, Christian (2015). *Thoughts on Grammaticalization.* 3rd Edition. Berlin: Language Science Press. https://doi.org/10.26530/OAPEN_603353

Lobeck, A. (1995). *Ellipsis - Functional Heads, Licensing, and Identification.* Oxford: Oxford University Press.

Lohrmann, Susanne (2011). A Unified Structure for Scandinavian DPs. In Petra Sleeman, & Harry Perridon (Eds.), *The Noun Phrase in Romance and Germanic. Structure, Variation, and Change* (111–125). Amsterdam: John Benjamins. https://doi.org/10.1075/la.171.08loh

Lyons, Christopher (1999). *Definiteness.* Cambridge: Cambridge University Press. https://doi.org/10.1017/CBO9780511605789

McColl Millar, Robert (2000). *System Collapse, System Rebirth.* Oxford: Peter Lang.

Middle English Dictionary (MED). (1956–2001). Ann Arbor: University of Michigan Press. https://quod.lib.umich.edu/m/med/ (9 October, 2018).

Mustanoja, Tauno F. (1960) [2016]. *A Middle English Syntax.* Amsterdam: John Benjamins.

Nerbonne, John, & Mullen, Tony (1999). Null-headed nominals in German and English. In Ineke Schuurman, Frank van Eynde, & Ness Schelkens (Eds.), Computational Linguistics in the Netherlands 1998 (143–164). Amsterdam-Atlanta (GA): Rodopi.

Nykiel, Jerzy (2015). The Reduced Definite Article *th'* in Late Middle English and Beyond: an Insight from the Definiteness Cycle. *Journal of Germanic Linguistics* 27(2), 105–144. https://doi.org/10.1017/S1470542714000221

Nykiel, Jerzy (2016). Non-anaphoric use of reduced *th'* in the 15th century. Paper presented at XXVII SELIM, Granada, Spain.

Onions, C. T. (Ed.). (1966). *The Oxford Dictionary of English Etymology.* Oxford: The Clarendon Press.

Oxford English Dictionary (OED). (1933). Oxford: Oxford University Press, and OED online.

Plank, Frans (2003). Double Articulation. In Frans Plank (Ed.), *Noun Phrase Structure in the Languages of Europe* (337–395). Berlin: Mouton de Gruyter.

Quirk, Randolph, Greenbaum, Sidney, Leech, Geoffrey, & Svartvik, Jan (1985). *A Comprehensive Grammar of the English Language.* London-New York: Longman Inc.

Salmon, Vivian (1999). Orthography and Punctuation. In Roger Lass (Ed.), *The Cambridge History of the English Language*. Volume III, 1476–1776 (13–56). Cambridge: Cambridge University Press.

Schoorlemmer, Erik (2012). Definiteness Marking in Germanic: Morphological Variations on the Same Syntactic Theme. *The Journal of Comparative Germanic Linguistics* 15, 107–156. https://doi.org/10.1007/s10828-012-9048-5

Taraldsen, Knut Tarald (1990). D-projections and N-projections in Norwegian. In Joan Mascaró, & Marina Nespor (Eds.), *Grammar in Progress* (419–431). Dordrecht: Foris. https://doi.org/10.1515/9783110867848.419

Viereck, Wolfgang (1995). Realizations of the Definite Article in Dialectal English and How and When They Originated. In Jacek Fisiak (Ed.), *Medieval Dialectology* (295–307). The Hague: Mouton de Gruyter. https://doi.org/10.1515/9783110892000.295

Leveraging grammaticalization

The origins of Old Frisian and Old English

Rebecca Colleran

For a long time, the striking similarities between OFris (Old Frisian) and Old English (OE) were attributed to an exclusive shared ancestor (Anglo-Frisian), but in the late 20th century that view was ousted in favor of a dialect continuum model. Recent developments in genetics, textual analysis, and archaeology, however, suggest that the earlier model is more accurate. This paper explores a series of diagnostics to distinguish between shared grammaticalizations caused by linguistic relatedness and those caused by geographical proximity. Those diagnostics are then applied to two developments exclusive to OFris and OE: the grammaticalization of *aga(n)* 'have' into auxiliary 'have to', and the development of a verb complement based on the OE/OFris present participle. In both cases, the diagnostics indicate that the changes occurred due to a shared ancestor, supporting the Anglo-Frisian hypothesis.

Keywords: Anglo-Frisian hypothesis, inheritance, contact, drift, grammaticalization

1. Introduction

Since the 14th century, the striking similarities between Old Frisian (OFris) and Old English (OE) have been cause for comment (Bremmer, 1989; Nielsen, 1981) The source of these similarities, however, has been hotly debated. Some linguists attribute the numerous features shared exclusively between OFris and OE – sound changes, overlapping pronoun and morphological paradigms, numeral inflection and alliterative formulae – to an immediate Anglo-Frisian ancestor, while others credit them to neighboring positions in a North Sea coast dialect continuum.

Phonological comparison led the neogrammarians to propose 'genealogical' relatedness to explain the exclusive similarities. They posited an Anglo-Frisian (or 'Ingvaeonic') ancestor in their Germanic (Gmc) family tree, with OFris and OE as 'sister' nodes below it (Bremmer, 2001; see Stiles, 1995).

https://doi.org/10.1075/cilt.346.05col

In the late 20th century, evolving models of language change led linguists to scrap this neat family tree. The exclusion of Old Saxon (OS, a forerunner of Low German) and Old Low Franconian (OLF, an input for Dutch) from many of the early neogrammarian comparisons may have skewed the results (Bremmer, 1981; Markey, 1981; Stiles, 1995). Worse, fitting the exclusive OFris/OE phonological changes into a relative chronology valid for both languages, a central concern for innovation-based groupings, has proven difficult. The family tree model itself comes under fire for its failure to model post-split contact (Hogg, 2002). A dialect continuum model, encompassing the North Sea Germanic (NSG) languages (OFris, OE, OS and perhaps OLF), overtook Anglo-Frisian as the favored theory in the eighties, culminating in Stiles's (1995) article intending to 'nail down the coffin lid' on the idea of Anglo-Frisian (Århammar, 1990: 10; Bremmer, 2009: 128; Stiles, 1995, passim).

Certain assumptions underlie the historical attempts to account for similarities within NSG: Germanic Frisians have occupied the Frisian coastal area since Roman times; Frisian occupied a physical space between OE and OS while the differentiating features developed (e.g. Stiles, 2016: 33);[1] the North Sea acted as a barrier to shared developments. Recent developments in non-linguistic fields, including archaeology (Bos, 2001; Nieuwhof, 2009, 2013), textual history (Bazelmans, 2009; Bazelmans et al., 2012; Dijkstra, 2011; Härke, 2011), and genetics (Abdelaoui et al., 2013; Boomsma et al., 2014; Capelli et al., 2003; Forster et al., 2004; Schiffels et al., 2016; Weale et al., 2002) suggests that these assumptions are invalid. The extra-linguistic evidence indicates that the Frisians of Roman times deserted the Frisian coast almost completely in the 4th century (A.D.). In the 5th century, Frisia was populated again by the same waves of Angles who colonized Britain (Härke, 2011; genetic studies above). The Anglo-Frisian ancestor suggested by the neogrammarians is a historical reality, at least in a genetic sense. The Frisians are really Angles.

These findings place the dialect continuum model favored by linguists in direct contradiction with other disciplines. The linguistic data must be robust enough to stand on their own, even if the findings conflict with those in other fields; but at the same time, such a conflict demands that we at least re-examine the linguistic evidence. The interface between what we think we know about linguistics and what we think we know about history offers a testing ground for linguistic methods that have developed since the dialect continuum model was last examined, and a chance to ensure that our theories do not attempt to fit the linguistic data to a set of assumptions that have now proven to be invalid.

1. A revised version of Stiles, 1995.

New linguistic methods have developed in the last thirty years, giving us new approaches to an old (but not quite resolved) question. Diagnostics pertaining to grammaticalization – the development of a morpheme from more lexical to more grammatical functions – offer a principled method with which to distinguish between changes due to shared inheritance and those due to post-split contact or drift. One example of grammaticalization is the development of lexical verb 'have' into auxiliary 'have to', as seen in Examples (1–3) below.

(1) Frodo *has*$_V$ a ring$_N$.

(2) Frodo *has* a ring to destroy. (Ambiguous between 'Frodo possesses a ring, which he can destroy' and 'Frodo has before him the task of destroying a ring'.)

(3) Frodo *has*$_{AUX}$ to destroy a ring$_{Vinf}$.

This shift of 'have' into 'have to' closely mirrors the grammaticalization of OE/OFris cognate *aga(n)* 'have' into 'have to'. In section 3, I will apply the diagnostics presented in Section 2 to *aga(n)* to show how grammaticalization can shed light on the question of Frisian origins.

The fact that two languages share exclusive grammaticalizations seems, *prima facie*, to be evidence of an exclusive common ancestor, but there are other explanations. The innovations might have spread from one of the languages to the other through contact, or may have developed independently in each of the languages after they had diverged, a process known as 'drift'. If a grammaticalization is not rare cross-linguistically, it might even have arisen by chance, due to universal pathways in human cognition. To distinguish between these possible explanations, I propose the following research questions:

1. How can we distinguish between a grammaticalization that is shared between two languages due to a shared ancestor and one that develops due to proximity?
2. Do the grammaticalizations OFris and OE share point to an exclusive Anglo-Frisian ancestor or to a dialect continuum?

In this paper, I explore the use of various diagnostics to distinguish between 'genealogical' relatedness, post-split contact, and drift as causes of specific shared grammaticalizations. Factors that complicate these distinctions in the case of closely related languages (such as OFris and OE) are examined. Finally, I illustrate a number of the diagnostics using two test cases in OFris and OE: *aga(n)*'s development from 'have' to auxiliary 'have to' and the participle-based infinitive. I will argue that based on diagnostics set down by researchers working on a variety of language families, the exclusive grammaticalizations shared by OFris and OE were caused by an exclusive shared parent language, i.e. Anglo-Frisian.

2. Grammaticalization as a diagnostic tool

As mentioned above, the similarities between OE and OFris have historically been explained by one of two mechanisms: an immediate common ancestor (Anglo-Frisian) or a dialect continuum spanning all of the NSG languages more or less equally, with the possibility of further changes spread by contact between OE and OFris after they separated. Generally, these relationships have been approached in the neogrammarian tradition, working out relatedness based on the extent of participation in a series of ordered sound changes. In contrast, this section explores a method for using morphological and syntactic evidence to determine whether a given change common to OFris and OE is due to shared ancestry or post-split contact. I discuss the mechanisms that underlie the different types of change, the extra complications inherent in determining the origin of a change in closely-related languages like OFris and OE, and some diagnostics for using grammaticalization to distinguish between contact- and inheritance-based shared changes.

2.1 Comparing Old Frisian and Old English

Comparing morphemes between OE and OFris manuscripts presents some problems, however. The extant sources are not contemporaneous. The OE period ranges from roughly A.D. 700 to 1100 (Howe, 2013: 1; Quirk & Wrenn, 1955: 6), though as with OFris, its periodization is not uncontested (e.g. Lass, 2000). By the writing of the first surviving OFris manuscript, English had weathered the Norman Conquest and moved on to the early Middle English (ME) period. The period traditionally labelled "Old Frisian", in contrast, stretches from 1275 to 1550.[2] 1275 is the approximate date of the earliest extant manuscript, the *First Brokmer Codex*. 1550 represents the latest date of medieval Frisian charters.

In the end, the names given to medieval Frisian do not change the fact that aside from scanty runic inscriptions, the Frisian manuscripts dating from 1200 to 1550 are the closest attestations we have to compare with other medieval Gmc languages, such as OE. Because of the strong influence of the Norman tongue on English after 1066, OE is a much better source for comparison with OFris than ME is, despite the age gap.

That is not to say, however, that the difference in chronology may not have a strong effect on the results of this study. Indeed, close attention will be paid during the course of the research to determine whether any differences observed are caused by dialect geography or time depth. The directionality underlying many

2. For alternate periodizations, see Bremmer, 2009: 119–125.

of the differences, particularly grammaticalization (as explained below), will prove a valuable tool in this endeavor.

Similarly, the size and composition of the two corpora must be considered in determining comparability. At 350,500 words, the OFris corpus is a faint echo of the 1.5 million words of running prose in the *York-Toronto-Helsinki Parsed Corpus of Old English Prose* (YCOE). On the other hand, nearly a third of a million words provides a great deal of fodder for syntactic investigation. Moreover, the legal genre of most of the OFris texts makes it uniquely suited to investigating a construction (*aga* + *to*) that deals with ownership, debts and obligation, particularly in a legal system that functioned by payment of carefully calculated wergild, or monetary compensation, for crimes. Interestingly, it also yields a large number of tokens in the way of infinitives; infinitives form the basis of several formulae favored in some of the legal texts.

The fact that the OE corpus does not share this bias toward legal texts should not present a material obstacle to the investigation. Versloot & Adamczyk find that the study of comparative phonology and morphology is 'basically genre-independent and is not affected by the corpus size' (2014: 565). No comparisons between percentages of different syntactic structures in OE and OFris are drawn, so error is not introduced through comparison of disparate genres.

2.2 Mechanisms of language change in contact and inheritance scenarios

The kinds of changes that occur in a contact situation depend on a number of factors, including the age of the learners, the depth of contact (if any), and speaker attitudes. Consequently, determining what kind of linguistic changes emerge from a given scenario may shed light on the historical situation underlying the change. This section explores the mechanisms behind the situations that are summed up as *inheritance* and *contact* throughout this paper.

Inheritance is shorthand for direct transmission from one generation to the next generation within a largely monolingual community: the kind of development that would take place within a language whose speakers lived on an isolated island. Change will still occur, because language is non-static. Changes that occur in such a population may be called *internally/genealogically motivated*. Cognitively, the mechanism involved in such transmission is child (*perfect, full*) acquisition; learners acquire the full form of the language before a critical age threshold (Labov, 2007). This is the kind of change we would expect to see from a shared Anglo-Frisian ancestor.

Contact scenarios, on the other hand, involve adult acquisition. Adults have lost the brain plasticity necessary for perfect acquisition. Adults still learn enough to communicate, and enough to acquire enough of the other language (often called the *target, model,* or *source language*) to incorporate aspects of it into their own language (the *recipient* or *replica language*). The borrowed material need not be phonological; a speaker might re-purpose an existing word or morpheme in their own language. For example, a speaker might notice that the target language uses the noun 'back (of body)' as a preposition meaning 'behind', and start to use the noun 'back' to mean behind when speaking their native (recipient) language. This would be an example of grammaticalization inspired by contact with another language; what Aikhenvald would call a *contact-induced grammaticalization* (2013), or Heine & Kuteva *grammatical replication* (2005: 2). We would expect this borrowing of some aspects of a change if OE and OFris were merely neighboring languages in a dialect continuum.

The limits on borrowability are particularly loose when the languages in contact are closely related. '[Thomason] has shown that there are no absolute linguistic constraints on language change, and while not every change is equally probable, any change seems to be possible (and, in fact, attested)' (Epps, Huehnergard, & Pat-El, 2013: 210). The simple fact of a change occurring in the morphology (rather than phonology or lexicon, which were once believed to be more vulnerable to change) cannot be taken as evidence of internal motivation. It does, however, argue for either internal motivation, typologies that are similar to the point of probably being related languages, and/or a *very* intense contact situation.

One other factor makes it difficult to distinguish between a contact explanation for a given change, and an inheritance one: many of the changes that are nudged into happening by contact are the same kind of changes that occur in languages in isolation. As Thomason writes, 'all available evidence suggests that, although contact is indeed sometimes responsible for exotic changes, it is much more often responsible for garden-variety changes that are also common as strictly internal changes' (2001: 92).

Given the similarity between the results of internal and externally-motivated change, it is perhaps not surprising that in some cases, researchers attribute the same change to a combination of internal and external causes. According to Pat-El, in some cases it is 'misleading to assume a change is the result of only one mechanism … most changes have multiple causations' (2013: 313). Drinka emphasizes the importance of acknowledging the role contact does play as a 'more fundamental explanatory mechanism than is usually acknowledged' (2013: 638). Contact may, for example, reinforce a change that is taking place internally, contributing to the change in distribution and frequency of an already-existing pattern (Pat-El, 2013). Poplack & Levy, however, argue against too-liberal an application of contact as an explanation, claiming that '[c]ontact-induced change is not an inevitable, nor possibly even a common, outcome of language contact' (2010: 412). Which claim is correct remains to be seen as the field of contact linguistics, particularly among related languages, continues to develop.

2.3 Additional complications for related languages

> Most of the theoretical works on language contact pay little attention to genetically related languages, and seem to imply that the situation there is no different than when contact occurs among unrelated languages. (Epps et al., 2013: 211)

While contact between (closely) related languages like OE and OFris does share many characteristics with contact between unrelated or only distantly-related languages, it differs from traditionally-studied contact in a number of ways. Complicating factors include cognates; lower restrictions/thresholds on what kinds of things can be borrowed and under what circumstances; and the confusion between relatedness and other factors, such as typology. I will also touch on a few avenues of research which are particularly tempting in the case of related languages, but which on closer investigation turn out to be methodologically unsound.

As discussed above, morphology is relatively resistant to borrowing, but morphological borrowing is far more permissible in closely-related languages (Epps et al., 2013: 214; Thomason, 2001: 71). Typological similarity seems to be the key to facilitating this borrowing. Typological similarity, however, is difficult to disentangle from relatedness. Bowern (2013) sums up the difficulties:

> [D]egree of closeness between two languages in a family tree is not independent of other factors that may themselves be responsible for facilitating contact. (417)
>
> [S]tructural compatibility is considered more important for transfer than phylogenetic distance ... but it's hard to measure one without the other, as related languages are usually typologically similar. (418)

The correlation of relevant factors in typological similarity and relatedness has led to some methodologically problematic approaches to questions of linguistic genealogy. Emonds & Faarlund (2014), for example, disastrously mistake typological similarity in the present-day versions of English and Scandinavian languages for signs of a common inheritance. In fact, a look at earlier versions of the languages (which are well attested) shows that some of the shared features in question did not arise in the languages in question until *after* the time Emonds and Faarlund claim they diverged.[3] This serves to illustrate why it is best practice in historical linguistics to start with data from the oldest known attestations, and only conjecture further back in time as necessary (and be aware that these conjectures will be, at best, informed guesses).

3. For a full critique of Emonds & Faarlund, see Bech & Walkden (2015), Pereltsvaig (2015), and Thomason (2012).

Languages that are moderately related may turn out to be more like one another based in part because of (nearly) inevitable developments. For example, if loss of inflectional morphology can contribute to more fixed word orders, two languages that lose some of their inflectional morphology may develop similar (but often not identical) fixed word orders as coping strategies.

2.4 Demystifying drift

In order to prove or disprove an Anglo-Frisian ancestor, we must rule out drift as a cause of similarities. The fact that English and Scandinavian developed similarities in their systems, though with some striking differences in distribution and implementation, may be due to a phenomenon known as DRIFT (a.k.a. parallel drift, Sapirian drift, convergent/parallel development). The idea of 'drift' causing similar developments was articulated by Sapir as early as 1921: 'the momentum of … drift is often such that languages long disconnected will pass though the same or strikingly similar phases' (1921: 171–178). The classic case is Grassman's Law: Greek and Sanskrit both developed dissimilation of aspirated stops, but other, non-shared changes earlier in the relative chronology make it clear that Greek and Sanskrit had already diverged by that time (Aikhenvald & Dixon, 2001: 4; Bowern 2013: 428).

Drift has been treated as an almost mystical force or phenomenon, and the linguistic community has no clear-cut way of quantifying it (Joseph, 2013). The exact mechanism, and indeed definition, behind drift has not been agreed on yet. In 'Demystifying drift', Joseph attributes drift phenomena to prosodic variation (e.g. weak vs. strong intonation, as between auxiliaries and nouns) as a sort of internal stylistic variation ('phrasal/sentential sandhi') that might later resolve itself in predictable and similar ways in the daughter languages (2013: 50–52).

Some shared developments that occur after two lects have separated are clearly the result of changes that were already underway by the time of separation. In the case of grammaticalizations, Robbeets & Cuyckens (2013, 10–12) cite 'ancestral polysemy' as the cause of what they call 'inherited grammaticalization', in which language already showed meaning variation in a given morpheme before separation. Such developments hardly need the label of 'drift', as they are the only logical conclusion for a change already underway, save in instances of heavy interference from contact with another language or substrate. Hence, a change affecting both OE and OFris that was largely carried out before these two varieties split does not seem to qualify as drift. In phonology, common sound changes carried out before (too many) non-shared changes occur would be an indication that the languages had not yet split. Provided that the developments are the same in both form and function (see below), it does not seem unreasonable to interpret morpho-syntactic changes in the same way.

On the other hand, shared grammaticalizations that are the same in meaning but different in form *are* likely to have developed post-split. Aikhenwald (2013) and Csató (2013) suggest that new grammaticalizations will occur along the lines of existing ones to maintain existing categories; two related language may draw on non-cognate morphemes with similar meanings to accomplish similar purposes.

So how can we rule out drift as the primary cause behind similarities between OFris and OE? Joseph concludes that "[i]n general, variation in related languages that matches up in some crucial way is a good basis for reconstructing proto-language variation." Another good indication of proto-language variation are selectively shared elements, where (for example) the distribution in each language matches up, but the form differs (2013: 62). Thus, if developments in OE and OFris data match in some, but not all, crucial way(s), we may take the developments as the languages' separate mechanisms for resolving the variation that was present in the proto-language, at some time after they split. If, on the other hand, developments match in both form and function, the match might be more accurately attributed to direct inheritance, and drift (for that particular development, at least) may be ruled out.

Accruing a number of cases of parallel development between two languages may also rule out drift. Per Joseph,

> A single case could easily, and quite reasonably, be considered a matter of chance parallel independent developments, but when one has to invoke chance in case after case, there is more cause to look at a different scenario, especially since invoking drift alone is, as argued here, hardly compelling in and of itself. (2013: 64)

Thus, one similarity between OE and OFris morpho-syntax may be chance, but every successive instance increases the likelihood of an Anglo-Frisian ancestor.

I have spoken so far of ways to identify drift as the 'primary' source of a given change. Here (again), it is important to emphasize the possibility of multiple sources for a given change. Change based on a variation already present in the proto-language may 'be vulnerable to contact, because the contact conditions are likely to reinforce the biases that are already present in the languages' (Bowern, 2013: 428). Csató (2013), too, points out that strong contact between related languages reinforces parallel drift, whereas strong contact among less closely related languages would weaken the category. So it is possible that drift phenomena are more likely to appear in OE and OFris than in languages that have been separated entirely. I would argue, however, that the above criteria for differentiating drift similarities from those caused by immediate inheritance still hold; that developments due to drift will:

a. be similar in some respects but not others (e.g. function but not form) – they will have selectively shared characteristics
b. be more scattered than those due to direct inheritance.

Consequently, to rule out drift in the test cases in Sections 3 and 4, I want to find multiple grammaticalizations that share all characteristics (form, function, semantics, and distribution). Conveniently, these criteria are echoed in the diagnostics for classifying shared grammaticalizations, below.

2.5 Grammaticalization as a diagnostic tool

Here, then, is where we get down to brass tacks and synthesize all we know about how change happens in different environments into concrete diagnostics for distinguishing inheritance- from contact-based shared changes. Harris & Campbell (1995: 344–375) argue that it is possible to establish syntactic correspondences among related languages based on syntactic patterns. However, even if systematic syntactic correspondences can in principle exist, the methodological problem of actually identifying them remains (Walkden, 2013, 2014: 47–53). As a result, syntactic evidence for relatedness is only admissible in 'instances so distinctive they could not easily be explained by borrowing or accident' (Bech & Walkden, 2015: 79; Campbell & Poser, 2008: 177).

What kind of evidence is distinct enough to rule out borrowing? Bowern is confident that such evidence exists: "in many places we can, in fact, differentiate contact-induced change from transmission changes" (2013: 423). Robbeets suggests that shared morphology may be the key (2013: 148). Differences in patterns of grammaticalization may help us distinguish contact and inheritance.

Grammaticalization is the development of a morpheme along the cline from lexical meaning to grammatical meaning, such as the development of OE and OFris *aga(n)* 'have' into 'have to'. On the face of it, the fact that OE and OFris alone among the Germanic languages developed Germanic (Gmc) *agan* 'have' into a modal might suggest that OE and OFris were once a unified linguistic entity, but Robbeets presents four possible causes for any shared grammaticalization:

a. universal principles of grammatical change
b. language contact
c. contact reinforced by coincidence in form
d. common ancestorship, with inherited polysemy and Sapirian drift as subtypes (2013, 148)

In a previous section I discussed criteria for ruling out drift. Contact reinforced by coincidence in form is unlikely in both Anglo-Frisian and NSG dialect continuum scenarios, as morphemes and word orders with similar meanings are much more likely to be cognate than coincidence. Thus, this section addresses ways to use grammaticalization to distinguish between developments due to contact and recent inheritance.

These are the scenarios we need to distinguish between for each case study in Sections 3 and 4:

a. *contact*
   what Heine & Kuteva (2005) term '**replica grammaticalization**', by which speakers might perceive cognate relationships between roots and affixes in one language, and reduce corresponding roots to affixes in the other.
b. *direct inheritance*
   aga(n) was already developing not only auxiliary meanings, but also the complements that $aga(n)_{\mathrm{AUX}}$ can take (vs. $aga(n)_{\mathrm{V}}$), before OE and OFris became separate languages.

Compare these with the intermediate scenario described above:

c. *drift*
   aga(n) starts to develop the polysemy that will lead to $aga(n)_{\mathrm{AUX}}$, but the languages split before the full range of meanings or the complements really develop. It is conceivable that OFris and OE are so similar that they will develop identical coping mechanisms for a new auxiliary for the sole reason that they are so very similar; but if they're so very similar as that, it becomes difficult to make the case that they *have* become separate languages.

The distinctions discussed so far can be distilled into five diagnostics. These are the diagnostics that will be applied in Sections 3 and 4 to interpret the data as evidence either for or against an exclusive Anglo-Frisian ancestor (particularly diagnostics 1, 2 and 5).

1. Globally vs. selectively shared grammaticalizations. In a globally shared grammaticalization (GSG), all semantic and combinatorial features are shared, as well as the phonological form. In a selectively shared grammaticalization (SSG), on the other hand, the grammaticalization will share some semantic or combinatorial elements but not all. According to Robbeets and Cuykens (2013: 8), SSGs tend to be borrowed, while GSGs tend to be genealogically motivated. GSGs are considered 'a strong indication of genealogical relatedness'; there are very few counterexamples in the linguistic literature to the tendency for contact-induced grammaticalization to be selective (Robbeets, 2013: 147–150).

SSGs share some semantic and/or combinational elements. One example would be the development of the rise of BE and HAVE perfects in the Standard Average European language area (*Charlemagne Sprachbund*), despite some of the languages being Gmc and some Romance (Drinka, 2013). The HAVE/BE perfects illustrate an important point about borrowed constructions: the precise implementation of the construction may vary from language to language.

If SSGs are present in two languages, that is an indication of contact, and their distribution may help determine which language is the borrowing (recipient) language. Two specific subtypes of selective sharing are relevant to our case.[4]

a. *reduction*
   Older (i.e. model language) categories may show more semantic erosion, phonetic erosion, and/or irregular morphology than the ones in the replica language (Heine & Nomachi, 2013: 92).
b. *restriction*
   Constraints may appear in the replica language where there are not any in the model language: the replica is less frequent, less productive and/or limited to a narrower range of contexts (Pat-El, 2013: 325; Heine & Nomachi, 2013: 92). For instance, Russian and Yiddish share a focus construction, in which constituents are fronted with a particle (*eto* in Russian, *dos* in Yiddish) for emphasis. Yiddish only allows subjects to be fronted, while Russian allows a wider range of constituents. This imbalance suggests that Yiddish borrowed the construction from Russian (Heine & Nomachi, 2013: 92).

Universals of human cognition are another source for SSGs. Due to the way the human brain is wired, certain pathways of grammaticalization – such as $back_{\text{NOUN}}$ to $back_{\text{ADVERB}}$ – are likely to occur in in many languages, to the point that Heine and Kuteva (2002) have compiled a book listing some of the common pathways in multiple languages. That two languages share a cross-linguistically common grammaticalization thus cannot be taken as evidence of relatedness. Such grammaticalizations share some semantic core, but will generally differ in distribution and form. The exceptions are languages in which forms are either coincidentally similar, which is a statistically unlikely occurrence, or cognates, which is generally due to some degree of relatedness. Details of distribution, too, tend to vary, though there may be some overlap where two languages are typologically very similar. As closely related languages often are similar, this sometimes obscures a shared grammaticalization's origins.

While Robbeets presents the difference between globally and selectively shared grammaticalizations as a powerful diagnostic tool – and rightly so – she has reservations as to how it will perform on closely related languages:

> Globally shared grammaticalization may be contact-induced across dialects or languages with a high degree of mutual intelligibility … grammatical accommodation usually does not produce globally shared grammaticalization, *unless the model and recipient languages are genealogically related in the first place.*
>
> (2013: 151–152, emphasis mine)

4. For a comprehensive list of diagnostics, see Heine & Nomachi (2013).

Nonetheless, the difference between GSGs and SSGs may still serve us. If GSGs are that much more likely to be shared by languages that are related, even when the grammaticalization is caused by contact and not genealogy, the *absence* of a globally shared grammaticalization can only be that much more damning for an inheritance explanation.

2. Intermediate stages. If the various stages of a process are attested in one language, while the other shows only the final result, the grammaticalization is caused by contact (Pat-El, 2013: 325).

3. Clustering of multiple grammaticalizations for a given function. The appearance of a given path of grammaticalization appears in more than one cognate set suggests genealogical motivation (Heine & Nomachi, 2013: 289; Robbeets, 2013: 157). An example of multiple grammaticalizations occurring along the same path would be the development in ModE of two separate possessives, *have* and *got*, into (quasi-)modal deontic auxiliaries 'have to' and 'got to/gotta'. This is reminiscent of one of the diagnostics proposed by Joseph (2013, 64) to rule out drift; one development can be written off as chance, but multiple developments render chance a questionable motivation.

4. A globally shared grammaticalization is not restricted to contact zones. (Robbeets, 2013: 155) This diagnostic presents some difficulties for OE/OFris: we would have to both localize the manuscripts to their places of origin and show that some of the OFris locations had greater post-split contact with OE than others.

5. A globally shared grammaticalization involves the development of a less grammaticalized to a more grammaticalized bound morpheme. The rare instances of GSGs that are not genealogically motivated involve the grammaticalization of borrowed lexical item. Bound morphemes are more resistant than independent lexemes to code-copying. Therefore, it is even more difficult to find instances of globally copied grammaticalization where the source is a bound morpheme. Consequently, such cases provide even stronger support for genealogical retention. (Robbeets, 2013: 156).

English and Frisian alone among the North Sea languages bring the present participle into verb complementation, resulting in such alternations as *I saw him cross the street/I saw him crossing the street*. Tracing the distribution of this exclusive non-finite complement back to OE and OFris will show us whether this shared participle-cum-infinitive can be considered a GSG or whether there are differences in form or distribution, suggesting drift or contact. If it is a GSG, its status as bound morpheme will make it an even stronger indicator of genealogical relatedness than a free morpheme (such as *aga*).

Summary: Shared grammaticalizations present different features, which reflect the historical linguistic situation they developed in. Changes that occurred before two related languages diverged will tend to be GSGs (sharing all characteristics of form, function, and distribution), show intermediate stages of the change, appear with other, similar changes, not be restricted to contact zones, and may involve bound morphemes. Conversely, grammaticalizations shared due to contact will share only some features, lack intermediate stages in one of the languages, appear only haphazardly in one or both languages, appear only in contact zones, and seldom involve bound morphemes. In the case of closely related languages, disentangling the various possible causes of a shared change presents particular challenges, but is by no means impossible. By applying the diagnostics explored in Section 2 to grammaticalizations that OE and OFris share, we can determine whether the similarities developed due to a shared Anglo-Frisian ancestor or neighboring positions in a dialect continuum.

3. Test case 1: *aga(n)*

The first test case to apply these diagnostics will be auxiliary *aga(n)*. Among the NSG languages, only English and Frisian among the Gmc languages have lighted on *aga(n)* 'have to' as an auxiliary. In other Gmc languages, the equivalent obligation is expressed by reflexes of OGmc *skulan* 'to owe': ModHG *sollen*, ModDu *zullen*, Present-Day English (PDE) *should*. The fact that OE and OFris are the only NSG languages to grammaticalize *aga* into an auxiliary appears to point to an exclusive shared ancestor for OFris and OE, but that is not the only possible explanation.[5]

To test the Anglo-Frisian ancestor hypothesis, I turned to diagnostics 1 and 2 from the last section:

1. GSGs. Does *aga(n)* show the same form, distribution and semantics in OFris and OE?
2. Intermediate stages. Does the development of aga(n) from verb to auxiliary show all of the same intermediate steps in OFris and OE, or does one language skip steps or progress less far, suggesting borrowing?

Diagnostic 3, clustering of multiple grammaticalizations in the same function, cannot be applied without more grammaticalized modals. 4, restriction to contact zones, requires more knowledge of where the manuscripts were authored, and 5 does not apply, as *aga(n)* is not a bound morpheme.

To answer these questions, I searched the OFris corpus (Fryske Akademy, 2009) using the AntConc concordance tool (Anthony 2006) for instances of *aga*, including all spellings in the dictionary and several others not listed but found in the

5. The OFris data and conclusions presented in this section are summarized from Colleran (2015) and Colleran (2017).

manuscripts. I then tagged the tokens by meaning, complement type, and complement form, including infinitive ending and the spelling (if any) of *to*.

3.1 The grammaticalization of OE *agan*

OFris *aga* is cognate to Old Saxon *ēgan*, Middle Dutch *eigen*, Old High German *eigan, etc.*, and also to OE *agan* 'own', leading to PDE forms *owe* and *ought*. The *Oxford English Dictionary* (Anon, 2017, 'ought,') suggests that it 'originates in the Old English phrase *āgan to gieldenne*, with accusative and inflected infinitive, in the sense 'to have (something) to pay' shading imperceptibly into 'to have to pay (something)'. Dekeyser (1998) illustrates this development with several OE examples:

(4) *þa micles beþurfon þe* *micel* ***agan*** *willaþ*.
those much need that much own will
'those are in need of much who want/wish **to possess** much'. c 888 *Boethius*

(5) *geld þæt þu* ***aht*** *to geldanne*.
pay what you have to pay
'pay what you **have** to pay/owe'. c 950 *Lindisfarne Gospels*

(6) *þes we ahte(n) to beon þe edmoddre*
thus we ought to be the humbler
'thus we **ought** to be the humbler (ones)'. c 1175 *Lamb. Homilies*

Kuteva (2001: 1–2) describes this grammaticalization of auxiliaries as 'a morphosyntactic change whereby the lexical structure *verb – complement* turns into the grammatical structure *grammatical marker – verb*.' This change can be viewed as three steps: *untypical contexts*, where the meaning is still a part of the word's original sense (Example 4), lead to *critical contexts*, where the context might be interpreted in either the old or a newer sense (Example 5), and then to *isolating contexts*, in which the construction unambiguously has the newer meaning (Example 6) (framework from Diewald, 2002). As forms become increasingly grammaticalized, they often undergo phonological reduction. Older meanings may persist even after the new meaning becomes common, a process known as *layering*. Uses of the new meaning, however, tend to outnumber uses of the old due to the increased range of contexts available (Bybee, 2003).

3.2 Semantic layering: Intermediate stages and a semantic GSG

If OFris *aga* can be shown to have undergone all of the intermediate stages of development from common Gmc 'have/own' to exclusively Anglo-Frisian 'have to', this is evidence against one of the languages having borrowed the grammaticalization from the other due to contact (diagnostic 2). Moreover, a full overlap in semantic distribution will indicate that semantically, this grammaticalization is a candidate for a GSG, suggesting shared inheritance (diagnostic 1).

To trace the semantic development of *aga*, I divided the tokens into seven classes. Complements (or in categories E-G, the verbs heading complements) are underlined.

Category codes:

A. owns.

(7) soe *schel hi, deer dat land* ***aegh****, habba dine kere*
so shall he, who the land owns, have the choice'
'so shall he who owns the land have the choice'. (*Jus*)

B. *the injured party* (or *lawkeeper*) has a right to.

(8) *Sa* ***ach*** *thi frana of tha xij. merkum fiarda*
Then deserves/should-get the judge of the twelve marks 4
twedene scill.
2/3 shillings
'Then the judge should get 4 2/3 shillings of the 12 marks.' (*Fivelgo*)

C. owes something to someone/belongs to someone.

(9) *Sa* ***achma*** *tha frana of tha tuelef merkum fiarda tuede scill.*
Then owes-one the judge of the twelve marks 4 2/3 shillings
'Then one owes the judge 4 2/3 shillings of the twelve marks.' (*Hunsigo 1*)

D. *the crime* or *body part* requires a certain penalty.

(10) *Benes onstall* ***ach*** *en eth.*
bone's trapping requires one oath
'A lodged bone fragment deserves an oath.' (*Jus*)

E. 'have to': + bare infinitive OR + infinitive without TO.

(11) oe ***aegh*** *ma him oenthingia mit aefta tioege*
then must one him bring-to-law with lawful witness
'then one must bring him to law with lawful witness'. (*Jus*)

F. 'have to' + TO + bare infinitive (no <n>).[6]

(12) *Tetther nen moder ne* ***ach*** *te sella hire birnes erue er*
That-there no mother not ought to sell her child's inheritance before
thet bern ierich wirthe.
the child of-age becomes
'That a mother ought not sell her child's inheritance before the child comes of age'. (*Emsingo 1*)

6. With only three tokens, this pattern may be defective (i.e. scribal mistakes rather than a grammatical option).

G. ‘have to’ + TO + long infinitive (*includes* <n>).

(13) soe *aegh di asega ti delane, dat* …
then ought the law-speaker to decree, that …
‘then should the law-speaker decree that ….’ (*Jus*)

Breaking the OFris manuscripts into fifty-year date ranges,[7] we can view the distribution of these categories across the course of the OFris corpus.

Category G, *aga* used as an auxiliary with an inflected *to*-infinitive, comprises a strong majority in all date ranges. B, ‘having a right to’ something, maintains a small but robust presence, with A, ‘having’ something, also present in all time frames.

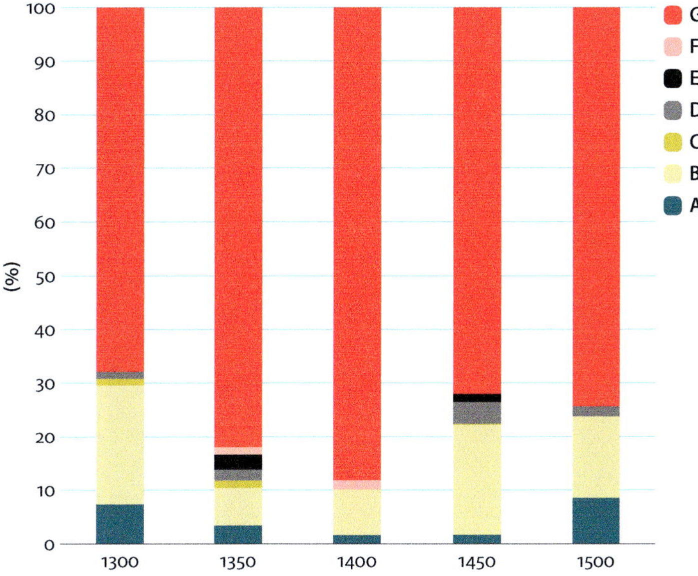

Figure 1. Proportion of *aga* categories at varying date ranges (n = 1034)

This distribution suggests that the grammaticalization of *aga* took place before these manuscripts were written, as the most grammaticalized form (G) is in the majority even in the earliest manuscripts. In accordance with Bybee’s (2003) observation, grammaticalized uses outnumber non-grammaticalized ones due to the expanded number of the contexts in which they can be used. The process of developing auxiliary *aga* in OFris took place prior to the writing of manuscripts of the OFris corpus, placing the grammaticalization of OFris *aga* prior to 1200 and bringing it potentially in line with the same change in OE. (If the grammaticalization occurred within the date range of the OFris corpus, it would have greatly postdated the same change in

7. *1300* is shorthand for 1275–1324, *1350* for 1325–1374, etc.

OE.) Unfortunately, we have almost no data for Frisian prior to the 13th century (the earliest extant manuscript dates to the late 1200s), so this kind of inference is the only method we have for making comparisons of dates between the two languages.

OFris *aga* definitively shows signs of having developed through the intermediate semantic stages of auxiliation, as all of these meanings are attested in the corpus: 'have' > 'have a right to' > 'owe as a penalty' > 'have to (often as a penalty)'. This suggests that OFris did not merely borrow the results of grammaticalization from OE, fulfilling diagnostic 2. Moreover, the range of meanings is the same between OFris and OE *aga*, indicating a GSG, at least in semantic variation (diagnostic 1).

3.3 Another marker of intermediate stages: *to*

Like its OE counterpart (Los, 2005), OFris *to* has a full preposition form and an infinitive marker form. In the complement of *aga*, the latter shows phonological reduction over time. This reduction correlates with its grammaticalized function, a correlation Heine and Kuteva (2005: 80) lead us to expect for grammaticalized forms.

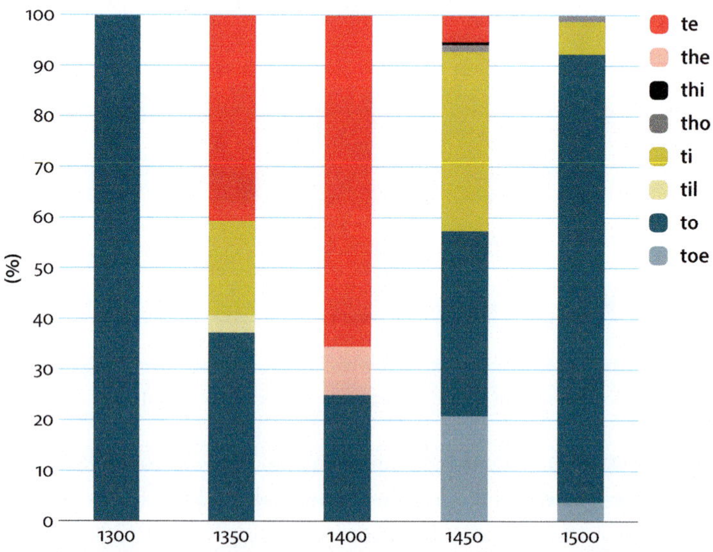

Figure 2. Spelling of infinitive *to* across date ranges in the complement of *aga* (n = 764).[8]

8. *Til* is a separate lexical item, similar in meaning to the preposition *to*. It enjoyed a brief run in OFris as an infinitive marker, but as in OE (Callaway, 1913; Fischer, 1997: 266; Los, 2015: 144), *to* remained the only preposition to grammaticalize into an infinitive marker for a sustained period. In English, other prepositions (e.g. *æt*, *til*) did not appear with infinitives until Middle English, and even then may have been dialectal markers (Fischer, 1997: 266) (See Colleran, 2017: 111–113).

> Variation in the spelling of infinitival *to* increases, suggesting reduction in the pronunciation, which generally co-occurs with grammaticalization. In this data set, toward 1500, variation remains, but <to> again starts to take over as the preferred spelling. In data sets that include matrix verbs besides *aga*, however, <ti> and <tho>/<toe> remain strongly represented in the 1500 range, and <tho>/<toe> handily outnumbers <to> in the 1600 range, possibly due to increasing Dutch influence. (Colleran, 2017: 107–111)

This reduction is reflected by increased variation in spelling over time; owing to the lack of a written standard, OFris spelling is very likely to reflect genuine spoken variation (Versloot, 2008: 255).

This grammaticalization of infinitival *to* from preposition to infinitive marker, with concomitant phonological reduction, is another sign of OFris participation in the intermediate stages of *aga*'s grammaticalization (diagnostic 2).

3.4 Infinitive inflections in *aga's* complement

The distribution of inflectional endings in the complement of *aga* provides more evidence of intermediate stages: OFris does not borrow an infinitive ending ready-made for the complement of *aga*. Rather, OFris goes through several stages with increasing phonological reduction.

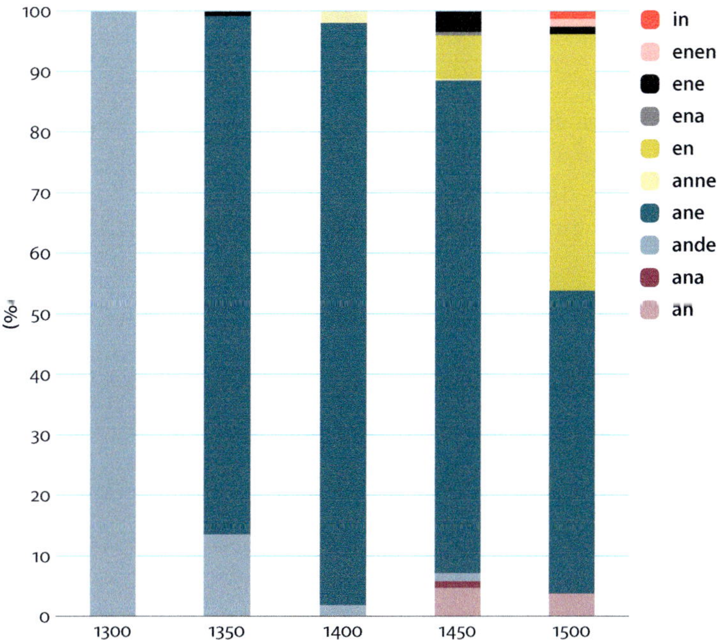

Figure 3. Distribution of inflected infinitives by date range (n = 764)

The infinitive ending develops from early *-ande* (formally identical to a canonical OFris present participle inflection and very like OE present participle inflection *-ende*, which may have added to the confusion) through nearly universal *-ane*, and is eventually reduced by frequent omission or reduction of the final vowel and reduction of the first vowel, signaled by orthographic variation.

Thus we see that *aga(n)* fulfills diagnostic 1, performing as a GSG in every test: it shows the same range of semantics and the same *to*-infinitive complement as its OE counterpart. Likewise, OFris *aga* shows the same intermediate stages as in OE, both semantically and in its complement, satisfying diagnostic 2. *Aga(n)* argues firmly for a shared ancestor.

4. Test case 2: The participle-based complement[9]

4.1 The participle-as-verb-complement: A potential GSG

Grammars of OFris and OE present two non-finite verb complements, often called the long/inflected[10]/*to*-infinitive and the *short/bare* infinitive. Where OFris and OE differ from other West Germanic languages is that they also show signs of drawing the present participle in as a third form of non-finite verb complement. This phenomenon has been remarked on in OE as a fully grammatical option with some matrix verbs, notably verbs of perception, motion and rest (Los, 2005: 34; Ringe & Taylor, 2014: 488).

(14) *Ic* ***geseah*** *ða englas dreorige* *<u>wepan</u>* *and ða sceoccan* *<u>blissigende</u>* *on*
I saw the angels bitterly weep$_{\text{INF}}$ and the demons rejoicing$_{\text{PRES PART}}$ at
eowerum forwyrde
your destruction
'I saw the angels weep bitterly and the demons rejoicing at your destruction.'

This usage has not been considered an option in OFris, but, as we shall see below, this omission may be due to other complicating factors: highly variable spelling; later attestation compared to OE, leading to more reduced forms; the difficulty of categorizing contracted verbs (e.g. OFris *sta(e)n* vs. *stonda* 'stand$_{\text{INF}}$'); and the paucity of studies on OFris grammar compared to OE.

9. This concept was presented as the "third infinitive" in Colleran (2017). The terminology has been changed for clarity.

10. Historically, both long and short infinitives derived from inflected forms (Ringe & Taylor, 2014: 483), but 'inflected' has traditionally been used to refer to the long/*to*-infinitive in OE.

For both OE and OFris, grammars note the use of an occasional present-participle-like ending where we would expect a long infinitive ending (Bremmer, 2009: 84; Callaway, 1913: 2). Fast-forward several centuries, and we find that PDE still uses the present participle as a complement to verbs of perception (e.g. 'see') and position (e.g. 'stand', 'sit').

(15) I saw John crossing the street.

Meanwhile, in the West-Fries dialect of modern Dutch, a dialect with a strong Frisian substrate, verbs of perception and position are consistently set apart by a complement ending in *-n*, while other verbs take an infinitive ending in *-e* (Eric Hoekstra, 1993, 1994). This is in contrast to Standard Dutch (SDu), whose bare infinitive ending (now formally identical to the SDu *to*-infinitive) varies between *-e* and *-n* depending on whether the following word begins with a consonant. Something has caused the complements of perception and position verbs to remain set apart from other complements in West-Fries Dutch, blocking the phonological conditioning of endings found in SDu.

Present-Day Frisian (PDFris), like West-Fries, sets the complement of perception and position verbs apart from modals and 'let' with an *-n* ending, and apart from *to*-infinitives by use of *to* (keeping *-n* as the *to*-infinitive ending) (de Haan, 2010: 153). Thus we find a three-fold split of infinitives in PDFris:

	Features	
Infinitive	*To*	Nasal
To-infinitive	+	+
Bare infinitive	–	–
Position/perception infinitive*	–	+

* Henceforth *position infinitive.*

Figure 4. Features of infinitives

Anticipating my results, I will confirm that all three complements are attested in OFris:

(16) *to* -infinitive:
soe *aegh di asega ti delane, dat ...*
then ought the law-speaker to decree, that ...
'then should the law-speaker decree that ....' (*Jus*)

(17) Bare:
dat *hit* ***gunghe*** *sitta in syn vaders ief moders stede*
that it go sit in his father's or mother's place
'that it [a child] go sit in it's father's or mother's place'. (*Aysma, 55*)

(18) Position, etc.:
Disse xij ***ghingen*** *om disse born* <u>*sitten*</u>
these twelve went by this well sit
'These twelve went and sat by this well'. (*Aysma, Gesta Fresonum V: 17*)

Note that the bare infinitive ending had eroded to *-a* in OFris by the earliest manuscripts, save in the contracted verbs.[11]

The etymological origin of this perception infinitive ending in PDFris has not yet been determined. Eric Hoekstra (1993, 1994, 2001) rejects an earlier claim (Daan, 1956) that this *-n* ending derives from a past participle. Jarich Hoekstra (1992), commenting on Fering Frisian, offers a plausible derivation for the *-n* form from the present participle. While the presence in PDFris of a present participle ending in *-ende* may seem to undermine this etymology, a split is well within the common patterns of grammaticalization: the present participle form as verb complement (to perception and aspectually-used position verbs) was reduced to *-n* and no longer associated with the present participle, while the present participle that builds adverbial clauses remained. Alternatively, the present participle in *-ende* may have been reintroduced through Dutch influence.

If Jarich Hoekstra is correct, we may have another shared grammaticalization: the use of present participle as verb complement (further reduced in PDFris so that it no longer looks like the modern present participle). To test this hypothesis, we need to answer several questions:

1. Can the OFris position infinitive plausibly be derived from the OE/OFris present participle?
2. Is there a position infinitive – the *-n* infinitive that is not a *to*-infinitive – in OFris, as there is in PDFris? Does its distribution match that of the present participle in OE?

If the answer to both is *yes*, the development of the Germanic (Gmc) present participle into a verb complement in OFris and OE is likely a GSG (diagnostic 1). Sharing a novel method of verb complementation is not, in itself, evidence of shared development at any deep level. However, if the formal characteristics of the positional infinitive (e.g. the form of the endings) and its distributional properties (the verbs it complements) match with those of the OE present participle, that makes the participle-as-verb-complement a candidate for the status of a GSG. Every small detail in which the OE and OFris participle-cum-infinitives are congruent decreases

11. Part of this difference between OFris and OE bare infinitives is doubtless the result of the difference in dates; by the time of the OFris texts, OE had turned into MidE, and was likewise losing its final *-n* in uninflected infinitives and in other word classes. The Northumbrian dialect was already losing *-n* during the OE period (Bremmer, 2009: 126; Minkova, 2016).

the probability that this feature developed independently in each language, or spread by low-level contact, and increases the probability of a shared Anglo-Frisian ancestor. Moreover, the fact that the grammaticalized form is a bound morpheme increases the weight of the evidence (diagnostic 5).

4.2 Erosion in Old Frisian infinitive and participle endings

Answering the first of the infinitive research questions rests on deriving the PDFris *-n* position infinitive ending from the OFris present participle *-ande/ende*,[12] and there is evidence that the present participle ending was already undergoing just such a phonological reduction within the OFris period. While Bremmer has commented on the formal correspondence between the long infinitive and the present participle in *-ande/-ende* in the dialect of Old East Frisian (OEFris) (2009: 84, 113), the corpus indicates that the correspondence actually has a much broader distribution. The present participle is often formally indistinguishable from the long infinitive in their reduced *-ane* and *-en* endings, as well as the *-ande/–ende* ending:

(19) der *hi* **is** *kapien ende vorkapien ende da haechtiden* **is** *fyriane*
where he is buying and selling and the holy-day is celebrating
'where he is buying and selling and celebrating the holy day'. (*Aysma, 518*)

(20) *Hwa soe faereth oenbiraedadis mit onriochter wald ti ene*
Who so goes unannounced with unlawful force to a
standane hus
standing house
'Whoever goes unannounced with unlawful force to a standing house'.
(*Jus, 16: 1*)

The ensuing correspondence between the forms of the long (and position?) infinitive and the present participle suggests that these forms were not entirely distinct in speakers' minds in many varieties, whether because speakers had 'adopted the same [*ande*] ending as that of the present participle' for their inflected infinitives, as in OEFris (Bremmer, 2009: 113), or reduced the participle ending from *-ande* to *-en(e)/-an(e)* as part of a larger simplification of *nd* > *n*, as in the Old West Frisian dialect.[13] Indeed, it would be difficult for a speaker to acquire a distinction between the infinitive and participle endings, given this input. It is therefore not surprising that some matrix verbs may be complemented by *-n* endings either with or without *to* (see below).

12. Forms from Bremmer, 2009: 84.

13. There is also a diachronic axis to this division, as OEFris manuscripts are largely older than OWFr ones (Bremmer, 2009: 15–18).

Contributing even further to the overlap of various infinitive and participle endings in speakers' minds is the uncertain status of the 'contracted' verbs. Particularly in the (later-attested) OWFris dialect, monosyllabic verb stems may show 'contracted' infinitive forms: *gan* < *gunga* 'go', *sta(e)n* < *stonda* 'stand', etc. (Bremmer, 2009: 84). The contracted verbs are often analyzed as bare infinitives in grammars (e.g. Bremmer, 2009: 103). These contracted verbs, however, may show identical forms in contexts where we might reasonably expect a bare (after modals), *to-* (after *aga*) or position infinitive.

(21) da ***scel*** *hy* <u>*staen*</u>
then shall he stand
'then he shall stand'. (*Aysma, 522*)

(22) dat *nenne trouwa* ***agen*** <u>*to*</u> <u>*staen*</u>
that no agreements ought to stand
'that no agreements ought to stand'. (*Aysma, 475*)

(23) *Dae* ***ghinghen*** *hia allegaer to efara den paeus ende koning* <u>*staen*</u>
Then went they all-together to right the pope and king $\text{stand}_{\text{INF}}$
'Then they all went together to stand at the right hand of the pope and the king'. (*Jus, 5: 11*)

This formal similarity raises questions as to how we decide that a given infinitive is a bare infinitive. If the form of the infinitive does not distinguish between non-finite types, have we been basing our analysis of the status of contracted infinitives on assumptions as to what kind of complement the matrix verb selects? For verbs of motion, perception, and rest, which have been shown to take either a position infinitive or a present participle in OE, this kind of assumption may be one of the reasons the position infinitive has been overlooked for so long in OFris.

For *sta(e)n* 'stand', in fact, contexts without *to* (e.g. as complements of modal verbs) overwhelmingly select the shorter spellings of contracted verb *sta(e)n*, without final *-e*. *To*-infinitives, however, select as many tokens without final *-e* (*stane, staene*) as with it. If the forms of bare contracted infinitives are indistinguishable from *to*-infinitives, we cannot assume that any instance of *sta(e)n* we find in the corpus (or, by extension, any contracted infinitive) is a bare infinitive rather than a position infinitive because it lacks final *-e*.

Interestingly, the tokens of *sta(e)n* with verbs of motion and rest (five with *bliwa* 'stay', five with *gan* 'go', and one with *halda* 'hold') invariably appear without final *-e* – exactly the same as their PDFris counterparts. The bare infinitive *stonda* is most likely to appear with modals, where a bare infinitive is the standard West Germanic complement.

4.3 The distribution of Old Frisian infinitives

Despite these complications, a brief comparison of matrix verbs in OFris with their counterparts in OE (as described by Los, 1999, and Ringe & Taylor, 2014) shows that they share the same (often idiosyncratic) distribution. In OE, matrix verbs vary; a given verb may select bare infinitives, *to*-infinitives, present participles, or a combination of these as its complement. Those that take a bare infinitive tend to be toward the auxiliary end of the verb scale (e.g. core modals); those that take the *to*-infinitive are either less auxiliary-like or only became an auxiliary at a later period (e.g. *agan* 'to own'); and a small group of aspectualizers and perception verbs can take either, or a present participle, possibly with a semantic difference depending on which is used (e.g. *onginnan*) (Los, 1998, 2000, 2005: 1). Comparing these classes with their counterparts in OFris, we find that the classes of verbs that select each complement are so consistently the same between OFris and OE that drift, coincidence and contact cannot be considered reasonable explanations. When paired with the formal similarity traced in Section 4.2, this shared distribution suggests that the participle-as-verb-complement is a GSG (diagnostic 1) that is also a bound morpheme (diagnostic 5), indicative of a common Anglo-Frisian ancestor.

This part of the study aims to establish what complementation structures were attested for OFris and how they match with their OE counterparts. As the corpus is not lemmatized, and spelling is variable to a problematic degree, the goal was to collect enough instances for each category of verb to determine that the results were not hapax legomena and might be considered a fair representation of at least the most common complementation options. This was achieved by searching for forms of matrix verbs with obvious verbal inflections, which reduced the number of unrelated homographs.

4.3.1 *Verbs of motion and rest*

In OE, verbs of motion and rest (e.g. *cierran* 'turn, go'; *cuman* 'come', *gangan*/*gan*/*gengan* 'go', *sittan* 'sit') take a bare infinitive or present participle as a complement, or a *to*-infinitive as a purpose adjunct (Los, 2005: 34). The OFris corpus shows the same results for matrix verbs *kuma* 'come'; *fara* 'travel, go'; *gunga* 'go'; and *sitta* 'sit', including clear examples of the present participle in *-ande*.

(24) *Sa hwersa thi tegothere clagande* ***kumth***
So wheresoever the tithe-collector complaining comes
'Wherever the tithe collector comes bringing a charge'. (*Rustringen 1, 20: 11*)

(25) dat *hit* ***gunghe*** *sitta in syn vaders ief moders stede*
that it go sit in his father's or mother's place
'that it [a child] go sit in it's father's or mother's place'. (*Aysma, 55*)

(26) *Disse xij* ***ghingen*** *om disse born* *sitten*
these twelve went by this well sit
'These twelve went and sat by this well'. (*Aysma, Gesta Fresonum V: 17*)

(27) *Hwerso twa kinden to gader* ***comet*** *binna vij jerum op aefte to*
Wherever two children to gether come within seven years on law to
dwane ende to halden
do and to hold
'Wherever two descendents have come together within seven years to carry out and uphold the law' (*to*-infinitive indicates purpose). (*Aysma, 332*)

Endings of *-n* without *to* are most likely to appear in contracted verbs (see Section 4.2).

4.3.2 *Accusativus cum Infinitivo (AcI) verbs: Perception and true causatives*

As in PDE, OE AcI verbs are mainly verbs of perception and causation. They are two-place predicates, and the matrix and embedded verbs take separate subjects, as in the PDE examples below.

(28) Mary saw [John win the race].

(29) Mary made [John study].

In OE and PDE, true causatives, such as *lætan* 'let', only allow bare infinitives, not *to*-infinitives or *that*-clauses. Verbs of perception select both bare infinitives and present participles (Los, 1998: 27; Ringe & Taylor, 2014: 484–485).

(30) *Ic* ***geseah*** *ða englas dreorige wepan and ða sceoccan blissigende*
I saw the angels bitterly weep$_{\text{INF}}$ and the demons rejoicing$_{\text{PRES PART}}$
on eowerum forwyrde
at your destruction
'I saw the angels weep bitterly and the demons rejoicing at your destruction.'

This is also the pattern we find with the PDFris *-en* infinitive without *to*; it appears with verbs of perception, but not causative *litte* 'let' (de Haan, 2010: 153).

In OFris, too, we find that the *to*-infinitive never appears with verbs of perception and causatives, only the bare and *-n* (position?) infinitives. The matrix verbs searched for in the OFris corpus were *leta* 'let, make' and *sia*, 'see'. For the latter, it was not possible to find many tokens by corpus search, owing in part to the sheer number of homographs and the irregularities in spelling attendant on such a short word.

For *leta* 'let' complements, a lot of the *-n* endings are in forms of *gunga* 'go' or *stonda* 'stand', which commonly appear with contracted *-n* forms even as unambiguous bare infinitives, but there are a number of *-n* endings on other verbs as well (e.g. *bliwa* 'stay', *echta* 'judge').

(31) zo *scelma* *da* *bokingha* ***leta*** *onstaen*
so must one the bequest let stand
'then must one let the bequest stand'. (*Aysma, 541*)

(32) *Wye* *hem* *echten* *sal* ***laten***
Who him judge shall make
'The one who will have him judged'[14] (*Aysma, 2*)

(33) *Sa* *ach* *hi* *thenna* *thene* *kere.* *wether* *hine* *vr* *driwe* *sa* *hine*
Then has he then the choice, whether him away drive or him_{ACC}
sitta ***lete***
sit_{INF} let (*Fivelgo, 7: 3*)

As we find present participles in PDE only after perception verbs, and not after causatives, our hypothesis would predict that the position infinitive should not be found with *leta* in OFris. However, while complements ending in vowels (usually *-a*) – i.e. unambiguous bare infinitives – predominate in *leta*'s complement in OFris, *-n* forms do occur. In the complement of *leta*, the *-n* forms – and thus the divergence from OE causatives – appear only from the mid-15th century, so they don't necessarily reflect on the early years of the construction, and thus may not argue against a common Anglo-Frisian origin.

For *sia*, the OFris complement was still always a bare or position (*-n*) infinitive. It was (marginally) more likely to end in *-n* than *-a*, even in complements that were not contracted verbs, such as *spreka* 'speak' and *bleda* 'bleed'. This mirrors the distribution found in PDE and OE, with bare AcIs and present participle constructions both appearing as the complement of perception verbs.

4.3.3 Ditransitive object control: *biada* 'order'.

Los refers to this class of verbs, including *don* 'cause', *biddan* 'ask', and *(be)beodan* 'command', as 'directives'. In OE, *biodan/bebeodan* and *biddan* can appear with either a *to*-infinitive (ditransitive object control) or a bare infinitive (AcI) complement (Los, 1999: 181; Ringe & Taylor, 2014: 487).[15]

---

14. From the dictionary definition of *echta*, the passive seems to be encoded in the lexical item: 'abschätzen, bewerten, beurteilen (lassen)' ('appraise, valuate, (allow to be) judge(d)', trans. RC) (Hofmann & Popkema, 2008).

15. In English, the once-separate verbs '*biddan*, *bebeodan* and *beodan* coalesced into ME *bidden/beden*, and further into the PrDE reflex *bid*' (Los, 1998: 20). The forms are analysed as a single lemma in MidE. In OFris, the most recent dictionary recognizes two lemmata, *biada* 'order' and *bidda/bedda/bidia* 'ask, recommend', but notes that it may be difficult to distinguish between them in the preterite (Hofmann & Popkema, 2008, "biada", "bidda"). As *(be)beodan* and *biddan* have the same syntactic distribution in OE, and there is no principled way to distinguish between them in the preterite in OFris, the OFris results are separated only according to the different spellings, not by semantics.

In OFris, we do not see the competing infinitival complementation of *to*-infinitive and bare infinitive we find in OE. <Bad> takes either a *to*-infinitive or a *that*-clause. <Biot> takes a *to*-infinitive, or twice a ditransitive with two NPs (rather than an NP subject and an infinitive, as in OE), ordering something to someone else. Whether OFris never used bare infinitives with these verbs or resolved the competition between bare and *to*-infinitives before the time of the corpus, this category does not provide a strike against the position infinitive's possible status as a GSG. Based on the OE patterns, I did not expect to find a position infinitive with these verbs in OFris. I searched these verbs to be certain that the distribution of the position infinitive (with *-n*, without *to*) was not wider than that of the OE present participle. With regard to ditransitive object control verbs, it appears that it is not.

4.3.4 *A control group for modals: skela* 'shall'

In both OE and OFris, modals are listed among the matrix verbs that take a bare infinitive complement. (Bremmer, 2009: 102–103; Mitchell & Robinson, 2012, § 205). A corpus search for OFris showed that this is indeed the case with regards to the first verbal element in the complement. The first element in a conjoined complement to *skela* is nearly always bare (or occasionally contracted, in *-n*), as expected.

However, there are a number of cases in which a *to*-infinitive does appear in the complement of *skela*: as the second element of a conjoined complement. This mismatch may be due to an ellipsis of *ma ach* 'one ought', which would call for a *to*-infinitive complement (Bremmer, 2009: 103), or to conjunctions of non-identical tense/mood combinations, which are characteristic of older stages of Germanic languages (de Haan, 2010: 60–61) and are often found in OE as well (Los, 2005: 157–158). In either case, the (surface) conjunction does not give rise to any dissimilarity between modal complementation in OFris and OE.

We started with the observation that in addition to the *to*-infinitive and the bare infinitive, PDFris has an infinitive characterized by an ending that includes <n> and a lack of infinitival *to*, which complements position and perception verbs. As these are the same contexts where OE and PDE bring the present participle into verb complementation, this raises the possibility that the grammaticalization of the present participle into a verb complement may have been be a grammaticalization shared by OE and OFris. Section 4.2 demonstrates that the OFris position infinitive may plausibly have started out identical to the OE present participle, as there is evidence in the OFris corpus of the *-ande/ende* participle ending being reduced to *-en*. This meets the criterion of formal similarity. Section 4.3 demonstrates another criterion, distributional similarity; the posited OFris positional infinitive appears (especially in the early manuscripts) only with classes of verbs where the present participle is licensed in OE. Thus the present-participle-based verb complement can be classed as a GSG for form, function and distribution (diagnostic 1). Its weight as evidence is strengthened by the fact that it is a bound morpheme (diagnostic 5), suggesting even more strongly that it derives from a time when pre-OE and pre-OFris were both part of an Anglo-Frisian ancestor.

5. Conclusion

The question of Anglo-Frisian origins has long been explored through phonological comparison, but only occasionally through other methods. Recent finds in archaeology, genetics and textual history suggest that we revisit the question using a new approach. Shared grammaticalizations offer a methodologically rigorous way to determine whether certain similarities shared between two languages are likely to be due to genealogical relatedness (inheritance), contact, or post-separation drift. In Section 2, I establish five diagnostics for distinguishing shared grammaticalizations due to a shared ancestor from those due to contact. Changes that occurred before two related languages diverged will tend to be GSGs (sharing form, function, and distribution), show intermediate stages of the change in both languages, cluster with similar grammaticalizations, not be restricted to contact zones, and may involve bound morphemes. In section 3, I show that the development of *aga(n)* 'own' to auxiliary 'have to', a grammaticalization exclusive in the West Germanic languages to OFris and OE, displays all of the intermediate stages of grammaticalization in both languages (diagnostic 2) and is a GSG (diagnostic 1). Section 4 traces back an anomalous infinitive ending in Present-Day Frisian to show that OFris and OE may both have grammaticalized the present participle into a verb complement; it has the same form, function and distribution in both languages (diagnostic 1) and as a bound morpheme, provides weighty evidence (diagnostic 5). Taken together, these studies make a strong case for an exclusive Anglo-Frisian ancestor, confirming recent developments in extralinguistic fields.

Acknowledgement

The majority of this article is drawn or adapted from various chapters of Colleran (2017). Many thanks to the anonymous reviewer(s), whose suggestions greatly improved the readability of this paper.

References

Abdelaoui, Abdel et al. 2013. Population Structure, Migration, and Diversifying Selection in the Netherlands. *European Journal of Human Genetics* 21, 1277–1285. https://doi.org/10.1038/ejhg.2013.48

Aikhenvald, Alexandra 2013. Areal Diffusion and Parallelism in Drift: Shared Grammaticalization Patterns. In Martine Robbeets, & Hubert Cuyckens (Eds.), *Shared Grammaticalization: With special focus on the Transeurasian languages* (23–42). Amsterdam: John Benjamins. https://doi.org/10.1075/slcs.132.07aik

Aikhenvald, Alexandra, & Dixon, Robert M. W. (Eds.). 2001. *Areal Diffusion and Genetic Inheritance: Problems in Comparative Linguistics.* Oxford: Oxford University Press.

Anon. 2017. *OED (Oxford English Dictionary Online).* Oxford: Oxford University Press. Retrieved September 6, 2017 (http://www.oed.com/).

Anthony, Laurence 2006. *AntConc Concordance Software.*

Århammar, Nils 1990. Friesisch und Sächsisch. Zur Problematik ihrer gegenseitigen Abgrenzung im Früh-und Hochmittelalter. In *Aspects of Old Frisian Philology.* German: Amsterdamer Beiträge zur älteren Germanistik (1–25).

Bazelmans, Jos 2009. The Early-Medieval Use of Ethnic Names from Classical Antiquity: The Case of the Frisians. In Ton Derks, & Nico Roymans (Eds.), *Ethnic Constructs in Antiquity* (321–338). Amsterdam: Amsterdam University Press.

Bazelmans, Jos, Meier, Dirk, Nieuwhof, Annet, Spek, Theo, & Vos, Peter 2012. Understanding the Cultural Historical Value of the Wadden Sea Region. The Co-Evolution of Environment and Society in the Wadden Sea Area in the Holocene up until Early Modern Times (11,700 BC-1800 AD): An Outline. *Ocean & Coastal Management* 68, 114–126. https://doi.org/10.1016/j.ocecoaman.2012.05.014

Bech, Kristin, & Walkden, George. 2016. English Is (Still) a West Germanic Language. *Nordic Journal of Linguistics* 39(1), 65–100. https://doi.org/10.1017/S0332586515000219

Boomsma, Dorret et al. 2014. The Genome of the Netherlands. *The European Journal of Human Genetics* 22, 221–227. https://doi.org/10.1038/ejhg.2013.118

Bos, Jurjen. M. 2001. Archaeological Evidence Pertaining to the Frisians in the Netherlands. In Horst Haider Munske (Ed.), *Handbuch des Friesischen/Handbook of Frisian Studies* (487–492). Tübingen: Max Niemeyer. https://doi.org/10.1515/9783110946925.487

Bowern, Claire 2013. Relatedness as a Factor in Language Contact. *Journal of Language Contact* 6(2), 411–432. https://doi.org/10.1163/19552629-00602010

Bremmer, Rolf H. J., Jr. 1981. Frisians in Anglo-Saxon England: A Historical and Toponymical Investigation. *Friske Nammen* 3, 45–94.

Bremmer, Rolf H. J., Jr. 1989. Late Medieval and Early Modern Opinions on the Affinity between English and Frisian: The Growth of a Commonplace. *Folio Linguistica Historia* 9, 167–191.

Bremmer, Rolf H. J., Jr. 2001. The Study of Frisian to the End of the 19th Century. In Horst Haider Munske, & Nils Århammar (Eds.), *Handbuch des Friesischen/Handbook of Frisian Studies* (1–11). Tübingen: Max Niemeyer. https://doi.org/10.1515/9783110946925.1

Bremmer, Rolf H. J., Jr. 2009. *An Introduction to Old Frisian.* Amsterdam: John Benjamins. https://doi.org/10.1075/z.147

Bybee, Joan 2003. Mechanisms of Change in Grammaticalization: The Role of Frequency. In Joseph, B. D., & Janda, R. D. (Eds.), *The Handbook of Historical Linguistics.* Malden, MA: Blackwell. https://doi.org/10.1002/9780470756393.ch19

Callaway, Morgan 1913. *The Infinitive in Anglo-Saxon*. Washington, D.C.: Carnegie Institution of Washington.

Campbell, Lyle, & Poser, William 2008. *Language Classification: History and Method*. Cambridge: Cambridge University Press. https://doi.org/10.1017/CBO9780511486906

Capelli, Christian et al. 2003. A Y Chromosome Census of the British Isles. *Current Biology* 13(11), 979–984. https://doi.org/10.1016/S0960-9822(03)00373-7

Colleran, Rebecca 2015. 'To have' and 'to have to': Addressing Old Frisian inheritance through auxiliation. In Eric Hoekstra, Janneke Spoelstra, & Hans Van de Velde (Eds.), *Philologia Frisica Anno 2014* (41–63). Leeuwarden: Fryske Akademy.

Colleran, Rebecca 2017. "Keeping It in the Family: Disentangling Contact and Inheritance in Closely Related Languages." Doctoral dissertation, University of Edinburgh, Edinburgh.

Csató, Éva Ágnes 2013. Growing Apart in Shared Grammaticalization. In Martine Robbeets, & Hubert Cuyckens (Eds.), *Shared Grammaticalization: With special focus on the Transeurasian languages* (251–258). Amsterdam: John Benjamins. https://doi.org/10.1075/slcs.132.18csa

Daan, Jo 1956. *Onze Friese familie. West-Frieslands Oud en Nieuw* 23, 106–110.

Dekeyser, Xavier 1998. The Modal Auxiliary Ought: From 'possession' to 'obligation'. In Johan van der Auwera, Frank Durieux, & Ludo Lejeune (Eds.), *English as a Human Language: to honour Louis Goossens* (109–119).

Diewald, Gabriele 2002. A Model for Relevant Types of Contexts in Grammaticalization. *Typological Studies in Language* 49, 103–120. https://doi.org/10.1075/tsl.49.09die

Dijkstra, Menno 2011. *Rondom de Mondingen van Rijn & Maas: Landschap en bewoning tussen de 3e en 9e eeuw in Zuid-Holland, in het bijzonder de Oude Rijnstreek*. Leiden: Sidestone Press.

Drinka, Bridget 2013. Sources of Auxiliation in the Perfects of Europe. *Studies in Language* 37(3), 599–644. https://doi.org/10.1075/sl.37.3.06dri

Emonds, Joseph, & Faarlund, Jan 2014. *English: The Language of the Vikings*. Palacký University.

Epps, Patience, Huehnergard, John, & Pat-El, Na-ama 2013. Introduction: Contact among Genetically Related Languages. *Journal of Language Contact* 6(2), 209–219. https://doi.org/10.1163/19552629-00602001

Fischer, Olga 1997. The Grammaticalization of Infinitival to in English Compared with German and Dutch. In Raymond Hickey, & Stanislaw Puppel (Eds.), *In Language History and Linguistic Modelling. A Festschrift for Jacek Fisiak on his 60th Birthday* (265–280). Berlin: Mouton de Gruyter. https://doi.org/10.1515/9783110820751.265

Forster, Peter, Romano, Valentino, Calì, Francesco, Röhl, Arni, & Hurles, Matthew 2004. mtDNA Markers for Celtic and Germanic Language Areas in the British Isles. In Martin Jones (Ed.), *Traces of Ancestry* (99–114). Cambridge: Cambridge University Press.

Fryske Akademy 2009. *Frisian Language Databases*. Leeuwarden. Retrieved (http://argyf.fryske-akademy.eu/files/tdb/).

de Haan, Germen 2010. *Studies in West Frisian Grammar*. Amsterdam: John Benjamins.

Härke, Heinrich 2011. Anglo-Saxon Immigration and Ethnogenesis. *Medieval Archaeology* 55, 1–28. https://doi.org/10.1179/174581711X13103897378311

Harris, Alice C., & Campbell, Lyle 1995. *Historical Syntax in Cross-Linguistic Perspective*. Cambridge: Cambridge University Press. https://doi.org/10.1017/CBO9780511620553

Heine, Bernd, & Kuteva, Tania 2002. *World Lexicon of Grammaticalization*. Cambridge: Cambridge University Press. https://doi.org/10.1017/CBO9780511613463

Heine, Bernd, & Kuteva, Tania 2005. *Language Contact and Grammatical Change*. Cambridge: Cambridge University Press. https://doi.org/10.1017/CBO9780511614132

Heine, Bernd, & Nomachi, Motoki 2013. Contact-Induced Replication: Some Diagnostics. In Martine Robbeets, & Hubert Cuyckens (Eds.), *Shared Grammaticalization: With special focus on the Transeurasian languages* (67–100). Amsterdam: John Benjamins. https://doi.org/10.1075/slcs.132.09hei

Hoekstra, Eric 1993. Over de implicaties van enkele morfo-syntactische eigenaardigheden in West-Friese dialecten. *Taal en Tongval* 45, 135–154.

Hoekstra, Eric 1994. Positie- en Bewegingsaspect bij Selectie van de Infinitief op -E of -EN in het Westfries en het Fries. *Taal en Tongval* 46, 66–73.

Hoekstra, Eric 2001. Frisian Relics in the Dutch Dialects. In Horst Haider Munske (Ed.), *Handbook of Frisian Studies* (138–142). Tübingen: Max Niemeyer Verlag. https://doi.org/10.1515/9783110946925.138

Hoekstra, Jarich 1992. Fering Tu-Infinitives, North Sea Germanic Syntax and Universal Grammar. *Friesische Studien I*, 99–142. https://doi.org/10.1075/nss.8.05hoe

Hofmann, Dietrich, & Popkema, Anne Tjerk 2008. *Altfriesisches Handwörterbuch*. Heidelberg: Winter.

Hogg, Richard 2002. Dutch Dialects and Stammbaum Theory. In *Of Diuersitie & Chaunge of Langage: Essays Presented to Manfred Görlach on the Occasion of his 65th Birthday* (212–223). Heidelberg: Winter.

Howe, Stephen 2013. North Sea Germanic Pronouns. *The Bulleting of the Central Research Institute, Fukuoka University* 12(4), 5–18.

Joseph, Brian 2013. Demystifying Drift. In Martine Robbeets, & Hubert Cuyckens (Eds.), *Shared Grammaticalization: With special focus on the Transeurasian languages* (43–65). Amsterdam: John Benjamins. https://doi.org/10.1075/slcs.132.08jos

Kuteva, Tania 2001. *Auxiliation: An Enquiry into the Nature of Grammaticalization*. Oxford: Oxford University Press.

Labov, William 2007. Transmission and Diffusion. *Language* 83(2), 344–387. https://doi.org/10.1353/lan.2007.0082

Lass, Roger 2000. Language Periodization and the Concept 'Middle'. In Irma Taavitsainen, Terttu Nevalainen, Päivi Pahta, & Matti Rissanen (Eds.), *Placing Middle English in Context*, 7–41. Berlin: Mouton de Gruyter. https://doi.org/10.1515/9783110869514.7

Los, Bettelou 1998. The Rise of the to-Infinitive as Verb Complement. *English Language and Linguistics* 2, 1–36. https://doi.org/10.1017/S1360674300000678

Los, Bettelou 1999. *Infinitival Complementation in Old and Middle English*. The Hague: Theseus.

Los, Bettelou 2000. *Onginnan/Beginnan* with Bare and to-Infinitive in Ælfric. In Olga Fischer, Anette Rosenbach, & Dieter Stein (Eds.), *Pathways of Change: Grammaticalization in English* (251–274). Amsterdam: John Benjamins. https://doi.org/10.1075/slcs.53.13los

Los, Bettelou 2005. *The Rise of the TO-Infinitive*. Oxford: Oxford University Press. https://doi.org/10.1093/acprof:oso/9780199274765.001.0001

Los, Bettelou 2015. *A Historical Syntax of English*. Edinburgh: Edinburgh University Press.

Markey, Thomas L. 1981. *Frisian*. The Hague: Mouton Publishers. https://doi.org/10.1515/9783110815719

Minkova, Donka 2016. *The Interaction of Phonology-Morphology-Syntax-Pragmatics in Final -n Loss*. Presented at ICEHL XIX, Essen, August 2016.

Mitchell, Bruce, & Robinson, Fred 2012. *A Guide to Old English*. 8th edition. Chichester: Wiley-Blackwell.

Nielsen, Hans Frede 1981. *Old English and the Continental Germanic Languages*. Innsbruck: Institut für Sprachwissenschaft der Universität Innsbruck.

Nieuwhof, Annet 2009. Discontinuity in the Northern-Netherlands Coastal Area at the End of the Roman Period. In Titus Panhuysen (Ed.), *Transformations in North-Western Europe (AD 300–1000): Proceedings of the 60th Sachsensymposion 19.-23. September 2009 Maastricht.* Hanover: Niedersächsischen Landesmuseum Hannover.

Nieuwhof, Annet 2013. Anglo-Saxon Immigration or Continuity? Ezinge and the Coastal Area of the Northern Netherlands in the Migration Period. *Journal of Archaeology in the Low Countries* 5(1), 53–83.

Pat-El, Na-ama 2013. Contact or Inheritance? Criteria for Distinguishing Internal and External Change in Genetically Related Languages. *Journal of Language Contact* 6(2), 313–328. https://doi.org/10.1163/19552629-00602006

Pereltsvaig, Asya 2015. Is It English or Engelsk? Parts 1–3. *Languages of the World.* Retrieved September 24, 2015 (http://www.languagesoftheworld.info/bad-linguistics/english-engelsk-part-3.html).

Poplack, Shana, & Levey, Stephen 2010. Contact-Induced Grammatical Change: A Cautionary Tale. In Peter Auer, & Jürgen Erich Schmidt (Eds.), *Language and Space: An International Handbook of Language Variation* (391–419).

Quirk, Randolph, & Wrenn, Charles Leslie 1955. *An Old English Grammar.* Methuen.

Ringe, Donald, & Taylor, Ann. 2014. *The Development of Old English.* Oxford: Oxford University Press. https://doi.org/10.1093/acprof:oso/9780199207848.001.0001

Robbeets, Martine 2013. Genealogically Motivated Grammaticalization. *Shared Grammaticalization: With special focus on the Transeurasian languages* (147–176). Amsterdam: John Benjamins. https://doi.org/10.1075/slcs.132.13rob

Robbeets, Martine, & Cuyckens, Hubert 2013. Towards a Typology of Shared Grammaticalization. In Robbeets, Martine, & Cuyckens, Hubert (Eds.), *Shared Grammaticalization: With special focus on the Transeurasian languages* (1–20). Amsterdam/Philadelphia: John Benjamins. https://doi.org/10.1075/slcs.132.05rob

Sapir, Edward 1921. *Language: An Introduction to the Study of Speech.* New York: Harcourt, Brace and World.

Schiffels, Stephan et al. 2016. Iron Age and Anglo-Saxon Genomes from East England Reveal British Migration History. *Nature Communications* 7:10408. https://doi.org/10.1038/ncomms10408.

Stiles, Patrick V. 1995. Remarks on the 'Anglo-Frisian' Thesis. In Volkert F. Faltings, Alastair Walker, & Ommo Wilts (Eds.), *Friesische Studien II* (177–220). https://doi.org/10.1075/nss.12.11sti

Stiles, Patrick V. 2016. Remarks on the 'Anglo-Frisian' Thesis (revised version, unpublished).

Thomason, Sarah 2001. *Language Contact: An Introduction.* Edinburgh: Edinburgh University Press.

Thomason, Sarah 2012. English or Engelsk? *Language Log.* Retrieved September 24, 2015 (http://languagelog.ldc.upenn.edu/nll/?p=4351%20English%20or%20Engelsk).

Versloot, Arjen 2008. Mechanisms of Language Change: Vowel Reduction in 15th Century West Frisian. PhD, Rijksuniversiteit Groningen, Groningen.

Versloot, Arjen, & Adamczyk, Elzbieta 2014. Corpus Size and Composition: Evidence from the Inflectional Morphology of Nouns in Old English and Old Frisian. In Rolf H. J. Bremmer , Jr., Stephen Laker, & Oebele Vries (Eds.),. *Directions for Old Frisian Philology, Amsterdamer Beiträge zur älteren Germanistik* (539–569).

Walkden, George 2013. The Correspondence Problem in Syntactic Reconstruction. *Diachronica* 30(1), 95–122. https://doi.org/10.1075/dia.30.1.04wal

Walkden, George 2014. *Syntactic Reconstruction and Proto-Germanic*. Oxford: Oxford University Press. https://doi.org/10.1093/acprof:oso/9780198712299.001.0001

Weale, Michael E., Jager, Deborah A., Bradman, Neil, & Thomas, Mark G. 2002. Y Chromosome Evidence for Anglo-Saxon Mass Migration. *Molecular Biology and Evolution* 19(7), 1008–1021. https://doi.org/10.1093/oxfordjournals.molbev.a004160

Old English *wolde* and *sceolde*

A semantic and syntactic analysis

Ilse Wischer

The Old English (OE) pre-modals *willan* and **sculan* are generally considered less grammaticalized than their Modern English counterparts *will* and *shall*; nevertheless they most often function as auxiliary verbs (cf. Wischer, 2006: 173). Their present tense forms have already been studied in considerable detail, often in the context of their development into future tense markers, while their morphologically past tense forms have received comparatively little attention. In this paper I examine the past forms of *willan* and **sculan* in the poetry texts from the *Dictionary of Old English Corpus* and categorize them according to their syntactic contexts and the lexical or grammatical meanings they express. Thus, the aim of this paper is to shed light on their past and non-past time-reference, their main verb use versus auxiliary use and the type of modality or other function they can express in periphrastic constructions, and hence their degree of grammaticalization in Old English.

Keywords: grammaticalization, modality, Old English, *sculan*, *willan*

1. Introduction

In Old English, the distinction between *wille/wolde* and *sceal/sceolde*[1] is basically one of present versus past tense, while Modern English *will/would* and *shall/should* express different concepts of modality. The historical development of the English modals has been extensively documented (e.g. Plank, 1984; Goossens, 1987; Denison, 1993; Warner, 1993), and in particular *will* and *shall* have been in the centre of interest in connection with the evolution of the English future tense (e.g. Arnovick, 1990; Gotti, 2006). The past forms of *will* and *shall*, however, have hardly been of major interest.

1. The forms *wolde* and *sceolde* are used here as representatives for all inflected past tense forms such as *woldest*, *woldon*, etc.

https://doi.org/10.1075/cilt.346.06wis

Bybee (1995) describes the Old English use of *wolde* and *sceolde* in the following way: "...*wolde* is used almost exclusively to signal volition of the subject in the past, just as *wylle* was used to express volition in the present" (505); "[In Old English] we find many clear instances of *should* signalling destiny, duty or obligation of the subject in the past, corresponding to *sceal*, which has the same meaning in the present" (504). Changes in the past reference of *wolde* and *sceolde*, according to Bybee, must have occurred, however, from Old English to Middle English, as she states that "[b]y the Middle English period, however, both *should* and *would* had made their way into present contexts, especially with first and second person" (505). As changes do not occur abruptly from one moment to the next, but are gradual processes, there must have been occurrences of *wolde* and *sceolde* without their original past time reference in late Old English.

Mitchell (1985: 426) claims that "[t]he use of *wolde* 'would' to express a polite wish for the present or future begins in OE", providing an example from the OE Boethius: *Ac ic þe wolde acsian* ... ('But I wanted/would like to ask you ...'). Kohnen (2011) is an enlightening study concerning the cultural and social background of such (directive) requests. Looking at the OED, we can find a similar observation for *shall*: "As with other auxiliaries, the pa. tense (orig. subjunctive) of *shall* is often used to express, not a reference to past time, but a modal qualification of the notion expressed by the present tense." (OED, s.v. *shall*). Although this statement is not specifically related to Old English, but rather refers to PDE use of *should*, there are nevertheless very early OE examples of such uses provided. It is interesting to note that these early examples of modal uses of *sceolde* in the OED occur in the past subjunctive or are formally ambiguous with regard to indicative or subjunctive mood.[2] Anderson (1991: 27) similarly admits that "there are signs [...] of a dissolution of the past/non-past relationship" of *sceolde* in Old English, but he denies its status as an auxiliary.[3]

Visser (1978: III.1) lists a wide range of timeless or modal uses of OE *wolde* and *sceolde*: Thus, he provides evidence for *wolde* being used as a marker of posterior past ('was about to') (*ða hit on mergen dagian wolde* 'when it was about to dawn in the morning') (§ 1591), habitual aspect ('consuetudinal *would*') (*wild deor ðær woldon to irnan* 'wild animals used to come there') (§ 1710), pure futurity,

2. As *sceolde* is a weak past tense form, indicative and subjunctive mood could hardly be distinguished as early as in Old English due to reductive and analogical linguistic changes. It is possible that the modal meaning formerly expressed by the past subjunctive came to be assigned to the past tense form.

3. He claims that "the massive evidence for a central syntactic role for [...] a subcategory auxiliary [...] in the form of the "nice" properties and others [...] is quite absent from Old English" (Anderson, 1991: 14).

without any connotation of volition, intention or promise ('future in the past'), mostly in reported speech or thought acts (§ 1716) (*ongitan mihte, hu þis gewinn wolde gangan* 'might understand how this fight would proceed'), and possibility or contingency in the apodosis of conditional or hypothetical propositions (§ 1610) (*gif Maria unbeweddod wære & cild hæfde, þonne wolde þæt folc mid stanum hi oftorfian* 'If Mary were unmarried and had a child, the people would pelt her with stones'). Similarly, for *sceolde*, he identified timeless uses to express moral or social obligation (§ 1530) (*þu ne sceolde stelan* 'you should not steal anything'), unreality of a supposition (§ 1532) in the apodosis of (hypothetical) conditional clauses (*gif heo dyde ..., min fæder sceolde ...* 'if she had done ..., my father should/would have ...') and "in oblique report to indicate that what is said is only a rumour ... or unbelievable ... or ... untrue" (§ 1610) (*sædon þæt hio sceolde mid hire scinlace beornas forbredan* 'it was said that she should have bewitched people with her sorcery'; cf. also (17) below).

The following study is based on a data analysis from the poetry texts[4] of the *Dictionary of Old English Corpus*. The past tense forms of *willan* and **sculan* are identified and categorized with regard to the lexical or grammatical meanings they express. The study focuses on the full verb and auxiliary uses of *wolde* and *sceolde* as well as on the more specific grammatical functions expressed by periphrastic constructions with *wolde* and *sceolde*.

2. Theoretical considerations: Modality and grammaticalization

The evolution of modality and modal verbs has been extensively studied and discussed within the framework of grammaticalization theory.[5] There is general agreement that modal verbs have their origin in lexical verbs, which have been decategorialized into function words signaling various concepts of modality, whereby different types of modality mirror various degrees of grammaticalization (see my suggestions for the semantic pathways to epistemic modality below). The concept and classification of modality varies a lot in the literature. Therefore it is necessary to first present an outline of my theoretical approach to modality as a basis for the empirical analysis.

4. Poetry texts were chosen since they represent the oldest and most authentic layer of the OE language. In a future study, the analysis will be extended to prose texts as well.

5. For references to the most important literature cf. Ziegeler (2011).

Following Palmer (2001: 8) I draw a basic distinction between event modality and propositional modality, the first being "directive" and subject-related and the latter being "assumptive" and speaker-related, cf. Figure 1.

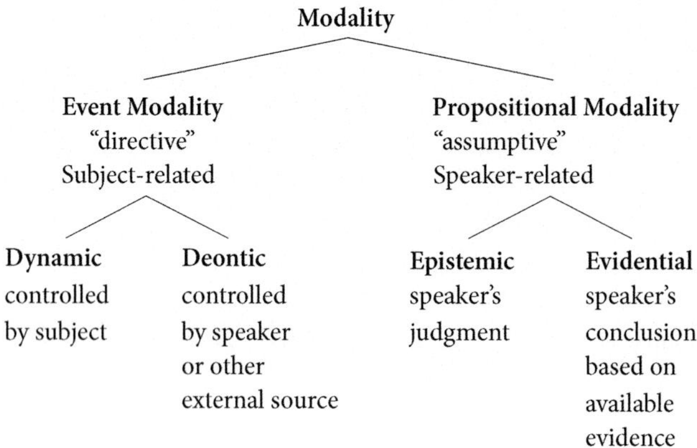

Figure 1. The concept of modality, based on Palmer (2001)

Event modality can be further divided into dynamic and deontic modality. With dynamic modality the event is controlled by the subject of the clause, while with deontic modality the speaker or some other external source has control over the event. Propositional modality, on the other hand, can be subdivided into epistemic and evidential modality. With epistemic modality the speaker makes a judgment about the likelihood of the event; with evidential modality the speaker draws a conclusion on the likelihood of an event on the basis of some available evidence.

According to Palmer (1990: 36), dynamic modality indicates the ability or volition of the subject of the sentence. It is directly related to the root meaning of the verb (*can* 'to know (how to …)' → ability; *will* 'to desire, wish' → volition),[6] while the concept of deontic modality is less directly, but still closely, related to the root meaning of the verb (*shall* 'to owe' → obligation/promise/threat; *may* 'to have power' → permission). Palmer (2001: 70–73) makes a difference between 'directives', where some authority tries to get the 'subject' to do something (permission, obligation) (*You/He must eat your/his breakfast.*) and 'commissives', where the speaker guarantees that something will necessarily happen to the subject (promise, threat, necessity) (*You/He must/shall be punished for what you/he did.*), cf. Figure 2.

6. For a discussion of 'dynamic modality' cf. also Gisborne (2007), who denies the existence of dynamic modality – which is usually only postulated for *can* and *will* – altogether and argues that it is "simply the retention of an earlier sense which persists after CAN has joined the modal verb system of English" (45). Although I generally agree with this argument, I will continue to use the term 'dynamic modality' to distinguish it from the 'root meaning' of the former lexical verbs.

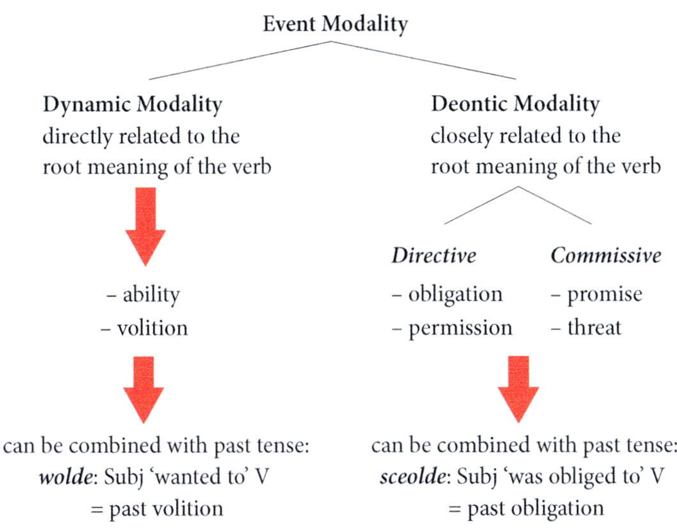

Figure 2. The concept of event modality, based on Palmer (2001: 70–73)

I am now turning to 'Propositional Modality': The concepts of epistemic and evidential modality are metonymically related to the root meaning of the verb (*can* 'to know how to ...' → possibility; *will* 'to desire, wish' → probability or report evidence; *shall* 'to owe' → necessity or report evidence; etc.), cf. Figure 3.

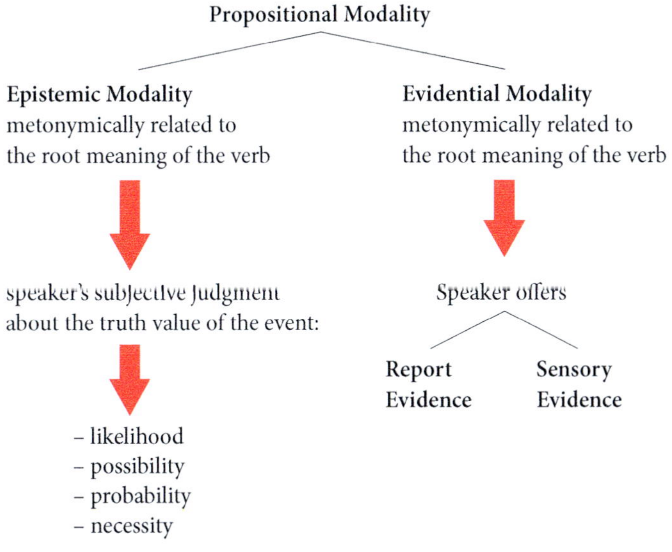

Figure 3. The concept of propositional modality, based on Palmer (2001: 8f.)

The grammaticalization of a modal verb begins with the auxiliarization of a former lexical or main verb. This process, which involves morphosyntactic changes (decategorialization) and semantic changes (lexical meaning > grammatical meaning), had been very well advanced for the OE pre-modals.[7] Further grammaticalization of auxiliaries usually comprises morphophonological changes (cliticization) and phonetic changes (erosion). These processes are irrelevant for Old English, i.e. they did not happen with OE pre-modals.

Grammaticalization of modal auxiliaries presupposes the gradual development of specific modal meanings. Thus, it is generally assumed that epistemic modality derives from non-epistemic modality; however, there is no general agreement on the path towards epistemic modality, or even to irrealis mood (cf. Ziegeler, 2011). On the basis of the modality concept outlined above and in line with my findings in the present study, I suggest a semantic pathway from the root meaning of a verb to dynamic or deontic modality and from there to epistemic or evidential modality, which finally can develop into a grammatical category of mood.[8] It is also possible that deontic modality does not directly emerge from the root meaning of a verb, but via dynamic modality, as illustrated in Figure 4.

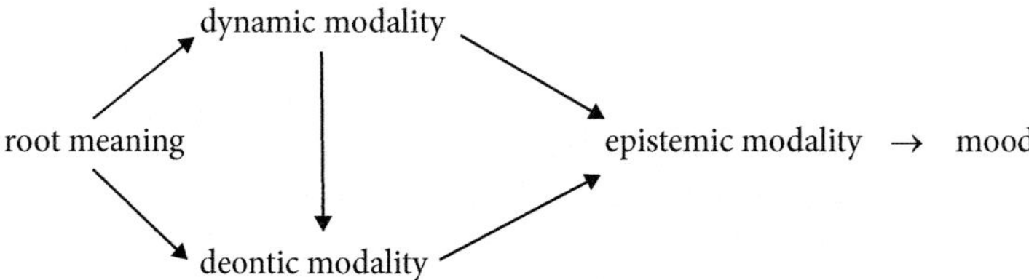

Figure 4. The semantic pathway towards epistemic modality

Depending on the root meaning of a verb, the path towards epistemic modality can vary: In the case of OE *wolde*, dynamic modality (volition, intention) is the source for the rise of epistemic modality, and even for a habitual aspect sense, as well as for the deontic obligation meaning, cf. Figure 5.

7. For the present tense forms of OE *willan* and *sculan*, whose interpretation in terms of their original lexical meaning does often not make sense anymore, cf. Wischer, 2006 and Diewald & Wischer, 2013.

8. Cf. Lehmann's (2015: 30–31) remarks on possible transformations of modal verbs into verbal mood affixes.

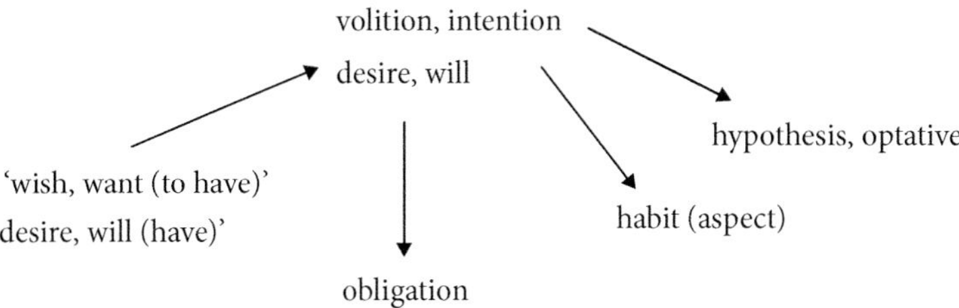

Figure 5. The semantic pathway of *wolde*

With *sceolde*, on the other hand, the root meaning is the direct source for its deontic obligation sense, and this, in turn, gave rise to a number of epistemic and evidential meanings, as outlined in Figure 6.

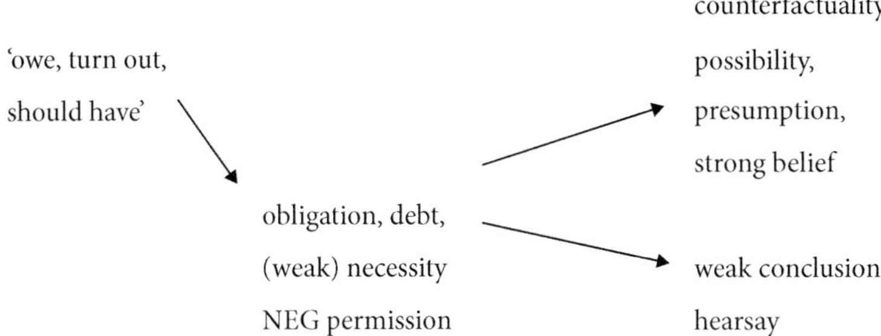

Figure 6. The semantic pathway of *sceolde*

Concerning the pathways of the semantic developments of *wolde* and *sceolde*, it can be expected that there should have been certain successive stages in the history of English, but also a considerable amount of parallel, overlapping uses of various modality concepts at the same time. In the following section, this shall be analysed in more detail with regard to the Old English period.

3. *Wolde* and *sceolde* in Old English: Analysis of the data

It is difficult to determine the category status of the OE pre-modals. As members of the group of preterite-present verbs they share a certain irregular morphology, which also holds true for *willan*, the only pre-modal that does not belong to that group but was an anomalous verb. For most of them non-finite forms are generally not recorded. Whether there really appears a past participle of *will* in Middle English, as stated by Warner (1993: 101) cannot be proven on the basis of my analysis.

Both *willan* and **sculan* can occur independently in Old English, i.e. having full verb status, or as auxiliaries in combination with the bare infinitive of a lexical verb. The independent use, however, is often questioned, especially in combination with a prepositional phrase (PP), e.g. *þæt he sceolde to his huse* 'that he should [go] to his house', or a directional adverb, as e.g. *togædere woldon* 'would/wanted [to come/go] together'. Kellner (1974 [1892]: 222) considers such cases as elliptical uses, while Mitchell (1985: 419f.) rather describes such constructions as ambiguous with regard to independent use or ellipsis. For elliptical uses he defines clear contexts:

1. if an infinitive is not repeated with one of two 'modal' auxiliaries (ex.: ... *hwæt hie ... don sceoldon, hwæt ne scolden*)
2. if an infinitive can clearly be supplied from a preceding finite verb or participle (ex.: *Ne man god ne lufað swa swa man scolde*).

I followed Mitchell here and analysed all examples of *wolde* and *sceolde* for which a related infinitive could be supplied from the context as ellipses and not as independent uses. All other examples, including Mitchell's ambiguous constructions, were analysed as main verb uses (ex.: *no ic fram him wolde*).

For the present study, I analysed all instances of *wolde*[9] and *sceolde* in the verse texts of the *Dictionary of Old English Corpus*, where *wolde* (277/58%) occurred slightly more often than *sceolde* (203/42%). The distribution of their uses is shown in Table 1.

Table 1. Quantitative distribution of the uses of *wolde* and *sceolde* in the corpus

	wolde		sceolde	
		%		%
Main Verb Use	33	11.9	2	1.0
Dynamic Modality	151	54.5	0	0
Deontic Modality	1	0.4	99	48.8
Epistemic Modality	30	10.8	13	6.4
Evidential Modality	1	0.4	6	3.0
Habitual Aspect	12	4.3	0	0
Accomplishment	19	6.9	8	3.9
Future in the Past*	30	10.8	75	36.9
Total	**277**	**100**	**203**	**100**

* "Future in the Past" is assigned a special status here, as a concept between tense and modality. It refers to a state-of-affairs that is posterior to a reference point in the past without putting special emphasis on a particular modal concept; most typical examples occur in reported speech.

9. Fused negated forms of *nolde* are not included in the study.

Here it becomes obvious that the most frequent use of *wolde* is to express dynamic modality (volition, intention, desire, will) in the past (54.5%) and that of *sceolde*, respectively, to express deontic modality (obligation, debt, necessity) in the past (48.8%), cf. Examples 1 and 2.

(1) *Wæron Egypte eft oncyrde, flugon forhtigende, fær ongeton,* ***woldon*** *herebleaðe hamas* ***findan****, gylp wearð gnornra.* (Exodus, 452–455)
'The Egyptians were turned back, they flew timidly, they understood the danger, they cowardly *wanted to find* dwellings, pride had become more sorrowful.'

(2) *Forþon he* ***sceolde*** *grund* ***gesecean*** *heardes hellewites, þæs þe he wann wið heofnes waldend.* (Genesis, 302–303)
'Therefore he *was forced to seek* the cruel pain of hell's abyss because he had fought against the ruler of heaven.'

Main verb uses of *sceolde* are extremely rare, while those of *wolde* amount to almost 12%, most of which are constructions with *that*-clause complements. Despite this relatively high proportion of main verb *wolde*, a similarly high amount of epistemic modality uses (10.8%) of *wolde* could be identified. With regard to the frequency of epistemic and evidential modality uses *sceolde* behaves more or less like *wolde*, with 9.4%, if epistemic and evidential modality are taken together.

Besides main verb and modality uses there are periphrastic constructions with *wolde* and *sceolde* that convey an aspectual or a mere temporal sense: Habitual aspect is only expressed with *wolde* (4.4%), a sense of accomplishment is found with both verbs; and both verbs are also used to express future in the past. The latter is especially frequent with *sceolde*, with 36.9% of all occurrences, although it must be admitted that most of the examples imply an additional modality sense, cf. also Table 2 on the time references of *wolde* and *sceolde*.

Table 2. Time reference of *wolde* and *sceolde* in the corpus

	wolde		sceolde	
		%		%
Past-time reference	212	76.5	112	55.1
Future in the past	30	10.8	75	36.9
Non-past-time reference	35	12.7	16	8.0
Total	277	100	203	100

Only about half of the *sceolde* examples in my corpus are used with a clear reference to past time, i.e. denoting an obligation or a necessity in the past. With *wolde* this percentage is much higher (76.5%), which corresponds to the higher proportion of its main verb uses compared to *sceolde*, because main verb uses always have a past reference. This might be evidence of a more advanced grammaticalization process of *sceolde* as compared to *wolde*. Nevertheless, clear non-past uses, i.e. those that express a modal sense with reference to the present or future, do not dominate with *sceolde* (because of a higher proportion of future-in-the-past with *sceolde*), but are even slightly higher in frequency with *wolde*.

4. Discussion of the results

4.1 *wolde*

The most typical use of *wolde* is to express dynamic modality, i.e. desire, volition, intention in the past (54.5%). Especially in paratactic clause constructions *wolde* is found to mark a purpose relationship, where in Present Day English a subordinate infinitive construction is used, as in (3).

(3) *... and þa on bæl ahof Isaac geongne, ...,* ***wolde*** *his sunu* ***cwellan*** *...*
(Genesis, 2904–2906)
'... and then he lifted the young Isaac up onto the fire ..., *to kill* his son ...'

In temporal clauses and negative contexts *wolde* is often used to express an accomplishment rather than a desire in the past, as exemplified in (4).

(4) *... drihtne guldon god mid gnyrne,* ***oðþæt*** *gasta helm, ...* ***leng ne wolde*** *torn* ***þrowigean****, ac him to sende stiðmod cyning strange twegen aras sine, ...*
(Genesis, 2421–2426)
'...they repaid good from the lord with evil, *until* the protector of spirits, ... *did (would) no longer endure* his anger, but the resolute king sent two of his strong messengers to them, ...'

Such accomplishment uses often overlap with habitual uses, depending on the context. If the event is no longer understood as an intention in the past, but rather as an accomplished fact that took place regularly or over a longer period of time, or is negated as such a regular event, as in (5), it may be interpreted as a habitual event.[10] It is possible that such accomplishment uses gave rise to the habitual use of *wolde* (one of the uses of PDE *would*).

(5) *Þone heht Astrias in Albano, hæðen ond hygeblind, heafde beneotan, forþan he ða hæðengild* ***hyran ne wolde****, wig weorðian.* (The Fates of the Apostles, 45–48)
'Whom Astrias commanded in Albania, heathen and blind of mind, to be deprived of his head, because he *would not obey* the idols, worship idols.'

10. An early occurrence of habitual *wolde* had already been attested by Kellner (1974 [1892]: 220). He observes that "'Will' as an auxiliary expressing customary action is met with at an early date," even though he only provides examples from Middle English.

Besides dynamic modality (desire, volition, intention) and aspectual uses (accomplishment, habit) with past-time reference, there was one single example of *wolde* expressing deontic modality. This type of modality is very rare with *wolde* since a directive meaning, a compulsion cannot directly be derived from its volitional sense. Nevertheless, it is found in one of the earliest OE poems, cf. (6). Here the potential deontic meaning is supported by the verb *gebædon* 'constrain'.

(6) *..., ne hie to þam gebede mihte* ***gebædon*** *hæðen heriges wisa, þæt hie þider* ***hweorfan wolden****, ...* (Daniel, 200–203)
'..., nor could the leader of the heathen people *constrain* them unto prayer, that they *(would) should turn* in that direction, ...'

Non-past-time reference occurs only with 12.7% of the examples. Nevertheless, there are several different uses of *wolde*. A dynamic modality meaning, like a wish, can be expressed in the context of a hypothesis, e.g. in the apodosis of a conditional sentence. Here the past tense of *wolde* serves to express the hypothetical sense, maybe because the past indicative and subjunctive in the 3rd person singular are identical (*wolde*), so that the past tense form is used to express the past subjunctive, or a counterfactual meaning, cf. (7).

(7) *Biowulf maþelode ...: Nu ic suna minum* ***syllan wolde*** *guðgewædu, þær me gifeðe swa ænig yrfeweard æfter wurde, lice gelenge.* (Beowulf, 2724–2732)
'Beowulf spoke – ... I *would have wanted to present* the war-garb to my son, if it had been granted that any heir belonging to my body should succeed me.'[11]

In such contexts the volitional sense may fade more or less into the background. Such uses in hypothetical contexts may have led to epistemic interpretations denoting a mere hypothesis, as in (8), or even an optative sense in exclamations, as exemplified in (9).

(8) *Gif mon ðonne* ***wolde*** *him* ***awindan*** *of þæs cynegerelan claða gehwilcne, ..., ðonne meaht ðu gesion þæt he bið swiðe gelic sumum ðara gumena þe him geornost nu mid ðegnungum ðringað ymbeutan;* (The Meters of Boethius, 25.22–28)
'If then any one *would* from him *strip off* these kingly robes – each of his garments – ... then you might see that he is very like any of those men, who now most anxiously with services crowd about him.;'[12]

(9) *Eala, gif he* ***wolde****, ðæt he wel meahte, þæt unriht him eaðe* ***forbiodan****.*
(The Meters of Boethius, 9.53–54)
'Oh, that he *would* only, as he easily might, soon *forbid* him such injustice!'

11. Michael Swanton's (1978) translation.

12. Based on the translation by Fox (1835).

Another use of *wolde* with non-past-time reference occurs mainly in first person contexts, where *wolde* can express an intention in a more distanced, or polite way, as 'I would like to', cf. (10), see also Kohnen (2011).

(10) *Him þa Andreas eaðmod oncwæð:* **Wolde** *ic þe* **biddan**, *..., þæt ðu us gebrohte brante ceole, hea hornscipe, ofer hwæles eðel on þære mægðe.*

(Andreas, 270–275)

'Andreas then humbly answered: "I *would like to ask* you ..., to bring us aboard that steep vessel, that beaked ship, and over the whale's home to the country.'

Besides a clear past-time reference and a non-past-time reference *wolde* can express a future in the past. This is typically the case in subordinate clauses after verbs of promising, knowing and in reported speech. Yet, the original meaning of 'desire, wish' may be more or less foregrounded to render the promise more emphatic, as it is not only a future event that is promised, but at the same time an event that the subject (often when identical with the speaker) likes or intends to do, cf. (11).

(11) *Wiglaf maðelode, ... Ic ðæt <mæl> geman, ..., þonne <we> geheton ussum hlaforde in biorsele, ..., þæt we him ða guðgetawa* **gyldan woldon** *...*

(Beowulf, 2631–2636)

'Wiglaf spoke, ... 'I remember the time, ..., when we promised to our lord in the beer-hall, ..., that we *would (wanted to) repay* him for the armour, ...'

4.2 *sceolde*

Goossens (1987: 125ff.), on the basis of a sample analysis of 100 present tense (*sceal* and *scealt*) and 100 past tense forms (*sceolde, sceoldon* and *sceolden*) in late OE texts (from Ælfric and Wulfstan), came to the conclusion that it was not a full verb any more in Old English. It lacked any non-finite forms, almost always combined with an infinitive and could often be related to a non-animate subject.[13] Furthermore, his data implied that the *sceold*-forms were considerably more advanced in terms of grammaticalization than their present tense counterparts.

He further noticed that the *sceold*-forms only exceptionally functioned as the past tense equivalent of *sceal* to mark past necessity or obligation (three of 100 examples). This could not be confirmed by my analysis based on the poetry texts. In my sample roughly half of the examples of *sceolde* occur still with past time

13. The original lexical meaning of **sculan* 'to owe' is typically combined with animate subjects, and more specifically, even with humans. For Fischer (2007: 189) it is particularly constructions with inanimate subjects that contribute to the development of epistemic readings. Hogg & Denison (2008: 133) consider only those constructions with inanimate subject as "[c]lear examples of ongoing grammaticalisation".

reference (55.1%). Most of them express deontic modality, i.e. obligation or necessity in the past, cf. (12).

(12) ***Sceolde*** *forht monig blachleor ides bifiende* ***gan*** *on fremdes fæðm; feollon wergend bryda and beaga, bennum seoce.* (Genesis, 1969–1972)
'Many a frightened, white-cheeked woman *had to go* trembling into a stranger's embrace, the defenders of wives and rings fell, physically impaired with wounds.'

Deontic modality, however, can be weakened, so that something (that was predetermined) indeed happened in the past, and so *sceolde* can also, like *wolde*, express an accomplishment, rather than a necessity, cf. (13). This use occurs typically in temporal clauses, where an objective necessity is often additionally implied, but no longer predominant. Obviously, we are dealing here with a special narrative style in Old English.

(13) *Us gewritu secgað þæt her eahta hund iecte siððan mægðum and mæcgum mægburg sine Adam on eorðan; ealra hæfde nigenhund wintra and XXX eac, þa he þas woruld þurh gastgedal* ***ofgyfan sceolde.*** (Genesis, 1121–1127)
'The Scriptures tell us that Adam afterwards increased his tribe on earth with women and men for 800 years; all in all he was 930 years old when he *left (was to leave)* this world due to his death.'

Besides past-time reference, *sceolde* shows a very high frequency of references to future in the past (36.9%). This supports Goossens' (1987: 135f.) observation that *sceolde* often functioned as a marker of future in the past. This type of reference is most often combined with deontic modality, i.e. an obligation or a necessity for this future event, and the vast majority of such occurrences is found in object clauses after verbs of saying or commanding, as e.g. *bebead* 'commanded' in (14).

(14) *Forþon he unc self* ***bebead*** *þæt wit unc wite* ***warian sceolden,*** *hearma mæstne.* (Genesis, 800–802)
'because he himself commanded us that we must guard ourselves from pain, greatest of harms.'

In certain contexts the deontic modality sense is weakened, e.g. after verbs of knowing. Nevertheless, if *sceolde* is used, the future event seems to be more determined compared to similar constructions with *wolde*, cf. (15) as against (16).

(15) *and þæt* ***wiste*** *eac weroda drihten, þæt* ***sceolde*** *unc Adame yfele* ***gewurðan*** *ymb þæt heofonrice, þær ic ahte minra handa geweald.* (Genesis, 386–388)
'and the lord of the hosts also *knew*, that it *would (should) turn out* badly between me and Adam, concerning the kingdom of heaven, if I had the power of my hands.'

(16) *Hæfde se alwalda engelcynna þurh handmægen, halig drihten, tene getrimede, þæm he* ***getruwode*** *wel þæt hie his giongorscipe* ***fyligan wolden****, wyrcean his willan, forþon he him gewit forgeaf and mid his handum gesceop, halig drihten.* (Genesis, 246–251)
'The ruler of all, the holy lord, had arranged ten orders of angels by the power of his hands, whom he well trusted *would follow* in his obedience, work his will – because he, the holy Lord, granted them intelligence and created them with his hands'

In (15) the original sense of necessity is still implied, while in (16) the original sense of volition is very much driven into the background. It might be speculative, but in both cases there seems to be an incipient development of two different types of evidential modality. A clear case of evidential modality, in the sense of hearsay, is found in (17).

(17) *Ða ongunnon wercan werðeoda spell, sædon þæt hio* ***sceolde*** *mid hire scinlace beornas* ***forbredan****, and mid balocræftum wraðum* ***weorpan*** *on wildra lic cyninges þegnas,* ***cyspan*** *siððan and mid racentan eac* ***ræpan*** *mænigne.* (The Meters of Boethius, 26.73–78)
'Then people started making up stories, and said that with her sorcery she (should have) *transformed* people and with magic cruelty (should have) *cast* the king's thanes into bodies of wild animals, and afterwards (should have) *bound* many of them into chains and fetters.'

Epistemic modality can be expressed by *sceolde* with all three types of time reference. With past-time reference it is used to convey a hypothesis or a presumption or strong belief that something happened in the past, particularly after verbs like *wenan* 'believe', as in (18). With non-past-time reference epistemic *sceolde* denotes an ideal (19), possible, hypothetical or counterfactual event. When *sceolde* has a rather temporal function to refer to future in the past, epistemic modality can be additionally implied, as in (20), where a high probability is inferred.

(18) ***Wende*** *ic þæt þu þy wærra* ***weorþan sceolde*** *wið soðfæstum swylces gemotes* (Juliana, 425–426)
'I *assumed* that you *should have become* the more cautious over such a contest with one steadfast in truth,'

(19) *Swylc* ***sceolde*** *secg* ***wesan****, þegn æt ðearfe.* (Beowulf, 2708–2709)
'so *ought* a man *to be*, a thane in need'

(20) *... swylce oft bemearn ærran mælum swiðferhþes sið snotor ceorl monig, se þe him bealwa to bote gelyfde, þæt þæt ðeodnes bearn* ***geþeon scolde****, fæderæþelum onfon, folc gehealdan, hord ond hleoburh, hæleþa rice, //eþel// Scyldinga.* (Beowulf, 907–912)

'... likewise did many a wise churl in earlier times often lament the career of the strong-hearted man, having believed as a cure for their evils that this king's son *would thrive*, receive his father's noble rank, guard his nation, hoard, and citadel, the kingdom of heroes, the Scyldings' inherited land.'

Examples like (20) are also provided by Kaita (2015: 97f.), who calls the modality expressed "epistemic necessity" and claims that "[t]he analysis of logical necessity or certainty (i.e. epistemic use) of *sculan* in OE awaits further examination" (*ibid.*, 98).

5. Conclusion

My analysis has supported the view that both *wolde* and *sceolde* were predominantly used as auxiliaries in OE poetry (*wolde*: 88.1%; *sceolde*: 99%). While *wolde* was mostly used to express dynamic modality (volition) (54.5%), *sceolde* typically conveyed deontic modality (necessity) (48.8%). Both could be used with a bleached modality sense and express an accomplishment in the past: *wolde*: 6.9% and *sceolde*: 3.9%. Epistemic modality occurred with both, *wolde* (10.8%) and *sceolde* (6.4%). Evidential modality was rare; if at all, it occurred with *sceolde* (3%). There is only one single example of *wolde* in the sample which might be interpreted with an evidential modality sense. Of the two modals only *wolde* had developed a habitual use as early as in OE poetry (4.3%), maybe from its accomplishment use, whose original modal meaning of volition/intention had almost completely disappeared.

Both verbs can be used with non-past-time reference: *wolde* (12.7%) and *sceolde* (8%); additionally, they often refer to future in the past: *wolde* (10.8%) and *sceolde* (36.9%). The latter use is often combined with a modal sense (dynamic, deontic, or even epistemic modality). However, it is noteworthy that both can be bleached of their modal meaning in such contexts and express merely or predominantly a temporal meaning, namely future in the past. This bleaching is much stronger with *wolde* than with *sceolde*. 28 of all 30 examples of *wolde* with a reference to future in the past have been completely rid of their modal meaning and are used as mere temporal, i.e. future (in the past), markers; while with *sceolde* only three of all 75 examples with a reference to future in the past show this complete loss of the modal meaning. Here, in most cases some kind of deontic modality, and sometimes also epistemic modality, is implied. Nevertheless, it can be assumed that the uses of *wolde/sceolde* as markers of future in the past may have contributed essentially to the development of *will/shall* as future markers in English.

Further analyses on the basis of more texts from the *Dictionary of Old English Corpus* will include the questions whether there are any texts, authors or genres that stand out in their use of modal *wolde* or *sceolde* and whether there can be observed an increasing degree of their grammaticalization from earlier to later text samples.

Furthermore, a comparison with German *wollte/sollte* might reveal new insight into the divergent development of English and German with respect to their modal categories. It is possible that the special behaviour of OE *wolde/sceolde* in contrast to Old High German *wolta/scolta* might have had an influence on the divergent development of future markers in English and German.

References

Anderson, John (1991). "*Should*" In Dieter Kastovsky (Ed.), *Historical English Syntax* (11–30). Berlin & New York: Mouton de Gruyter.

Arnovick, Lesley Katherine (1990). *The Development of Future Constructions in English. The Pragmatics of Modal* Shall *and* Will *in Middle English*. (= *Berkeley Insights in Linguistics and Semiotics*, 2). Frankfurt/M.: Peter Lang.

Bybee, Joan L. (1995). The Semantic Development of Past Tense Modals in English. In Joan L. Bybee, & Suzanne Fleischmann (Eds.), *Modality in Grammar and Discourse* (503–517). Amsterdam & Philadelphia: John Benjamins. https://doi.org/10.1075/tsl.32.22byb

Denison, David (1993). *English Historical Syntax*. London: Longman

Dictionary of Old English Web Corpus, compiled by Antonette diPaolo Healey with John Price Wilkin and Xin Xiang. (2009). Toronto: Dictionary of Old English Project.

Diewald, Gabriele, & Wischer, Ilse (2013). Markers of Futurity in Old High German and Old English: A Comparative Corpus-Based Study. In Gabriele Diewald, Leena Kahlas Tarkka, & Ilse Wischer (Eds.), *Comparative Studies in Early Germanic Languages – With a focus on verbal categories* (195–215). Amsterdam & Philadelphia: John Benjamins. https://doi.org/10.1075/slcs.138.09die

Fischer, Olga (2007). *Morphosyntactic Change: Functional and Formal Perspectives*. Oxford: Oxford University Press.

Fox, Samuel (1835). *King Alfred's Anglo-Saxon Version of the Meters of Boethius*. London: William Pickering.

Gisborne, Nikolas (2007). Dynamic Modality. *Journal of Theoretical Linguistics* 4, 44–61.

Goossens, Louis (1987). The Auxiliarization of the English Modals: A functional Grammar View. In Martin Harris, & Paolo Ramat (Eds.), *Historical Development of Auxiliaries* (111–143). Berlin: Walter de Gruyter. https://doi.org/10.1515/9783110856910.111

Gotti, Maurizio (2006). Prediction with SHALL and WILL: A diachronic perspective. In Antoinette Renouf, & Andrew Kehoe (Eds.), *The Changing Face of Corpus Linguistics* (99–116). Amsterdam: Rodopi. https://doi.org/10.1163/9789401201797_009

Hogg, Richard, & Denison, David (2008). *A History of the English Language*. Cambridge: Cambridge University Press.

Kaita, Kousuke (2015). *Modal Auxiliaries from Late Old to Early Middle English: With Special Reference to* āgan, sculan, *and* mōtan. München: Herbert Utz Verlag.

Kellner, Leon (1974) [1892]. *Historical outlines of English syntax*. New York: Gordon Press.

Kohnen, Thomas (2011). Understanding Anglo-Saxon 'politeness': directive constructions with "ic wille / ic wolde. *Journal of Historical Pragmatics* 12, 230–245. https://doi.org/10.1075/jhp.12.1-2.10koh

Lehmann, Christian (2015). *Thoughts on Grammaticalization.* (3rd ed.). Berlin: Language Science Press. https://doi.org/10.26530/OAPEN_603353
Mitchell, Bruce (1985). *Old English Syntax. Vol. I: Concord, the parts of speech, and the sentence.* Oxford: Clarendon Press. https://doi.org/10.1093/acprof:oso/9780198119357.001.0001
OED = The Oxford English Dictionary. (2nd ed.). OED Online. Oxford University Press. 23.03.2017 Retrieved from http://dictionary.oed.com/
Palmer, Frank R. (1990). *Modality and the English Modals.* (2nd ed.). London & New York: Longman.
Palmer, Frank R. (2001). *Mood and Modality.* (2nd ed.). Cambridge: Cambridge University Press. https://doi.org/10.1017/CBO9781139167178
Plank, Frans (1984). The modals' story retold. *Studies in Language* 8(3), 305–364. https://doi.org/10.1075/sl.8.3.02pla
Swanton, Michael (Ed.). (1978). *Beowulf.* Manchester: Manchester University Press.
Visser, Frederic Theodor (1978) [1969]. *An Historical Syntax of the English Language. Part III*: 1. Leiden: E.J. Brill.
Warner, Anthony R. (1993). *English Auxiliaries: Structure and History.* Cambridge: Cambridge University Press. https://doi.org/10.1017/CBO9780511752995
Wischer, Ilse (2006). Markers of Futurity in Old English and the Grammaticalization of *shall* and *will*. *Studia Anglica Posnaniensia* 42, 165–178.
Ziegeler, Debra (2011). The Grammaticalization of Modality. In Heiko Narrog, & Bernd Heine (Eds.), *The Oxford Handbook of Grammaticalization* (595–604). Oxford: Oxford University Press.

A corpus-based study on the development of *dare* in Middle English and Early Modern English

Sofia Bemposta-Rivas

This study argues that the changes undergone by *dare* in late Middle English cannot be explained solely in terms of the phonological similarity between *dare* and *tharf*, but also by the relationship between *tharf* and the verb *need*, plus the influence that the latter exerted on *dare*. The aim of this study is to analyse the semantic and structural changes that the verbs *dare*, *tharf* and *need* undergo in the period between Middle English and Early Modern English. The data are drawn from *The Penn-Helsinki Parsed Corpus of Middle English*, *The Penn-Helsinki Parsed Corpus of Early Modern English* and *The Penn Corpus of Early English Correspondence*. The analysis confirms that the verbs *dare* and *tharf* were confused in Middle English in non-assertive and 'fear' contexts. With the obsolescence of *tharf*, *dare* begins to occur more frequently in assertive contexts, and also starts to exhibit lexical features due to the influence exerted by *need*.

Keywords: pre-modal verbs, regularisation, assertivity, blend construction, impersonal verbs

1. Introduction[1]

The complex nature of the verb *dare* and its development in the history of English are reflected in the proliferation of studies on the directionality of grammaticalization (Duffley, 1994; Traugott, 2001; Haspelmath, 2004; Taeymans, 2006; Schlüter,

1. The research reported in this article was funded by the Spanish Ministry of Economy and Competitiveness (grant no. BES-2014-069851). I am also grateful to the following institutions for generous financial support: the Spanish Ministry of Economy and Competitiveness and the European Regional Development Fund (grant no. FFI2013-44065-P), and the Autonomous Government of Galicia (grant no. ED431C 2017/50). I thank Dr. Ann Taylor, Aaron W. Ecay and the members of the "Grammatical Variation and Change" reading group of the University of York, Dr. Willem Hollmann and the anonymous reviewers for helpful comments, suggestions and help. All remaining errors are my own.

https://doi.org/10.1075/cilt.346.07riv

2010). The "hypothesis of unidirectionality" states that "the changes which fall under the rubric of grammaticalization always move in the direction from more to less lexical or from less to more grammatical" (Börjars & Vincent, 2011: 163). In OE *dare* shows auxiliary features of the pre-modal group of verbs but from Late Middle English onwards it starts to exhibit some full-verb features. Within this context, the historical evolution of the verb *dare* is one of the most cited counterexamples of the unidirectionality principle of grammaticalization (Beths, 1999; Schlüter, 2010). However, little attention has been paid to the factors causing the divergence of *dare* from the other pre-modal verbs (see Section 2).

The aim of this study is to explain the reasons why the pre-modal verb *dare* begins to exhibit certain lexical features and does not continue along its path of grammaticalization at the end of the Middle English period. For this purpose, I will carry out a qualitative and quantitative analysis of the meanings and structural patterns associated with the verb *dare* from Middle English (henceforth ME) to Early Modern English (EModE). I will argue that both the syntax and the interpretation of *dare* can be explained in terms of the confusion between *dare* and the obsolete verb *thurven* in late Old English (OE) and ME (see, in this respect, Loureiro-Porto, 2009; Taeymans, 2006; Visser, 1963–1973) and also the influence that the verb *need* exerts on *dare* in Late ME (LME) and EModE, as illustrated in (1a)–(b).

Example (1a) shows the cliticised form of the verb *dare* and the second person pronoun *thow*, i.e. *darstou*, expressing necessity rather than 'courage', as the gloss in square brackets indicates with the synonymous construction *thow nedest*. Likewise, the cliticised form *þerftou* of the verb *tharf* plus the second pronoun *thou* in (1b) means 'to have the courage to do something' rather than 'necessity', 'obligation' or 'possibility', which are the modal meanings that this verb used to convey (see also Section 2.3). The glosses in square brackets in (1a)–(b) reflect strings attested in different manuscripts. This suggests these words are synonymously used.[2]

(1) a. Ne *darstou* [vr. *thow nedest*] on erþe þenchen elles nouht
(c1390 Castle Love(1) (Vrn) 975)(MED, s.v. *durren* 2(a) a.)
Not dare you on earth think else not
"you don't need to think on anything else on earth"

b. Clement..*þerftou* [Ld: *darstþov*] þi moder pulte? Cri hire merci.
(c1300 SLeg.(Hrl 2277) 521/193)(MED, s.v. *thurven* 8(a))
Clement.. tharf you your mother strike? Cry her mercy
"Clement... do you dare strike your mother? Cry her mercy"

2. In the case of *XXXVIII. Castel of Loue. [folio CCXCII]*, the MED indicates that the various readings to XXXVIII from Halliwell's MS may be the result of "deteriorations or arbitrarily made to help the sense; some few contain the original reading or help to find it, where the Vernon-text is spoiled; none can with certainty be ascribed to a later or new revision with the French text" (*The minor poems of the Vernon ms*. Corpus of Middle English Prose and Verse).

The study is structured as follows: Section 2 deals with the distinctive features of the pre-modal verbs *dare* and *tharf* and the verb *need* in Old English and ME. The morphological features of these three verbs are discussed in Section 2.1. Section 2.2 goes on to deal with their syntactic features. Section 2.3 considers the semantics of *dare* and *tharf* (plus the confusion) attested in dictionaries and in Visser's (1963–1973) grammar, as well as the semantic changes *need* undergoes in the periods under analysis. The data and methodology are explained in Section 3. Section 4 compares the evolution of *dare, tharf* and *need* and the contexts in which these verbs are confused. Finally, Section 5 summarises the main issues.

2. The ancestors of the modal verbs and the status of *dare, tharf* and *need* in OE

The verbs *dare* and *tharf* differ historically from *need* as the former are preterite-present verbs in OE, like the majority of PDE modals. The group of modal auxiliaries begins to form a distinct grammatical category only in the ME period, but it is not radically distinguishable from the group of full verbs until the second half of the 15th century or the first half of the 16th century (Warner, 1993: 92–235; see Wischer, this volume). Modern English is a period of rapid change in which the status of modals and auxiliaries was clarified to a great extent. However, Warner (1993: 103) considers that a modal verb can be distinguished from a lexical verb on the basis of a number of distinctive features on different linguistic levels, and that these have a high level of mutual predictivity since OE onwards (see Wischer, this volume):

a. Occurrence in ellipses, like modern post-auxiliary ellipsis and pseudogapping.
b. Occurrence within impersonal constructions where the subordinate verb controls the case of nominal arguments.
c. Restriction of some of these words to finite forms.
d. Use of past-tense forms without past time reference, outside a motivating context.
e. Subcategorisation for the plain infinitive, but not for the *to*-infinitive.
f. Preterite-present morphology.
g. The availability of negative forms in *n-* in OE.
h. Failure to occur as the antecedent to pro-verbal *do*.
i. Word order patterns involving "verb raising".

The semantics of these verbs also confers identifiable features on this group which are different from those exhibited by other verbs in OE and ME. One of these features affects the behaviour of pre-modal verbs as "sentence modifiers". In other words, pre-modals do not generally select their subjects but typically qualify the event or proposition as a whole (Warner, 1993: 157). Warner claims that subjectivity is another characteristic which distinguishes the modal group from (indicative) verbs. Subjectivity refers to the speaker's judgements and intentions, and is said to constitute a significant source of semantic change associated with grammaticalization (see Wischer, this volume). Finally, pre-modal verbs expressed semantic notions central to PDE modals such as necessity and possibility, obligation and permission, futurity, prediction, hypotheticality, and report (Warner, 1993: 156–179). In what follows, I will present a detailed overview of the morphological, syntactic and semantic features that *dare* and *tharf* showed in OE and which categorise these verbs as pre-modals in comparison with the status of *need* in that period.

2.1 Morphological features

Since the OE period, *dare* and *tharf*, as well as most PDE modal verbs (other than *will*), have been considered special verbs because of their morphology, in that they show preterite-present morphology and a defective paradigm. As for the historical evolution of the verbs, preterite-present verbs can be subdivided into "non-modals" and so-called "pre-modals" (Loureiro-Porto, 2009: 57, quoting Traugott, 1992: 193 and Denison, 1993: 296).[3] In the pre-modal group, the one of interest to us here, Mitchell (1985: § 990) includes *agan* 'own', *cunnan* 'can', **durran* 'dare', *magan* 'may', **motan* 'must', **sculan* 'shall' and *þurfan* 'need'.[4] The origin of each of these verbs is the preterite of a strong verb, which, after losing its past time reference, had to develop a new preterite, following the productive weak conjugation in OE (Loureiro-Porto, 2009: 56).

A further morphological characteristic of the OE pre-modals is their defective paradigm; that is, their non-finite forms are very infrequent and they lack the inflections for third person singular -*þ* ending, as in (2), and corresponding simple past forms. In Example (2), *dear* does not show overt agreement morphology with its subject *he*. Most of these preterite-present verbs have survived in PDE, and belong either to the class of central modal verbs or to what Krug (2000: 167) calls the group of "emerging modals" or, alternatively, "neomodals", to which *dare* belongs.

3. The non-modal/modal distinction of preterite-present verbs is important here. The preterite-present non-modal verbs include *beneah/geneah* 'suffice', *deah* 'avail, be of use', *gemunan* 'remember', (*ge*)*unnan* 'love, grant', *witan* 'know' (Denison, 1993: 296). These verbs disappeared from the language in the late 15th century.

4. The symbol '*' indicates that the verb was not recorded in the infinitive form (Mitchell, 1985: § 993).

The term "emerging modals" refers to the new process of modalization which does not produce elements that share all the characteristics of the central modals, i.e. *can, could, may, might, shall, should, will/'ll, would/'d* and *must.*

(2) Gif *he* gesecean *dear.* (OE Beowulf 684) (OED, s.v. *dare* v.[1] c. α.)
If he seek dares
"If he dares seek"

Loureiro-Porto (2009: 59) observes that these verbs were already defective in OE, since "the original infinitive is no longer valid for the meaning they have acquired". The verbs **durran* 'dare', **motan* 'must' and **sculan* 'shall' do not show infinitive, present or past participle forms in OE. The non-finite forms are no longer attested for *dare* in late ME. As for *tharf,* Campbell (1959: § 767) provides the infinitive form *þurfan* and the present participle *þearfende,* but he does not give any examples of these forms.

By contrast, the verb *need* is not a preterite-present verb. It behaves as a full verb and shows the inflections for third person singular in (3), past simple and non-finite forms, i.e. (*to*) *need* and the bare infinitive (BI, henceforth) form in (4), *needed* and *needing.* However, from LME onwards it starts to show some modal features, such as the lack of inflections and non-finite forms. Krug (2000: 167) also classifies this verb as neomodal since it shows modal verb features in PDE.

(3) Thenke first hou flexe cometh oute of the erthe and with gret labour is maad white, [...] and atte last, to make it moor whyte, *it nedeth to haue both fire and water.* (CMAELR4, 15.429)

(4) 'Hit *shall* nat *nede,*' seyde Merlion, 'thes two kynges to com agayne in the wey of warre; (CMMALORY, 31.992)

2.2 Syntactic features

The possibility of coordination is one of the unique syntactic features that modal verbs exhibit in OE within the group of verbs which can select BI clauses, as in (5) (Beths, 1999: 1078–1079). Moreover, Example (5) shows verb phrase (VP) deletion, an option that has been possible for modals since the OE period (Beths, 1999: 1079; Warner, 1993: 110–134). In Example (5) the complement of the coordinated verbs *mæg* and *dear* is retrievable from the post-verbal complement of the previous clause, i.e. *onsacan frymþe & werfæhðe*:

(5) ælc mon mot *onsacan frymþe & werfæhðe,* gif he *mæg oððe dear.*
"each man may dispute origin and breach of the peace, if he can or dare."
(Law I 110.46.2) (Beths, 1999: 1079)

In OE and ME *dare* can select as its complement a *that*-clause, as in (6), and a BI clause, the latter being the more frequent in use as the analysis of my data indicates. In turn, *tharf* could select both noun phrases (NPs) and BI clauses, but ceased to select NPs in ME and began to be used exclusively with BI clauses, expressing modal meanings as in (7) (Taeymans, 2006: Chapter 3).

(6) Ne *dear* ich *þt ha deopluker ne witerluker schriue hire to ġeung Preost her abuten* (CMANCRIW-2, II.255.148)
Not dare I that she more thoroughly and more fully confess herself to young priest her about
"I dare not [recommend] that she should confess more fully concerning this to young priests"

(7) that were popys of Rome, reseyved þis writyng and sayd, "Hosoeuer bere þis writyng abowte hym, *he thar not drede* hym of non enmy ner sodeyn deth, ner fyer, ner watyr, ner poyson" (CMREYNES, 247.412)
"who were popes of Rome, received this letter and said, 'whosoever has this letter with him, he needs not fear him about no enemy nor sudden death nor fire nor water nor poison"'

Need could select a wider range of complement types, i.e. *to*-infinitive complements as in (3) and (4), *that*-clauses, prepositional phrases (PP) and NP, as in (8). From 1350 onwards, *need* starts to be attested with BI complementation, as in (9).

(8) 'What hast þou do þat þou *nedist so many men*?' (CMCAPCHR, 41.278)

(9) Certes, the trouthe of this matiere, or of this conseil, *nedeth* nat diligently *enquere*, for it is wel wist whiche they been that han doon to yow this trespas and vileynye (CMCTMELI, 228.C1.427)

An additional syntactic feature is the occurrence of *dare*, *tharf* and *need* in so-called "impersonal constructions". These structures lack an argument inflected for the nominative and "the verb is always in the form associated with the third person singular" (Anderson, 1986: 167–168). Allen (1995: 20) distinguishes two types of themes that an impersonal/experiencer verb can select in OE, i.e. nominal theme and sentential theme. Since *tharf* and *dare* do not appear with a nominal theme in my data, I will restrict my analysis to sentential themes (see Section 4). Based on Allen, three types of impersonal constructions can be distinguished: (i) Type "S" with an non-nominative experiencer and no formal subject, e.g. the second person singular *the* in (10a), which is the understood subject, is in the oblique form; (ii) Personal Type which consists of an experiencer in the nominative case, as in (10b) *Ye*; and (iii) Types "Hit" and "DEM", which contain a third person pronoun '(*h*)*it*' or a demonstrative pronoun in subject position, as in (10c).

(10) a. Soden deth ... *The dar not drede.* (?a1425 Const.Masonry(1) (Roy 17.A.1) 674) (MED, s.v. *durren*, 2 (b))
Sudden death ... You-obl. exp. dare-3SG not fear
"Sudden death ... You need not fear"
b. *Ye need to care* if ye folow my sawe. (1460 Towneley Myst. xii 163) (OED, s.v. *need*, III. 8a)
You-NOM need to care if you follow my message
"You need to be careful if you follow my message"
c. It nedeþ to leuen in þe huyue hony meneliche. ((a1398) *Trev. Barth. (Add 27944) 273a/a) (MED, s.v. *need* v^2 1b. (a))
It-NOM needs to leave in the hive honey common
"It needs to leave the common honey hive"

Summing up, *dare* and *tharf* show syntactic features characteristic of modal verbs (coordination and VP deletion) and are more frequently attested with BI clausal complements than with *that*-clauses or NP complements. As regards *need*, it selects complements typical of lexical verbs until 1350. *Dare, tharf* and *need* can occur in personal and impersonal constructions.

2.3 Semantics

As regards *dare*, both the *Oxford English Dictionary* (OED) and the *Middle English Dictionary* (MED) indicate that this verb means 'to have boldness or courage (to do something); to be so bold as' when it is followed by an infinitive clause, as in (2) above (Section 2.1), or by the ellipsis of the verbs *go* or *venture*, as in (11a). The MED also mentions the use of *dare* in emphatic questions and asseverations, as in (11b).

(11) a. Ferrer ne *draste* þay noȝt for fere.
(c1380 Sir Ferumbras (1879) l. 3725) (OED, s.v. *dare* v^1. 9)
Further not dare they not for fear
"They don't dare further for fear"
b. How hast *thou dorre be* so hardi? (c1450 *Pilgr.LM* (Cmb Ff.5.30) 78) (MED, s.v. *durren* 1b. (a))
"How dare you be so brave?"

As a modal verb, *tharf* expresses necessity, as in (12a); obligation based on duty, superior authority, divine law, etc.; it can also be used with reduced semantic force in reference to the interpretation of an emotional state, with *asken* in negative contexts; it can express what is fitting, right or proper: should (do sth., believe sth., etc.); ought (to do sth., etc.); possibility: to have occasion (to do sth., to be in a certain state, etc.), have the opportunity, be able; may (do sth., etc.), can, could, as in (12b) (MED, s.v. *thurven* 2a, 3a, 4a, 5, 6a, 7a, respectively).

(12) a. Beo stalewurðe ant stont wel: Ne *þearf* þu [Roy: *þerftu*] *drede* na deð.
(c1225(?c1200) St.Kath.(1)
(Bod 34) 96/672) (MED, s.v. *thurven* 2a. (a))
"Be stalwart and stand firm. You need not fear death"
b. Þou ert full meke; A meker man thar noman seke.
(a1425 NPass.(Cmb Gg.5.31) 35/324) (MED, s.v. *thurven* 7a(a))
"You are really humble; A more humble man who anyone can seek"

The entries, examples and/or etymological sections for these two verbs in the OED (s.v. *dare*, v^{1}. 9) and the MED (s.v. *thurven* 8) indicate that *dare* and *tharf* show considerable confusion and overlap in function and form in ME. In the etymology section of the verb *dare*, the OED points out that "in Middle English there was some confusion between them, *dar* being sometimes written for *thar*, while, on the other hand, [the] *th-* forms [...] appear with the sense of *dar*: see Forms 9" (s.v. *dare* v^{1}). Example (13) shows the cliticised form of the verb *tharf*, i.e. *therstou*, in a context expressing 'courage'.

(13) Hou *therstou* ... bifore him nemne his name? (c1300 St. Brandan 585)
How tharf you ... in front of him mention his name?
"How dare you ... mention his name in front of him? "

There is also some confusion noted in the MED entry of *tharf*, as in (14). As modal auxiliary, it expresses

> volition, determination, free choice, etc.: to have the will (to do sth.), be willing; venture (to do sth.), have the courage, *dare*;—usu. in negative contexts; ~ seien, venture to say (sth., that sth. is so), *dare say* [many quots. in 8. show confusion with, or influence from, *durren* v.]. (MED, s.v. *thurven* 8)

(14) [She] *thurst* [Auch: wold] *speke* a worde ne mo. (a1500 Amis (Dc 326) 1187)
"She doesn't dare speak one more word"

In addition, the MED states that *dare* is found expressing "to be under necessity or obligation; (one) must (do sth.), ought, needs, should; – with neg., (one) need not (fear, blame, seek, say, etc.)", as in (15a). The first example of *dare* attested in the MED with a meaning related to necessity/obligation is dated around the year 1200, given in Example (15b) below. Even though *dare* and *tharf* differed semantically in origin, the orthographical similarity between them explains the confusion attested in (13), (14) and (15a)–(b). In ME, a period in which orthographical variability was common, the letter, which represented the sound <v>, is sometimes dropped and/or the initial dental fricative consonant is replaced with the plosive stop *d-*. (Molencki, 2002: 378; 2005; Loureiro-Porto, 2009: 71–72).

(15) a. 3e ne *dorre* me *blamie* nou3t.
(c1300 SLeg.Dunstan (LdMisc 108) 83) (MED, s.v. *durren* 2. (a))
You not dare me blame not
"You shouldn't blame me"

b. Ne *dert* þu nauere *adrede*... þæt æuere æine modi cniht at þine borde makie fiht.
(c1275(?a1200) Lay. *Brut* (Clg A.9) 22923) (MED, s.v. *durren*, 2a (a))
Not need you never fear ... that ever any brave knight at your table fight
"You need never fear ... that any brave knight ever fight at your table"

The confusion between *dare* and *tharf* is confirmed when an explicit contrast is made between citations in the OED, MED and in Visser (1963–1973). Different sources classify the same example under both the entry of *dare* and *tharf*. In fact, seven of the nine examples in the MED (s.v. *durren*, 2 (b)) are also found either in the OED or in Visser (1963–1973) in the entry for *thurven*. Examples (16a)–(16b) and (17a)–(17b) are two of the three instances found in both the OED (s.v. *tharf*) and the MED (s.v. *durren*, 2 (b)), respectively. In Examples (16a)–(16b), the second person singular form *þow* cliticises with the verb *dare* or *tharf* in the form *darstow*. *Darstow* takes a BI as its complement and occurs in a non-assertive context expressing necessity. As for (17a)–(17b), the form *darh* occurs in an impersonal construction, with the non-nominative *him* which functions as the subject of the clause and the BI complement *fail*.

(16) a. Bi so þat þow be sobre ... Darstow [v. rr. Tharst þow, Thardestow] neuere care for corne, ne lynnen cloth ne wollen.
(1377 LANCL. *P. Pl. B.* xiv. $_{55}$) (OED, s.v. *tharf*, A 1. b. ɣ3)
"be so that you be sober ... neither need care for corn, nor for linen clothes nor for wool."

b. Darstow neuere care for corne, ne lynnen cloth ne wollen.
(c1400 (c1378) *PPl.B* (LdMisc 581) 14.55) (MED, s.v. *durren*, 2 (b))

(17) a. Nou is Edward kyng of engelond al aplyht..*of gode knyhtes darh him nout fail.* (c1325 (c1307) Death Edw.I (Hrl 2253) 80)
(MED, s.v. *durren*, 2 (b))
"Now is king Edward of England completely ... he dare not fail the good knights"

b. of gode knyhtes *darh him nout fail*
(a1327 *Pol. Songs* (Camden) 250) (OED, s.v. *tharf*, A 1.c. ɣ3)

In addition, four out of the nine examples provided by the MED (s.v. *durren*, 2 (b)) correspond to the examples given by Visser (1963–1973: 1424) for *thurven*, as illustrated in (18). Examples (16a)–(16b) to (18) evince the difficulty in determining which verb, or combination of features of *dare* and *tharf*, is at work.

(18) 'A sone,' he seide, 'dar þe [vr. þu nedis] nouht wepe, þauh ischulle from þe falle.'
(c1390 *St.Greg.* (Vrn) 8/57) (MED, s.v. *durren*, 2b (b))
(Visser 1963–73: 1424)
'Ah son', he said, dare you not weep, though I should from you fail.'
'"Ah son', he said, 'you do not dare weep, even if I fail you."'

As for *need*, the OED provides two entries (*need* v.[1] and *need* v.[2]). Loureiro-Porto (2009: 204) points out that "in OE and ME [Middle English], *need* v.[1] is the most common *need*-verb", first expressing physical forces and then conveying social forces. It is with this second meaning that *need* v.[1] exhibits coalescence with *need* v.[2] in M[iddle English]3 (1350–1420) (see Section 3). In M3 *need* v.[2] replaces *need* v.[1] with a meaning of force based on external, internal, general and logical factors (Loureiro-Porto, 2009: 204). With these new meanings, *need* starts to compete with *tharf* (see Taeymans, 2006 and Loureiro-Porto, 2009) since both occur syntactically in personal and impersonal constructions, and in terms of semantics cover participant-external and participant-internal necessity senses when followed by an infinitive clause (Taeymans, 2006: Chapter 3).

Even though the verbs *dare* and *tharf* are recorded in separate entries with their own meanings in the OED, MED and Visser, these sources comment on the confusion and overlap that these verbs show in certain contexts. In this vein, in this section I have claimed that *need* becomes a competitor of *tharf* from M3 onwards, that is, once *need* has developed a necessity meaning.

3. Data and methodology

In this section I will discuss, on the one hand, the orthographical confusion between *dare* and *tharf* and, on the other, the syntactic and semantic contexts in which *dare*, *tharf* and *need* occur in ME and EModE using data from three corpora: *The Penn-Helsinki Parsed Corpus of Middle English* (PPCME2), a 1.1 million-word database divided into four periods, M1 (1150–1250), M2 (1250–1350), M3 (1350–1420) and M4 (1420–1550);[5] *The Penn Corpus of Early English Correspondence* (PCEEC), consisting of 2.8 million words covering the final years of the period

5. I will follow Taeymans' (2006) corpus design and I will give precedence to the manuscript dates. For instance, MX/2 and M1/2 texts are both classified as M2.

M3 (1410–1419), the period M4 (1420–1550) of ME and the three periods of Early Modern English, i.e. E1 (1500–1569), E2 (1570–1639) and E3 (1640–1710); and the 1.7 million-word *Penn-Helsinki Parsed Corpus of Early Modern English* (PPCEME) for the EModE period (1500–1710), which follows the same three sub-periods as the PCEEC.[6] Thus, together these corpora cover the time span under study, have the same compilation format, and are syntactically annotated.

The tool Corpus Studio was used to extract all relevant examples of the verbs *dare, tharf* and *need.* My query retrieved all the spelling variants of *dare, tharf* and *need* attested in the OED, MED and Visser. The corpus results were contrasted with examples from the OED, the MED and Visser's (1963–1973) grammar.

4. Blurred categorisation

The distribution of *dare, tharf* and *need* from ME to EModE illustrates the confusion attested between *dare* and *tharf* and the various morphosyntactic and semantic changes that these two verbs and *need* underwent in that period. In M1, the verbs *dare* and *tharf* show similar proportions in use, but from this period onwards their frequency of use changes radically (see Figure 1). *Dare* increases in use progressively from M1 to E2, whereas *tharf* decreases significantly from M1 to M4 (χ^2 $P < 0.0001$).[7] Since the increase in the use of the verb *need* from M1 to M4 is not statistically significant (χ^2 $P = 1$), I conclude that the confusion between *dare* and *tharf* is responsible for the decrease in the use of the *th-/þ* forms and the increase in the use of the *d-* spelling forms in ME. The starting point of the verb *need* in M1 is lower than that of *dare* and *tharf*, but its frequency increases significantly from M4 to E1 (χ^2 $P = 0.0007$). In E1, both *need* and *dare* are found in the same number of examples (154 (n.f. 46.94) each).

Alongside the changes observed in their distribution (Figure 1), six criteria have been explored here to explain the relationship between *dare, tharf* and *need* as regards (i) spelling and pronunciation; (ii) the type of subordinate verb that these verbs select; (iii) the contexts in which they are found; the occurrence of these verbs in (iv) impersonal constructions and (v) (non-)assertive contexts; and (vi) their semantics.

6. Since there is an overlap between the PCEEC and the PPCEME, I decided to delete the following texts from the PPCEME because they were included in the PCEEC: Kpaston-E2-h, Joxiden-E2-p2, Knyvett-1620-E2-p1, Morelet1-E1-h and Conway2-E3-p2.

7. The increase in the use of the verb *dare* is already significant from M1 to M4 (χ^2 $P = 0.0397$). As for *tharf*, the decrease is extremely significant in the same period of time (χ^2 $P = < .0001$).

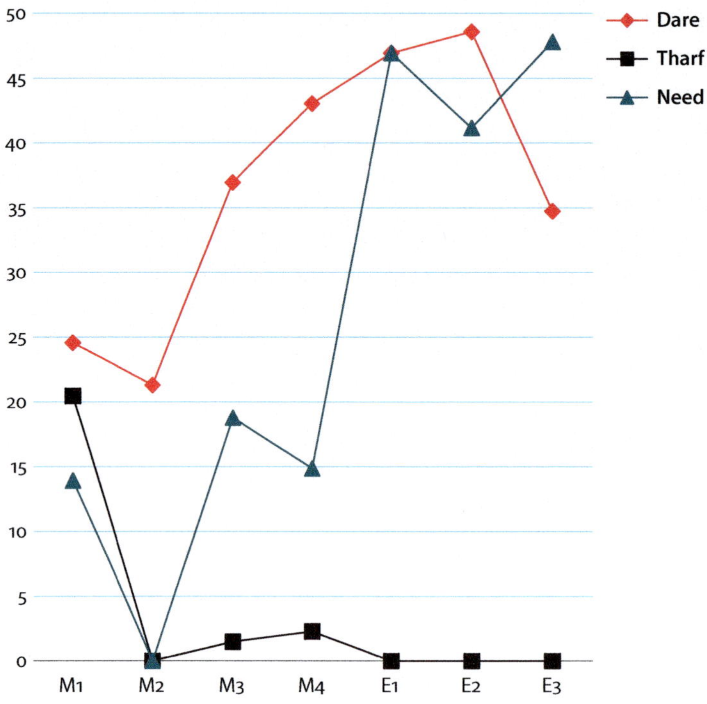

Figure 1. Distribution of *dare*, *tharf* and *need* from ME to EModE (normalised frequencies /10,000 IP-MATs)[8]

With respect to confused spelling and pronunciation (criterion (i)), my data corroborate the observations in dictionary entries and also comments in Loureiro-Porto (2009: 71–72) and Molencki (2002: 378; 2005) (see Section 2.3). *Tharf* is found in one instance from M4 showing *d*-spelling and expressing necessity meanings, in (19). Likewise, *dare* is attested in one example from M3 with *th*-spelling and 'courage' meaning, in (20).

(19) 'So God me helpe,' seyde the quene, 'ye *darfnat* shame, for he ys the goodlyest knyght, and of the beste men of the worlde commyn, and of the strene, of all partyes, of kynges.' (CMMALORY, 636.3826)

(20) And ells thay say that they *thernot* take it vppon hem, for they dwelle so ney to the othere many that thay knowe well thay shold neuer be in ease yf thay dyde soo whyle that thay dele a-mongys hem. (PASTON, I, 304.101.2991)

8. The Penn corpora and the PCEEC use the abbreviation *IP-MAT* for matrix clauses, i.e. main clauses with a subordinate clause embedded.

Criterion (ii) is related to the type of verbs that *dare*, *tharf* and *need* select in the lower clause. As the MED (s.v. *durren* 2a. (a)) indicates, *dare* can express necessity when verbs such as *fear*, *blame*, *seek*, *say*, etc. occur as its complement.[9] Based on the MED, Table 1 below shows the co-occurrence of *dare*, *tharf* and *need* plus the subordinate verb phrases *be afraid*, *be ashamed*, *be frightened* or the verbs *shame*, *doubt*, *dread*, *grieve* and *seek*. The verb *tharf* is found in 13 instances in ME selecting these types of subordinate verbs, as in (21) with the lower verb *drede* 'to fear'. The verb *dare* is attested in five occurrences, two in ME, as in (22a) with the lower verb *eisian* 'to frighten', and three in the last two periods of EModE, as in (22b) from E2 with the verb *doubt*. Out of these five instances, *dare* occurs in one example, in (22c), expressing 'courage' rather than 'necessity' with the verb *seek* in the subordinate clause. The verb *need* is found in four examples in the last two periods of ME, but it is in EModE when it begins to co-occur more frequently with these subordinate verbs, as in (23) from E3 (see Table 1).

Table 1. *Dare*, *tharf* and *need* plus 'fear' subordinate verbs (raw and normalised frequencies /10,000 IP-MATs)

	M1	M3	M4	E1	E2	E3	Total
Dare	1 (0.82)	0	1 (0.38)	0	2 (0.33)	1 (0.26)	5 (1.79)
Tharf	8 (6.54)	1 (0.29)	4 (1.52)	0	0	0	13 (8.37)
Need	0	3 (0.89)	1 (0.38)	15 (4.57)	27 (4.44)	25 (6.53)	71 (16.82)
TOTAL	9 (7.36)	4 (1.18)	6 (2.28)	15 (4.57)	29 (4.77)	26 (6.79)	89 (26.98)

(21) Beo stalewurđe & stont wel *ne þearf þu drede* na deđ. (CMKATHE, 42.373)
"Be stalwart and stand firm. You need not fear death"

(22) a. þet he his men *eisian* ne *der* ne to nane wisdome heom nule wissien. (CMLAMBX1, 111.1060)
That he his men fear not dare not to none wisedom them will not teach
"That he does not need to be afraid of his men nor he won't give them no wise teaching"

b. If that confidence did not refresh me, this journey would be very sad; but *I dare not doubt* the tender compassions of our heavenly Father to you, because I have alwaies experienced your tenderness to me. (HARLEY, 217.068.1811)

9. I decided not to consider examples of *dare* plus the verb *say* in the subordinate clause within this criterion, due to the difficulty of determining whether *dare* really means necessity or courage in such cases.

c. The old man answeres, A poore Shropshire man; and demands if there were not a gentleman in the court dwelling, called by the name of M. Will Sommer? for the country hearing him in fauour in the court, said hee was so at least. The courtier answered, Here is such a one indeede. For fault of a worse, saies hee, I am his uncle; and wept with joy that hee should see him. Marry, sayes the man, I'll help you to him straight; for, I tell you, *not any in the court durst but haue sought him*, which this man did, and it was told him. (ARMIN-E2-H, 43.282)

(23) Y. Fash. Giving her his Hand. Come, Madam, dare you venture your self alone with me? Miss. O dear, yes, Sir, I don't think you'll do any thing to me *I need be afraid on*. (VANBR-E3-H, 64.715)

As for criterion (iii), *dare* and *need* differ from *tharf* in their semantic contexts. *Dare* and *need* are attested in contexts expressing 'fear' and 'doubt' with collocates such as *terrible, fearful, be afraid, make doubt, dangerous*, etc. As Table 2 illustrates, *dare* occurs in these contexts in both ME and EModE and mainly expresses meanings of 'courage' or 'boldness', as in (24). It is at the end of ME and in EModE when *need* is attested in these environments, as in (25). No instances of *tharf* in contexts of 'fear' or 'doubt' were found in my data.

Table 2. *Dare* and *need* in 'fear' contexts (raw data)

	M1	M2	M3	M4	E1	E2	E3	Total
Dare	7	1	13	11	11	19	9	71
Need	0	0	0	2	3	8	4	17
TOTAL	7	1	13	13	14	27	13	88

(24) he was *so aferde* that *he dorst neuere lifte vp* his eyen from the erthe. (CMAELR4, 13.359)
"He was so frightened that he dared never raise up his eyes from the ground"

(25) And for your towne stey *you shall not nede to make any doute* therein but that you maie tarry at home till the nexte terme or els have a *dedimus potestatem* for your othe in the countrey. (BACON, II, 87.219.3756)

Criterion (iv) analyses the use of the three verbs in impersonal constructions (see Section 2.2). As Table 3 indicates, no examples of *dare* in impersonal constructions are obtained from my data (cf. MED, s.v. *durren* 2 (b)). In the case of *tharf*, this verb is attested in four (out of 25) instances in M1, as in (26). However, in M3 and M4 this number increases to half of the total occurrences attested in each period (three out of five and three out of six examples, respectively). *Need* also occurs in the impersonal construction in ME, as in (27) from M3, and in EModE.

In Example (26), *tharf* selects the experiencer *us* in the oblique case and the coordinated BI complement clauses *gramien* and *shamien*, whereas the dative *þee* and the *to*-infinitival *to haue discrecion* function as subject and clausal complements of *need* in (27).

Table 3. *Tharf* and *need* in the impersonal construction with sentential theme (raw data)

	M1	M3	M4	E1	E2	E3	Total
Tharf	4	3	3	0	0	0	10
Need	2	7	7	2	0	2	20

(26) þanne ne *þarf us* nođer *gramien.* ne *shamien.* (CMTRINIT, 69.965)
then not need us-obl.exp. neither to-be-grieved nor to-be-ashamed
"then we will not need either to-be-grieved or to-be-ashamed"
(translation from Warner 1993: 126)

(27) Bot in þis sorow *nedeþ þee to haue discrecion* on þis maner: (CMCLOUD, 83.441)
But in this sorrow needs you-obl.exp. to have discretion in this manner
"But in this pain you need to be discreet in this manner"

The fifth criterion tackles the occurrence of *dare, tharf* and *need* in non-assertive contexts. Modality is related to non-assertive clauses: negative, interrogative, conditional, comparative, concessive, *before*-clauses, lightly stressed adverbs such as *hardly, never* or *seldom* and negative items (Jacobsson, 1974: 62; Duffley, 1994: 219; Quirk et al., 1985: 138–139; Beths, 1999; Taeymans, 2006; Schlüter, 2010). Molencki (2002: 369–370; 2005) notes that *þearf* and *dearr* are restricted to non-assertive contexts and that whereas *þearf* is replaced by periphrastic constructions, *gedyrstigan* is used as an equivalent to *dearr* in affirmative sentences. This is corroborated in the case of *tharf* which only occurs in non-assertive context, as in (26) above. *Dare* is also restricted to non-assertive contexts in M1 and M2, but from this period onwards its presence in assertive examples increases.[10] (28) is an instance of the new type of environment in which *dare* occurs. The incidence of *need* in (non)-assertive contexts is more uneven in ME. However, this verb is restricted to non-assertive contexts in EModE, as in (29).

(28) And than he sayd, '*I dare swere vppon a boke* that the Duchesse of Suffolk hath no knowlych therof.' (PASTON, II, 374.443.11397)

10. The increase of *dare* in assertive contexts is only statistically significant when the M3 and E1 subperiods are compared (χ^2 P = 0.0001).

(29) Yt when hee was well, ye receipts and payments were managed by other hands and yt this thing was of yt nature yt *it neither needed*, nor would I feared *stay* for his recovery. (ESSEX, 105.025.682)
"Yet when he was well, the receipts and payments were managed by other hands and yet this thing was of such nature that it did not need, nor would I feared, stay for his recovery"

Criterion (vi) looks at the confusion of *tharf* and *dare* in the semantic contexts of necessity, possibility and volition (see MED, s.v. *durren* 2, (a) and s.v. *thurven* 7. (a) and 8). *Tharf* is only found expressing volition in two examples, in (20) above from M3, and in (30) below from M1. The remaining 34 occurrences of this verb in my data correspond to meanings of necessity and obligation. In the case of *dare*, necessity and obligation are the most frequent meanings of the verb in M1, M4 and in EModE and examples of these types are present in the two periods under study, as in (22a)–(22b) above and (31) below from E2 (see Table 4). Possibility is attested in 15 occurrences from M3 onwards, as in (32) from M4. Finally, volition is the most frequent meaning in M2 and M3 and is found in a total of 16 examples from M2 to E2, as in (33).

Table 4. Semantics of *tharf* and *dare* from ME to EModE (raw and normalised frequencies -10000 IP-MATs)

	M1	M2	M3	M4	E1	E2	E3	Total
Necessity/ Obligation	3 (2.45)	1 (1.64)	3 (0.89)	3 (1.14)	4 (1.22)	15 (2.47)	5 (1.3)	34 (11.13)
(Im)possibility	0	0	2 (0.59)	3 (1.14)	3 (0.91)	6 (0.99)	1 (0.26)	15 (3.9)
Volition	0	2 (3.28)	4 (1.19)	1 (0.38)	1 (0.3)	8 (1.31)	0	16 (6.47)
TOTAL	3 (2.45)	3 (4.91)	9 (2.68)	7 (2.66)	8 (2.44)	29 (4.77)	6 (1.57)	65 (21.5)

(30) Ðat seiđ sanctus Ieronimus: *Est autem penitere peccata ante acta deflere, et flenda non repetere*, "Swa scal," he seiđ, "mann his senne berewsen, đat he eft ne do đat *he* eft *đurue be-riwsin*." (CMVICES1, 121.1492)
That said Saint Jeronimus: ... "So shall", he said, "man his sin repent, which he afterwards not do what he afterwards wants to repent."
"That said Saint Jeronimus: "Est autem penitere peccata ante acta deflere, et flenda non repetere", "So shall", he said, "man repent his sin, which he afterwards does not do what he wants to repent.""

(31) Exit. T. S. what shift she'll make now with this peece of flesh In this strict time of Lent, I cannot imagine, Flesh *dare not peepe abroad* now, I haue knowne This Citie now aboue this seuen yeers, (MIDDLET-E2-H, 16.334)

(32) & do þer-to ambros, burnet & þe crispe malue &, if þer be bane broken & *þu dare noghte serche it ġit*, gyf hym þis to drynke (CMTHORN, 69.484)
and do thereto Ambrose, Burnet and the crisp mallow &, if there be bone broken & you dare not probe it yet, give him this to drink
"And do for this purpose Ambrose, Burnet and the crisp mallow and, if there be bone broken and you cannot probe it yet, give him this drink "

(33) but for sweats in his cloaths without any exercise abroad, you shall giue them either when the weather is so much vnseasonable, that you cannot go forth, or when your horse is so much in danger of lamenes, *that you dare not straine him,* (MARKHAM-E2-P2,1,82.48)

The six criteria analysed in this section have given support to the orthographic, syntactic and semantic confusion between *dare* and *tharf* and the competition between *tharf* and *need* from ME onwards. The *th*-spelling is found with the 'courage' meaning and the *d*-spelling is attested expressing necessity meanings. *Dare, tharf* and *need* express necessity when they select subordinate verbs denoting fear and doubt, and they mainly occur in non-assertive contexts. However, whereas *tharf* and *need* can occur in impersonal constructions, *dare* is only attested in personal ones in my database (cf. MED, s.v. *durren* 2 (b).

5. Conclusions

It is difficult to understand the historical changes undergone by *dare*, and also to analyse this verb in isolation, without dealing with the OE verbs *tharf* and *need*. In the light of my data and information from the OED, MED and Visser (1963–1973), I have shown that *dare* and *tharf* are two independent verbs with their own meanings in OE, i.e. "to have the boldness or courage (to do something); to be so bold as" (OED, s.v. *dare*, v^1 B.I.1) and "to be under the necessity or obligation", "to need" (Visser, 1963–1973: 1423; MED, s.v. *thurven*), respectively. In ME, these two verbs come to be confused (Molencki, 2002: 378; 2005; Loureiro-Porto, 2009: 71–72). Such confusion must be explained in terms not only of orthographical/phonological similarity but also of the semantic and syntactic influence between the minimal pair *thurven* and *need*, in both cases expressing necessity.

With *dare* and *tharf*, my data corroborate the confusion attested in the dictionaries in the ME period. As a consequence of this, *dare* is still found in contexts expressing necessity/obligation and possibility in EModE. The close relationship between *need* and *thurven* has a direct influence on *dare* in that the latter occurs in the syntactic environments of *thurven* with collocations related to the field of fear, expressing an absence of necessity, and also in non-assertive contexts and in some impersonal constructions (MED, s.v. *durren* 2 (b)). The analysis of the distribution of *dare* and *tharf* demonstrates that the confusion between these two verbs is responsible for the decrease in use of *tharf* and the increase of *dare* in M2 and M3.

It is from M3 onwards that *need* begins to express meanings of force based on external, internal, general and logical factors (Loureiro-Porto, 2009: 204) and hence to compete with *tharf* in the field of necessity. *Need* is first attested in 'fear' contexts and with 'fear' verbs in LME. Once the verb *tharf* becomes obsolete in EModE, the incidence of *need* in these two contexts increases, as does the overall frequency of the verb. Also, with the obsolescence of *thurven*, *dare* starts to select NPs and *to*-infinitives as its complements and occurs as a ditransitive verb in EModE, as in (34), three complementation options that *need* exhibited but which *dare* had not displayed before.

(34) We go by trouthe, noghte by syghte, þat es, we lyff in trouthe, noghte in bodily felynge; *we dare* and hase *gud will* to be absent fra þe body, and be present to Godd (CMROLLTR, 36.752)

As a result of these semantic and morphosyntactic changes, in LME and particularly from EModE onwards, *dare* shows the features that it characteristically exhibited in OE, that is, coordination, VP deletion, desemantisation, BI-complement selection, but also develops lexical verb features, such as the use of non-finite forms, the new weak past form *dared* for past simple, and the possibility of NP and *to*-infinitive complementation. The influence that *need* exerts on *dare* is motivated by the fact that both *need* and *dare* may express necessity meanings, and may occur in 'fear' contexts and with 'fear' verbs and in non-assertive environments. I suggested that the obsolescence of *tharf* and the increasing use of *need* may have caused the verb *dare* to stop developing modal features and to start showing lexical characteristics. Hence, *dare* is attested in modal, blend and lexical constructions at the end of EModE.

The fact that *dare* starts showing lexical features may counter the unidirectionality hypothesis. Further research is needed here in light of data from periods following EModE so as to ascertain whether the development of *dare* and *need* either continued along similar grammaticalization paths or diverged, as well as to determine possible reasons for such changes.

Primary sources

Kroch, Anthony & Taylor, Ann (2000). *The Penn-Helsinki Parsed Corpus of Middle English* (PPCME2). Department of Linguistics, University of Pennsylvania. CD-ROM, second edition, release 4. Retrieved from http://www.ling.upenn.edu/ppche-release-2016/PPCME2-RELEASE-4

Kroch, Anthony, Santorini, Beatrice & Delfs, Lauren (2004). *The Penn-Helsinki Parsed Corpus of Early Modern English* (PPCEME). Department of Linguistics, University of Pennsylvania. CD-ROM, first edition, release 3. Retrieved from http://www.ling.upenn.edu/ppche-release-2016/PPCEME-RELEASE-3

MED = Kurath, Hans, Kuhn, Sherman McAllister, & Lewis, Robert E. (Eds.). (1952–2001). *Middle English Dictionary*. Ann Arbor, MI: University of Michigan Press. Retrieved from http://quod.lib.umich.edu/m/med/

OED= Oxford English Dictionary, online edn. (2016). Oxford: Oxford University Press. Retrieved from http://www.oed.com

Taylor, Ann, Nurmi, Arja, Warner, Anthony, Pintzuk, Susan, & Nevalainen, Terttu (2006). *The York-Helsinki Parsed Corpus of Early English Correspondence* (PCEEC). Department of Linguistics, University of York. Oxford Text Archive, first edition. Retrieved from http://www-users.york.ac.uk/~lang22/PCEEC-manual/index.htm

References

Allen, Cynthia L. (1995). *Case Marking and Reanalysis: Grammatical Relations from Old to Early Modern English*. Oxford: Clarendon Press.

Anderson, John M. (1986). A Note on Old English Impersonals. *Journal of Linguistics* 22, 167–177. https://doi.org/10.1017/S0022226700010604

Beths, Frank (1999). The History of Dare and the Status of Unidirectionality. *Linguistics* 37, 1069–1110. https://doi.org/10.1515/ling.37.6.1069

Börjars, Kersti, & Vincent, Nigel (2011). Grammaticalization and Directionality. In Heiko Narrog, & Bernd Heine (Eds.), *The Oxford Handbook of Grammaticalization* (163–176). Oxford: Oxford University Press.

Campbell, Alistair (1959). *Old English Grammar*. Oxford: Oxford University Press.

Denison, David (1993). *English Historical Syntax: Verbal constructions*. London: Longman.

Duffley, Patrick J. (1994). Need and Dare: The Black Sheep of the Modal Family. *Lingua* 94, 213–243. https://doi.org/10.1016/0024-3841(94)90010-8

Haspelmath, Martin (2004). On Directionality in Language Change with Particular Reference to Grammaticalization. In Olga Fischer, Muriel Norde, & Harry Perridon (Eds.), *Up and Down the Cline – The Nature of Grammaticalization* (17–44). Amsterdam: John Benjamins Publishing Company. https://doi.org/10.1075/tsl.59.03has

Jacobsson, Bengt (1974). The Auxiliary Need. *English Studies* 55, 56–63. https://doi.org/10.1080/00138387408597603

Krug, Manfred (2000). *Emerging English Modals: A Corpus-based Study of Grammaticalization*. Berlin: Mouton de Gruyter. https://doi.org/10.1515/9783110820980

Loureiro-Porto, Lucía (2009). *The Semantic Predecessors of Need in the History of English (c750–1710)*. Oxford: Wiley Blackwell.

Mitchell, Bruce (1985). *Old English Syntax* (2 vols.). Oxford: Claredon Press. https://doi.org/10.1093/acprof:oso/9780198119357.001.0001

Molencki, Rafał (2002). The Status of Dearr and þearf in Old English. *Studia Anglica Posnaniensia* 38, 363–379.

Molencki, Rafał (2005). The Confusion between Tharf and Dare in Middle English. In Nikolas Ritt, & Herbert Schendl (Eds.), *Rethinking Middle English: Linguistic and Literary Approaches* (147–160). Frankfurt am Main: Peter Lang.

Quirk, Randolph, Greenbaum, Sidney, Leech, Geoffrey, & Svartvik, Jan (1985). *A Comprehensive Grammar of the English Language*. London: Longman.

Schlüter, Julia (2010). To Dare To or Not To: Is Auxiliarization Reversible? In An van Liden, Jean-Christophe Verstraete, & Kristin Davidse (Eds.), *Formal Evidence in Grammaticalization Research* (289–325). Amsterdam: Benjamins. https://doi.org/10.1075/tsl.94.11sch

Taeymans, Martine (2006). An Investigation into the Emergence and Development of the Verb Need from Old to Present-Day English: A Corpus-Based Approach. Ph.D. dissertation, Universiteit Antwerpen.

Traugott, Elizabeth Closs (1992). Syntax. In Richard M. Hogg (Ed.), *The Cambridge history of the English language*, Vol. I: *The Beginnings to 1066* (168–289). Cambridge: Cambridge University Press.

Traugott, Elizabeth Closs (2001). Legitimate Counterexamples to Unidirectionality. Paper presented at the *University of Freiburg*, 17 October 2001. Retrieved from http://www.stanford.edu/~traugott/papers/FreiburgUnidirect.pdf

Visser, F. Thomas (1963-1973). *An Historical Syntax of the English Language*, Vol. I-III. Leiden: E.J. Brill.

Warner, Anthony R. (1993). *English Auxiliaries: Structure and History*. Cambridge: Cambridge University Press. https://doi.org/10.1017/CBO9780511752995

Counterfactuality and aktionsart

Predictors for *BE* vs. *HAVE* + past participle in Middle English

Judith Huber

In Middle English (ME), manner of motion verbs occur in perfect periphrases with both *BE* and *HAVE* as auxiliaries (e.g. *is/has run*, *is/has ridden*), the *BE*-variant being the older, the *HAVE*-variant the more recent form with these verbs. Los (2015) hypothesizes that the choice of auxiliary with manner of motion verbs in ME might depend systematically on aktionsart in that *HAVE* is chosen when the verb denotes a controlled process (e.g. *he has run fast for an hour*), and *BE* when the verb denotes a change of location (e.g. *he is run into town*), much as in Present-Day Dutch. Also taking into account other factors that have been suggested to influence the choice of *BE* vs. *HAVE* in Middle English (such as counterfactuality, infinitive, or past perfect), I test this hypothesis on data from the *Corpus of Middle English Prose and Verse*. I show that aktionsart is indeed a very reliable predictor, but overridden by counterfactuality.

Keywords: perfect, auxiliary selection, Middle English, counterfactuality, aktionsart, construal, manner of motion verb, mixed logistic regression

1. Development of periphrases with *BE*/*HAVE* + past participle in English

In Old and Middle English, both *BE* and *HAVE* combined with past participles of verbs to form perfect periphrases. Both periphrases have their prehistoric origin in resultative structures: Originally, *HAVE* combined with transitive verbs (cf. (1)) in a meaning of 'possession' ('they had him as a killed one') or, according to de Acosta (2013), one of 'attained state', where the subject achieves a result ('they had killed him'). *BE* originally combined as a copula with participles of mutative intransitive verbs, i.e. verbs which denote a change of state (e.g. 'become', 'grow') or a change of location (e.g. 'arrive', 'come') (cf. (2)).

https://doi.org/10.1075/cilt.346.08hub

(1) *hie hine* ***ofslægenne hæfdon*** (*ChronA* 252 (755), DOEC)
they him killed had
'They had killed him' (trans.)

(2) *ealswa heo ham* ***wæren gecumene*** (*LS* 29 (Nicholas) 0094 (261), DOEC)
when they home were come
'When they had (lit. 'were') come home' (mutative intrans.)

With the grammaticalization of the *HAVE*-periphrasis into a more general perfect (see e.g. Wischer, 2004; Macleod, 2014; on the high frequency of perfect meanings in attestations of *HAVE* + past participle in Old English, cf. Johannsen, 2016), the combinational range of *HAVE* – originally restricted to transitive verbs as in (1) – had increased already in Old English to include intransitives, especially non-mutatives (such as *gesyngod* 'sinned' in (3), which does not denote a change of place or condition), but sometimes also mutatives (such as *inʒeþrungen* 'entered' in (4)).

(3) *we* ***habbað gesyngod*** *þæt we swa spræcon ongean þone ælmihtigan God* (ÆHom 21 319, from Łęcki 2010: 158)
'We have sinned when we spoke so against the almighty God' (non-mutative)

(4) ***hæfde*** *þa se æðeling* ***inʒeþrungen*** (*And* 303(990), DOEC)
'Then the noble one had pressed inwards/entered' (mutative)

Typically, however, mutative intransitive verbs still combine with *BE* (cf. (2)) throughout Middle English and Early Modern English, except in a range of contexts identified in the literature as favouring *HAVE* over *BE* already in these periods (e.g. Fischer, 1992: 256–262; Kytö, 1997; Łęcki, 2010: 159; Mustanoja, 1960: 502): These are predominantly combinations with modal verbs, past perfects, perfect infinitives, hypothetical statements, iterative/durative contexts, and contexts highlighting process/activity. These factors will be discussed in more detail in the next section. The *BE*-periphrasis drops out of use in standard English only in the Late Modern English period (cf. e.g. Anderwald, 2014), becoming almost entirely replaced by the perfect with *HAVE* around 1900 (e.g. Rydén & Brorström, 1987: 198), so that there is a long period of variation in which mutative intransitive verbs can occur with both *BE* and *HAVE*.

Los (2015: 76) links the variation between *BE* and *HAVE* in the history of English to the auxiliary selection hierarchy (ASH) proposed by Sorace (2000): This implicational hierarchy applies to intransitive verbs classified according to their aspectual and thematic characteristics; it suggests that in languages that have two perfect auxiliaries *BE* and *HAVE*, *BE* will be used most consistently with verbs that denote a change of location, *HAVE* with verbs denoting controlled processes, with a gradient in between (cf. Figure 1). The cutoff point in the hierarchy will be different in different languages, and the verb groups around the cutoff point will display more auxiliary variation than the core ones ('change of location' and 'controlled process' respectively).

```
CHANGE OF LOCATION                          selects BE (least variation)
CHANGE OF STATE
CONTINUATION OF A PRE-EXISTING STATE
EXISTENCE OF STATE
UNCONTROLLED PROCESS
CONTROLLED PROCESS (MOTIONAL)
CONTROLLED PROCESS (NON-MOTIONAL)           selects HAVE (least variation)
```

Figure 1. Auxiliary selection hierarchy (Sorace, 2000: 863)

Los points out that manner of motion verbs are a particularly interesting type of mutative intransitive in this respect since they regularly denote both 'controlled processes' and 'changes of location' as in (5) and (6) respectively:

(5) *'Saw ye,' quod she, 'as ye* ***han walked wyde****, Any of my sustren walke you beside [...]?'* (Chaucer *LGW* 3, 978)
'Did you, she said, while you were walking far and wide, see any of my sisters walking beside you?'

(6) *Arcite* ***unto the temple walked is*** */ of fierce Mars, to doon his sacrifise* (Chaucer *CT.KT* II, 2368–9)
'Arcite has walked to the temple of fierce Mars to make his offering'
(both examples and translations from Los, 2015: 76–77)

On the basis of the ASH (Figure 1), manner of motion verbs in 'process' contexts, as *walked wyde* in (5), are therefore expected to combine with *HAVE*, whereas in contexts which highlight a change of location, as *unto the temple* in (6), they are expected to combine with *BE*. Based on a few examples, Los (2015: 77) hypothesizes that the difference between (5) and (6) might be systematic in Middle English manner of motion verbs, but points out that to substantiate this claim, "further research, with other verbs than just *walk*, is needed".

The present paper attempts to do precisely that, and investigates perfect auxiliary alternation in eight frequent manner of motion verbs as attested in the *Corpus of Middle English Prose and Verse* (Section 3). In addition to the ASH-type ('controlled process' vs. 'change of location'), other factors that have been reported to influence auxiliary selection in the history of English (see Section 2) are investigated too (Section 4.1–4.3), and their effects on the writers' choice of *BE* or *HAVE* are evaluated in a mixed-effects logistic regression analysis (4.4). The implications of the results for different accounts of the development of the *BE*- and *HAVE*-periphrases in the history of English are discussed in Section 5. This section also discusses a reconceptualization of the ASH-types 'process' and 'change of location' in terms of construal, as put forward by Beliën (2012, 2017) for Dutch, which could explain a few otherwise unexpected attestations of the *HAVE*-periphrasis.

2. *BE/HAVE* + past participle with mutative intransitives in Middle English – a case of auxiliary selection in the perfect?

The traditional account of the development of the *HAVE*- and *BE*-periphrases is one of a gradual and long-term replacement of *BE* by *HAVE*: *HAVE* increasingly encroaches on mutative intransitive verbs, which had originally constituted the domain of *BE*. Early examples of *HAVE* with mutative intransitives date from the Old English period (cf. (4)), but only after 1350 does *HAVE* occur more regularly with this kind of verb. It takes until the 18th century, however, for *HAVE* to become more frequent than *BE* with mutative intransitives, and until around 1900 until the development is completed (Kytö, 1997).[1]

A range of contexts have been identified in which the spread of *HAVE* to mutatives takes place earliest (e.g. Łęcki, 2010: 156–162 on Old English; Fridén, 1948 on Middle and Early Modern English; Rydén & Brorström, 1987 on Late Modern English; Kytö, 1997 on Middle English to Late Modern English.) These are listed and illustrated in (a)–(f):

a. Combinations with modal verbs, as in (7)

(7) *And ferther* ***wolde han riden*** *out of doute / fful fayn*
(a1425(c1385) Chaucer *TC* (Windeatt), 68)
'And undoubtedly [Troilus] would have ridden further very gladly'

b. Past perfects, as in (8) (see also the Old English Example 4)

(8) *For he* ***hadde riden*** *moore than trot or paas*
((c1395) Chaucer *CT.CY.* (Manly-Rickert) G.575)
'Because he had ridden faster than trot or amble'

c. Perfect infinitives, as in (9) (see also *han riden* in (7), and *have cropen* in (10a))

(9) *Hym had ben bettere* ***to haue ygo****; þan so fer* ***to haue iryde***
(c1400 *King Solomon's Book of Wisdom* (LdMisc 622))
'It would have been better for him to have gone than to have ridden so far'

1. On continued or new uses of *BE*-perfects in different varieties of English, however, cf., e.g., Werner, 2016; Yerastov, 2015.

d. Hypothetical/counterfactual statements, as in (10a)–(10b) (see also *wolde han riden* 'would have ridden' in (7) and *hym had ben bettere to haue ygo* 'It would have been better for him to have gone' in (9)). Counterfactuals also tend to take *HAVE* in Middle Dutch and Middle Low German, cf. Shannon (1995: 138–141).

(10) a. *he* ***wende have cropen*** *by his felawe john / And by the millere in he creep anon* ((c1390) Chaucer *CT.Rv.*)
'He thought he had crept in next to his friend John, but he crept in next to the miller right away'

b. *and hys hors had be slayn yf he* ***had not lept*** *a syde* (c1485 Caxton *Charles the Grete* (Herrtage))
'And his horse would have been slain if it had not leapt aside'

e. Iterative and durative contexts, as in (11a) (*many tymes*) and (11b) (*al niht*) respectively.

(11) a. *for I* ***hafe many tymes*** *passed and* ***riden*** *it* (?a1425 *Mandev.*(2) (Eg 1982))
'Because I have passed and ridden it [i.e. the way] many times'

b. *we* ***habb[eþ] hii-riden al niht*** (c1300 Lay.*Brut* (Otho C.13))
'We have ridden all night'

f. Contexts which highlight the process (or 'activity') character of an event rather than emphasizing the resulting change of state or location (as an 'accomplishment'), as in (7–9) and (11). In the following, I will call this factor "aktionsart" (cf. Brown & Miller, 2013; Shannon, 1995: 134). In (7), for instance, Troilus is accompanying his lover Criseyde to the Greeks, where she is going to be exchanged for a Trojan prisoner of war. This means that the lovers have to part once they arrive, which is why Troilus would prefer the ride to take longer, in order to delay their separation. *Ferther wolde han riden* in (7) therefore can be characterized as highlighting the process of riding, not the change of location. The same is true for (8), where *moore than trot or paas* specifies the manner of riding, and where no change of location is predicated. In (9), the prophet Habakkuk is about to bring food to reapers in the field, when an angel tells him to bring it to Daniel in the lion's den instead. Habakkuk refuses, upon which the angel grabs him by his hair and carries him through the air to Daniel (Dan 14,33–36). The narrator's comment in (9) is that Habakkuk would probably have preferred to have walked (*ygo*) himself than to have "ridden" in this uncomfortable way – the focus, therefore, is again on the process of riding rather than on the resulting change of location. The same is true in (11a), where the narrator announces that he will tell the reader how to get to Jerusalem, claiming expertise on the basis of having travelled the way numerous times himself: The focus is on the process of getting to Jerusalem, rather than on the fact that the author has been there. In (11b), finally, it is the temporal adverbial *al niht* that puts the focus on the process of riding. This difference between 'process' and 'change of location' aktionsart is exactly the parameter that is said to govern the variable auxiliary selection (*hebben* vs. *zijn*) with manner of motion verbs in Modern Dutch (Gillmann, 2015: 342–344; Sorace, 2000: 875).

All of the factors above have been reported to correlate with a use of *HAVE* as opposed to *BE* in the history of English. Yet they often overlap – the use of a modal verb (a), for instance, entails the use of a perfect infinitive (c), and often goes along with a hypothetical, counterfactual reading (d), as in (7). Similarly, also a past perfect (b) may be used to convey a hypothetical, counterfactual reading (d), as in (10b). Furthermore, as in (7–9) and (11), all factors (a–e) may coincide with process aktionsart rather than change of location.

These overlaps have been pointed out by McFadden & Alexiadou (2006, 2010; McFadden, 2017), who argue that essentially the early spread of *HAVE* (in the Middle and Early Modern English periods) can be reduced to the effect of counterfactuality (d) and to the fact – as they claim – that only the *HAVE*-periphrasis, but not the one with *BE*, develops into a more general perfect: The *BE*-periphrasis, they emphasize, remains resultative ("a copula construction built around a stative resultative participle" (2010: 421)), with the resulting state holding at the reference time (cf. similarly Mitchell, 1985: §§ 740–742; Brunner, 1962: 299). The *BE*-periphrasis with its resultative semantics would therefore hardly be compatible with iterative, durative, or process readings (e, f) anyway. According to this alternative account of the development of the *HAVE*- and *BE*-periphrases, the early spread of *HAVE* in the Middle and Early Modern English periods crucially does not happen at the expense of *BE*, because the latter was never possible in the contexts (a–f) to which *HAVE* spreads in the first place (McFadden & Alexiadou, 2010: 421). On the contrary, the *BE*-periphrasis is said to remain "stable throughout ME and EModE"; the actual replacement of *BE* by *HAVE* being a "separate and later change" (2010: 422) taking place in the Late Modern English period.

Therefore, whether the variation between *BE* and *HAVE* + past participle in Middle and Early Modern English should be viewed as a matter of auxiliary selection in the perfect – and therefore as a potential candidate for the application of the auxiliary selection hierarchy – crucially depends on the status of the periphrasis with *BE*: Has it grammaticalized into a perfect on a par with the *HAVE*-periphrasis, or is it still the copula + past participle, denoting a resulting state? The first view, with *BE* + past participle as a perfect, and hence the choice of *BE* vs. *HAVE* as a case of auxiliary selection, appears to be the traditional account, and is adopted, for instance, in Rydén & Brorström (1987), Kytö (1997), and many textbooks on the history of English or English historical syntax, such as Brinton & Arnovick

(2017: 228–229, 301, 372–373), Denison (1993: Chapter 12), Faiß (1989: 298), Fischer (1992: 256–261), Hogg (2002: 80–81), or Los (2015: 72–77). In the context of this traditional account, the present paper contributes an analysis of the respective weight of the different predictor variables on the choice of auxiliary in Middle English, exemplified on manner of motion verbs as a group of verbs which regularly occur in both relevant aktionsarten.

In the context of McFadden & Alexiadou's alternative account, in which only the *HAVE*-, but not the *BE*-periphrasis develops into a more general perfect (hence no 'auxiliary selection' in the perfect), the present paper's focus on manner of motion verbs provides an interesting test case: In McFadden & Alexiadou's data for Middle English (all 676 attestations of verbs that show *BE*/*HAVE* variation in *PPCME2* (Kroch & Taylor, 1999)), more than 40% are instances of *come* (McFadden & Alexiadou, 2006: FN5; see also McFadden, 2017: 168 for the very high share of *come* and *go* among the verbs taking a *BE* perfect in the history of English). *Come*, of course, is an "inherently telic" verb (Shannon, 1995: 141) which is typically used when the focus is on a change of location, but rather unlikely to be employed with a focus on 'process' or 'activity' (i.e. atelic), as the questionable outcome of a classic test for atelicity (e.g. Filip, 2011: 1189–1190), the combination with *for an hour* shows: *?They have come for an hour*. Following *come*, the next frequent verbs in McFadden & Alexiadou's Middle English data are *go* and *fall* (2006, FN5), which are arguably likely to be predominantly used for changes of location rather than processes as well. Considering moreover that verbs like *arrive* and *land* (both inherently highlighting change of location) and verbs denoting a change of state, like *become, cease, end, grow*, and *vanish* will equally have a penchant for resultative uses as opposed to process ones, the data are likely to be dominated by prototypical mutative intransitives (or in ASH-terms, by verbs denoting change of location or change of state). Manner of motion verbs, by contrast, are less prototypically mutative in that they are equally likely to be used for processes as they are for changes of location.[2] Consequently, they are also likely to show greater variation between *BE* and *HAVE*, they therefore form a critical group of verbs against which McFadden & Alexiadou's findings can be tested.

2. In the attestations of manner of motion verbs in *BE*/*HAVE*-periphrases from the CME, the ratio of process vs. change of location uses is almost fifty-fifty (120 process vs. 119 change of location), though note that with regard to the individual verbs, only *run* and *sail* are roughly equally used in both kinds of aktionsart (42/37 and 5/4 respectively) while *climb, creep, leap* and *swim* are more frequent in change of location contexts (2/10, 1/20, 2/30, 0/2), and *ride* and *walk* more frequent in process contexts (39/10 and 29/6).

3. Data and classification

In a first step, the *Corpus of Middle English Prose and Verse* (CME) was searched for attestations of the past participle forms of *climb*, *creep*, *leap*, *run*, *ride*, *sail*, *swim*, and *walk* in various spellings. These verbs were selected because they had emerged as the most frequent Middle English manner of motion verbs in Huber (2017: 188–190). In a next step, those attestations in which the participle combined with an auxiliary *BE* or *HAVE*, i.e. appeared in a perfect periphrasis, were filtered out manually, resulting in a total of N = 257 attestations from 110 different texts. The numbers of occurrences of the individual verbs in perfect periphrases with *BE* and *HAVE* respectively are given in Table 1:

Table 1. Periphrases with *BE*/*HAVE* + past participles of manner of motion verbs in CME

verb	BE	HAVE	total
climb	11	1	12
creep	15	6	21
leap	21	11	32
run	41	50	91
ride	10	40	50
sail	3	7	10
swim	–	2	2
walk	4	35	39
total	105	152	257

Beside the dependent variable of 'type of auxiliary verb' (*HAVE* vs. *BE*), I annotated the attestations according to the following predictor variables taken from the literature (see Section 2) and illustrated below:

- 'subperiod': ME 2, ME 3, ME 4[3]
- 'counterfactual semantics': yes, no
- 'aktionsart': process, change of location, ambiguous
- 'form of auxiliary': present, past, infinitive

I had originally also classified the attestations according to the variable 'presence of modal verb' (factor (a) in Section 2), but it turned out that in the data set, all attestations with modal verbs simultaneously had counterfactual semantics (cf. (13)),

3. For the variable 'subperiod', the periodization from the Helsinki Corpus – ME 2 (1250–1350), ME 3 (1350–1420), ME 4 (1420–1500) – was applied to the texts based on the manuscript date given for each text in the MED.

though not vice versa, cf. (12)).[4] This is why an extra variable 'presence of modal verb' would not have made much sense. The variable 'counterfactual semantics' therefore also includes the attestations with modal verbs. Examples for attestations with counterfactual semantics are (12)–(13) (see also (10a)–(10b)).

(12) *As thou right now* ***were cropen*** *out of the ground, / Ne nevere er now ne haddest knowen me* ((c1395) Chaucer *CT.Fkl.*)
'As if you had crept out of the ground right now, and had never known me before'

(13) *He* ***wolde have ronne*** *upon that other / Anon [...] ne hadde be that Uluxes / Between hem made accord and pes* ((a1393) Gower *CA* (Frf 3))
'He would have run against that other one immediately [...], if Uluxes had not reconciled them'

Next, each attestation was categorized as to whether, in terms of aktionsart (and also in terms of the ASH), it describes a process or a change of location. In (14), for instance, the lack of a directional adverbial and the presence of the adverb *wel* makes it clear that a process is described. Also the classic test for atelicity, adding *for an hour*, works perfectly fine (cf. also Examples 5, 7–9 and 11).

(14) *He telth hire [...] hou his houndes* ***have wel runne*** ((a1393) Gower *CA* (Frf 3))
'He tells her how his dogs have run well'

In (15a), by contrast, the directional adverbial *þerinne* 'into there' is responsible for the telic, change of location reading. Such a directional adverbial is present in 114 of the 119 attestations that were classified as describing changes of location (cf. also Examples (6), (10), (12)–(13). Five attestations, however, were classified as describing a change of location despite the lack of such an adverbial: in (15b), it is the presence of the prefix *at-* 'away' that telicizes the verb; in (15c), the fact that the guests have departed (and that Gamelyn therefore is alone) is stressed, i.e. their change of location rather than the process of their riding and going. The three remaining attestations that were classified as 'change of location' despite the lack of a directional adverbial are all of the same type as (15c).[5]

4. Two thirds of the counterfactual attestations (22/33) feature a modal verb.

5. Note that this type of attestation calls for a slight modification of McFadden & Alexiadou's claim that manner of motion verbs like *run* or *ride* only take *BE* "when there is additional material containing a target state, like a goal PP" (2010: 418) – the target state need not necessarily be expressed in "additional material", but may also be contextual, as shown by (15c).

(15) a. *þe dore wes ope / Hennen weren* ***þerinne I-crope***
(?a1300 *Fox & W.* (Dgb 86))
'The door was open, hens had crept into there'

b. *heo [...] qualden alle þa ilke; þe aniht weoren* ***atcropene***
(c1275(?a1200) Lay.*Brut* (Clg A.9) 2828)
'They [...] killed all those that had crept away by night'

c. *ho Gamelynes gestes were* ***riden*** *and y-gon / Gamelyn stood anoon* ***allone*** *[...]* (c1415 *Gamelyn* (Corp-O 198), 348)
'When Gamelyn's guests had ridden and gone, Gamelyn stood suddenly alone'

Some attestations could not with any certainty be classified as highlighting either change of location or the process of moving and were therefore classified as 'ambiguous' with respect to aktionsart. This is the case in (16a), for instance, where both a change of location reading 'was near the place as a result of having walked there' and a process reading 'had been walking near the place' is possible. The same is true for (16b), where *þerynne* could be both directional 'into it' (i.e. change of location) and locational '(around) in it' (i.e. process). 18 out of the 257 attestations had to be classified as ambiguous.

(16) a. *afftyr stylle he stode for to here/Yff ony seruaunt* ***had walkyd ther nere***
((1449) Metham *AC* (Gar 141), 254)
'And then he stood still to listen whether any servant had walked near there'

b. *meny men haueþ* ***i-walked þerynne*** *and i-seie ryueres and stremes, but nowher konneþ þey fynd non ende* ((a1387) Trev.*Higd.* (StJ-C H.1))
'Many people have walked in it [a cave in Cherdhole] and seen rivers and streams, but they could not find an end anywhere'

The literature usually further identifies durative and iterative contexts as favouring *HAVE* (factor (e) in Section 2). In the present data set – and probably with manner of motion verbs in general – durative and iterative readings go hand in hand with the process of moving being highlighted rather than the resulting change of location, as has been discussed with respect to (11a)–(11b) in Section 2, cf. also the durative (18b) (*a while*). Vice versa, none of the attestations classified as highlighting change of location had a durative or iterative context, which is why this factor was not included as a separate variable.

Finally, each attestation was categorized according to the form of auxiliary – present (17), past (18), or infinitive (7), (9), (10a), (13).

(17) a. *Arcite* ***is*** *riden anon unto the toun* ((c1385) Chaucer *CT.Kn.*, 1628)
'Arcite has ridden to the town at once'

b. *and sir Gawein* **hath** *so riden till he com [...] a-gein the wyndowe*
(a1500(?c1450) *Merlin* (Cmb Ff.3.11))
'And Sir Gawain has ridden so [long] until he came [...] to the window'

(18) a. *Whan Gemelyn þe ȝonge* **was** *riden out atte gate*
(c1425 *Gamelyn* (Petw 7), 191)
'When the young Gamelyn had ridden out at the gate'

b. *when he* **hadde** *a while walkude þus Among þe children*
(a1450 *St.Editha* (Fst B.3))
'When he had walked a while like this among the children'

With these variables, all the factors listed in Section 2 are covered: Factors (b) and (c) (past perfect or perfect infinitive) are captured by the variable 'form of auxiliary', factors (a) and (d) (modal verb and hypothetical statements) by 'counterfactuality', and factors (e) and (f) (durative or iterative semantics, or process readings) are covered by 'aktionsart'. The variable 'period' covers the possibility that the incidence of *HAVE* may increase throughout the Middle English period, as suggested in the traditional account of *HAVE* gradually encroaching onto *BE*-territory.

4. Results and discussion

This section will present and discuss the results, starting with the general results for the single variables (4.1). As counterfactual attestations turn out to almost categorically feature *HAVE* as auxiliary, I control for counterfactuality in Section 4.2 and additionally for aktionsart in Section 4.3. Section 4.4 presents the evaluation of the effects of the variables in a mixed-effects logistic regression model.

4.1 General results (N = 257)

4.1.1 *Period*

Table 2 shows that throughout the Middle English period, the share of *BE* vs. the one of *HAVE* is decreasing in the periphrasis with manner of motion verbs, from 62% in ME 2 to 33% in ME 4. In the traditional account, this would be interpreted as reflecting the spread of *HAVE* which starts to gradually replace *BE* in the perfect; in McFadden & Alexiadou's account, alternatively, it would represent the grammaticalization of *HAVE* with its spread to new contexts, not at the expense of *BE*. The rising numbers of the periphrases in general will be due to the fact that the amount of extant text equally grows over time (the CME does not aim at balance with respect to period).

Table 2. *BE/HAVE*-periphrases with manner of motion verbs: period (N = 257)

	ME 2 (1250–1350)	ME 3 (1350–1420)	ME 4 (1420–1500)
BE	13 (62%)	38 (51%)	54 (33%)
HAVE	8 (38%)	36 (49%)	108 (67%)
	21	74	162

4.1.2 *Counterfactuality*

As shown in Figure 2 and Table 3, attestations with counterfactual semantics almost invariably (with a single exception only) feature *HAVE* as auxiliary, which makes counterfactuality a nearly categorical predictor for *HAVE*. This result is fully in line with earlier research (cf. e.g. Fischer, 1992: 261; McFadden & Alexiadou, 2010: 395).[6]

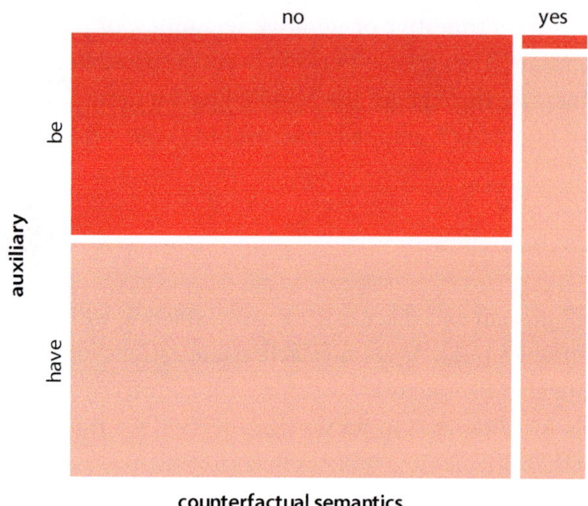

Figure 2. *BE/HAVE*-periphrases with manner of motion verbs: counterfactuality (N = 257)

6. The one attestation where *BE* is used despite the counterfactual semantics of the clause is given in (12) above and fits well to McFadden & Alexiadou's (2010: 406) explanation of exceptional *BE* in counterfactuals as "*present* counterfactuals of result states" as opposed to normal past counterfactuals, which "convey […] that the proposition being considered was contrary to fact at a particular time in the past" (ibid: 395): (12) is uttered by the "philosopher" in the Franklin's Tale, who generously cancels a large debt that Aurelius owes him, basically saying 'let's start from scratch and act as if we had never met before': *sire, I releesse thee thy thousand pound, / As thou right now **were cropen** out of the ground, / Ne nevere er now ne haddest knowen me* 'Sir, I release your thousand pounds to you as if you had crept out of the ground right now, and had never met me before now.' Arguably, and highlighted by the *right now*, the emphasis in *were cropen out of the ground* is on Aurelius' sudden first appearance as a "contrary-to-fact present state" (ibid: 405) rather than on the counterfactual idea of his creeping out of the ground prior to the moment of speaking.

Table 3. *BE/HAVE*-periphrases with manner of motion verbs: counterfactuality (N = 257)

	counterfactual semantics	
	no	yes
BE	46% (104)	3% (1)
HAVE	54% (120)	97% (32)

4.1.3 *Aktionsart*

Attestations with emphasis on the process of riding/walking etc. strongly tend to feature *HAVE* as auxiliary (in 95% of the cases), but the reverse tendency is less pronounced: Attestations in which the resulting change of location is emphasized do tend to have *BE* as auxiliary, but only in 74% of the cases, as shown in Figure 3 and Table 4.

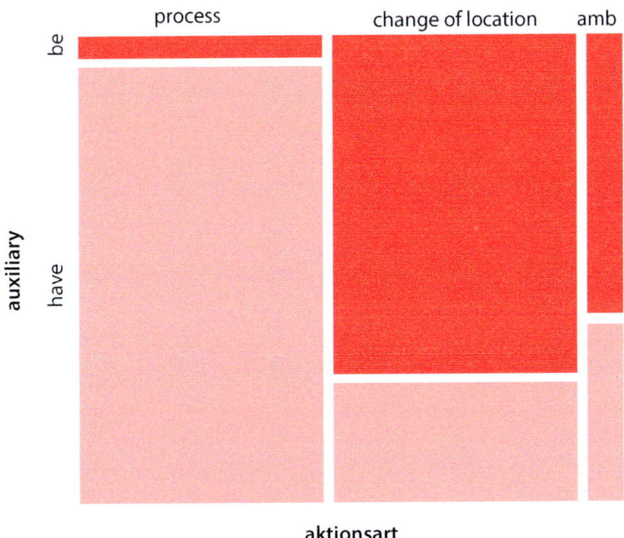

Figure 3. *BE/HAVE*-periphrases with manner of motion verbs: aktionsart (N = 257)

Table 4. *BE/HAVE*-periphrases with manner of motion verbs: aktionsart (N = 257)

	aktionsart		
	process	change of location	ambiguous
BE	5% (6)	74% (88)	61% (11)
HAVE	95% (114)	26% (31)	39% (7)

4.1.4 *Form of auxiliary*

With respect to the form of the auxiliary, Figure 4 and Table 5 show that infinitives indeed occur as *HAVE* most often (93%). The tendency for past to co-occur with *HAVE* is less strong (63%), and there is a slight tendency (55%) towards *BE* in the present.

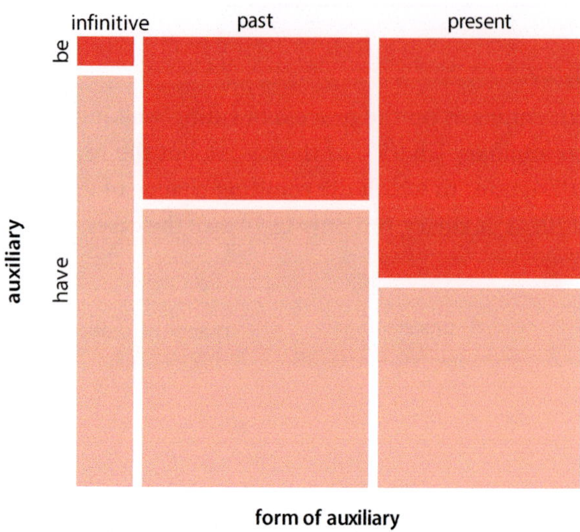

Figure 4. *BE/HAVE*-periphrases with manner of motion verbs: form of auxiliary (N = 257)

Table 5. *BE/HAVE*-periphrases with manner of motion verbs: form of auxiliary (N = 257)

	form of auxiliary		
	infinitive	past	present
BE	7% (2)	37% (44)	55% (59)
HAVE	93% (28)	63% (75)	45% (49)

4.2 Controlling for the "counterfactual effect"

Since counterfactuality turned out to correlate almost categorically with *HAVE* (Section 4.1.2), the next step in the analysis is to focus on the non-counterfactual attestations only (N = 224) to find out about the respective influence of the other variables independent of this "knock-out" factor.

4.2.1 *Period*

As shown in Table 6, there is an increase of the proportion of *HAVE* in the periphrasis throughout the Middle English period also in the non-counterfactuals. Disregarding the counterfactuals does not really change the picture: The increase of *HAVE* from ME2 to ME4 is almost the same as in Table 2.

Table 6. *BE/HAVE*-periphrases with manner of motion verbs (non-counterfactuals): period (N = 224)

	period		
	ME 2 (1250–1350)	ME 3 (1350–1420)	ME 4 (1420–1500)
BE	65% (13)	57% (37)	39% (57)
HAVE	35% (7)	43% (28)	61% (85)
	20	65	142

4.2.2 *Aktionsart*

This is quite different for the variable 'aktionsart': Once the counterfactuals with their strong tendency toward *HAVE* are disregarded, the correlation of 'change of location' with *BE* becomes a lot more pronounced (89% as opposed to 74%), as can be seen by comparing Figure 5 and Table 7 with Figure 3 and Table 4 in Section 4.1.3. The effect of aktionsart on the choice of auxiliary in manner of motion verbs, as hypothesized by Los (2015), is therefore quite systematic indeed, though clearly overridden by counterfactuality.

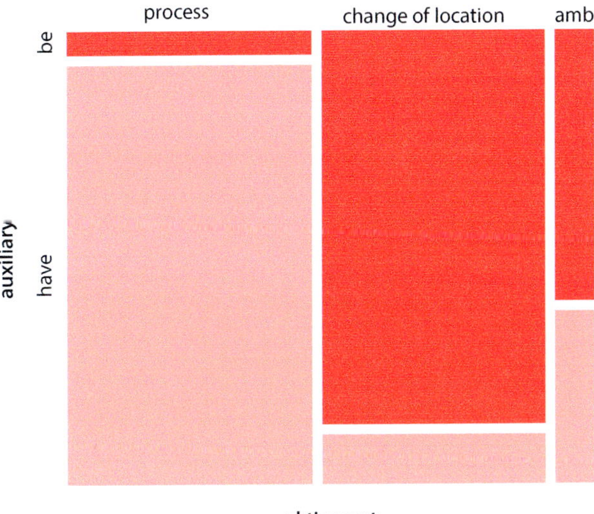

Figure 5. *BE/HAVE*-periphrases with manner of motion verbs (non-counterfactuals): aktionsart (N = 224)

Table 7. *BE*/*HAVE*-periphrases with manner of motion verbs (non-counterfactuals): aktionsart (N = 224)

	aktionsart		
	process	change of location	ambiguous
BE	6% (6)	89% (87)	61% (11)
HAVE	94% (102)	11% (11)	39% (7)

4.2.3 *Form of auxiliary*

Also in the non-counterfactual attestations, the slight tendency for past to co-occur with *HAVE* remains (62%), i.e. *had walked* is more frequent than *was walked*, for instance. These results markedly contradict the ones in McFadden & Alexiadou (2010: 397), who find only less than 7% *HAVE* in Middle English past perfect non-counterfactuals (as opposed to 14.5% in the present perfect), and therefore conclude that the alleged effect of past on *HAVE* does not exist, but is only a by-product of the counterfactual effect, since counterfactuals are often in the past tense. The different results shown in Figure 6 and Table 8 are probably due to the fact that the present study focuses on manner of motion verbs only. These are much more likely also to be used in process contexts (and hence with *HAVE*) than other mutative intransitives: As argued in Section 2, other mutatives, particularly *come*, the verb that dominates the data in McFadden & Alexiadou (2010), typically occur in resultative contexts, which, in turn, strongly favour *BE* anyway (cf. 4.2.2).

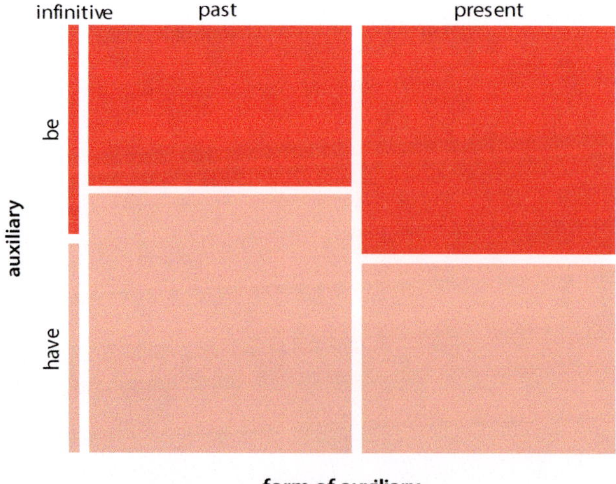

Figure 6. *BE*/*HAVE*-periphrases with manner of motion verbs (non-counterfactuals): form of auxiliary (N = 224)

Table 8. *BE/HAVE*-periphrases with manner of motion verbs (non-counterfactuals): form of auxiliary (N = 224)

	form of auxiliary		
	infinitive	**past**	**present**
BE	50% (2)	38% (43)	55% (59)
HAVE	50% (2)	62% (69)	45% (49)

4.3 Controlling for counterfactuality and aktionsart (N = 97)

In 4.1–4.2, we have seen that both the variables 'counterfactuality' [+ counterfactual] and 'aktionsart' [process] strongly correlate with *HAVE*. If we remove these attestations and narrow down the dataset further to only those 97 attestations that are both non-counterfactual and emphasize a change of location, and hence are highly likely to occur with *BE*, we see that the remaining attestations with *HAVE* all have their auxiliary in the past tense (see Table 9).

Table 9. *BE/HAVE*-periphrases with manner of motion verbs (non-counterfactuals, change-of-location): form of auxiliary (N = 97)

	form of auxiliary	
	past	**present**
BE	76% (34)	100% (52)
HAVE	24% (11)	–

Although at this level of detail, the numbers of attestations are necessarily rather low (N = 97), these results lend cautious support to the findings in 4.2.3 above: They suggest that the factor 'past' indeed favours *HAVE*, and, moreover, does so increasingly in the course of the Middle English period, as shown in Table 10 and Figure 7, where all the attestations with *HAVE* have their auxiliary in the past (i.e. occur with *had*).

Table 10. *BE/HAVE*-periphrases with manner of motion verbs (non-counterfactuals, change-of-location): period (N = 97)

	period		
	ME 2 (1250–1350)	ME 3 (1350–1420)	ME 4 (1420–1500)
BE	100% (12)	96% (27)	82% (47)
HAVE	–	4% (1)	18% (10)

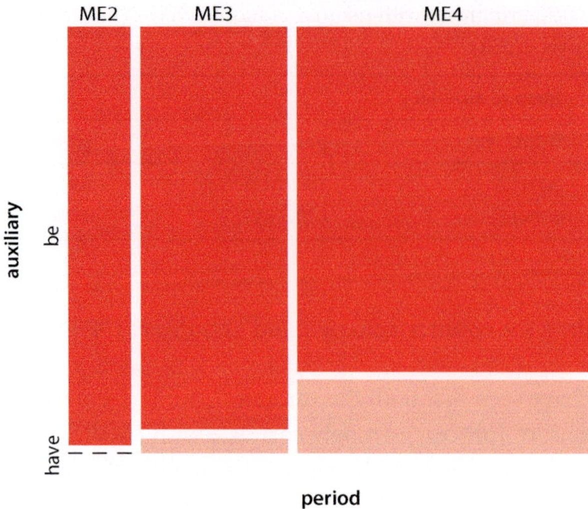

Figure 7. *BE*/*HAVE*-periphrases with manner of motion verbs (non-counterfactuals, change-of-location): period (N = 97)

4.4 Mixed-effects logistic regression analysis

In 4.1, the variable 'counterfactuality' was shown to have an almost categorical effect on the choice of auxiliary. To evaluate the effects of the other variables – 'aktionsart', 'form of auxiliary', and 'period' – on the choice of *BE* or *HAVE*, a mixed-effects logistic regression model was fitted to the data, limited to the non-counterfactual attestations (N = 224), using the glmer function of the lme4 package (Bates et al., 2015) in R 3.1.2. A random effect was included for the individual verbs (with a variance of 2.058).[7] Table 11 shows the model estimates.

Table 11. Estimated mixed-effects logistic regression model for the perfect auxiliary with manner of motion verbs data. Auxiliary *HAVE* is treated as the success

	estimate coefficient	exp(coefficient)	std. error
intercept	−4.1900	0.0151	1.2661
period: ME3	0.5961	1.8150	1.0957
period: ME4	1.6965	5.4548	1.0891
aktionsart: amb	1.7710	5.8767	0.7738
aktionsart: process	5.5533	258.0878	0.7528
auxform: infinitive	−0.5363	0.5849	1.5757
auxform: past	1.5766	4.8385	0.6110

7. Many thanks are due to the StaBLab at LMU Munich, particularly to Andreas Hueck, for their help with the logistic regression.

Generally in Table 11, an exponentiated coefficient greater than one means that, *ceteris paribus*, the odds of *HAVE* are greater than in the reference category (ME2; change of location; present); an exponentiated coefficient smaller than one means that the odds for *BE* are greater than in the reference category. More specifically, the odds of *HAVE* are higher in periods ME3 and ME4 compared to the reference period ME2; they are roughly five times higher if the auxiliary is in past form compared to the reference form present, and more than 250 times higher in process aktionsart compared to change of location (the reference aktionsart).

In a likelihood ratio test – which evaluates the effect of each of the variables as a whole on the null-hypothesis (i.e. the hypothesis that the variable has no influence on the auxiliary) – the variables 'aktionsart' and 'form of auxiliary' were shown to be significant predictors (χ^2 (2) = 119.2, p = 2.2e-16 (***) for 'aktionsart' and χ^2 (2) = 8.5052, p = 0.01423 (*) for 'form of auxiliary'), while 'period' was no significant predicting variable (χ^2 (2) = 4.7785, p = 0.0917). Hence, in addition to confirming 'aktionsart' as a highly significant predictor, this analysis suggests that, despite the low numbers we saw in Section 4.3, 'form of auxiliary' is a significant predictor for the choice of *HAVE* vs. *BE* as well.

5. Implications for different accounts of the *BE*/*HAVE*-periphrases

Two different accounts of the *BE*/*HAVE*-periphrases in the history of English were sketched in Section 2: On the one hand, the traditional view that sees both as perfect periphrases, with a gradual replacement of *BE* by *HAVE* as auxiliary over several centuries starting in Middle or even Old English; on the other, McFadden & Alexiadou's (2006, 2010) account according to which only the *HAVE*-periphrasis develops into a more general perfect, while the *BE*-periphrasis remains resultative until it starts to fall out of use around 1800. How do the results presented in Section 4 relate to these two accounts respectively?

In the frame of both accounts, manner of motion verbs are a rewarding object of study: Among the mutative intransitive verbs, they can be expected to show the highest degree of variation with respect to factor (f) in that they are most likely to be used in 'process' and 'resultative' (i.e. change of location) contexts alike. That other mutative intransitives – particularly the highly frequent *come* – are less likely to occur in 'process' contexts, in turn, may entail the danger of underrating this factor in a general corpus analysis of verbs that show *BE*/*HAVE* variation. Concentrating on manner of motion verbs avoids this danger.

With regard to the respective weight of the factors influencing auxiliary selection in manner of motion verbs, the analysis in Section 4 confirms McFadden & Alexiadou (2010) in showing that counterfactuality is not only one among many predictor variables, but the most categorical one: In counterfactual statements, the auxiliary is almost always *HAVE*, irrespective of any other factors that would predict *BE* (4.1.2).

A restriction of the data to non-counterfactual attestations (4.2, 4.4) shows that aktionsart correlates with choice of auxiliary quite systematically: Change of location contexts usually feature *BE* (in 89% of the cases), process contexts *HAVE* (in 95% of the cases). With regard to the traditional account, this corroborates Los' hypothesis (2015: 77), though with the qualification that the influence of aktionsart is overridden by counterfactuality. The strong correlation of *BE* with change of location contexts also conforms with McFadden & Alexiadou's assessment of the Middle English *BE*-periphrasis as a mere resultative.

Form of auxiliary (past vs. present tense) turns out to be a third significant predictor variable, though of lesser influence than the other two: The odds of *HAVE* are higher if the auxiliary is in the past tense compared to the present tense, even in non-counterfactuals. This is in line with the traditional account of a gradual replacement of *BE* by *HAVE* in the perfect, according to which past tense is a context to which *HAVE* spreads early on. In McFadden & Alexiadou's scenario (2010), by contrast, in which the spread of *HAVE* at the expense of *BE* is only dated to the Late Modern period, this is unexpected: The present study finds a slight encroachment of *HAVE* onto *BE*-territory (non-counterfactual change of location contexts) in manner of motion verbs already starting in the late Middle English period. It should be stressed, however, that this only concerns eleven attestations, and that their use of *HAVE* may perhaps be explained in other ways, as discussed in the following.

First, in five of the attestations, the unexpected *HAVE* could arguably be due to a priming effect of a preceding occurrence of *HAVE*, as in (19a)–(19b) (see also 21).[8]

(19) a. *And whanne Aaron* **hadde** *do this, and* **hadde runne** *to the myddis of the multitude* ((a1425(c1395) *WBible(2)* Num 16, 47)
'And when Aaron had done this [i.e. taken the censer with incense] and had run into the midst of the assembly'

b. *Thus ledde hym the devell that he* **hadde** *serued, that he* **hadde lepte** *in to the ryver and drowned hym-self* (a1500(?c1450) *Merlin* (Cmb Ff.3.11))
'The devil whom he had served had led him so that he had leapt into the river and drowned himself'

Second, the occurrence of *HAVE* in these attestations could also more generally be due to the fact that manner of motion verbs combine with *HAVE* more often than

8. Note that the function of the past form in *had lept* in (19b) is hard to explain anyway: It can neither be a counterfactual past, because the parson in the story in fact leaps into the river and drowns himself, nor does anterior past make sense for *had lept* (in contrast to the clearly anterior *had served*).

other mutatives because they are more frequently used in process contexts.[9] This might lead to a strengthened mental association of these individual lexemes to auxiliary *HAVE*, an entrenchment which could then also bring about combinations with *HAVE* in change of location contexts, i.e. the former domain of *BE*.

Third, even though the eleven attestations in question are telic (and therefore categorized as 'change of location' in the present paper), it is possible that the choice of the auxiliary *HAVE* is motivated by a construal of the event as a 'type of act' rather than a 'change of location'. This is the argument put forward by Beliën (2012, 2017) for Present-Day Dutch, in order to account for attestations such as (20), in which the auxiliary *hebben* 'have' is used with a manner of motion verb and a telic PP (*in het zwembad* 'into the pool'), thus violating the allegedly "perfect relation between telicity and auxiliary choice" (2012: 12) in Dutch (where usually auxiliary *zijn* 'be' is used in telic contexts, auxiliary *hebben* 'have' in atelic ones).

(20) *En ze **heeft** dinsdag eindelijk **in het zwembad gesprongen**! Ze is nu over d[']r angst heen*
'And she finally jumped into the pool on Tuesday! She is over her fear now'
(Beliën, 2012: 12)

According to Beliën (2012, 2017), this kind of attestation shows that auxiliary choice in Dutch is not merely a function of telicity, but depends on the speaker's construal of the event, in the cognitive grammar sense in which "differences in grammatical structure [...] highlight one facet of the conceived situation at the expense of another" (Langacker, 1987: 39). Choosing *hebben* 'have' as auxiliary means construing the motion event as a type of act. This typically coincides with atelicity, but it also works with telic events: In (20), for instance, the use of *hebben* foregrounds the girl's feat of jumping into the pool, as a "remarkable act" (Belien, 2012: 21), while backgrounding the change of location that was part of the motion event.

If this analysis is adopted for Middle English, it could be an explanation for *HAVE* in the apparent counterexamples to Alexiadou & McFadden's (2010) account. In (19a), for instance, Aaron's running into the middle of the assembly with the censer to prevent the people from dying of the plague could equally be construed as a 'remarkable act'; likewise the suicidal leap into the river in (19b). Another such example of *HAVE* used in a non-counterfactual change of location context is (21), from the story of the missionary journey of the apostles Barnabas and Saul to Cyprus. Due to the PP *to Pafum*, the motion event is clearly telic. Yet,

9. In the present dataset, restricted to manner of motion verbs, 59% of the attested periphrases have the auxiliary *HAVE*, as opposed to only 19% in McFadden & Alexiadou's data with all verbs that show *BE/HAVE* variation (2010: 396, Table 1). See also FN 2 for the share of process contexts in the individual verbs.

here again, one could argue along the lines of Beliën (2012, 2017) that the use of *HAVE* points towards a construal of the motion event as a 'type of act' rather than a 'change of location'. The PP *bi al the ile* 'through all the isle', which refers to stages of the journey prior to the endpoint in Paphos, supports this reading.

(21) *[...] and wenten forth to Seleucia, and fro thennus thei wenten bi boot to Cipre. And whanne thei camen to Salamyne, thei prechiden the word of God in the synagogis [...] And whanne thei* ***hadden walkid bi al the ile to Pafum****, thei founden a man, [...] to whom the name was Bariesu*

(a1425(c1395) *WBible(2)*, Acts 13: 4–6)

'And they went on to Seleucia, and from there by boat to Cyprus. And when they came to Salamis, they preached the word of God in the synagogues [...] And when they had walked through all the isle to Paphos, they found a man [...] whose name was Bar-jesus'

A reason for the higher odds for *HAVE* in the past tense (i.e. as anterior past) in this type of attestation might be that perhaps anterior events, even though they may be telic, tend to be presented more generally as 'types of act' (*when they had DONE this*) rather than 'changes of location' in narrative texts.

Seen this way, the use of *HAVE* in these attestations does not disagree with Alexiadou & McFadden's (2006, 2010) account at all. On the contrary, it would constitute an instance precisely of the experiential perfect into which the *HAVE*-periphrasis is grammaticalizing – only that it in these cases, it combines with telic events.

In sum, therefore, although these attestations at first sight contradict McFadden & Alexiadou's account, they cannot really be read as counterevidence: They can too easily be explained in other ways and, if one allows for construal of telic events as type of act, they go perfectly well with the experiential perfect meaning of the *HAVE*-periphrasis.

6. Conclusion

In this paper, I have investigated the variation between *BE* and *HAVE* with past participles of manner of motion verbs in Middle English on the basis of 257 attestations of the verbs *climb*, *creep*, *leap*, *run*, *ride*, *sail*, *swim*, and *walk* in the relevant periphrases from the CME. Their analysis shows that the effect of counterfactual semantics on *HAVE* is almost categorical (cf. also McFadden & Alexiadou, 2006, 2010). Overridden only by the counterfactual effect, aktionsart is also a very systematic predictor, with *HAVE* occurring in 95% of the 'process' contexts and *BE* in 89% of the (non-counterfactual) 'change of location' contexts, which confirms the hypothesis put forward in Los (2015: 77). The results of a mixed-effects logistic regression analysis (Section 4.4) indicate that, next to aktionsart as a highly significant predicting variable, the form of auxiliary is a significant predictor as well, with higher odds for *HAVE* in the past tense. This finding agrees with the traditional account of *HAVE* gradually replacing *BE* as perfect auxiliary in intransitive verbs, in which the past tense is one of the *HAVE*-favouring contexts. At first glance, the finding is problematic in McFadden & Alexiadou's (2010) scenario, according to which this replacement only happens in Late Modern English. However, as discussed in Section 5, the attestations on which this predictor ultimately hinges are few and their use of *HAVE* might well be motivated by other factors such as priming or construal of a telic event as a 'type of act'.

References

de Acosta, Diego (2013). The Old English *Have*-Perfect and its Congeners. *Journal of English Linguistics* 41(3), 33–64. https://doi.org/10.1177/0075424212441706

Anderwald, Lieselotte (2014). The Decline of the *BE*-perfect, Linguistic Relativity, and Grammar Writing in the Nineteenth Century. In Marianne Hundt (Ed.), *Late Modern English Syntax* (13–37). Cambridge: Cambridge University Press. https://doi.org/10.1017/CBO9781139507226.004

Bates, Douglas, Maechler, Martin, Bolker, Ben, & Walker, Steve (2015). Fitting Linear Mixed-Effects Models Using lme4. *Journal of Statistical Software* 67(1), 1–48. https://doi.org/10.18637/jss.v067.i01

Beliën, Maaike (2012). Dutch Manner of Motion Verbs: Disentangling Auxiliary Choice, Telicity and Syntactic Function. *Cognitive Linguistics* 23(1), 1–26. https://doi.org/10.1515/cog-2012-0001

Beliën, Maaike (2017). Auxiliary Choice with Particle Verbs of Motion in Dutch. *Acta Linguistica Hafniensia* 49(2), 212–231. https://doi.org/10.1080/03740463.2017.1352438

Brinton, Laurel J., & Arnovick, Leslie (2017). *The English Language: A Linguistic History*. Oxford: Oxford University Press.

Brown, Keith, & Miller, Jim (2013). *Cambridge Dictionary of Linguistics*. Cambridge: Cambridge University Press. https://doi.org/10.1017/CBO9781139049412

Brunner, Karl (1962). *Die englische Sprache: Ihre geschichtliche Entwicklung / 2: Die Flexionsformen und ihre Verwendung*. Tübingen: Niemeyer.

CME=Corpus of Middle English Prose and Verse. Retrieved from http://quod.lib.umich.edu/c/cme.

Denison, David (1993). *English Historical Syntax: Verbal Constructions*. London: Longman.

Faiß, Klaus (1989). *Englische Sprachgeschichte*. Tübingen: Francke.

Filip, Hana (2011). Aspectual Class and Aktionsart. In Klaus von Heusinger, Claudia Maienborn, & Paul Portner (Eds.), *Semantics: An International Handbook of Natural Language Meaning* (= HSK 33.2) (1186–1217). Berlin/New York: de Gruyter Mouton.

Fischer, Olga (1992). Syntax. In Norman Blake (Ed.), *The Cambridge History of the English Language*. Volume II. 1066–1476 (207–408). Cambridge: Cambridge University Press. https://doi.org/10.1017/CHOL9780521264754.005

Fridén, Georg (1948). *The Tenses of the English Verb from Chaucer to Shakespeare*. Uppsala: Almqvist & Wiksell.

Gillmann, Melitta (2015). Auxiliary Selection in Closely Related Languages: The Case of German and Dutch. In Rolf Kailuweit, & Malte Rosemeyer (Eds.), *Auxiliary Selection Revisited. Gradience and Gradualness* (333–358). Berlin: de Gruyter.

Hogg, Richard (2002). *An Introduction to Old English*. Edinburgh: Edinburgh University Press.

Huber, Judith (2017). *Motion and the English Verb: A Diachronic Study*. Oxford: Oxford University Press. https://doi.org/10.1093/oso/9780190657802.001.0001

Johannsen, Berit (2016). From Possessive-Resultative to Perfect? Re-Assessing the Meaning of [*hæbb-* + Past Participle] Constructions in Old English Prose. In Valentin Werner, Elena Seoane, & Cristina Suárez-Gómez (Eds.), *Re-assessing the Present Perfect* (23–42). Berlin: de Gruyter Mouton. https://doi.org/10.1515/9783110443530-004

Kroch, Anthony & Taylor, Ann (1999). *The Penn-Helsinki Parsed Corpus of Middle English* (PPCME2). Department of Linguistics, University of Pennsylvania.

Kytö, Merja (1997). *Be/Have* + Past Participle: The Choice of Auxiliary with Intransitives from Late Middle to Modern English. In Matti Rissanen, Merja Kytö, & Kirsi Heikkonen (Eds.), *English in Transition: Corpus-Based Studies in Linguistic Variation and Genre Styles* (17–86). Berlin: Mouton de Gruyter. https://doi.org/10.1515/9783110811148.17

Langacker, Ronald W. 1987. *Foundations of Cognitive Grammar. Volume 1: Theoretical Prerequisites*. Stanford: Stanford University Press.

Łęcki, Andrzej M. (2010). *Grammaticalisation Paths of 'Have' in English*. Frankfurt a. M.: Peter Lang. https://doi.org/10.3726/978-3-653-00288-1

Los, Bettelou (2015). *A Historical Syntax of English*. Edinburgh: Edinburgh University Press.

Macleod, Morgan (2014). Synchronic Variation in the Old English Perfect. *Transactions of the Philological Society* 112(3), 319–343. https://doi.org/10.1111/1467-968X.12029

McFadden, Thomas (2017). On the Disappearance of the BE perfect in Late Modern English. *Acta Linguistica Hafniensia* 49(2), 159–175. https://doi.org/10.1080/03740463.2017.1351845

McFadden, Thomas, & Alexiadou, Artemis (2006). Auxiliary Selection and Counterfactuality in the History of English and Germanic. In Jutta M. Hartmann, & Lászlo Molnárfi (Eds.), *Comparative Studies in Germanic Syntax* (237–262). Amsterdam: Benjamins. https://doi.org/10.1075/la.97.12mcf

McFadden, Thomas, & Alexiadou, Artemis (2010). Perfects, Resultatives, and Auxiliaries in Earlier English. *Linguistic Inquiry* 41(3), 389–425. https://doi.org/10.1162/LING_a_00002

Mitchell, Bruce (1985). *Old English Syntax*. Oxford: Clarendon. https://doi.org/10.1093/acprof:oso/9780198119357.001.0001

Mustanoja, Tauno F. (1960). *A Middle English Syntax*. Helsinki: Société Néophilologique.

R Development Core Team. (2014). *R: A Language and Environment for Statistical Computing*. Vienna: R Foundation for Statistical Computing. Retrieved from www.R-project.org.

Rydén, Mats, & Brorström, Sverker (1987). *The* Be/Have *Variation with Intransitives in English: With Special Reference to the Late Modern Period*. Stockholm: Almqvist & Wiksell.

Shannon, Thomas F. (1995). Toward a Cognitive Explanation of Perfect Auxiliary Variation: Some Modal and Aspectual Effects in the History of Germanic. *American Journal of Germanic Linguistics and Literatures* 7(2), 129–163. https://doi.org/10.1017/S1040820700001578

Sorace, Antonella (2000). Gradients in Auxiliary Selection with Intransitive Verbs. *Language* 76(4), 859–890. https://doi.org/10.2307/417202

Werner, Valentin (2016). Rise of the Undead? BE-perfects in World Englishes. In Valentin Werner, Elena Seoane, & Cristina Suárez-Gómez (Eds.), *Re-assessing the Present Perfect* (259–294). Berlin: de Gruyter Mouton. https://doi.org/10.1515/9783110443530-012

Wischer, Ilse (2004). The *Have*-Perfect in Old English. In Christian Kay, Simon Horobin, & Jeremy Smith (Eds.), *New Perspectives on English Historical Linguistics* (243–255). Amsterdam/Philadelphia: Benjamins. https://doi.org/10.1075/cilt.251.15wis

Yerastov, Yuri (2015). A Construction Grammar Analysis of the Transitive *Be* Perfect in Present-Day Canadian English. *English Language and Linguistics* 19(1), 157–178. https://doi.org/10.1017/S1360674314000331

Conservatism or the influence of the semantics of motion situation in the choice of perfect auxiliaries in Jane Austen's letters and novels

Nuria Calvo Cortes

The present study focuses on the analysis of the choice of either *be* or *have* in combination with the past participles of eleven motion verbs (*arrive, become, come, enter, fall, go, get, grow, pass, return* and *run*) to form perfective structures in Jane Austen's letters and novels. She has previously been considered conservative in her grammar, specifically in relation to her preference for *be* as opposed to *have* in this type of structure. A corpus-based study shows that although she could indeed be considered conservative, the option of the auxiliary might also have been motivated by the different components of the motion situation involved in each instance. The conclusions show that some tendencies can be observed in relation to the behaviour of some of these verbs, despite the low number of occurrences of some of the verbs included in the analysis.

Keywords: perfect, auxiliary, motion verbs, cognitive approach, stylistics

1. Introduction

Despite the popularity of Jane Austen as a writer, not many studies have been carried out of her work from a linguistic point of view (Phillips, 1970; Page, 1972; Cederlöf, 1985; Wijitsopon, 2013; Tieken-Boon van Ostade, 2014). She has often been classified as a conservative writer in relation to her usage of language in general (Phillips, 1970; Rydén & Brorström, 1987), while occasionally she has been considered to be conservative in her use of vocabulary but "experimental and adventurous" in her syntax (Page, 1972: 187). For these reasons, more comprehensive analyses of her use of some grammatical structures could lead to a better understanding of her writing style as well as to a clarification of whether she was in fact conservative or not.

The present study focuses on a very specific aspect, Jane Austen's choice of auxiliary verb in perfective structures in combination with the past participle forms

https://doi.org/10.1075/cilt.346.09cor

of the verbs *arrive, become, come, enter, fall, go, get, grow, pass, return* and *run*. These verbs indicate motion, either in a physical or in a metaphorical way, and the perfective structures with this kind of verb have been analysed before in more general studies (Rydén & Brorström, 1987; Kytö, 1997). However, in the present study a cognitive linguistics approach is taken (Talmy, 2000) and the focus is placed on the components that surround the verbs in the motion situation structure and how these different components may influence the choice of auxiliary verb. More specifically, the main semantic components that are part of a motion situation together with the verb are the *figure*, the *ground* and the *path*. The *figure* refers to the object that moves, the *ground* is the location of the destination of the movement, and the *path* indicates the direction of the movement.

Some of these verbs continued to be used in combination with *be* in perfect structures for a longer time than other verbs. They include those indicating basic motion, such as *come* and *go*, as well as others that refer to a change of state, namely *become* and *grow* (Rydén & Brorström, 1987; Kytö, 1997; Anderwald, 2014). In the case of *gone*, the combination with the auxiliary *be* even prevails in some varieties of English spoken today (Quirk et al., 1985; Anderwald, 2014; McCafferty, 2014).

Jane Austen wrote in a period that coincides with the time when the verb *have* began to be used much more frequently in perfective structures than the verb *be* (Rydén & Brorström, 1987; Denison, 1998; Beal, 2004; Tieken-Boon van Ostade, 2009; Barber et al., 2011). For this reason, an analysis of her usage of both auxiliary verbs could provide very useful information regarding her conservativeness.

Editorial interventions are not uncommon in the publication of literary works. The resulting texts may, therefore, contain features that do not fully reflect the original author's individual linguistic characteristics. As regards Jane Austen's editors' possible influence, a project led by Kathryn Sutherland might contribute to the clarification of such a possible influence. 2010 witnessed the completion of this project in which part of the original manuscripts of some of Jane Austen's works were compiled (https://janeausten.ac.uk/index.html). Her studies of the manuscripts point to the likely manipulation of Jane Austen's fiction works by her editors, more specifically by William Gilford (Sutherland, 2012: 124). In addition to the novels, a considerable number of private letters by Jane Austen has been preserved until today. This offers researchers the possibility to analyse Austen's unpublished language, which might not have undergone any changes by third persons. Tieken-Boon van Ostade (2014: 209) points to the writing process underlying novels and letters due to the novel being "intended for public consumption", as opposed to the private character of letters. Her analysis also confirms that the grammar in Jane Austen's novels was edited. This is exemplified by the participial form *eaten*, present in *Emma*, but not in the letters, where *ate* is the form used (Tieken-Boon van Ostade, 2014: 230). A comparison between the author's novels and letters might, consequently, show differences if the former also involved change by other people.[1] Furthermore, most of the preserved letters written by Jane Austen were addressed to relatives and friends, which means they were informal letters, in which writers are likely to be less careful in their writing style. In contrast, the novels represent a more formal type of writing. These differences may also contribute to finding specific linguistic features in one type of text and not in the other.

1.1 Previous studies

Previous studies that concern the present study are, on the one hand, those that analyse Jane Austen's language and, on the other hand, those that focus on perfective structures in the Late Modern English period. Whereas the former are scarce, the latter have offered a fairly comprehensive description of the usage of the auxiliaries *be* and *have* in the period in question. However, no studies have analysed these structures using a cognitive linguistic framework, or more specifically concentrating on the semantics of motion situations.

As regards the lack of linguistic studies of Jane Austen's work until recently, this coincides, to a certain extent, with the little interest shown in the Late Modern English period from a linguistic point of view until recently. Only a few studies have focused their attention on analysing aspects of Jane Austen's language (Phillips, 1970; Page, 1972; Cederlöf, 1985; Wijitsopon, 2013; Tieken-Boon van Ostade, 2014). While the studies of Phillips (1970) and Page (1972) seem to have attempted a general description of Jane Austen's language, their analyses still leave many specific aspects unanalysed. Cederlöf (1985) focuses on the structures discussed in this paper, but he only chooses some Austen novels and compares them with novels by other writers of the Late Modern English period. In a more recent analysis, Wijitsopon (2013) carries out a corpus-based study, focusing mainly on lexis, and exclusively on Jane Austen's six major novels. Tieken-Boon van Ostade (2014) concentrates on the study of the language of Jane Austen's letters. This is the most comprehensive

1. For practical reasons in the present study the examples have been extracted from electronic versions of the two editions of both the novels and the letters (see Section 2). This means that both types of texts went through an editing process. However, the editor of the letters is not expected to have altered grammatical features such as the ones analysed here, since the concern would probably be with the content rather than the grammatical forms, whereas the editors of the novels would have most likely adapted some linguistic features to fit the prescribed grammatical rules of the 18th and 19th century. Today, it is also possible to analyse the language of the novels and working drafts that Jane Austen wrote, but did not publish, since, as mentioned before, they have been collected in a digital collection in facsimiles (http://www.janeausten.ac.uk/index.html), which will contribute to more studies where the manipulation of editors would not have occurred at all.

study of this writer's letters so far, but, as the same scholar suggests, more studies are required to contribute to a better understanding of Jane Austen's usage of the language. For example, she indicates that "a closer comparative analysis of the novels in the light of what we now know about her private usage will (…) bring up more differences between the texts" (Tieken-Boon van Ostade, 2014: 230). Furthermore, it is also suggested that further studies will help to draw precise conclusions about her conservativeness when referring to her language use. In this respect, Tieken-Boon van Ostade refers to Rydén & Brorström's (1987) conclusions on Jane Austen's language regarding the use of *be* and *have* with perfective structures, which "should perhaps be revised" (Tieken-Boon van Ostade, 2014: 206), given the fact that other grammatical aspects do not appear to be conservative.

Regarding differences between the language Jane Austen uses in her novels and in her letters, there are contrasting opinions. Whereas Page (1972) states that important differences can be observed between one genre and the other, mainly in the sense that she uses colloquialisms in her letters and not in the novels, other researchers cannot conclude that the use of *be* or *have* as an auxiliary verb shows any "significant differences (…) between her letters and her novels" (Rydén & Brorström, 1987: 202).

In relation to the distribution of auxiliaries in Jane Austen's writings, according to Rydén & Brorström (1987), she uses *have* in perfective forms exclusively in grammatical structures that involve a conditional sentence or a verb in infinitive form, which, in their opinion, implies that she is a conservative writer in this respect. The reason which these two authors provide for her conservative use is Jane Austen's interest in using the English language correctly. Furthermore, the fact that her circle of acquaintances was small is also indicated as a possible factor for her conservative writing (Rydén & Brorström, 1987: 202). The analysis of all the syntactic structures in which the perfect tenses are used (e.g. if they appear in a particular type of sentences, such as the conditional sentences, or following a modal verb) is not the focus of this study, but it could be observed that Jane Austen used *have* in other structures apart from the ones indicated by Rydén & Brorström (1987).

Nevertheless, the implied conservative aspect of Jane Austen might not have been an exclusive individual characteristic of hers, but of the women writers of that time. Kytö (1997) points to a possible conservativeness of women writers in the 18th and 19th centuries in relation to the choice of auxiliary in perfective constructions, since her survey identifies that women in that period preferred to use *be* rather than *have*.[2] Kytö (1997: 59) also refers to "the presence of a complement" in a sentence as a reason to opt for the auxiliary *have*.

2. At present I am carrying a complementary study in which I am analysing the use of these auxiliaries by five women writers contemporary with Jane Austen. The results found so far confirm

Finally, even though it is not clear if Jane Austen had read the prescriptive grammar books of the time or not (Tieken-Boon van Ostade, 2014: 169), some studies suggest that she was probably following the rules of grammarians such as Dr. Johnson (Phillips, 1970: 151). This statement needs to be treated with some care, however, since the linguistic features in question might have been her editor's rather than her own, as suggested by Sutherland when she explains that "Gifford was a classical scholar known for being quite a pedant. He took Austen's English and turned it into something different – an almost Johnsonian, formal style" (Sutherland, as cited in Singh, 2010).

Despite the alleged lack of information about Jane Austen's familiarity with the grammar rules of the 18th century, both Dr. Johnson (1755) and Lowth (1763) refer to verbal forms including the verb *be* as an auxiliary verb. According to Lowth (1763: 67) "the neuter verb [...] admits in many instances of the passive form, retaining still the neuter signification; chiefly in such verbs as signify some sort of motion or change of place or condition". The examples he provides in relation to this explanation include "I am come" and "I was gone", which are considered passive forms, while the perfective forms are formed with the auxiliary *have*. As early as 1688, Miège already indicated that *be* was used as an auxiliary in combination with verbs such as *come, gone, arrived, returned, fallen, grown*, which happen to be some of the verbs that retained *be* for a longer time, and are analysed here.

Rydén & Brorström (1987) analysed a great number of grammar books of the time and concluded that the distribution of the uses of *be* and *have* is not present in all of those books. When it is present, the grammarians do not seem to show much opposition to the increasing usage of *have*, indicating that this topic does not seem to be of deep concern to them. However, they also find that Dr Johnson "recommends the use of *be* with (some) mutatives" (Rydén & Brorström, 1987: 202). Tieken-Boon van Ostade (2014) also states that the grammarians of the 18th century did not seem to pay much attention to the alternation between the uses of *be* and *have* in their prescription of grammatical rules. However, it is not unreasonable to think that if Miège already referred to this in the 17th century, there was something in these structures that aroused the attention of the grammarians, and it might have also been of interest for the editor(s) of Jane Austen's novels. Furthermore, if Dr Johnson's grammar is the one that seems to have influenced Jane Austen's novels the most, as indicated above, there may be reasons to think that the prescriptive rules could possibly have had an influence.

that there is a similar tendency in the choice of auxiliary and that they might have been both slightly more conservative than men, and influenced by the elements of the motion situation.

1.2 The present study

The present paper aims at analysing the use of the auxiliary verbs *be* and *have* in combination with the participial forms *arrived*, *become*, *come*, *entered*, *fallen*, *gone*, *got*, *grown*, *passed*, *returned* and *run* in perfective verbal forms, both in the letters and the novels written by Jane Austen. The reason for the choice of these eleven verbs lies in the fact that they were the most frequent verbs used in combination with *be* in Kytö's study (1997). Her list of these most frequent verbs also included *departed*, which did not occur in the two corpora used, however. Since Kytö's study encompassed a wide variety of authors, text types and periods of the language, the chosen set of verbs was expected to be sufficiently frequent in Jane Austen's texts as well.

While the verb *be* was the one chosen to create perfective verbal forms when the main lexical verb was a verb indicating motion in the older periods of the English language, the verb *have* was the auxiliary used in combination with the remaining verbs (Visser, 1973; Denison, 1993). However, the situation is different in present-day standard British English, where only the verb *have* is used to form the perfect tenses. It was precisely in the period in which Jane Austen wrote that the forms with *have* began to consolidate (Tieken-Boon van Ostade, 2009) and *be* remains today being used only in non-standard varieties of English (McCafferty, 2014) and in some fixed expressions (e.g. *he is gone*).

Different reasons justify the limitation of this study to one author and to a close set of lexical verbs. Focusing on some of the verbs that resisted the combination with *have* for a longer time, as well as in a specific writer, may contribute to learning about the reasons why these were more reluctant to admit the auxiliary verb *have* and if a particular author followed the tendency of the time or not. Moreover, the chosen author has not been studied in detail from a linguistic point of view and also, since both letters and novels written by her have been preserved, a comparison between the two types of genre can be carried out.

The analysis of these verbal structures might contribute to a clarification of whether Jane Austen's use of *be* was an indication of being conservative or whether, on the contrary, she was simply using the auxiliary verb that was common at the time. The similarities and/or differences shown in relation to the use of either auxiliary verb in her letters and novels could provide a new insight into these differences according to genres.

The main focus of this study lies in the analysis of the components of the motion situation involved in the perfective structures with the eleven lexical verbs chosen. Although all these verbs involve motion events, two groups can be established according to whether the idea of motion is more or less physical. The first group includes verbs that primarily refer to physical motion, that is *arrive*, *come*, *enter*, *fall*, *get*, *go*, *pass*, *return* and *run*, whereas the second group contains verbs whose meaning of motion is more metaphorical, specifically *become* and *grow*.[3]

As will be described below (see 1.3), these verbs are clear examples of verbs of motion, and the structures where they are present should incorporate a *figure*, that is, the object that moves and a *ground*, or the place to which the *figure* moves. The possible differences found in relation to these two basic components could explain the choice of auxiliary.

1.3 Basic motion situation

The research on perfect structures so far has not involved an insight into motion situations. However, motion situations have been the object of cognitive linguistics attention in the last decades, mainly since Talmy's description of lexicalization patterns (1987). These studies have concentrated on the description of the elements of motion situations (Talmy, 1975, 1987, 2000), in their connection with metaphorical contexts (Ramscar et al. 2009), and in the classification of languages in the world depending on the representation of the different components of the motion situation in the surface structure (Matsumoto, 1996; Slobin, 1996; Talmy, 2000).

A basic motion situation (see Figure 1) involves the following elements, the *figure*, or object that moves or is located somewhere; the *ground*, the place where the *figure* is moving to or where it is located; the *path*, which refers to the trajectory of the movement; and the *motion*, which could be represented either by a deep Be-located verb (e.g. *be*) or a deep Move verb such as *go* (Talmy, 2000).

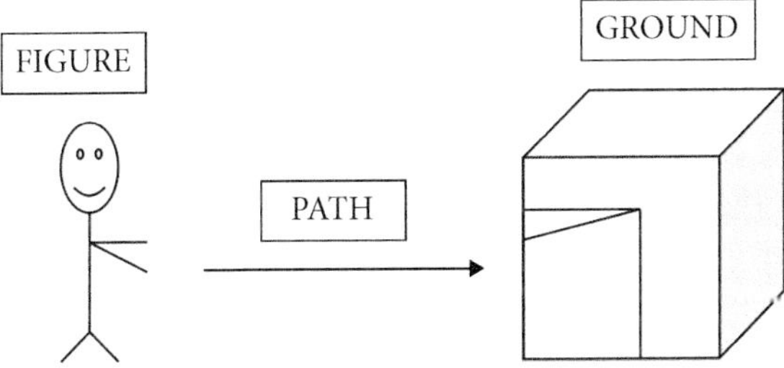

Figure 1. Basic motion situation

The verbs analysed in the present study are deep Move verbs, which means that their basic semantic meaning is one of movement, either physical (e.g. *come* or *run*) or metaphorical (e.g. *become* or *grow*). These other semantic components described

3. *Fall* and *get* can also be included in this subgroup, as they can also be used with a metaphorical meaning similar to *become*.

above may be present only in the deep structure or both in the deep structure and the surface structure, that is, they will always be implied in the semantics of the sentence (its deep structure), but will not always be represented in the syntactic realisation of the sentence (its surface structure). For instance, in "She is gone",[4] the *figure* (*she*) is present in the surface structure as well as in the deep structure, whereas the *path* and the *ground* are only interpreted as part of the deep structure, since there is a trajectory that *she* has followed and a location that *she* is in or is aiming to be in.

The analysis of these components in the instances found in the letters and in the novels will prove essential in order to understand the choice of the auxiliary. Therefore, the study will concentrate on the types of *figures* (human, for example, *she* in "she had gone to church"; or non-human, such as *the room* in "The room had then become useless"), the types of *ground* (physical, for instance, *Plymouth* in "The Laconia had come into Plymouth"; or abstract, as *misfortune* in "who had since fallen into misfortune"), the presence of *path* without an explicit *ground* (as, for example, in "the gentleman who is just gone away", where the reader does not know what the final destination of *the gentleman* is, since the *ground* is not found in the surface structure, and only the *path*, *away*, is present), and the absence of *ground* in the surface structure (as in "my trunk is come already", where the *ground* is interpreted as the place where the speaker is located, but is not present in the surface structure).

This interpretation can provide a richer analysis than studies concentrating exclusively on syntactic structures, as is the case with previous studies on the choice of auxiliaries in perfective structures with motion verbs or mutative verbs (see 1.1).

1.4 Hypotheses

Three hypotheses are suggested in this study. The first one refers to the differences predicted between the use of auxiliaries in the letters and in the novels. Jane Austen's usage of the auxiliary forms of *be* and *have* has been considered to be conservative, as mentioned before. If this is the case, the letters are expected to contain more perfect forms with the verb *be*, since they are a more personal type of text and would probably not have undergone much (if any) manipulation by editors or publishers in relation to grammatical features. In contrast, the possible changes in the editing process of the novels pointed out above may have included the alteration of grammatical structures to accommodate to the rules prescribed by grammarians.

The second hypothesis states that Jane Austen's novels would have followed more faithfully the grammar rules of the time than the letters, due to the more

4. All the examples provided in this and the following sections of this paper have been extracted from the two corpora used for the analysis (see Section 2).

familiar and informal style of the latter as opposed to the more formal and public character of the novels. This means that, as regards perfective structures, she would have used the auxiliary verbs that were suggested to be more appropriate in combination with one type of verb or another. Even though it cannot be proved if Jane Austen was familiar with the grammar books written in her lifetime, she had received some formal education before her teens (Le Faye, 1997; Grant, 2010; Warren, 2018), which implies that she would have been taught some grammar, as was common practice in schools at the time. In addition, she would have read books that her father kept, many of which he would have used for teaching (Corry, 2014). Furthermore, she was aware of the English novels written at the time by other authors, as evidenced by the presence of many titles of novels mentioned in *Northanger Abbey* (e.g. *The mysteries of Udolpho* or *Sir Charles Grandison*). It is, therefore, most likely that she would have received some information related to correct grammar usage, both directly in school and indirectly through her reading practices, and she would have wanted to keep a good writing style, which would guarantee better possibilities of publication of her work.

Thirdly, as mentioned before, there is a possibility that the different components of the motion situations could have influenced the author's choice of *be* or *have*. The main components of motion situations (see 1.3), *figure*, *ground*, *path* and *motion* are represented in the syntactic representation of the sentence by lexical elements that can be more or less physical. The more physical they are, the more likely the situation is expected to be represented by the verb *be*, since this is the verb that was traditionally used in combination with motion verbs. However, the more metaphorical they are, the more likely it is for the verb *have* to be used in combination with any of these verbs.

2. Method

In constructing the corpora, the novels were taken from one edition digitalized in the Gutenberg Project (2010), and the letters from the second edition by Chapman from 1952, taken from the *Oxford Text Archive*. The corpus of novels includes *Persuasion, Northanger Abbey, Mansfield Park, Emma, Lady Susan, Pride and Prejudice, Sense and Sensibility, Love and Friendship* and other early works, that is, most of her published works, and totalling 782,457 words. The corpus of letters contains 151,344 words in total. The disparity in numbers between the two corpora made it necessary to normalise the figures, as will be seen in the tables below. If both corpora were analysed together, the number would come to almost a million words, which is considered to be large enough to provide reliable results. However, as they are compared and analysed separately, the results found in the corpus of novels will produce more significant results than the results of the corpus of letters.

Despite this, some interesting trends can be traced in the comparison and they can contribute to encouraging further research, in which a larger sample including other authors might support the results of the present study.

The software *Antconc* was used to retrieve the occurrences from both corpora, which were then compiled in a document for analysis. Some instances were excluded from the analysis. These were cases that included the combination of the auxiliary verb *have* followed by the past participle form *got* meaning 'possession', as well as cases that contained the auxiliary verb *be* in a passive rather than a perfect construction. These were basically combinations with verbs such as *enter, passed* and *returned.*

3. Results

The total number of instances of perfective forms containing the eleven lexical verbs found in the letters is 193, whereas in the novels there are 819. Normalisation of these figures, as presented in Table 1 (see Appendix), shows that the apparent disparity of frequency mostly disappears.

As can be observed in Figure 2 (see Table 1 in appendix), when figures are normalised, there are in fact more instances of these participles in the letters than in the novels. This difference is not significant for the present study, since it is not the frequency of the lexical verbs that is being analysed or the use of the perfect structures, but the choice of auxiliary preceding the lexical verbs. Figure 3 (Table 2 in appendix) shows the distribution of occurrences in which the eleven participles appear, either preceded by *have* or *be* in the letters. Figure 4 (Table 3 in appendix)

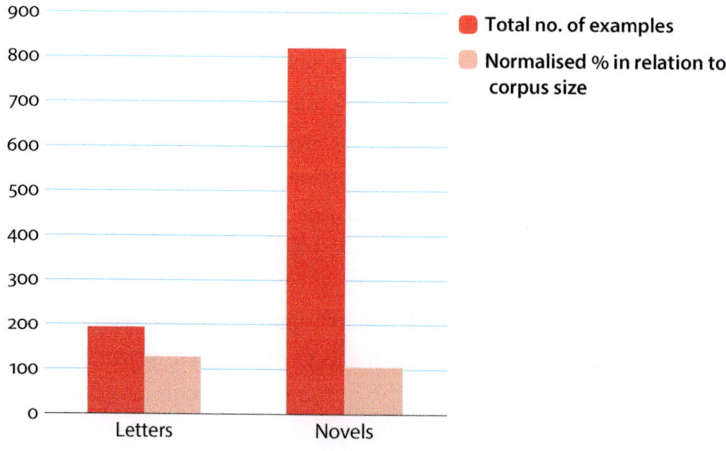

Figure 2. Total number of instances, including normalised figures (%)

contains the instances in which the participles are present in the novels with either auxiliary verb. As shown in the percentages, there is an appreciable difference in the choice of auxiliaries. Whereas *have* seems to be more common in the novels than in the letters, *be* is significantly the preferred option in the letters, with the exception of three verbs, *fall*, *get* and *pass*. Nevertheless, both types of texts display a far higher number of instances with *be* in general, with the exception of *enter*, *fall*, *pass* and *run*, which seem to prefer *have* in most or all cases. In addition, no examples of *run* in perfect forms were found in the letters.

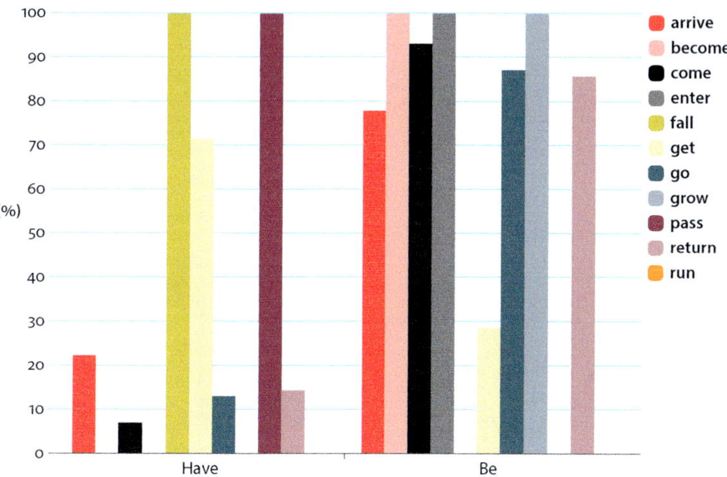

Figure 3. Distribution of instances in percentages of each verb in the letters

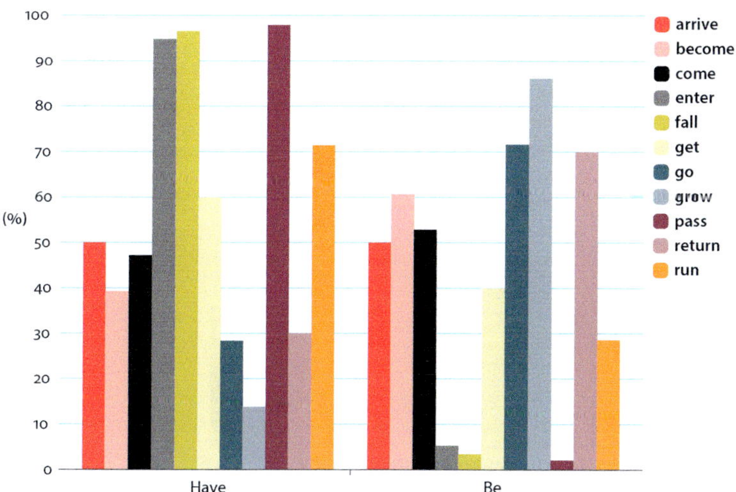

Figure 4. Distribution of instances in percentages of each verb in the novels

3.1 Motion situations in Jane Austen's letters

As can be observed in Figure 3 (Table 2 in appendix), *be* is the preferred auxiliary verb in perfect structures in most cases, except for the lexical verbs *fall*, *get* and *pass*. However, *have* is present in a notably lower number of examples in combination with the other verbs. Nevertheless, these results would not be complete without the analysis of the components of the motion situations, which are summarised in Figures 5, 6 and 7 (Tables 4, 5 and 6 in appendix).

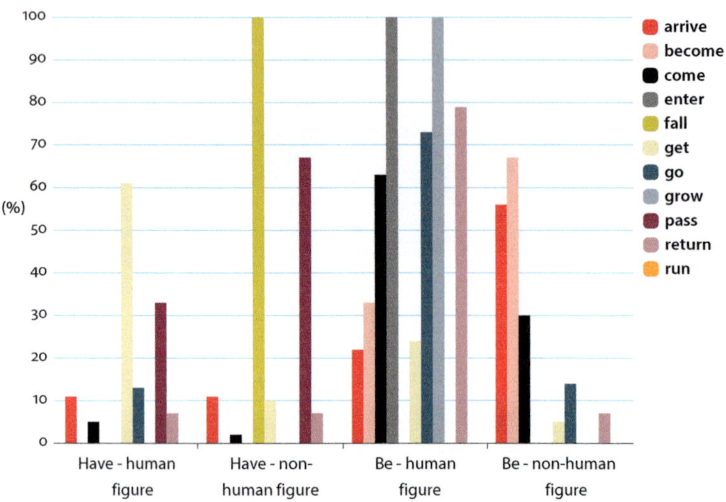

Figure 5. Types of *figure* in motion situations in Jane Austen's letters

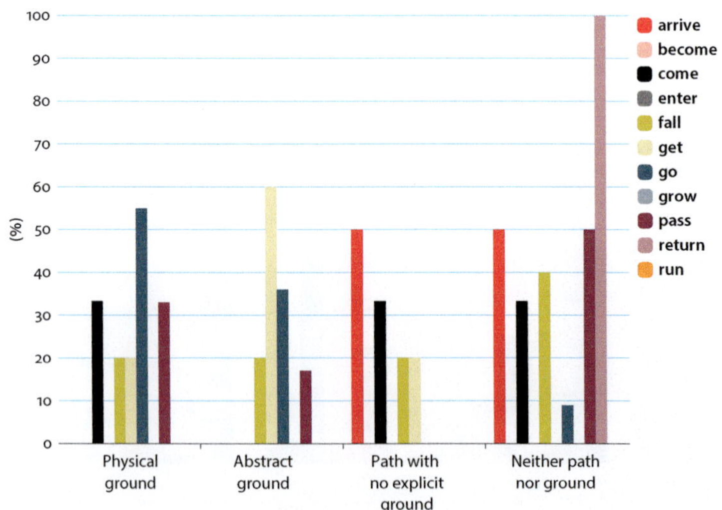

Figure 6. Types of *ground* and *path* in motion situations with auxiliary *have* in the letters

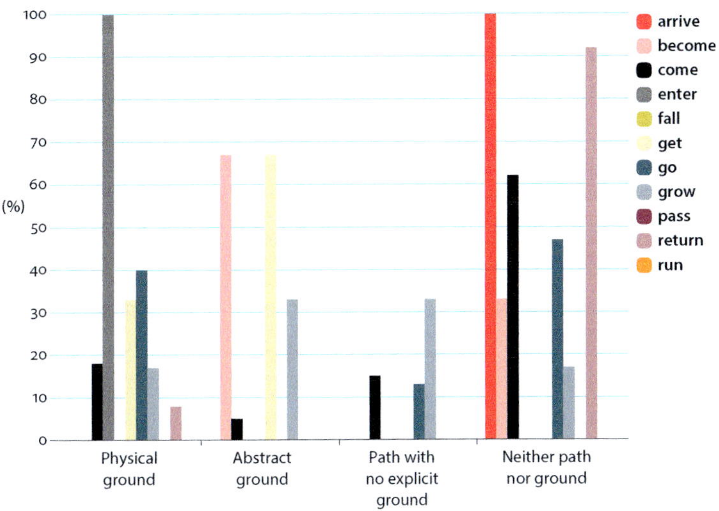

Figure 7. Types of *ground* and *path* in motion situations with auxiliary *be* in the letters

Given the lower number of examples of *have* compared to those with *be*, the results will, on some occasions, be either inconclusive or they will merely hint at tendencies. However, the comparison with the results found in the novels will provide a wider view of the use of the auxiliaries and it will allow drawing more accurate conclusions.

The distribution of figures seems fairly similar for both auxiliaries. However, it has to be remembered that there is an appreciably higher number of instances with *be* than with *have* (see Figure 3 or Table 2 in appendix). It is not surprising to find more human *figures* than non-human ones due to the intrinsic meaning of the lexical verbs involved. For this reason, the interest lies in the analysis of the non-human *figures* and, more specifically, of those examples where this type of *figure* is the predominant one. In the analysis of the *figures* with *have*, it can be observed that *fall* is only preceded by non-human *figures*, three of which are connected to the weather (e.g. "the little *snow* that had fallen") or to an object and the other two refer to situations (e.g. "*matters* have fallen out"). A similar verb is *pass*, in which case most of the *figures* are also non-human and refer either to time (e.g. "*three days and a half* which have passed") or to a situation (e.g. "after *all that* had passed"), both providing a more abstract context than a human *passing* somewhere. In contrast, the instances in which *be* is the auxiliary and the *figure* is non-human, these *figures* mainly refer to objects that people carry or move, such as *a letter*, *a note* or *parcels* in the case of the lexical verb *arrive* (e.g. "a very kind and feeling *letter* is arrived today"), whereas in the examples with *become* the non-human *figures* are a place, *London* (e.g. "*London* is become a hateful place to him"), or an abstract concept, *shyness*. As regards the examples of non-human *figures* with lexical verbs where the human *figures* are dominant, mainly *come*, *get* and *go*, the non-human *figures* are mostly something that people carry, such as *letters*, *a hamper of apples* and *a cough* (e.g. "my *letter* is gone"); only occasionally is there a physical object not moved by a person, like *the sun* (e.g. "*the sun* was got behind everything"); it is also unusual to find a more abstract *figure*, for example, one referring to time (e.g. "the *day* is come").

Figures 6 and 7 (Tables 5 and 6 in appendix) show the distribution of examples according to the *ground* and the *path* of the motion situation. Unfortunately, on many occasions there are very few instances in total, which does not contribute to achieving conclusive results. However, some general comments and ideas can be extracted from the data shown in both tables. First of all, it seems clear that the meaning of the verb and the type of *figure* determine in many cases the type of *ground* present in each given structure. Therefore, those verbs with a more metaphorical meaning of motion such as *become*, *get* and *grow* tend to prefer more abstract *grounds*. Secondly, the lack of explicit presence in the surface structure of either *ground* or *path* is more commonly the preferred option when the auxiliary verb is *be* rather than *have* although often the *ground* can be inferred from the lexical verb, as in the examples with *arrive*, *come*, *go* and *return*. Finally, most of the instances which contain the *path* without an explicit *ground* show a preference for an implied physical *ground*, which is not needed in the surface structure because of the meaning of the lexical verb.

3.2 Motion situations in Jane Austen's novels

As in the case of the letters, the analysis of the *figure* (Figure 8 and Table 7 in appendix) and the *ground* (Figures 9 and 10, and Tables 8 and 9 in appendix), two key components of the motion situation, will contribute to a better understanding of the results.

Human *figures* are dominant (see Figure 8, Table 7 in appendix), but the percentage of non-human *figures* is also high, particularly in some cases. Whilst all the verbs appear preceded by human *figures*, not all of them are realised by non-human *figures*, as is the case of *get*, where non-human *figures* are never present. In addition, although most verbs show a similar tendency in relation to the percentages both with human and non-human *figures*, there are two verbs which display a reverse situation, namely *become* and *grow*, which are two of the verbs that retained *be* longer.

The non-human *figures* include a variety of lexical items, such as *time, a carriage, conditions of the day, my heart, an event* or *a cake*. Both physical objects carried or moved by people (*a carriage* or *a cake*) and more abstract objects (*time* or *conditions of the day*) are found. There does not seem to be a tendency for one type or the other to prefer the combination with one type of auxiliary or another, with the exception of the verbs mentioned above (*become* and *grow*), which tend to opt

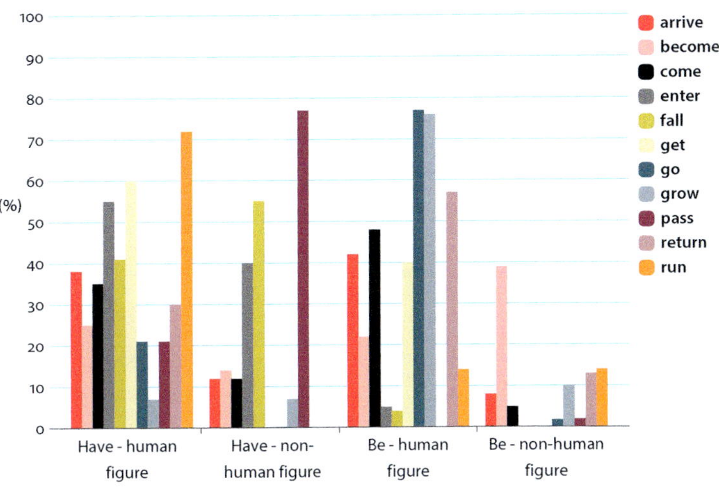

Figure 8. Types of *figure* in motion situations in Jane Austen's novels

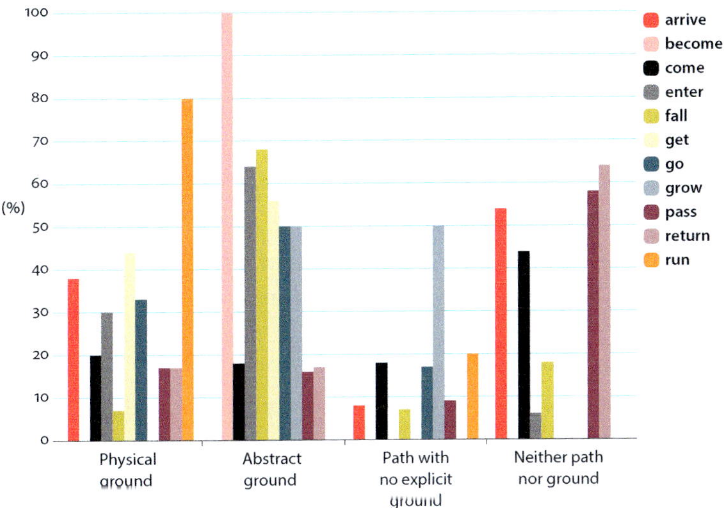

Figure 9. Types of *ground* and *path* in motion situations with auxiliary *have* in the novels

for *have* when the *figure* is human (e.g. "*she* too must have become indifferent to me" and "*Reginald* had not in any degree grown cold towards me") and *be* when it is non-human (e.g. "*the doubts and alarms* as to her conduct (…) were become of little consequence now" and "*the apricot* (…) which is now grown such a noble tree").

As in the case of the *figures*, most of the verbs seem to follow the same pattern with both auxiliaries, that is, they tend to prefer the same types of *grounds* (*path* or absence of both) independently of the auxiliary (see Figures 9 and 10, Tables 8

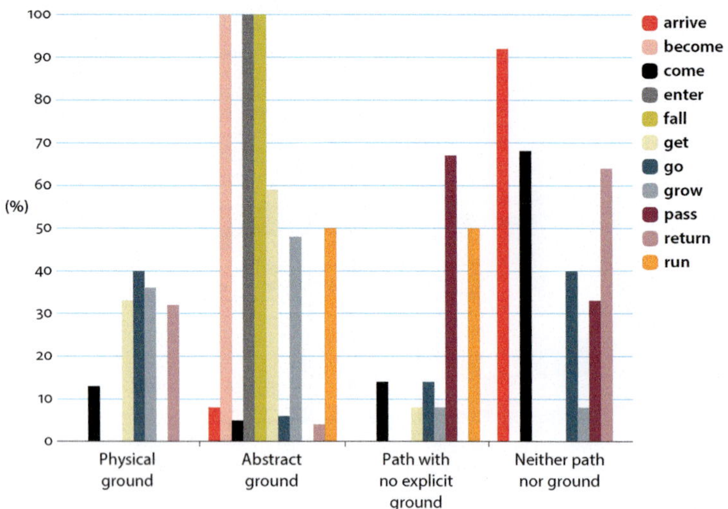

Figure 10. Types of *ground* and *path* in motion situations with auxiliary *be* in the novels

and 9 in appendix). Furthermore, when the number of instances is very low with one of the auxiliaries in opposition to the other (e.g. *enter*, *fall* or *pass* are much more often combined with *have* rather than with *be*), the comparison cannot be established in a conclusive way.

Nevertheless, there are a few verbs that do display some variation. The most significant one is *go*. Whereas no instances were found with *have gone* with the absence of *ground* in the surface structure, 40% of the occurrences of *be gone* belong to this category. Similarly, 56% of the instances with *have gone* are followed by an abstract *ground*, while only 6% contain the same type of *ground* in the *be gone* group. Other verbs that show a slightly different tendency are *arrive* and *run*. They are never used together with a physical *ground* with the auxiliary *be*; on the contrary, they seem commonly used in that context with the auxiliary *have*. Generally, there are more verbs that tend to opt for *have* when accompanied by a physical *ground*.

4. Letters versus novels

A comparison of the results found in the letters and in the novels certainly contributes to clarifying the uses of auxiliary verbs in perfect tenses. Despite the low figures of the occurrence which have been found in the letters and of some verbs, the normalization of the raw figures as well as the aspects analysed provide clearer insights into this situation.

As regards the *figure* element of motion situations, both in the letters and in the novels, human *figures* are the most common ones, with the exceptions of the *figures* accompanying the verbs *become*, *fall* and *pass* (see Tables 4 and 7). Even though both types of texts show a similar tendency, the novels present a higher number of human *figures* than the letters. This might be due simply to the topics discussed in one type of text or the other, rather than to any other linguistic factors. Also, it can be observed that whereas the auxiliary verb *be* seems to be more often present in motion situations with human *figures*, with the exception of the verb *become*, *have* shows more balance in this respect, with the exception of the verb *pass*, which both in the letters and the novels is used much more frequently with non-human *figures*. However, it is important to emphasise that the non-human *figures* show differences as well. Whereas the verb *be* seems to appear in combination with *figures* relating to objects that people carry or move, the verb *have* is more frequently found in slightly more abstract contexts (e.g. "forget *all that* has passed"). This is particularly found in the examples with *gone* (e.g. "*everything* has gone wrong"), which is the verb with the most instances and, therefore, the results can be regarded as more decisive. What is more, one of the verbs that show a reverse situation in the novels, *become*, also shows the same reverse situation in the letters.

In the analysis of the *ground* and *path* components, a similarity between the letters and the novels can also be seen. When the four tables are compared (see Appendix, Tables 5, 6, 8 and 9), the results stand out as being strikingly similar in some aspects and different in others. Despite the low number of instances of some verbs, the tendency in both types of texts is the same. First of all, some verbs show the same preference both in the letters and in the novels, for example, *become* is very often accompanied by abstract *grounds* independently of the auxiliary verb. Likewise, while *have* is often preferred when there is an abstract *ground* particularly in the novels, *be* is used very similarly with no explicit *ground* both in the letters and the novels. Similarly, whereas in the letters there seems to be a preference for not including the *ground* explicitly in the surface structure, this is also common in the novels, but with higher percentages of abstract *grounds* and physical *grounds*, very often accompanying *have*. The two verbs with a higher number of occurrences in total provide the most relevant results. *Come* displays a much more varied distribution of *grounds* in combination with *have*, than in combination with *be*, where the most common option is the absence of *ground* or *path*. In the case of *go*, whereas in the letters *go* seems to prefer combination with *have* if a physical or an abstract *ground* are present, *be* is the chosen auxiliary in the absence of an explicit *ground* or *path*. In the novels, *go* also prefers abstract *grounds* with *have* and the absence of *ground* or *path* with *be*.

5. Conclusion

The present study does confirm some conservativeness of Jane Austen writing in relation to the use of *be* or *have* as the auxiliary verb to express the perfect aspect. The tendency shown in her letters, albeit based on little data, points to a significant discrepancy in the use of both verbs, with the verb *be* being more frequent (see Figure 3 and Table 2). Whereas *have* is the preferred auxiliary verb with the verbs *fall, get* and *pass*, the remaining verbs (with the exception of *run* that displayed no hits), *arrive, become, come, enter, gone, grown* and *return* appear to prefer the combination with *be*. In her novels, despite the similarities found with the results in the letters, there is an increase in the use of *have* as an auxiliary verb (see Figure 4 and Table 3). It can be observed that there is a more balanced situation as regards the choice of auxiliary, with less drastic differences in proportions (e.g. in the letters *come* shows 7% of frequency with *have* and 93% with *be*, whereas in the novels these figures are 47% with *have* and 53% with *be*). In fact, five verbs seem to prefer *have* (*enter, fall, get, pass* and *run*) and five verbs opt for *be* more often (*become, come, go, grown* and *return*), while the verb *arrive* shows identical results for both auxiliaries. Interestingly, the verbs that appear more frequently combined with *be* include most of the verbs that Miège mentioned in his grammar (with the exception of *fall*), and they are also the ones that took longer to take the auxiliary *have*.

The increase in the use of *have* in the novels is probably justified by the fact that the editors might have changed some grammatical features in these texts before they were finally published or that the author herself might have been more conscious of her linguistic choices while writing. This consciousness could have been caused by her being in contact with the grammar rules of the time or simply by the presence of this type of structures in other novels of the time that she would have certainly been familiar with, as evidenced in *Northanger Abbey*. The fact that the grammarians of the time did not seem to be extremely concerned about the choice of the auxiliary in these particular verbal forms might lead one to conclude the latter as the more likely possibility. Nevertheless, before ruling out the editorial intervention as one possible factor, it needs to be considered that the alleged editor, William Gilford, has been described as a "pedant" by Sutherland (as cited in Singh, 2010), which points to the possibility that he might have applied the grammar rules that, despite not being of great concern for the grammarians, were in fact "recommended" by them.

Both types of texts, the letters and the novels, in fact show similar tendencies regarding the use of one auxiliary or the other, which may mean that Austen was not as conservative as may have been thought in previous studies. However, the slight increase of *have* in the novels might still point to a likely degree of conservatism.

As regards the influence of the components of motion situations, the analysis indicates that together with the influence of the grammarians through the editor, the choice of auxiliary verb may have been caused by these components to a certain extent. The figures show a very similar distribution both in the letters and in the novels in the sense that some verbs show preferences for one particular auxiliary verb or the other, which is also conditioned by the type of *figure*, either human or non-human. Not only does the type of *figure* seem to condition the presence of one or the other auxiliary verb, but also the semantic content of the non-human *figures* appears to have a slight effect on the choice of the auxiliary, *figures* referring to something that people carry tend to appear more often in combination with *be*, while *have* is the preferred option for more abstract *figures*. The *figure* may have, therefore, influenced the choice of auxiliary slightly. Also, the *ground* and the *path* on its own have proved to be influential components in this choice. The presence of a *ground* in the surface structure seems to condition the use of *have* as opposed to *be*. In a similar way, the absence of a *ground* or a *path* is often seen to appear in combination with *be*. However, it is also important to notice that abstract *grounds* also combine with *be*, particularly in the case of the verbs *become*, *get* and *grow*, which usually imply a more abstract type of movement. Although the presence of a complement in a sentence had been identified as one of the reasons contributing to the use of *have* (Kytö, 1997), the results shown in relation to the concept of *ground* are different. First, the complement is a syntactic concept and it is only present in the surface structure, whereas the *ground* is a semantic one, which also encompasses differences, that is, a *ground* may be present in the surface structure or not, and it may also be more or less physical or abstract. In addition, the *path* component is also determinant in some cases for the choice of the auxiliary. Therefore, both the *ground* and the *path* appear to influence to some extent the type of auxiliary used.

The limitation of this study to one writer is not enough to conclude that motion situations would have been the main driving force to opt for one auxiliary or another in the creation of the perfect tenses. Nevertheless, it offers the possibility of taking this factor into consideration when analysing these structures in a broader context, that is, with more lexical verbs and more authors.

In future studies, the analysis will be expanded to include more verbs as well as a comparison of different writers – some of them are already being analysed (see footnote 4) – in order to obtain an accurate result of the uses of these two auxiliaries to form perfect tenses in the Late Modern English period, the time when *have* is supposed to have extended its uses to combine with all lexical verbs.

References

Anderwald, Lieselotte (2014). The Decline of the Be-perfect, Linguistic Relativity, and Grammar Writing in the Nineteenth Century. In Marianne Hundt (Ed.), *Late Modern English Syntax* (13–37). Cambridge: Cambridge University Press. https://doi.org/10.1017/CBO9781139507226.004

Austen, Jane (2010). *The Complete Works of Jane Austen*. Ed. by David Widger. Project Gutenberg. *Retrieved from* www.gutenberg.org.

Barber Charles, Beal, Joan C., & Shaw, Philip A. (2011). *The English Language. A Historical Introduction*. (2nd ed.). Cambridge: Cambridge University Press.

Beal, Joan C. (2004). *English in Modern Times*. London: Arnold.

Cederlöf, M. (1985). *Be and Have as Perfect Auxiliaries with Mutative Verbs in Some Novels by Jane Austen, Charles Dickens and George Eliot*. University of Stockholm (mimeographed).

Chapman, Robert W. (1952). *Jane Austen's Letters To Her Sister Cassandra and Others*, 1796–1817, 2nd ed. London: Oxford University.

Corry, Pearl (2014, January, 10). *The Education of Jane and Cassandra*. Retrieved from: https://byuprideandprejudice.wordpress.com/2014/01/21/the-education-of-jane-and-cassandra-austen/

Denison, David (1993). *Historical English Syntax*. London: Longman.

Denison, David (1998). Syntax. In Suzanne Romaine (Ed.), *The Cambridge History of the English Language*, (Vol. 4, 1776–1997, 92–329). Cambridge: Cambridge University Press.

Grant, T (2010, September, 20). *Jane Austen Went to School*. Retrieved from: https://janeaustensworld.wordpress.com/2010/09/20/jane-austen-went-to-school/

Johnson, Samuel (1755). *A Dictionary of the English Language*. London: Times Books Ltd.

Kytö, Merja (1997). Be/have + past participle: The choice of the auxiliary with intransitives from Late Middle to Modern English. In Matti Rissanen, Merja Kytö, & Kirsi Heikkonen (Eds.), *English in transition: Corpus-based studies in Linguistic Variation and Genre Styles* (17–84). Berlin: Mouton de Gruyter. https://doi.org/10.1515/9783110811148.17

Le Faye, Deirdre (1997). Chronology of Jane Austen's life. In Edward Copeland, & Juliet McMaster (Eds.), *The Cambridge Companion to Jane Austen* (1–11). Cambridge: Cambridge University Press. https://doi.org/10.1017/CCOL0521495172.001

Lowth, Robert (1763). *A Short Introduction to English Grammar*. (2nd ed.). London.

Matsumoto, Yo (1996). Subjective motion and English and Japanese verbs, *Cognitive Linguistics* 7, 138–226. https://doi.org/10.1515/cogl.1996.7.2.183

McCafferty, Kevin (2014) '[W]ell, are you not got over thinking about going to Ireland yet': the Be-perfect in Eighteenth and Nineteenth century Irish English. In Marianne Hundt (Ed.), *Late Modern English Syntax* (13–37). Cambridge: Cambridge University Press. https://doi.org/10.1017/CBO9781139507226.025

Miège, Guy (1688). *The English Grammar*. London.

Page, Norman (1972). *The Language of Jane Austen*. Oxford: Basil Blackwell.

Phillips, K. C. (1970). *Jane Austen's English*. London: Andre Deutsh.

Quirk, Randolph, Greenbaum, Sidney, Leech, Geoffrey, & Svartvik, Jan (1985). *A Comprehensive Grammar of the English Language*. London: Longman.

Ramscar, Michael, Matlock, Teenie, & Boroditsky, Lera (2009). Time, motion and meaning: the experiential basis of abstract thought. In Kelly S. Mix, Linda B. Smith, & Michael Gasser (Eds.), *The Spatial Foundations of Language and Cognition* (67–82). Oxford: Oxford University Press. https://doi.org/10.1093/acprof:oso/9780199553242.003.0004

Rydén, Mats, & Brorstöm, Sverker (1987). *The Be/Have Variation with Intransitives in English.* Stockholm: Almqvist & Wiksell International.

Singh, A (2010, October, 22). *Jane Austen's famous prose may not be hers after all.* Retrieved from: https://www.telegraph.co.uk/culture/culturenews/8080832/Jane-Austens-famous-prose-may-not-be-hers-after-all.html

Slobin, Dan I. (1996). Two ways to travel: Verbs of Motion in English and Spanish. In Masayoshi Shibatani, & Sandra A. Thompson (Eds.), *Grammatical Constructions* (195–219). Oxford: Clarendon Press.

Sutherland, Kathryn (2012). Jane Austen's dealings with John Murray and his firm, *RES The Review of English Studies* 64(263), 105–126. https://doi.org/10.1093/res/hgs020

Talmy, Leonard (1975). Semantics and Syntax of motion. In John P. Kimbali (Ed.), *Syntax and Semantics* (Vol. 4, 181–238). Nueva York: Academic Press.

Talmy, Leonard (1987). Lexicalization Patterns: Semantic Structure in Lexical Forms. In Timothy Shopen (Ed.), *Language Typology and Syntactic Description* (57–149). Cambridge: Cambridge University Press.

Talmy, Leonard (2000). *Towards a Cognitive Linguistics.* Vols. 1 & 2. Cambridge: MIT Press.

Tieken-Boon van Ostade, Ingrid (2009). *An Introduction to Late Modern English.* Edinburgh: Edinburgh University Press

Tieken-Boon van Ostade, Ingrid (2014). *In search of Jane Austen: The Language of the Letters.* Oxford: Oxford University Press. https://doi.org/10.1093/acprof:oso/9780199945115.001.0001

Visser, Fredericus Th., (1973). *An Historical Syntax of the English Language.* I-III. Leiden: E. J. Brill.

Warren, Renee (2018, April, 10). *Jane Austen Life Timeline.* Retrieved from: https://www.janeausten.org/jane-austen-timeline.asp

Wijitsopon, Raksangob (2013). A Corpus-based Study of the Style in Jane Austen's Novels. *MANUSYA: Journal of Humanities* 16(1), 41–64.

Appendix

Table 1. (Figure 2, including the total number of words corresponding to each corpus) Total number of words and instances, including normalised figures (%)

	Total number of words	Total number of instances
Letters	151,344	193 (0.127%)
Novels	782,457	819 (0.105%)

Table 2. Distribution of instances and percentages of each verb in the letters

	Have	**Be**
Arrive	2 (22.22%)	7 (77.77%)
Become	0	3 (100%)
Come	3 (6.98%)	40 (93.02%)
Enter	0	1 (100%)
Fall	5 (100%)	0
Get	15 (71.43%)	6 (28.57%)
Go	11 (12.94%)	74 (87.06%)
Grow	0	6 (100%)
Pass	6 (100%)	0
Return	2 (14.29%)	12 (85.71%)
Run	0	0

Table 3. Distribution of instances and percentages of each verb in the novels

	Have	**Be**
Arrive	13 (50%)	13 (50%)
Become	11 (39.29%)	17 (60.71%)
Come	50 (47.17%)	56 (52.83%)
Enter	36 (94.74%)	2 (5.26%)
Fall	28 (96.55%)	1 (3.45%)
Get	18 (60%)	12 (40%)
Go	98 (28.41%)	247 (71.59%)
Grow	4 (13.79%)	25 (86.21%)
Pass	138 (97.87%)	3 (2.13%)
Return	12 (30%)	28 (70%)
Run	5 (71.43%)	2 (28.57%)

Table 4. *Figure* in motion situations in Jane Austen's letters

	Have Human *figure*	*Have* Non-human *figure*	*Be* Human *figure*	*Be* Non-human *figure*
Arrive	1 (11%)	1 (11%)	2 (22%)	5 (56%)
Become	0	0	1 (33%)	2 (67%)
Come	2 (5%)	1 (2%)	27 (63%)	13 (30%)
Enter	0	0	1 (100%)	0
Fall	0	5 (100%)	0	0
Get	13 (61%)	2 (10%)	5 (24%)	1 (5%)
Go	11 (13%)	0	62 (73%)	12 (14%)
Grow	0	0	6 (100%)	0
Pass	2 (33%)	4 (67%)	0	0
Return	1 (7%)	1 (7%)	11 (79%)	1 (7%)
Run	0	0	0	0

Table 5. *Ground* and *path* in motion situations with auxiliary *have* in the letters

	Physical *ground*	Abstract *ground*	*Path* with no explicit *ground*	Neither *ground* nor *path*
Arrive	0	0	1 (50%)	1 (50%)
Become	0	0	0	0
Come	1 (33.3)	0	1 (33.3%)	1 (33.3%)
Enter	0	0	0	0
Fall	1 (20%)	1 (20%)	1 (20%)	2 (40%)
Get	3 (20%)	9 (60%)	3 (20%)	0
Go	6 (55%)	4 (36%)	0	1 (9%)
Grow	0	0	0	0
Pass	2 (33%)	1 (17%)	0	3 (50%)
Return	0	0	0	2 (100%)
Run	0	0	0	0

Table 6. *Ground* and *path* in motion situations with auxiliary *be* in the letters

	Physical *ground*	Abstract *ground*	*Path* with no explicit *ground*	Neither *ground* nor *path*
Arrive	0	0	0	7 (100%)
Become	0	2 (67%)	0	1 (33%)
Come	7 (18%)	2 (5%)	6 (15%)	25 (62%)
Enter	1 (100%)	0	0	0
Fall	0	0	0	0
Get	2 (33%)	4 (67%)	0	0
Go	30 (40%)	0	9 (13%)	35 (47%)
Grow	1 (17%)	2 (33%)	2 (33%)	1 (17%)
Pass	0	0	0	0
Return	1 (8%)	0	0	11 (92%)
Run	0	0	0	0

Table 7. *Figure* in motion situations in Jane Austen's novels

	Have Human *figure*	*Have* Non-human *figure*	*Be* Human *figure*	*Be* Non-human *figure*
Arrive	10 (38%)	3 (12%)	11 (42%)	2 (8%)
Become	7 (25%)	4 (14%)	6 (22%)	11 (39%)
Come	37 (35%)	13 (12%)	51 (48%)	5 (5%)
Enter	21 (55%)	15 (40%)	2 (5%)	0
Fall	12 (41%)	16 (55%)	1 (4%)	0
Get	18 (60%)	0	12 (40%)	0
Go	65 (21%)	1(0.2%)	239 (77%)	8 (1.8%)
Grow	2 (7%)	2 (7%)	22 (76%)	3 (10%)
Pass	30 (21%)	108 (77%)	0	3 (2%)
Return	12 (30%)	0	23 (57%)	5 (13%)
Run	5 (72%)	0	1 (14%)	1 (14%)

Table 8. *Ground* and *path* in motion situations with auxiliary *have* in the novels

	Physical *ground*	Abstract *ground*	*Path* with no explicit *ground*	Neither *ground* nor *path*
Arrive	5 (38%)	0	1 (8%)	7 (54%)
Become	0	11 (100%)	0	0
Come	10 (20%)	9 (18%)	9 (18%)	22 (44%)
Enter	11 (30%)	23 (64%)	0	2 (6%)
Fall	2 (7%)	19 (68%)	2 (7%)	5 (18%)
Get	8 (44%)	10 (56%)	0	0
Go	32 (33%)	49 (50%)	17 (17%)	0
Grow	0	2 (50%)	2 (50%)	0
Pass	23 (17%)	22 (16%)	13 (9%)	80 (58%)
Return	2 (17%)	2 (17%)	0	8 (64%)
Run	4 (80%)	0	1 (20%)	0

Table 9. *Ground* and *path* in motion situations with auxiliary *be* in the novels

	Physical *ground*	Abstract *ground*	*Path* with no explicit *ground*	Neither *ground* nor *path*
Arrive	0	1 (8%)	0	12 (92%)
Become	0	17 (100%)	0	0
Come	7 (13%)	3 (5%)	8 (14%)	38 (68%)
Enter	0	2 (100%)	0	0
Fall	0	1 (100%)	0	0
Get	4 (33%)	7 (59%)	1 (8%)	0
Go	100 (40%)	12 (6%)	35 (14%)	100 (40%)
Grow	9 (36%)	12 (48%)	2 (8%)	2 (8%)
Pass	0	0	2 (67%)	1 (33%)
Return	9 (32%)	1 (4%)	0	18 (64%)
Run	0	1 (50%)	1 (50%)	0

Signs of grammaticalization

Tracking the GET-passive through COHA

Sarah Schwarz

In this study, I examine a large number of GET-passives from different genres and time periods in the *Corpus of Historical American English* for signs of grammaticalization by looking for evidence of semantic bleaching and morphosyntactic generalization. A comparable set of BE-passives is included as a control group throughout. The study shows a dramatic increase in the frequency of central GET-passives between the 1870s and the 1990s. Changes in situation type, subject type, and range of past-participle collocates, which are traced through all four genres in the corpus, provide further indications that the GET-passive is continuing to grammaticalize over the period.

Keywords: GET-passive, grammaticalization, semantic bleaching, morphosyntactic generalization, situation type

1. Introduction

1.1 Aim and scope

In this study, I make use of material from the *Corpus of Historical American English* (COHA) (Davies, 2010) to track changes in the use of the GET-passive, as in *she got arrested*. The aim of the paper is to study the development of central GET-passives across over one hundred years in different written genres of American English for signs of the kind of semantic bleaching and morphosyntactic generalization associated with the process of grammaticalization as the construction increases in frequency. Changes in the GET-passive are compared to changes in the BE-passive (as in *she was arrested*) throughout.

https://doi.org/10.1075/cilt.346.10sch

1.2 Grammaticalization and the GET-passive

Grammaticalization is the process by which a word or phrase undergoes a shift from a more lexical function to a more grammatical one (Hopper, 1991; Hopper & Traugott, 1993, 2003). The process of grammaticalization usually entails phonetic reduction and so-called semantic bleaching, which is a term for the "loss" of full lexical semantics and establishment of a more purely syntactic function, at least in certain contexts.[1] One of the classic examples of this is the *going to* future (see e.g. Hopper & Traugott, 1993: 82–84; 2003: 87–93), where the original motion sense was lost in some contexts (*I'm going to go to the store*) and a future-marking function established.

The GET-passive is a grammaticalized construction that has likely been undergoing further grammaticalization in recent years. An indication of this is the dramatic increase in frequency that it displays in the latter half of the 20th century, especially in American English (Mair, 2006; Leech et al., 2009; Schwarz, 2017). When a form undergoes semantic bleaching, it also becomes generalized to new morphosyntactic environments (Hopper & Traugott, 2003: 104), effectively increasing the number of contexts where it can be used and thus its frequency. However, while language corpora like COHA provide valuable natural language material from which empirical conclusions can more replicably be drawn, the frequency changes that we see in written material probably lag behind changes that are already well-established in spontaneous spoken language (see Mair, 2011: 244–245).

GET-passives in standardized written English are probably a particularly good example of this kind of corpus lag. The GET-passive is practically infamous for its association with spoken language, and Biber et al. (1999: 476) actually found that the GET-passive was almost exclusively attested in conversation in their *Longman Corpus*. The association of the GET-passive with informal, spoken language is further supported by a quick search of GET + past participle in the conversation section of the *British National Corpus* (accessed through the BYU interface, Davies, 2004), at 314.64 instances per million words (pmw), and in the Spoken (not conversation) section of the *Corpus of Contemporary American English* (Davies, 2008), at 264.51 instances pmw.[2] This can be compared to only 169.31 instances pmw in the 2000s in

1. Phonetic reduction will not be considered in this investigation of written data.

2. While it may seem surprising that the older data from the British National Corpus (BNC) contain a higher normalized frequency of GET + past participle than the newer data from the Corpus of Contemporary American English (COCA), an anonymous reviewer points out that this discrepancy actually only further highlights the association of the GET-passive with informal spoken language, as the COCA data come from radio and television broadcasts and the BNC data from casual conversation.

COHA, where only written language, but from a wider diachronic span, is included. Mair (2006: 113), Leech et al. (2009: 156), and Schwarz (2017: 314) have found increasing frequencies of GET-passives in written American English, especially in newspaper writing from the latter half of the 20th century, and have suggested that this increase is due to "colloquialization", a process by which spoken-language features are increasingly accepted in written genres (see Siemund, 1995: 357; Mair & Hundt, 1995: 118 and Mair, 1997: 203–205). It is thus likely that any changes in the use of GET-passives in COHA are traces of changes that had already taken place in spoken American English.

1.3 Parameters investigated in the present study

As a first step, the normalized frequency of GET-passives across four time periods and four genres in COHA is estimated (Sections 2.3 and 3.1). The data are then examined for signs of the semantic bleaching or morphosyntactic generalization that would signify that further grammaticalization is occurring. Specifically, the GET-passives in the collected data are examined by *situation type* (3.2), *subject type* (3.3), and by *past participle* (3.4).

One famous characteristic of the GET-passive which is *not* pursued in the present study is adversativity (Chappell, 1980; Haegeman, 1985; Givón & Yang, 1994; Carter & McCarthy, 1999; Leech et al., 2009). Adversativity means that what happens to the subject of a GET-passive is likely to be undesirable, as in *he got shot* or *she got fired*. However, recent work (e.g. Schwarz, 2015) has shown that GET-passives are also commonly found in *benefactive* contexts as in the examples *get paid* and *get promoted*. The GET-passive is thus not so much adversative as non-neutral, and studies have shown that the non-neutral restriction still holds (Leech et al., 2009: 156). Therefore, the GET-passive cannot yet be said to be undergoing semantic bleaching on this parameter.

The subject of a GET-passive is also supposed to bear some responsibility for whatever is happening to it (Lakoff, 1971). In a sentence like *he got shot*, subject responsibility would imply that the passive subject *he* has, at least to some degree, done something to bring the shooting upon himself. If the GET-passive is grammaticalizing further, we would expect to find fewer GET-passives over time that involve a sense of subject responsibility. Because of the inherent subjectivity involved in classifying sentences for subject responsibility, in this study, the focus is on whether or not the GET-passives are used with human subjects. Since human subjects will be more likely to be agentive and responsible for what is happening to them, this parameter may shed indirect light on subject agentivity.

While various suggestions have been made as to the origins and development of the GET-passive (Givón & Yang, 1994; Gronemeyer, 1999: 29; Hundt, 2001), Fleisher

(2006) has recently convincingly demonstrated that it does not originate in reflexive constructions like *he got himself fired*, but instead in GET + adjective constructions like *she got sick*. The GET-passive still shows traces of these origins in that it is often found in inchoative, change-of-state uses like *get fired* and *get appointed*. In a recent study (Schwarz, 2017: 321–323), I found that GET-passives favor the situation type Transitional Act, as in *he got killed* or *they got chosen*, which makes good sense considering their adjectival origins. However, in the most recent data, the Transitional Act situation type was no more frequent than the Accomplishment type, as in *the car got repaired*. This possible sign of morphosyntactic generalization will be further pursued across a wider diachronic stretch and across genres in the present study.

The final parameter in focus in this paper involves the past participles that occur with GET and BE in the data. It is hypothesized that morphosyntactic generalization of the GET-passive will allow for use with an increasingly wide range of past participles over time.

A central research question throughout the paper is the effect of genre on the development of the GET-passive. It is likely that genres will differ in their acceptance of the construction, and genre variation should provide valuable clues to the spread of the construction through stylistically different text-types.

2. Material and methods

2.1 COHA

Because the GET-passive is relatively rare in written language, a very large corpus is desirable. As Leech et al. (2009: 156) have shown that the GET-passive seems to be making inroads into written American English, that variety is a logical place to look for signs of grammaticalization. COHA, which contains over 400 million words of written, part-of-speech-tagged American English, fulfils both the size and dialect desiderata for this study. The corpus also covers a sufficient time span (from the 1810s up until the 2000s) and includes four genres (fiction, popular magazines, newspapers, and non-fiction books), enabling genre comparison.

The decade and genre samples of COHA are not evenly balanced; for instance, around 50% of the corpus consists of fiction texts, and there are no newspaper texts for the 1810s–1850s. Frequencies from decades and genres are therefore normalized per million words where compared in the study. Due to the dearth of data in the earlier decades, the present study begins in the 1870s and continues at forty-year intervals, thus including the 1870s, 1910s, 1950s, and 1990s. Even so, the earlier decades sometimes contain so little data, especially from Newspapers and Popular magazines, that results should sometimes be interpreted with extra caution, as in Section 3.3.

2.2 Data selection and retrieval

COHA's size presents both an advantage and a challenge. There are tens of thousands of instances of BE + past participle per decade, and it was necessary to perform manual analyses of randomized subsets of data and extrapolate normalized frequencies based on the percentages of those sets which qualified as passives. In order to find potential GET- and BE-passives in the four decades selected for analysis, the following search was performed:

> the lemma of GET/BE + (optional adverb) + past participle

Ideally, 200 randomized tokens of GET/BE + (adverb) + past participle from each genre and decade were collected. Wherever there were fewer than 200 search returns for GET, all instances were harvested for further study. In order to maximize comparability between the GET and BE data sets, certain sentences were eliminated prior to further analysis. The so-called GET-passive is problematic in that GET does not behave like a true auxiliary. For one thing, GET cannot function as an operator in questions and in negative statements (**got she shot? *no, she got not shot*).[3] This means that questions and negative statements were retrieved for GET, but not for BE, because only GET remains adjacent to the past participle when auxiliary DO is used.[4] Therefore, all tokens in which GET was used in questions (*did she get shot?*) or in negation (*she didn't get shot*), where they would not have been retrieved with BE, were removed from the database. The distribution of tokens from each decade and genre which were manually analyzed after the sets had been balanced is found in Table 1.

Table 1. Make-up of the datasets gathered from COHA for manual analysis

Genre	1870s		1910s		1950s		1990s		Total
	BE	GET	BE	GET	BE	GET	BE	GET	
Fiction	200	200	200	200	200	200	200	200	1600
Magazines	200	133	200	187	200	200	200	200	1520
Newspapers	200	35	200	29	200	88	200	200	1152
Non-fiction	200	94	200	129	200	99	200	136	1258
Total	800	462	800	545	800	587	800	736	5530

3. For more on the dubious status of GET as a passive auxiliary, see Section 2.2 and Haegeman (1985), Quirk et al. (1985: 160–161), Gronemeyer (1999: 17), Fleisher (2006: 227–228) and Leech et al. (2009: 145), among others.

4. The corpus tagger does not recognize *not* as an adverb.

As previously stated, it is important that what is said about the GET-passive in this study is considered against a control group of BE-passives, for at least two reasons. First, although the constructions are different in terms of frequency, style, and semantics, they perform the same basic information-structuring function; second, the BE-passive, as the more established, neutral expression, may set the standard for what can be considered canonical for passives in English.

2.3 Classification of passives in the data sets

Using Quirk et al.'s "passivity gradient" (1985: 167–171) as a guide, I assigned each token in Table 1 to one of three categories: central passive, semipassive, or pseudo-passive.[5] Central passives are those where only a verbal reading of the past participle is possible, as in Examples (1) and (2).

(1) For leaping the city wall, Remus *got killed* by Romulus. (COHA Fiction 1990s)

(2) It may here *be incidentally remarked*, that the other Asiatic kingdoms also reach a high antiquity. (COHA Non-fiction books 1950s)

For semipassives, the past participle is ambiguously verbal/adjectival, as in (3) and (4).

(3) "I love the sport, but I'm beginning to *get frustrated* because of the business side of it," says Johnson. (COHA Newspapers 1990s)

(4) The path soon became wider; we were now scarcely two hundred paces from the hut, and we *were astonished* not to hear the barking of dogs, which generally prowl round an Indian's dwelling. (COHA Non-fiction books 1870s)

Based on the proportions of central passives and semipassives in the data, it was possible to extrapolate normalized frequencies of each. Both central passives and semipassives, as in (1)–(4), were of potential interest in this study. Semipassives are probable predecessors of central GET-passives: GET + adjective is known to be the construction from which the verbal GET-passive is descended (Fleisher, 2006), so the ambiguous verbal/adjectival nature of semipassives may have laid the groundwork for the central GET-passive. Pseudopassives, on the other hand, which bear only a surface resemblance to passives, were not considered further. Examples of pseudopassives are given in (5) and (6).

5. For a detailed list of the exact criteria, based entirely on Quirk et al. (1985: 167–171), that were used to assign tokens to the three categories, see Schwarz (2015: 158–159; 2017: 311–312).

(5) He *was slumped* behind a mountainous deskload of papers, bound (literally) in red tape. (COHA Magazines 1950s)

(6) "Hi-ya!" exploded Jess. Then added: "Come' long, babies, an' *git dressed up*. Yo' all's gwine git yo' summons up yonder presen'ly." (COHA Fiction 1910s)

The number and percentage of constructions in the collected data sets for each of the categories central, semi-, and pseudopassive are given in Tables 2 and 3 for GET and BE, respectively. These percentages were used to extrapolate the normalized frequencies in Section 3.1.

Table 2. Central, semi- and pseudopassives in the GET data set*
Chi-square = 149; d.f. = 6; $p < 0.001$

	1870s		1910s		1950s		1990s		Total	
central	87	19%	117	21%	160	27%	337	46%	701	30%
semi	35	8%	38	7%	35	6%	63	9%	171	7%
pseudo	340	74%	390	72%	391	67%	336	46%	1457	63%
Total	462	100%	545	100%	586	100%	736	100%	2329	100%

* Tables 6–13 in the appendix show the results of centrality coding for each genre.

Table 3. Central, semi- and pseudopassives in the BE data set
Chi-square = 27.8; d.f. = 6; $p < 0.001$

	1870s		1910s		1950s		1990s		Total	
central	629	79%	604	76%	625	78%	555	69%	2413	75%
semi	54	7%	50	6%	40	5%	71	9%	215	7%
pseudo	115	14%	146	18%	135	17%	174	22%	570	18%
Total	798	100%	800	100%	800	100%	800	100%	3198	100%

As expected based on previous studies, there is a highly significant difference in the proportions of central passives between the GET and BE data sets, with only 30% of total instances qualifying as central passives in the GET set (see Table 2) and 75% central passives overall in the BE set (Table 3). Also unsurprisingly, the proportion of GET-passives which qualify as central passives increases fairly drastically over time (Table 2);[6] in Section 3.1, the normalized frequencies that were extrapolated from these percentages will be shown to be very dramatic indeed.

6. While it is interesting that there is a significant increase in the proportion of search returns which qualify as central passives diachronically, the three categories shown in Tables 2 and 3 cannot be said to be competing variants and are therefore not presented as figures.

3. Results and discussion

3.1 Diachronic frequency of central and semi-passives in COHA

The percentages from Tables 2 and 3 were used to extrapolate the normalized frequency of central and semipassives in each decade and genre of COHA. The frequency of GET/BE + (adverb) + past participle in a given decade and genre was multiplied by the relevant percent for that decade and genre, yielding the estimated raw frequency of passives for that sample. Their normalized frequency per million words was then calculated based on the section word count.[7]

The frequency of the central GET-passive, which increases dramatically in the material, seems to behave as expected with regard to genre, as seen in Figure 1.[8] Fiction, arguably the least formal genre, has the highest frequency of GET-passives, and the trajectories of Fiction and Popular Magazines virtually parallel each other. Non-fiction books, the most formal, conservative genre,[9] show the least dramatic increase in central GET-passives. For the newspaper genre, it initially seemed likely that the sudden mid-century jump in GET-passives was due to changes in the style guidelines of the papers; however, *The New York Times Manual of Style and Usage* (Siegal & Connolly, 2015: 134) actually still explicitly asks that contributors "do not substitute *get* for *is* or *are*". Other publications may of course have been more accepting of the GET-passive than *The New York Times*; such editorial acceptance would also indicate that the construction was becoming more acceptable in writing as newspaper publishers were realizing the financial benefits of a more accessible, speech-like writing style.

Figure 2 shows the decrease in central BE-passives by genre. There are some parallel but opposite trends in Figures 1 and 2. Magazines seem to be following Fiction in each graph. Newspapers undergo dramatic change between the 1950s and 1990s. Non-fiction is more resistant to change than the other genres in both graphs. Note that, although the BE-passive is becoming less frequent, it is still vastly more common than the GET-passive; the increase in GET-passives cannot be claimed to play much of a role in the decline in BE-passives.

---

7. Because interrogative and negated GET-passives were removed manually from the data set, the frequency trajectories of GET- and BE-passives are not completely comparable.

8. Anderwald (2016: 223–224) has very similar findings; however, her study also includes pseudo- and semipassives.

9. The genre Non-fiction books includes expository works that have been evenly sampled across the Library of Congress's classification system and thus includes materials from a wide variety of disciplines. The informational focus of these texts is likely to be less involved and more abstract (Biber, 1988) than the written language in the other, less formal genres of Fiction, Popular Magazines, and Newspapers.

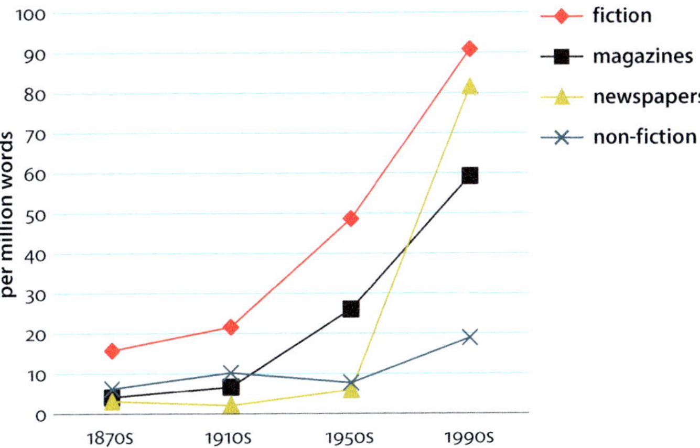

Figure 1. Estimated pmw frequencies of central GET-passives in each genre of COHA

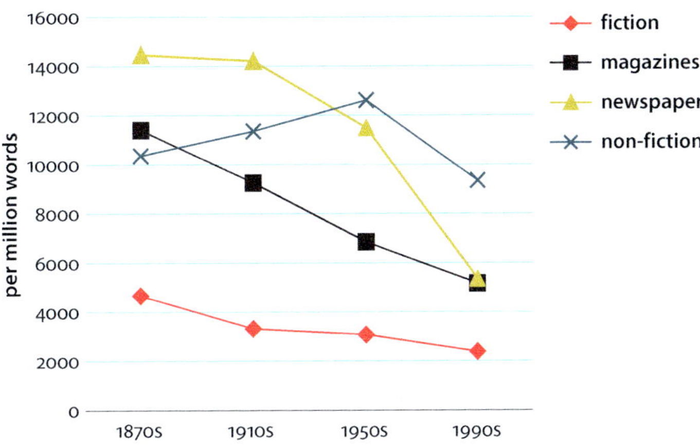

Figure 2. Estimated pmw frequencies of central BE-passives in each genre of COHA

The genre analysis shown in Figure 2 suggests that both stylistic proscription and colloquialization may be affecting the use of BE-passives. Leech (2004: 73) calls the decline of the BE-passive in written English a "negative manifestation of colloquialization", as its disappearance indicates a move towards a less formal, more spoken-like style. The decrease in BE-passives across genres of COHA does seem to spread from least to most formal, with Non-fiction books, the most conservative genre in COHA, holding out the longest, but eventually following the other, less formal text types in a downward trajectory.

Both GET- and BE-passives are constructions that writers may be aware that they are using, at least to some degree. However, as Pullum (2014) has pointed out, it is not necessarily the case that all writers have a working definition of passivity that matches the linguist's definition of passive voice. Semipassives especially, as in sentences 3 and 4 above, may certainly be seen as passive by writers if not by grammarians. If conscious, stylistic reasons are behind the changes in the frequency of passives, semipassives should also be considered. The extrapolated normalized frequencies for GET-semipassives are shown in Figure 3. To facilitate comparison with the central GET-passives, Figure 3 has the same scale as Figure 1.

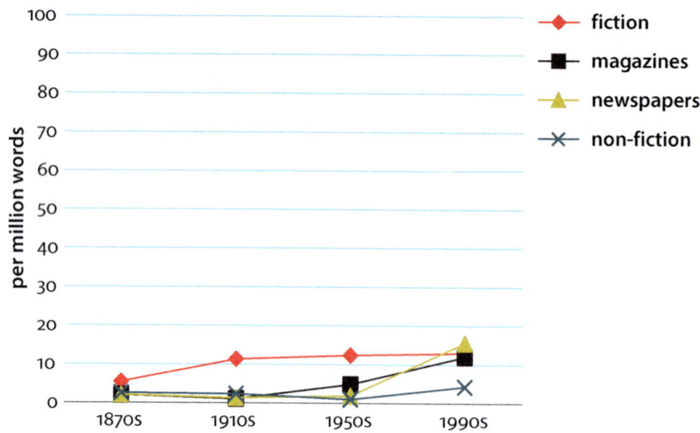

Figure 3. Estimated pmw frequencies of semipassives with GET in each genre of COHA

The increase in GET semipassives is slight compared with the verbal, central passives in Figure 1. However, the semipassives follow the same cross-genre trajectories as central GET-passives: while they increase earliest in Fiction, Non-fiction resists the increase until the latter half of the 20th century. Therefore, I conclude that although writers may *not* necessarily differentiate between semi- and central passives, the frequency change is mainly in the central passives, with semipassives possibly strengthening the category.

3.2 Situation type

Situation type, also known as Aktionsart, is based on Vendler's (1957) description of the temporal semantics that a verb confers on a sentence. His original categories have been developed and adapted slightly by different linguists (e.g. Brinton, 1988); the situation-type classification system used here is based on the version put forth by Quirk et al. (1985: 200–209). For the analysis of situation type, it was necessary to limit the scope to representative sub-samples of central passives. Wherever possible, 100 randomly selected central passives per auxiliary, decade, and genre were coded for situation type. Where there were fewer than 100 central passives in a sample, all instances were examined.

The tests for different situation types involved putting the active version of the passive sentence into the progressive.[10] The first distinction is whether a sentence is *stative* or *dynamic*. Statives are a very marginal category of passives, and virtually non-existent with GET-passives. A stative sentence usually resists being put into the progressive, as does the active version of the stative passive in (7), where *numerous small granules are surrounding each mitochondrion* is unlikely.[11]

(7) *Stative*: Each mitochondrion *is surrounded* by numerous small granules. (COHA Non-fiction books 1950s)

(8) *Durative & Conclusive:* You look at these letters, and you start to get a sense of some of the heartache that had to be endured before the little house in East Falls Church *got built.* (COHA Newspapers 1990s)

(9) *Durative & Nonconclusive:* It is a power such as has *been exercised* by the Clearing House, and always for good, although regarded with jealousy. (COHA Newspapers 1910s)

(10) *Punctual & Conclusive:* For about a year we was with Halleck over on the Mississippi, but after a while I *got transferred* to Burnside's division, when he was over in East Tennessee after the Rebs, and went with him up to Knoxville, and you see when I got there I was on my old stampin' ground. (COHA Magazines 1870s)

(11) *Punctual & Nonconclusive:* They called themselves the German Baptist Brethren, but because of their baptismal rites, which involve triple immersion, they *were widely referred* to as the Dunkers. (COHA Magazines 1950s)

The dynamic passives were further subcategorized according to whether they were *durative* or *punctual* and *conclusive* or *nonconclusive* (often called 'telic' and 'atelic'). Durative sentences are easily rendered in the progressive, as in (8) and (9), where *building a house* and *exercising a power* do not change the sense of the verb. Sentences such as (10) and (11), on the other hand, take on new verbal semantics when put into the progressive. For sentence (10), the progressive connotes the short period of time directly leading up to the moment where the decision to transfer him was made: a transition. And for sentence (11), the progressive version of the sentence, *people were widely referring to them as the Dunkers*, confers an iterative meaning: a momentary action happening again and again.

10. A more detailed account of this classification system can be found in Schwarz (2017: 317–320).

11. It is possible to imagine a sense of *small granules are surrounding each mitochondrion* where the granules are basically anthropomorphized, moving in deliberately on the mitochondrion, but this would entail a complete re-working of the sense of the sentence.

The test for whether the sentence is conclusive or nonconclusive has to do with the verb connoting an assumed end-point. The test for this, developed by Garey (1957: 105), is the question, "if one was *verb*ing, but was interrupted while *verb*ing, has one *verb*ed?" For sentences (8) and (10), an interruption means the verbal action has *not* been completed; one has not *built a house* or *transferred a soldier*. For sentences (9) and (11), the agents have at least been *exercising a power* or *referring to them as the Dunkers* up until the time they were interrupted. This means that sentences (8) and (10) are conclusive and sentences (9) and (11) are nonconclusive.

These distinctions lead to the five categories *Stative* (exemplified by sentence 7), *Accomplishment* (sentence 8), *Activity* (sentence 9), *Transitional Act* (sentence 10), and *Momentary Act* (sentence 11).

The data for each genre and auxiliary were considered separately with regard to situation type.[12] In examining the COHA data, it became increasingly clear that it was not necessarily the use of Transitional Acts that was undergoing change in the GET-passive, as suggested in Schwarz (2017), but instead the distribution of conclusive vs. nonconclusive situation types. This does not necessarily contradict the earlier findings, but may contribute to a better understanding of them. If GET-passives started out as change-of-state constructions (Fleisher, 2006), with their origins in GET + adjective uses like *get sick*, they would be most closely associated with conclusive situation types. The spread to new situation types may have progressed as follows: first, the GET-passive is used in Transitional Acts, which is the situation type bearing the closest semantic resemblance to GET + adjective. The GET-passive then begins to also be acceptable in Accomplishments, which involve both a process and a change of state. Finally, the GET-passive becomes generalizable to the nonconclusive situation types Activity and Momentary Act.

There is only one genre of GET-passives in COHA where this seems already to have taken place, and that is Fiction, as shown in Figure 4.[13] Fiction, probably the least formal of COHA's genres, also had the highest normalized frequency of central GET-passives overall (Figure 1), and is the genre where we expect spoken language features to be accepted most readily.[14]

12. The first two decades of GET-passives in Newspapers and the first decade of GET-passives in Magazines had to be excluded from the statistical analysis due to low expected frequencies.

13. Raw figures and results of Chi-square test in Table 14 in the Appendix.

14. There was also a genre which showed significant change as regards BE-passives; namely, Non-fiction books. However, this change displays no clear pattern, as seen in Table 15 in the Appendix.

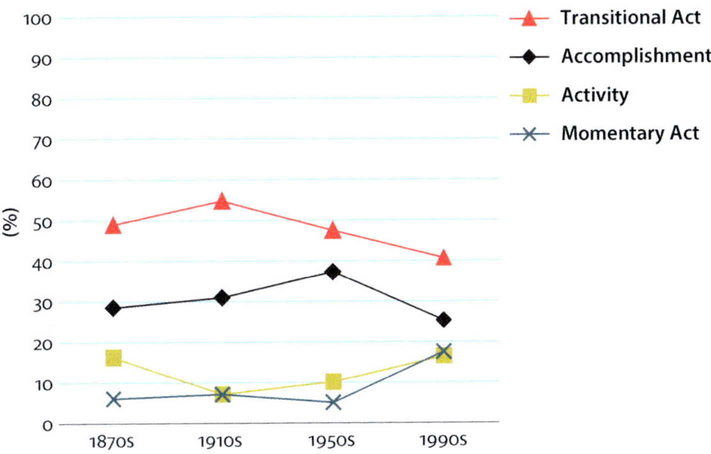

Figure 4. Proportion of central GET-passives in different situation types in the collected Fiction data

3.3 Subject type

The passive subjects in the COHA data were classified as *human*, *inanimate*, or *animal*. Human subjects, as in (12) and (13), and inanimate subjects, as in (14) and (15), accounted for the vast majority of instances. As it was difficult to determine the agentivity of animal subjects, this minor category was excluded when tests were run.

(12) The men were cut to pieces, the ground strewn horribly with their dead and dying bodies. *Those who lived to run away* were chased for twenty miles by Tarleton and his cavalry. (COHA Fiction 1950s)

(13) In essence, managed care tries to reverse the incentives of the traditional "fee for service" method, in which *providers* get reimbursed according to what they do – how many patients they treat, how many tests and procedures are performed, and so on. (COHA Magazines 1990s)

(14) In those days *the Times and the Eternities* got printed on the same sheet, as they always do when a hero appears. (COHA Magazines 1870s)

(15) *Evacuation of the big east coast port at Wonsan* was officially confirmed yesterday. (COHA Newspapers 1950s)

Figure 5 shows the proportion of human subjects of central GET-passives diachronically by genre. While Fiction, which has the highest frequency of GET-passives, displays diachronic stability (as do Newspapers, for which there was relatively little material in the corpus before the 1950s, see Section 2.1), the Magazine genre shows a statistically significant change away from use with human subjects in the recent data (Table 16). There is also a clear trend in this direction in Non-fiction books, although it does not reach statistical significance. The increased acceptability of GET with inanimate subjects in Magazines (and probably in Non-fiction books) is another good indication that the GET-passive is continuing to grammaticalize as its sphere of use widens.

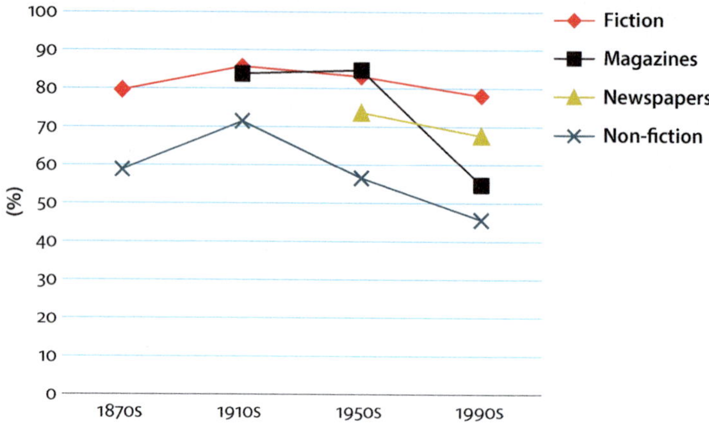

Figure 5. Proportion of human subjects used with central GET-passives across genres

One obvious question that arises from an examination of Figure 5 is whether Magazines and Non-fiction books have simply begun to include more inanimate subjects overall. However, the BE-passive data does not support this idea, as the BE-passives in Magazines and Non-fiction are diachronically stable on this parameter, as seen in Figure 6.

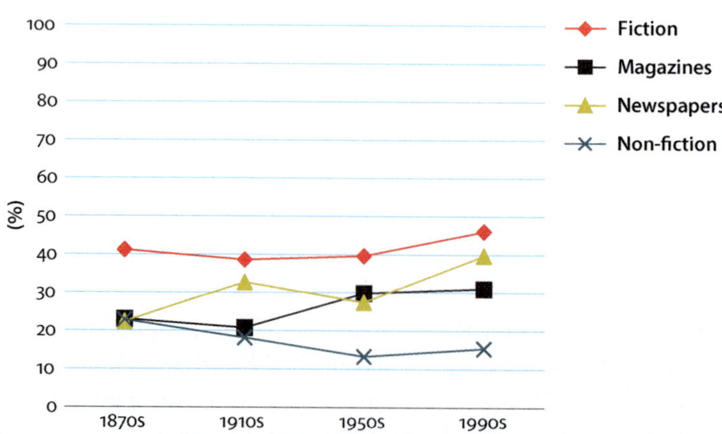

Figure 6. Proportion of human subjects used with central BE-passives across genres

There is a statistically significant increase in human subjects used with central BE-passives diachronically in newspaper texts (Table 17). Since BE-passives are assumed to be fully grammaticalized, this change was unexpected. While it is beyond the scope of this study to go into the reasons for this change, the fact that there are opposing changes for GET- and BE-passives shows that it is probably not the genres themselves which are changing in regard to subject-type.

3.4 Frequent past participles in GET- and BE-passives

The imbalance in the size of the data sets means that comparing the lists of past participles for each auxiliary and decade is no simple matter. Type/token ratios are misleading, showing GET as more productive than BE simply because there are so few tokens of the former. I have addressed the data-set imbalance (at least to some degree) by showing the proportions of past participles used most frequently with a given auxiliary in a given decade. Table 4 shows the most frequent past participles in the control group of central BE-passives. I have included only those participles which account for at least 2% of total instances for each auxiliary and decade. As the table shows, between 87% and 89% of tokens (those not present in Table 4) have past participles that account for less than 2% of the total each.

Table 4. Past participles in central BE-passives accounting for 2% or more of total instances per decade

1870s		1910s		1950s		1990s	
made	3%	*found*	3%	*made*	5%	*made*	3%
found	2%	*made*	2%	*taken*	2%	*found*	2%
allowed	2%	*known*	2%	*used*	2%	*considered*	2%
said	2%	*done*	2%	*given*	2%	*known*	2%
seen	2%	*said*	2%			*seen*	2%
		called	2%				
Total	11%	Total	13%	Total	11%	Total	11%

Table 5, which shows the most frequent past participles used with central GET-passives in each decade, paints a different and less stable picture. The 1870s are not included in the GET-passive table because the 1870s data set is too small to be comparable to those for the following decades. Because of the limited amount of data, it was also impractical to include a genre perspective on past participles.

There are semantic differences between the most frequent participles with BE and GET. While many of the frequent BE participles are likely stative (e.g. *seen* and *known*), the GET lists contain no frequent stative participles. Also, the GET participles are often non-neutral, as expected, but far from exclusively adversative: *paid* is

Table 5. Past participles in central GET-passives accounting for 2% or more of total instances per decade

1910s		1950s		1990s	
caught	7%	*paid*	14%	*paid*	7%
killed	6%	*elected*	5%	*caught*	7%
paid	6%	*caught*	4%	*done*	4%
hit	4%	*hurt*	4%	*hit*	4%
taken	3%	*killed*	4%	*killed*	3%
blown up	2%	*started*	3%		
elected	2%	*done*	2%		
fed	2%	*thrown*	2%		
fired	2%				
found out	2%				
hurt	2%				
kicked	2%				
knocked	2%				
licked	2%				
run	2%				
run in	2%				
scolded	2%				
sent	2%				
started	2%				
Total	54%	Total	38%	Total	25%

the top participle overall. The lack of overlap between participles used with BE and with GET further indicates that the increased use of the GET-passive is not responsible for the decline in the use of the BE-passive. There is also a marked productivity difference between the BE and GET lists; frequent participles with BE-passives account for a much smaller percentage of total tokens, which indicates that it is easier to use BE-passives creatively.

However, there is obvious diachronic development in the use of past participles with GET: a broadening of the range of past participles is clear. In the 1910s data, a full 54% of instances are accounted for by the participles that comprise 2% or more of total tokens for that decade. By the 1990s, only 25% of instances contain such participles. This diachronic change in productivity indicates morphosyntactic generalization and thus further grammaticalization of GET as a central passive auxiliary.

4. Conclusion

As regards the diachronic increase in the frequency of use of GET-passives, this study adds to earlier research (Leech et al., 2009, Schwarz, 2017) by increasing the diachronic span and including new genres of American English. It is this increase in frequency that raises the question of what other signs of grammaticalization we might find in a close examination of corpus material. While the increase in the frequency of GET-passives in written corpora almost certainly lags behind what has already occurred in spontaneous speech, the study of written data is far from useless; indeed, diachronic studies like this one offer a means of tracking a construction across time in authentic, natural linguistic material. The inclusion of a genre perspective helps provide a clearer picture of the acceptability of a construction.

In this study, semipassives were considered separately from central GET-passives, as semipassives are taken to be predecessors of central GET-passives based on the findings of Fleisher (2006). Semipassives with GET in COHA exhibited comparatively stable diachronic frequencies, indicating that they may already have reached saturation point even in relatively standardized written language. The central GET-passive was thus singled out as the GET construction currently undergoing change.

The frequency trajectories for each genre support the idea of delayed acceptance of the central GET-passive in written language. In the COHA data, the Fiction genre leads the way, with Popular magazines close behind. These two genres are the most likely of the four to contain informal language and a great deal of dialogue. Though the results from the Newspaper genre must be interpreted cautiously, it is interesting that they lag behind the frequency development in Fiction and Magazines until the latter half of the 20th century, at which point GET-passives suddenly become extremely frequent in Newspapers. While one interpretation of this development is increased editorial acceptance of the GET-passive, evidence from the latest edition of *The New York Times Manual of Style and Usage* (Siegal & Connolly, 2015: 134) suggests that the GET-passive is still overtly proscribed, which means the increase is happening in spite of double layers of proscription (against both passive voice in general and GET-constructions in particular). This means that the increased acceptability of GET-passives may be below the level of consciousness.

The semantic/morphosyntacic parameters under consideration in this study do indicate further grammaticalization of the GET-passive. Change in situation type suggests that informal language is paving the way for increased use of GET-passives in writing, as it is only in the arguably least formal genre of Fiction that we find significant change away from the situation types most closely related to the adjectival origins of the GET-passive. The study of subject types revealed that the proportion of human subjects, the preferred subject type of the GET-passive and the subject type most closely associated with subject responsibility, decreased in Magazines.

The weakening of the restriction to human subjects with GET-passives in this genre is another sign of semantic bleaching and thus of grammaticalization.

Finally, passive GET shows a clear diachronic change toward use with a wider range of past participles, which indicates increased productivity as the GET-passive grammaticalizes. Examining the past participles used with the passives in the material provided some of the most convincing evidence of the continuing grammaticalization of the GET-passive, highlighting the importance of considering the interaction of lexis and syntax in corpus studies of grammatical constructions.

The persistence of other uses of GET, such as semi- and pseudopassive GET, is nonproblematic in a study of grammaticalization (see, for instance, Mair, 2004 on layering and grammaticalization in corpus data). Nor is it necessary for GET to take over from BE as the English passive auxiliary. Rather, the grammaticalization of the GET-passive implies that the category of passives is being strengthened as the GET-passive becomes more and more generalizable to more contexts of use and becomes a more useful and used passive auxiliary.

Sources

Davies, Mark (2004). BYU-BNC. (Based on the *British National Corpus* from Oxford University Press). Retrieved from http://corpus.byu.edu/bnc/.

Davies, Mark (2008). *The Corpus of Contemporary American English*: 450 million words, 1990–present. Retrieved from http://corpus.byu.edu/COCA/.

Davies, Mark (2010). *The Corpus of Historical American English*: 400 million words, 1810–2009. Retrieved from http://corpus.byu.edu/coha/.

References

Anderwald, Lieselotte (2016). *Language between Description and Prescription: Verbs and Verb Categories in Nineteenth-century Grammars of English*. Oxford: Oxford University Press. https://doi.org/10.1093/acprof:oso/9780190270674.001.0001

Biber, Douglas (1988). *Variation across Speech and Writing*. Cambridge: Cambridge University Press. https://doi.org/10.1017/CBO9780511621024

Biber, Douglas, Johansson, Stig, Leech, Geoffrey, Conrad, Susan, & Finegan, Edward (1999). *Longman Grammar of Spoken and Written English*. London & New York: Longman.

Brinton, Laurel J. (1988). *The Development of English Aspectual Systems: Aspectualizers and Post-verbal Particles*. Cambridge: Cambridge University Press.

Carter, Ronald, & McCarthy, Michael (1999). The English *get*-passive in Spoken Discourse: Description and Implication for an Interpersonal Grammar. *English Language and Literature* 3(1), 41–58.

Chappell, Hilary (1980). *Is the get*-passive Adversative? *Papers in Linguistics* 13, 411–452.

Fleisher, Nicholas (2006). The Origin of Passive *get*. *English Language and Linguistics* 10(2), 225–252. https://doi.org/10.1017/S1360674306001912

Garey, Howard B. (1957). Verbal Aspect in French. *Language* 33(2), 91–110. https://doi.org/10.2307/410722

Givón, Talmy, & Yang, Lynne (1994). The Rise of the English *get*-passive. In Barbara Fox, & Paul J. Hopper, (Eds.), *Voice. Form and Function*. Amsterdam: John Benjamins. 119–149. https://doi.org/10.1075/tsl.27.07giv

Gronemeyer, Claire (1999). On deriving complex polysemy: The grammaticalization of *get*. *English Language and Linguistics* 3(1), 1–39. https://doi.org/10.1017/S1360674399000118

Haegeman, Liliane (1985). The *get*-passive and Burzio's Generalization. *Lingua* 66, 53–77. https://doi.org/10.1016/S0024-3841(85)90256-6

Hopper, Paul J. (1991). On Some Principles of Grammaticization. In Elizabeth Closs Traugott, & Bernd Heine (Eds.), *Approaches to Grammaticalization*, vol. 1: *Theoretical and Methodological Issues* (17–35). Amsterdam: John Benjamins. https://doi.org/10.1075/tsl.19.1.04hop

Hopper, Paul J., & Traugott, Elizabeth Closs (1993). *Grammaticalization*. Cambridge: Cambridge University Press.

Hopper, Paul J., & Traugott, Elizabeth Closs (2003). *Grammaticalization* (2nd ed.). Cambridge: Cambridge University Press. https://doi.org/10.1017/CBO9781139165525

Hundt, Marianne (2001). What Corpora Tell Us about the Grammaticalisation of Voice in *get*-constructions. *Studies in Language* 25(1), 49–87. https://doi.org/10.1075/sl.25.1.03hun

Lakoff, Robin (1971). Passive Resistance. In *Papers from the 7th Regional Meeting, Chicago Linguistic Society*. 140–163.

Leech, Geoffrey (2004). Recent Grammatical Change in English: Data, Description, Theory. In Karin Aijmer, & Bengt Altenberg (Eds.), *Advances in Corpus Linguistics* (61–81). Amsterdam: Rodopi.

Leech, Geoffrey, Hundt, Marianne, Mair, Christian, & Smith, Nicholas (2009). *Change in Contemporary English. A Grammatical Study*. Cambridge: Cambridge University Press. https://doi.org/10.1017/CBO9780511642210

Mair, Christian (1997). Parallel Corpora: A Real-time Approach to the Study of Language Change in Progress. In Magnus Ljung (Ed.), *Corpus-based Studies in English* (195–209). Amsterdam: Rodopi.

Mair, Christian (2004). Corpus Linguistics and Grammaticalisation Theory: Statistics, Frequencies, and Beyond. In Hans Lindquist, & Christian Mair (Eds.), *Corpus Approaches to Grammaticalization in English* (121–150). Amsterdam & Philadelphia: John Benjamins. https://doi.org/10.1075/scl.13.07mai

Mair, Christian (2006). *Twentieth-century English. History, Variation and Standardization* Cambridge: Cambridge University Press. https://doi.org/10.1017/CBO9780511486951

Mair, Christian (2011). Grammaticalization and Corpus Linguistics. In Heiko Narrog, & Bernd Heine (Eds.), *The Oxford Handbook of Grammaticalization* (239–250). Oxford: Oxford University Press.

Mair, Christian, & Hundt, Marianne (1995). Why is the Progressive Becoming more Frequent in English? A Corpus-based Investigation of Language Change in Progress. *Zeitschrift für Anglistik und Amerikanistik* 43(2), 111–122.

Pullum, Geoffrey K. (2014). Fear and Loathing of the English Passive. *Language and Communication* 37(7), 60–74. https://doi.org/10.1016/j.langcom.2013.08.009

Quirk, Randolph, Greenbaum, Sidney, Leech, Geoffrey, & Svartvik, Jan (1985). *A Comprehensive Grammar of the English Language*. London & New York: Longman.

Schwarz, Sarah (2015). Passive Voice in American Soap Opera Dialogue. *Studia Neophilologica* 87(2), 152–170. https://doi.org/10.1080/00393274.2015.1049831

Schwarz, Sarah (2017). 'Like Getting Nibbled to Death by a Duck': Grammaticalization of the GET-passive in the TIME Magazine Corpus. *English World-Wide* 38(3), 305–335. https://doi.org/10.1075/eww.38.3.03sch

Siegal, Allan M., & Connolly, William G. (2015). *The New York Times Manual of Style and Usage* (5th ed.). New York: Penguin Random House LLC.

Siemund, Rainer (1995). 'For Who the Bell Tolls': Or Why Corpus Linguistics Should Carry the Bell in the Study of Language Change in Present-day English. *Arbeiten aus Anglistik und Amerikanistik* 20(2), 351–376.

Vendler, Zeno (1957). Verbs and Times. *The Philosophical Review* 66(2), 143–160. https://doi.org/10.2307/2182371

Appendix

Table 6. Central, semi- and pseudopassives with GET in Fiction.
chi-square = 34.4; degrees of freedom = 6; probability < 0.001

	1870s		1910s		1950s		1990s		Total	
central	49	25%	42	21%	59	30%	91	46%	241	30%
semi	17	9%	22	11%	15	8%	13	7%	67	8%
pseudo	134	67%	136	68%	126	63%	96	48%	492	62%
Total	200	100%	200	100%	200	100%	200	100%	800	100%

Table 7. Central, semi- and pseudopassives with GET in Popular magazines
chi-square = 49.2; degrees of freedom = 6; probability < 0.001

	1870s		1910s		1950s		1990s		Total	
central	18	14%	37	20%	59	30%	84	42%	198	28%
semi	9	7%	6	3%	11	6%	17	9%	43	6%
pseudo	106	80%	144	77%	129	65%	99	50%	478	66%
Total	133	100%	187	100%	199**	100%	200	100%	719	100%

** One token in the 1950s Magazine section resisted classification for centrality and was removed from the table.

Table 8. Central, semi- and pseudopassives with GET in Newspapers.
Expected frequencies too low for significance testing with chi-square

	1870s		1910s		1950s		1990s		Total	
central	3	9%	3	10%	19	22%	105	53%	130	37%
semi	2	6%	2	7%	6	7%	20	10%	30	9%
pseudo	30	86%	24	83%	63	72%	75	38%	192	55%
Total	35	100%	29	100%	88	100%	200	100%	352	100%

Table 9. Central, semi- and pseudopassives with GET in Non-fiction books.
chi-square = 25.0; degrees of freedom = 6; probability < 0.001

	1870s		1910s		1950s		1990s		Total	
central	17	18%	35	27%	23	23%	57	42%	132	29%
semi	7	7%	8	6%	3	3%	13	10%	31	7%
pseudo	70	74%	86	67%	73	74%	66	49%	295	64%
Total	94	100%	129	100%	99	100%	136	100%	458	100%

Table 10. Central, semi- and pseudopassives with BE in Fiction.
chi-square = 15.9; degrees of freedom = 6; probability = 0.014

	1870s		1910s		1950s		1990s		Total	
central	136	68%	114	57%	116	58%	102	51%	468	59%
semi	21	11%	17	9%	22	11%	25	13%	85	11%
pseudo	42	21%	69	35%	62	31%	73	37%	246	31%
Total	199***	100%	200	100%	200	100%	200	100%	799	100%

*** Where figures do not add up to 200 in the tables for BE, there were examples that resisted classification and were removed from the table (one in Fiction in the 1870s and one in Non-fiction books in the 1870s).

Table 11. Central, semi- and pseudopassives with BE in Popular magazines.
chi-square = 8.34; degrees of freedom = 6; probability = 0.214

	1870s		1910s		1950s		1990s		Total	
central	165	83%	159	80%	161	81%	145	73%	630	79%
semi	11	6%	12	6%	9	5%	19	10%	51	6%
pseudo	24	12%	29	15%	30	15%	36	18%	119	15%
Total	200	100%	200	100%	200	100%	200	100%	800	100%

Table 12. Central, semi- and pseudopassives with BE in Newspapers.
chi-square = 19.7; degrees of freedom = 6; probability = 0.003

	1870s		1910s		1950s		1990s		Total	
central	170	85%	171	86%	175	88%	146	73%	662	83%
semi	9	5%	9	5%	4	2%	15	8%	37	5%
pseudo	21	11%	20	10%	21	11%	39	20%	101	13%
Total	200	100%	200	100%	200	100%	200	100%	800	100%

Table 13. Central, semi- and pseudopassives with BE in Non-fiction books.
chi-square = 5.65; degrees of freedom = 6; probability = 0.464

	1870s		1910s		1950s		1990s		Total	
central	158	79%	160	80%	173	87%	162	81%	653	82%
semi	13	7%	12	6%	5	3%	12	6%	42	5%
pseudo	28	14%	28	14%	22	11%	26	13%	104	13%
Total	199	100%	200	100%	200	100%	200	100%	799	100%

Table 14. Situation types of central GET-passives in Fiction.
chi-square on conclusive vs. non-conclusive situation types: chi-square = 9.85; degrees of freedom = 3; probability = 0.020 (Significance level < 0.025, Bonferroni correction)

	1870s		1910s		1950s		1990s		Total	
Accomplishment	14	29%	13	31%	22	37%	23	25%	72	30%
Activity	8	16%	3	7%	6	10%	15	16%	32	13%
Transitional Act	24	49%	23	55%	28	47%	37	41%	112	46%
Momentary Act	3	6%	3	7%	3	5%	16	18%	25	10%
Total	49	100%	42	100%	59	100%	91	100%	241	100%

Table 15. Situation types of central BE-passives in Non-fiction books.
chi-square on conclusive vs. non-conclusive situation types: chi-square = 14.8; degrees of freedom = 3; probability = 0.002 (Significance level < 0.025, Bonferroni correction)

	1870s		1910s		1950s		1990s		Total	
Accomplishment	35	35%	31	32%	26	27%	28	29%	120	31%
Activity	18	18%	29	30%	34	35%	33	34%	114	29%
Transitional Act	36	36%	26	27%	24	25%	16	19%	105	27%
Momentary Act	0	0%	4	4%	4	4%	6	6%	14	4%
Stative	10	10%	6	6%	8	8%	12	12%	36	9%
Total	99	100%	96	100%	96	100%	98	100%	389	100%

Table 16. Types of subject used with central GET-passives in Popular magazines.
chi-square on human vs. inanimate subjects, excluding the 1870s: chi-square = 20.6; degrees of freedom = 2; probability < 0.001 (Significance level < 0.025, Bonferroni correction)

	1870s		1910s		1950s		1990s		Total	
Human	9	50%	31	84%	50	85%	46	55%	136	69%
Inanimate	9	50%	5	14%	8	14%	37	44%	59	30%
Animal	0	0%	1	3%	1	2%	1	1%	3	2%
Total	18	100%	37	100%	59	100%	84	100%	198	100%

Table 17. Types of subject used with central BE-passives in Newspapers.
chi-square on human vs. inanimate subjects: chi-square = 12.9; degrees of freedom = 3; probability = 0.005 (Significance level < 0.025, Bonferroni correction)

	1870s		1910s		1950s		1990s		Total	
Human	38	22%	56	33%	48	27%	58	40%	200	30%
Inanimate	132	78%	114	67%	126	72%	88	60%	460	69%
Animal	0	0%	1	1%	1	1%	0	0%	2	0%
Total	170	100%	171	100%	175	100%	146	100%	662	100%

From *time-before-place* to *place-before-time* in the history of English

A corpus-based analysis of adverbial clusters

Susanne Chrambach

In Present-day English, place adverbials tend to precede adverbials of time in clusters (cf. Hasselgård, 1996). In this paper, this word order preference is investigated from a diachronic perspective. The corpus-based analysis shows that the preferred order changes from time-before-place in Old English to place-before-time towards the end of the Middle English period. In a number of binary logistic regressions this study explores which factors might motivate these preferences respectively. The obligatoriness of the adverbials and their realization form emerge as two crucial factors. Their effect can be related to the proximity principle (cf. Hasselgård, 2010), the principle of end weight, and the principle of given-before-new. Comparing the different periods of English from Old English to Early Modern English, this paper shows how the increasingly fixed position of the lexical verb can be linked to the reversal of the ordering preference from time-before-place to place-before-time.

Keywords: word order, adverbial, proximity principle, information structure

1. Introduction

Adverbials in Present-day English (PDE) have been characterized as special among the elements of the clause because of the vast range of their semantic roles, their many realizations forms and not least because of their positional flexibility. Not only do they occur in a number of different positions in the clause (*front*, *medial*, *end*; see Section 2 for the definition of these positions used in this study); what is more, they also co-occur in one position (cf. Quirk et al., 1985: 478). Two or more adverbials occurring in such immediate adjacency will be referred to as adverbial *clusters* here. (1) shows an adverbial cluster in clause-final position:

(1) *Are you going to stay* ***in London after you've retired?*** (BNC A0F, 291)

https://doi.org/10.1075/cilt.346.11chr

Although the placement of adverbials in PDE is often described as freer than that of other elements of the clause, adverbials in clusters (and adverbials in general) exhibit ordering preferences. The end position is the most common position for adverbial clusters in PDE and, in that position, adverbials of time and place are the most frequent types of adverbials (cf. Hasselgård, 2010: 115). The preferred order in these clusters is *place-before-time*, i.e. the place adverbial precedes the time adverbial, as in (1) for instance (cf. Biber et al., 2004: 812). This is the most prominent and best-established pattern that holds among co-occurring adverbials in a clause in PDE.

Cross-linguistic comparisons of the ordering preferences in adverbial clusters have shown that PDE contrasts with Dutch and German, which prefer the reverse order of adverbials.[1] In Dutch and German, adverbials of time occur predominantly before adverbials of place in clusters (*time-before-place*). This juxtaposition of preferences has been described as a "mirror-image" (e.g. Hinterhölzl, 2009) or as "Janus-faced" (Shannon & Coffey, 2004). We know that, typologically, older forms of English have a lot in common with Present-day German or Dutch. For instance, one of its clause patterns allows the verb to occur in clause-final position. It will be argued here that the position of the lexical verb is central in determining the order of the adverbials in clusters. Given how similar modern German and Dutch are to Old English with respect to the flexibility in the placement of the verb, it is plausible to assume that older forms of English might behave more like German or Dutch in terms of adverbial placement. In a previous study, I have demonstrated that this is indeed the case (cf. Chrambach, 2014). (2) is an Old English (OE) example that illustrates these findings. It shows a cluster in final position with a time adverbial (*on niht*) preceding an adverbial of place (more precisely, an adverbial of direction: *to Balaam*):

(2) *Þa com God* ***on niht*** ***to Balaam***
Then came God.$_{\text{NOM}}$ at night.$_{\text{ACC}}$ to Balaam
'Then God came to Balaam at night.' (cootest,Num: 22.20.4338, Heptateuch)

This paper picks up the thread and examines Middle English (ME) and Early Modern English (EModE) adverbial clusters of time and place. It will trace the decline of the preference for the order *time-before-place*, which begins in the ME period and continues steadily throughout the EModE period. For both periods, it will show which factors motivate the respective preference. For this purpose, the results of a number of multifactorial analyses will be discussed. Building on

1. Note that the notion of *preference* implies a default pattern of occurrence in terms of frequency. It does not suggest that the reverse order is ungrammatical, the reverse order simply does not occur as often.

these synchronic observations, the main focus will be on investigating how we can account for the change from *time-before-place* to *place-before-time* diachronically.

This study follows Hasselgård's semantic categorization of the adverbials of time and place (2010: 24f). Adverbials of place denote the spatial location of events or a situation, and motion as movement in space from a source or to a goal, as well as general direction along a path. In addition, this category of adverbials of place also includes adverbials which denote distance as spatial extent. Time adverbials locate events and states in time (time position), and specify duration and frequency. The temporal location of a situation or event may be a point in time or a period of time. Adverbials denoting the duration of a situation or event may either refer to the entire period (span) or just to the beginning (source) or end of that period (goal). The frequency of an action can be referred to with a definite adverbial, such as *every week,* or an indefinite adverbial, such as *often*. Finally, time adverbials may also denote a time relationship between two positions of time, e.g. *already* (see Table 4 in the appendix for EModE examples of each of these semantic subcategories). These adverbials of time or place may be realized as adverbs (e.g. *then*, *here*), noun phrases (*that night*, *seven miles*), prepositional phrases (*for two weeks*, *in my house*) or clauses (*when you've finished your paper*, *where we used to live*).

The literature on adverbials offers a variety of terms to distinguish different categories of adverbials. The labels *adverbial of time* and *adverbial of place* are used here for the sake of clarity. The adverbials discussed in this study belong in the category of *adjuncts* (Quirk et al., 1985), *circumstance adverbials* (Biber et al., 2004), or *adjunct adverbials* (Hasselgård, 2010). The main motivation for using the umbrella-term *adverbial* is to avoid confusion with the terms that differentiate between obligatory and non-obligatory adverbials, which will be referred to as *complements* and *adjuncts,* respectively. In this analysis of historical English, this distinction – which is summarized under the label *obligatoriness* when referring to the feature in general – emerges as one of the most influential factors that brings about the preferred order of the time and place adverbials in clusters.

The obligatoriness of the adverbials is one of the 15 features that have been annotated for each token. With the help of a regression model, this study investigates how well these features can predict the order of the adverbials of time and place in clusters. Thus, this study approaches this question with the underlying assumption that the preferred order of either *place-before-time* or *time-before-place* comes about as the result of a multifactorial process. The idea of adverbial placement as motivated by competing word order principles is well-established in current research (e.g. Hasselgård, 2010: 73). The following section will outline which factors have been put forward in that discussion and how they have been captured in this analysis.

2. Factors that motivate the order of adverbials in clusters – previous research and annotation of the data

The literature on placement of circumstance adverbials is mostly concerned with synchronic analyses of PDE. There are very few diachronic accounts of the positions that these adverbials may take in the clause (e.g. Daron, 1974). To my knowledge there are no diachronic investigations on clusters of circumstance adverbials.

Formal approaches explore how adverbials are integrated into the clause structure, discussing for instance the interaction between syntax and semantics, or the role of a parameter like OV/VO (e.g. Haider, 2000, 2004; Ernst, 2002; Cinque, 2004). The present study does not focus on how adverbial syntax can best be accounted for within one particular framework. Instead, it takes a more functional approach in asking what motivates the choice between two options that are both available to the speaker, namely which order the adverbials of time and place take in a cluster. In particular, the focus is on how we can account for one order being preferred over another.

In the literature on PDE, a number of factors are described as having an influence on adverbial placement. The present paper is largely inspired by the work of Hasselgård (1992, 1996, 2010), who comes to the conclusion that a number of word order principles interact to bring about a semantic pattern of *place-before-time* in PDE. In total, the present study investigates 15 features, of which two will emerge as central. In the remainder of this section, these features and how they have been operationalized will be presented. Let us will begin with the two most important features: the realization form of the adverbials and their obligatoriness, starting with the realization form.

The feature of REALIZATION FORM is an uncontroversial one: the adverbials may be either realized as adverb phrases, noun phrases, prepositional phrases or clauses (for examples see Section 1).

By contrast, the feature OBLIGATORINESS is not easily captured. Adverbials may be categorized into two main groups of obligatory (complements) and non-obligatory (adjuncts). However, differentiating between these two groups is not straightforward. Defining obligatoriness in terms of omissibility is not reliable because grammaticality judgments vary with context, as demonstrated by Pittner (1995). This problem is amplified when we attempt to evaluate historical data. Therefore, this study follows Pittner's suggestion as to how we can identify adverbials alternatively: An adverbial is classified as a complement if the statement in which it occurs would be rendered irrelevant were the adverbial omitted. Effectively, this alternative definition replaces the notion of *ungrammatical* with *irrelevant*, which circumvents the obstacle of how to evaluate the grammaticality of a clause when we omit the adverbial. Instead, the relevance of the statement becomes the decisive factor. (3) is an example from the ME data which serves to illustrate how the feature obligatoriness has been annotated. The obligatory adverbial is underlined, the entire cluster is in bold:

(3) *For in cas that the peler prevaylyd in that fyght he shulde be put* ***in preson ayen,***
'In case the thief prevails in that fight, he should be put in prison again.'
(CMGREGOR, 200.1624, Gregory's Chronicle)

I argue that there is no context imaginable in which the clause *He shall be put again* constitutes a relevant statement. Therefore *in preson* 'in(to) prison' has been classified as a complement. Secondly, I classify those adverbials as complements whose removal from the clause causes a change in the verb meaning. Adverbials which have this effect have been called culminative adverbials because they specify the culmination of a process of movement by indicating the source or goal of that movement. Hasselgård exemplifies this group of adverbials with the following example (cf. 2010: 48):

(4) *We didn't actually go inside.*

Removing *inside* from (4) changes the verb meaning from *enter* to *leave*. For the present study, it is postulated that such a change in verb meaning shows that the adverbial forms an essential part of the proposition and therefore should be classified as a complement. By contrast, adjuncts are defined as giving circumstantial information and as not describing features that are essential to the action denoted by the verb. Examples (5) and (6) illustrate this notion. In (5) we see a cluster (in bold) that is made up only of adverbials giving circumstantial information, i.e. adjuncts:

(5) ***Þat tyme at Dunstapil*** *þe signe of þe cros was i-seie in hevene*
'At that time the symbol of the cross was seen in the sky in Dunstable.'
(CMPOLYCH,VIII,89.3581, John of Trevisa's Polychronicon)

By contrast, Example (6) contains a motion verb (*rush*), which is complemented by a culminative adverbial specifying the goal of the motion (*into the King's Privy-Chamber*). Consequently, in this analysis this adverbial is classified as a complement:

(6) *If one should rush* ***into the King's Privy-Chamber, whilst he is alone,*** *and kill the King which God forbid and this Man be met coming with his Sword drawn all bloody; shall not he be condemned to death?*
(RALEIGH-E2-H,I,212.C2.315, state trial proceedings of Raleigh)

A similar notion is captured by the feature MOTION VERB. However, here, the focus is not on differentiating the adverbials into complements and adjuncts but on investigating the influence of lexical factors on the order of the adverbials. The classification of the verbs as motion verbs follows Levin (1993, 263–270). Levin describes verbs of motion as verbs of inherently directed motion (e.g. *advance, arrive, come*), leave-verbs (e.g. *abandon, desert*), manner of motion verbs (e.g. *bounce, roll, climb, stagger*), verbs of motion using a vehicle (e.g. *boat, paddle, ride*), waltz verbs (e.g. *boogie*), chase verbs (e.g. *chase, pursue, trail*), and accompany verbs (e.g. *accompany, escort, guide*). This feature could potentially consist of many more verb classes. This study focuses on the group of motion verbs because of the high frequency with which they occur. For instance, 47% of all OE tokens[2] contain a motion verb.

Next, we will turn to two features that are relatively similar and the terms used, COMPLEXITY and WEIGHT, are occasionally even used interchangeably in the literature. Overall, the use of one term rather than the other seems to come with the terminology used in different linguistic frameworks; *weight* is the term used in more traditional approaches, while *complexity* is used more in formal accounts (cf. Arnold & Wasow, 2000: 29). I measure weight in terms of number of words and – where these are equal – the number of syllables. By contrast, complexity is measured comparing the realization forms on a scale from least complex (adverb phrases) to most complex (clauses) with noun phrases and prepositional phrases as intermediate levels. If the elements in the cluster are modified, the number of nodes is counted. These two features often correlate, and I will show below how I address this issue in my regression analyses. The reason for looking at both features instead of deciding on one is to follow up different suggestions made in the literature about adverbial placement. A number of accounts refer to weight as a factor, arguing that lighter elements generally precede heavier ones (e.g. Quirk et al., 1985, or Hasselgård, 2010). Alternatively, Hawkins (2000) argues that structural complexity is at the base of what motivates element order in adverbial clusters. His approach analyses linear element order as arranged by increasing complexity. This, he argues, is geared at reducing the processing effort. Both perspectives seem plausible, and that is why both weight and complexity are considered here.

In addition, for each cluster it has been annotated where it occurs in the clause. This feature is called THE POSITION OF THE CLUSTER IN THE CLAUSE. Three positions are differentiated: front, medial, and end. These positions are simply defined as the first element in the clause (front), the last element in the clause (end), and as every element that occurs between these two positions (medial) (cf. Quirk et al., 1985: 491ff). The following three examples (7–9) from the EModE data set illustrate each of these positions:

2. A *token* consists of one sentence that contains an adverbial cluster.

(7) ***In the Sommer following, by the Townes of Bedforde and of Broklesward,*** *Monsters were seene oft times mornings and euenings to come out of the woods, [..]*
(STOW-E2-P1,553.69, John Stow: The Chronicles of England from Brute unto this present yeare of Christ)

(8) *And at Whitsunday-tyde, at the which tyme men say that Eadgar there was crounid, ther is a king electid* ***at Bath every yere*** *of the tounes men in the joyfulle remembraunce of King Edgar and the privileges gyven to the toun by hym.*
(LELAND-E1-H, 144.348, The itinerary of John Leland in or about the years 1535–1543)

(9) *On Thursday one came* ***into a bookseller's shop after dinner.***
(BURNETCHA-E3-H,1.2,164.355, Burnet's History of my own Time)

Another way of looking at the position of the cluster is to put it in relation to the position of the (lexical) verb (POSITION OF THE CLUSTER REGARDING THE LEXICAL VERB). In clauses that contain both a finite verb and a lexical verb, the latter is given prevalence here because this feature is geared at examining the idea that adverbials which specify a verb are naturally placed adjacent to that verb. Thus, this feature is binary (lexical verb – cluster vs. cluster – lexical verb). To illustrate this feature, I will give two examples from EModE: (10) illustrates the order *lexical verb – cluster*, while (11) shows the reverse order:

(10) *I came* ***home on the Sunday night***
(LISLE-E3-P1,4,109.218, Lisle state trial proceedings)

(11) ***At last to bed*** *I went, my man lying on the floore by mee*
(JOTAYLOR-E2-H,1,128.C2.25, The pennyles pilgrimage)

To investigate further whether the element order in the clause is related to the order of the adverbials in clusters, I have annotated the clause patterns for each clause based on the clause patterns outlined by Bech (2001) for OE and ME main clauses and Heggelund's (2010) application of the same patterns to subordinate clauses (CLAUSE PATTERN). The patterns used in the annotation are SVX, XVS, XSV, SXV, SXVX, SV_1XV_2, and verb-initial. S is the subject, V is the verbal element, and the X-element may be, for instance, an object, an adverbial or a subject/object complement. In addition, for EModE the following patterns have been added: infinitival clauses, participial clauses, and reduced relative clause. Since the ME and EModE data are analyzed separately statistically, the addition of these patterns does not compromise the comparability of the results, it merely acknowledges the ongoing change of clause patterns available to the speakers. To generalize over clause patterns, I have separately noted whether a clause is verb-final (VERB-FINAL VERSUS VERB-NON-FINAL).

I have also considered whether ADVERBIALS OF TIME AND PLACE OCCUR ELSEWHERE IN THE CLAUSE (a simple yes/no feature which investigates whether it makes a difference that some clauses have more adverbials in addition to those contained in the cluster) and how many adverbials make up the actual cluster (NUMBER OF ELEMENTS IN THE CLUSTER). The maximum number of adverbials in one cluster in the data is five. Such large clusters are very rare, though. The majority of clusters are composed of either two or three adverbials of time and place. (12)[3] illustrates a large cluster which contains four adverbials (taken from the EModE data), while (13) (taken from the ME data) consists of two adverbials and is thus representative of the majority of clusters, regardless of the period studied:

(12) *We'll bring Ireland* ***[now] [upon the 3d of August] [at Night,] [to my Lord Aston's House at Standen]****.*
(OATES-E3-H,4,75.C1.225, Oates state trial proceedings)

(13) ***[Þerafter] [at ȝork]*** *þey were compelled to defende hem self.*
'Thereafter at York they were forced to defend themselves.'
(CMPOLYCH,VI,339.2483, John of Trevisa's Polychronicon)

Finally, it has been noted for each token from which individual text and genre it is taken, whether the respective text is a translation and which period (and subperiod) it was composed in (GENRE, TRANSLATION, and PERIOD) based on the different categories provided by the corpora. The classification of the genres by text type follows the standard classification used in the Helsinki Corpus of English Texts. This classification of the genres is a grouping of texts both by function (e.g. handbook) as well as by topic (e.g. travelogue), which leads to some inner heterogeneity for each genre (cf. Meurmann Solin, 2001: 241f). Allocating the INDIVIDUAL TEXTS for each token serves to control whether the general trend in ordering preference is a matter of personal preference of some authors. This hypothesis turns out to be unfounded, as ordering preferences prove to be stable across different authors. Similarly, translated texts do not diverge in the preference from texts originally composed in English.

Most of the features outlined in this section are used as factors in the regression models that have been run to determine which factors motivate the order of the adverbials in clusters. However, some features are also used to further subdivide the data into smaller sets. For instance, the annotation of the feature realization forms allows us to study clusters made up of prepositional phrases only. In the following section more details on the technical aspects of this analysis will be given before moving on to the presentation and discussion of the results.

3. This sentence is taken from the Oates state trial proceedings and describes the plan to transport a Mr. Ireland from one location to the next.

3. Data and methodology

For this study, two corpora have been used, the *Penn-Helsinki Parsed Corpus of Middle English* (PPCME2) (Kroch & Taylor, 2000) and the *Penn-Helsinki Parsed Corpus of Early Modern English* (PPCEME) (Kroch et al., 2004). These parsed corpora are sister corpora to the *York-Toronto-Helsinki Parsed Corpus of Old English Prose* (YCOE) (Taylor et al., 2003), which was used for my previous study of adverbial clusters in OE (Chrambach, 2014). All three corpora exclusively contain prose texts and can be searched with the same search engine, CorpusSearch. The annotation of the corpora does not allow for a search of a label *adverbial* per se. A search of the corpora for clusters of adverbials of time and place therefore consists of a number of separate queries for all possible combinations of the realization forms of adverbials, i.e. adverbs, prepositional phrases, noun phrases, and clauses. This search output is then manually examined to only include clusters of adverbials of time and place and annotated for the features described above.

For the multifactorial analysis a binary logistic regression is carried out (cf. Gries, 2008: 284ff). A regression analyzes several variables with a focus on one dependent variable (here: the order of the adverbials as *time-before-place* or *place-before-time*) and one or more independent variables. The regression shows to what extent the values of the dependent variables can be predicted by the independent variables. More precisely, generalized linear models (glm) have been calculated using the software R (R Development Core Team, 2008). The goodness of fit of these models is evaluated by calculating Nagelkerke's R squared. This value indicates the percentage of the data which is explained with the help of the model.

Before being read into R, the data is further reduced by removing all variable values with fewer than five tokens. This is done to avoid skewed data. The independent variables used in the model are REALIZATION FORM, COMPLEXITY, WEIGHT, OBLIGATORINESS, ADVERBIALS OF TIME AND PLACE ELSEWHERE IN THE CLAUSE, THE POSITION OF THE CLUSTER IN THE CLAUSE, THE POSITION OF THE CLUSTER REGARDING THE VERB, THE CLAUSE PATTERN, MOTION VERB, GENRE as well as VERB-FINAL VERSUS VERB-NON-FINAL. The generalized linear model is first run with all of these variables. In a second step, a stepwise model selection by AIC (Akaike Information Criterion) chooses variables by measuring the relative goodness of different models in a weighing up of accuracy and complexity of each model (cf. Akaike, 1974). The variables chosen by the stepwise model selection are then entered into another generalized linear model and the results before and after the model selection are compared.

For each period, this process is carried out for the entire data set, as well as for subsets. These are the three subsets: one containing only clusters with two elements, one containing only pairs of prepositional phrases, and one subset containing only pairs of adverb phrases. Analyzing only clusters that contain two elements is geared at controlling that the results are not blurred by an imbalance of adverbials within one cluster, for instance in a cluster of one time adverbial followed by two place adverbials. Analyzing only clusters equal in realization form (eg. clusters only made up of adverb phrases) effectively levels out the factor realization form. On the one hand, these analyses show more clearly the effect of the remaining factors in the absence of the relatively dominant factor realization form. On the other hand, these analyses help check for effects that may come about as in consequence of unintended interactions between the two factors REALIZATION FORM and COMPLEXITY, whose annotation is at times parallel. In addition, unintended interactions between the two factors WEIGHT and COMPLEXITY might arise in the multifactorial analysis due to their similarity (multi-collinearity, cf. Hilpert, 2013: 50). Therefore, alternative models have been calculated with both as a variable as well as with each one of them separately. Below, I will restrict my presentation of the results to two exemplary analyses, one of the ME data and one of the EModE data, to illustrate the effects that emerge overall.

4. Results of the analyses

I begin this overview of my results with the general distribution of the order *time-before-place* v. *place-before-time* per period. To better show the main development I include the previous results for the OE period (taken from Chrambach, 2014) in this presentation and in Figure 1.

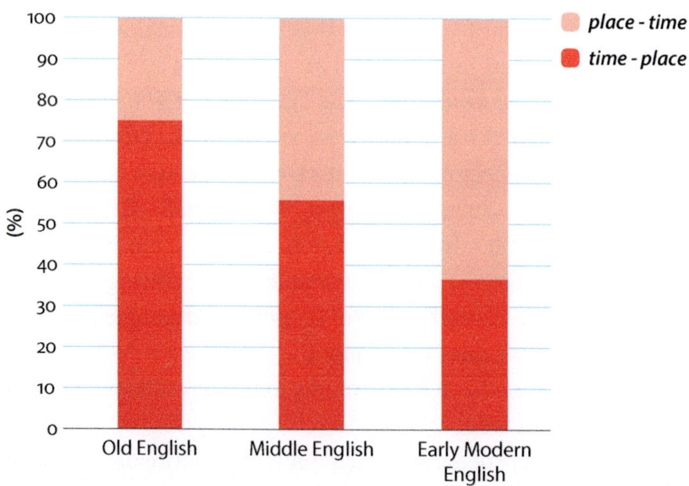

Figure 1. *time-before-place* vs. *place-before-time* in OE, ME, and EModE

The entire OE data set of 2131 clusters shows a preference of 75%*** for the order *time-before-place*.[4] The ME data set consists of 1167 clusters, of which 56%*** have the order *time-before-place*. The EModE data set is comprised of 1252 clusters. Of those, only 37%*** have the order *time-before-place*.

When we divide these three large periods into smaller stretches of time, it emerges that the first three subperiods of ME (from the second half of the 12th century to the early 15th century) show a preference for the order *time-before-place*. This preference decreases towards the third subperiod of ME, i.e. from the second half of the 14th century to 1420 (ME 3 60.71%*** for *time-before-place*). The final ME subperiod shows the reverse preference, i.e. a preference for the order *place-before-time*. In fact, the final subperiod of ME (1420–1500) shows nearly the same distribution as the first subperiod of EModE (ME4 44.6%* for *time-before-place*, EModE1 44.2%* for *time-before-place*). This shows that the changing of preference from one order to the other is gradual rather than abrupt. The preference for the order of the adverbials of time and place is reversed as of the subperiod ME 4, i.e. as of the 15th century, and the preference for the order *place-before-time* continues to grow in the EModE Period (EModE1 44%* for the order *time-before-place*, EModE2 35%*** for the order *time-before-place*).

The distribution of the clusters in terms of their size (two, three, four or five elements) remains relatively stable throughout the three stages of OE, ME, and EModE. Also, the proportion of clusters which only contain adjuncts, i.e. they do not contain complements, is similar for all three periods (OE 36%, ME 42%, EModE 33%).

What is different regarding the general distribution of the data is the position of the clusters in the clause. OE has many more clusters in medial position (44%), compared with both ME (11%) and EModE (5%). Accordingly, the latter two also show an increase of the number of clusters in end position, which totally dominates in EModE (91% in EModE vs. 53% in OE). Another steady change that can be observed in the data concerns the realization forms of the adverbials. The most striking development is the decrease of time adverbials realized as adverb phrases from 73% (OE) to 31% (EModE). I will return to this observation later on.

To illustrate the results of the multifactorial analyses in general, I will first outline the main findings and then give the exact results for two models in particular. Again, I also mention the main results of my analysis of the OE data (as presented in Chrambach, 2014) to show how they compare.

The results of the multifactorial analyses show that one factor emerges as highly influential in all models for each period. That is the factor OBLIGATORINESS.

4. The distributions of *time-before-place* vs. *place-before-time* are tested for their significance with the exact binomial test, conf. level = 0.95, $p < 0.001$***.

Secondly, the factor REALIZATION FORM is among those that are found to exert an influence on the order of adverbials in each stage of English, but with varying values and to different degrees.

For the OE data, the multifactorial analyses also show an influence for the factors WEIGHT and MOTION VERB. For ME, only the factor CLAUSE PATTERN is relevant in addition to the two main factors which exert an influence at each period of English. For EModE, THE POSITION OF THE CLUSTER REGARDING THE LEXICAL VERB, WEIGHT, COMPLEXITY as well as a number of CLAUSE PATTERNS are added to this list of factors which help explain the variance of the data.

Table 1 gives the exact results of two models calculated for the same subset of the ME and EModE data, respectively. The subset I have chosen to present here is the one that contains only two elements in the clusters. Both data sets have been calculated with WEIGHT and COMPLEXITY, but Table 1 only gives the results after the stepwise model selection. For the ME data the model selection drops the variables COMPLEXITY, ADVERBIALS OF TIME AND PLACE ELSEWHERE IN THE CLAUSE, THE POSITION OF THE CLUSTER IN THE CLAUSE, THE POSITION OF THE CLUSTER REGARDING THE VERB, MOTION VERB, and VERB-FINAL VERSUS VERB-NON-FINAL. For the EModE data set only three variables are dropped, namely ADVERBIALS OF TIME AND PLACE ELSEWHERE IN THE CLAUSE, CLAUSE PATTERN, and MOTION VERB.

Table 1. Results of the multifactorial analyses for the data set that comprises only two elements in the cluster for ME and EModE

Middle English n = 929, $R^2 = 0.916$	**Early Modern English** n = 1015, $R^2 = 0.89$
REALIZATION FORM (*advp pp*) *** +	REALIZATION FORM (*advp pp*) ** +
REALIZATION FORM (*pp advp*). –	REALIZATION FORM (*np pp*) *** +
REALIZATION FORM (*pp np*) *** –	COMPLEXITY (*more complex first*) * –
OBLIGATORINESS (*adjunct-complement*) ***+	OBLIGATORINESS (*adjunct-complement*) ***+
OBLIGATORINESS (*complement-adjunct*) ***–	OBLIGATORINESS (*complement–adjunct*) ***–
CLAUSE PATTERN (*XVS*) *** +	POSITION OF THE CLUSTER REGARDING THE VERB (*lexical verb – cluster*). –

The header row of Table 1 specifies the data set, indicating the number of tokens (n), the overall preference for the order of the adverbials of time and place for that particular data set, and the goodness of fit of the model (R^2). In the body of the table, I give the complete list of those factors that have a significant effect in the model. Each cell first names the variable, followed in parentheses by the particular value of the variable which is attributed to have that effect, and the respective significance level. Finally, the effect of that value is given. This effect may be either the order of *time-before-place* (indicated by the symbol +) or the order *place-before-time* (indicated by the symbol –).

Table 1 illustrates in two ways the overall result of the multifactorial analyses that I have carried out for each period. Firstly, it shows the dominance of the two main factors, OBLIGATORINESS and REALIZATION FORM. Secondly, it also shows that these analyses vary with respect to which other factors emerge as influential. It should not come as a surprise that the list of those factors that influence which adverbial occurs first in a cluster – the adverbial of place or the adverbial of time – is not uniform over the course of several centuries. It is probably to be expected that the status of an adverbial as complement or adjunct influences the word order regardless of which period we are studying. Other factors, such as the clause pattern, will not be as consistent in their effects because of the more the general development of English from a language with a more flexible word order towards one with a relatively fixed word order.

5. Discussion

5.1 Complements and their proximity to the lexical verb

In the multifactorial analyses of my data, the factor OBLIGATORINESS emerges as highly influential throughout. This factor captures how adverbials vary from being obligatorily selected by the verb (complements) to being optional clause elements describing circumstantial information (adjuncts). In my interpretation of the results presented above, the next step is to ask how and why this difference influences their position in a cluster. Hasselgård (2010: 143) describes a tendency for adverbial complements to be placed in proximity to the verb that they specify. Such complements are, for instance, directional adverbials which specify motion verbs (e.g. the motion verb *fly* and the directional *to London* in *fly to London*). Hasselgård captures this observation in the proximity principle. This principle states that elements which have a close relationship functionally, conceptually, or cognitively to one another will be put close to one another in the clause (cf. also Givón, 1990: 970; Behaghel, 1932, § 1426).

The effect of this general syntactic principle is linked to the semantic category of the adverbials because the different semantic categories of adverbials are not equally prone to being complements. Hasselgård finds for PDE that

> [t]he likelihood of an adverbial being obligatory is highly dependent on the semantic category it belongs to. [...] It is likely that the basic order of the adverbials in a cluster is influenced by the frequency with which each semantic category is obligatorily selected by the verb. (1996: 100)

In my data, most complements are adverbials of place. For instance, 98.8% of all complements which occur in clusters composed of two elements in the OE data are adverbials of place (n = 1085) (Chrambach, 2014: 57). However, it is important to consider that the reverse is not true, i.e. not all adverbials of place are complements, so the relationship is not as straightforward as these numbers may suggest at first. In what follows I will relate the idea of the proximity principle to the position of the lexical verb in the clause and show how this helps explain why the preference in clusters of time and place adverbials changed diachronically.

We know that, in the history of English, the position of the verb becomes more and more fixed. Above, I have described that, alongside this development, the position of the adverbial clusters becomes less flexible until we find a large majority of clusters in end position in EModE. Thus, the distribution of the clusters in relation to the position of the lexical verb is very different in OE from the distribution in EModE. Whereas in OE, 40% of all clusters are followed by the lexical verb, this percentage is down to 5% in EModE. Conversely, this means that the vast majority of EModE clusters is preceded by the lexical verb.

Bringing all these aspects together, we can describe the following process that takes place from ME onwards: As the lexical verb increasingly precedes the cluster, complements occur more often cluster-initially due to the proximity principle. These complements are predominantly adverbials of place, so a pattern of *place-before-time* is established. This process is supported by a shift in the proportion of the different realization forms of the time adverbials. This will be the focus of the following section.

5.2 Weight, realization form and the given-before-new principle

In the description of the general diachronic development of the adverbial clusters of time and place adverbials above, I have pointed out that there is one change in the make-up of the clusters that stands out. This change concerns the realization forms of the adverbials of time. In OE, the majority of time adverbials in clusters are realized by adverb phrases (73%) (for a discussion of the influence of *þa* in these clusters see Chrambach, 2013: 60). In EModE, this proportion has decreased to 31%. In general, the realization forms of the time adverbials are more evenly distributed in EModE. The amount of noun phrases increases from OE (12%) to ME (25%) and remains stable in EModE (26%). Similarly, the number of time adverbials realized as clauses increases from OE (1%) to ME (7%) and afterwards remains on that level (7%). The number of prepositional phrases grows more steadily from 13% in OE to 22% in ME to 36% in EModE. By contrast, the realization forms for adverbials of place are predominantly realized as prepositional phrases throughout the different periods (OE 68%, ME 82%, EModE 76%).

To begin with, a number of questions arise in light of the different proportions in the realization forms of the adverbials of time and place. The first question is this: Why do the adverbials of time and place differ in the distribution of their realization forms regardless of which period we compare? Secondly, why do we find a change in the proportions of the realization forms of the time adverbials from OE to EModE? And thirdly, why do we not find a similar development for place adverbials?

Adverbials of place and adverbials of time do not only differ with respect to the distribution of their realization forms in historical English, but also in PDE, where the distribution is very similar to the distribution in EModE (cf. Biber et al., 2004: 787). Biber et al. describe that adverbials prefer different realization forms depending on their semantics for a number of reasons. They remark on adverbials which are realized as prepositional phrases: "Prepositional phrases allow the information in the adverbial to connect more specifically with the clause content [...]. This is particularly useful for place and manner adverbials." (2004: 788). In contrast, Biber et al. observe for adverbials of time in PDE that

> [t]he semantic category of time is noteworthy in that is has a particularly wide range of syntactic realization. Prepositional phrases are typically used to indicate specific times: *On Monday morning* [...]. Single adverbs are used for times whose interpretation is tied to the context or situation (e.g. *then, later, today, now*), particular time frequencies (e.g. *weekly, monthly*), as well as vague references to time (e.g. *sometimes, occasionally*) [...]. (Biber et al., 2004: 788)

These observations can be approached from two angles. Firstly, Biber et al. claim that prepositional phrases lend themselves to expressing the "clause content" (ibid.) and to giving "specific" information (ibid). Biber et al. thus make a connection between the function of the adverbials and their realization form. This description is particularly focused on adverbials of place, which are overwhelmingly realized as prepositional phrases in PDE. Secondly, Biber et al. link the realization form of adverbials to their context-dependence. This observation is made for time adverbials realized as adverbs in PDE: "[s]ingle [temporal] adverbs are used for times whose interpretation is tied to the context or situation" (2004, 788).

This ties in with my data (Chrambach, 2013: 60), which show OE place adverbials as being realized more often as prepositional phrases than time adverbials. A closer look at the data shows that we find many time adverbials with deictic meaning which are expressed by short adverbs such as *þa* 'then' or *siþþan* 'afterwards'. The place adverbials, on the other hand, more often have specific referential meaning which is expressed using a prepositional phrase. The following sentence illustrates this point. In (13), the interpretation of the time adverbial *þa* 'then' depends on the context, while the place adverbial *to scipe* 'to the ship' gives concrete referential information:

(14) *Hi eodon* ***þa*** ***to scipe***
They went then to the ship.$_{DAT}$
'Then they went to the ship.'
(coaelive,+ALS_[Thomas]: 61.7579, Aelfric's Homilies Supplemental)

Hasselgård's (2010) also finds a systematic difference between adverbials of place and adverbials of time with regard to this aspect, which she relates to the text-type as well:

> [t]o a greater extent than space adjuncts [adverbials of place in my terminology, S.C.], time adjuncts [adverbials of time in my terminology, S.C.] have discourse-organizing functions. This is particularly visible in narrative passages where events may be structured along a time axis. (2010: 216)

In this context, one might assume that the concepts of discourse markers and adverbials with circumstantial meaning are being confused here. Regarding this concern, Hasselgård explicitly states that, in the cases she refers to, the temporal meaning of the adverbials stays intact, with the function of the adverbial being "mainly textual" (2010: 212). This claim is further substantiated in Hasselgård (1996): "It should be noted that the subsidiary discoursal functions of a time and space adverbial as defined here never eliminate its primary function. [...] an adverbial may very well have several functions at the same time" (241f). Similarly, Lenker (2010: 58ff) argues that adverbs expressing circumstantial information in Old English are semantically and syntactically polyfunctional and often referred to as ambiguous.

How does this relate to the different proportions of the realization forms of the adverbials of time and place in my data? Above, I described Biber et al.'s (2004) findings for PDE on the relationship between the function of adverbials, their context-dependence, and their realization form with their semantic classification. Biber et al. state that prepositional phrases are able to express specific information, which was found to be useful for adverbials of place. Adverbials of time, on the other hand, were found to be more often dependent on the context in their interpretation. Bringing together Hasselgård's (2010) observations with Biber et al.'s (2004) findings, we may postulate for this study: the higher proportion of the adverbials of time realized as short context-dependent adverbs (when compared to the adverbials of place) is related to their discourse-organizing function.

The next question to consider is why we find an increase in the number of prepositional phrases used to realize time adverbials from OE to EModE. Hasselgård (2010, 270ff) shows for PDE that text types differ with respect to the proportional distribution of the semantic types of adverbials as well as with respect to the realization types of these adverbials. Sports commentaries, for instance, have a high proportion of single adverbs, whereas the lowest proportion of single adverbs is found in academic writing. If the realization forms of adverbials vary by genre, we should explore from which genres the historical data studied here derives. The majority of the OE data – following the classifications of genre by text type as done in the Helsinki Corpus of English Texts – is derived from the three genres: history, biography, and homilies. These kinds of texts could also be subsumed under the text-type label *narrative* as defined by Virtanen (2010, 56). This definition uses the parameters of temporal sequentiality and participant-orientation. In other words, following this definition, narrative texts are characterized by a temporal continuity and a continuity of participants. In her earlier work, Virtanen demonstrates that sentence-initial temporal adverbials are text-structuring devices which are typically used in narrative texts to create temporal continuity (cf. Virtanen, 1992: 114). With respect to the question discussed here, it is interesting that many of the examples discussed by Virtanen in this context are deictic expressions realized by short adverbs, e.g. *presently, finally, then* (Virtanen, 1992: 93). Virtanen's observations focus on PDE, but we might assume that this is probably similar in OE narrative texts. In fact, Wårvik argues that the most prominent of the short temporal adverbs found in OE, *þa*, has just such a text-structuring function: "Old English *þa*, the temporal adverb, is primarily a connective element, creating cohesion in the narrative text by signalling the progress of the story-line and by keeping track of the main participants of the story" (2011, par. 3).

The ME data is not much more varied than the OE data: history (37%), religious treatise (21%), homilies (9%), and sermon (9%). By comparison, the EModE clusters stem from a wide range of texts. The biggest contributing genres are trial proceedings (19%), diary (13%), private letter (12%), travelogue (9%), and fiction (8%). Thus, we move from a relatively homogenous group of narrative texts to a much more varied collection of texts that include less formal language and shares more features with spoken discourse. It is to be expected that these texts will also differ regarding their use of temporal adverbials, in particular their use of short adverbs of time, as text-structuring devices. The different proportions of the realization forms of time adverbials in the different periods of English might thus be explained by acknowledging that the use of a particular realization form of time adverbial is text-type related: Short adverbs such as *then* often fulfill a deictic function in narrative texts and help to establish text cohesion. The change in the text types from OE to EModE is characterized by a decrease in the proportion of narrative texts. The high proportion of time adverbials realized as short adverbs in the two earlier periods and the subsequent decrease of the number of short adverbs can thus be attributed to this change in the proportions of text types.

At this point in the analysis, it may appear as if the change in preference from *time-before-place* to *place-before-time* can be attributed merely to the increased variation in text type as we progressively have access to more and more types of texts. Let me point out two aspects regarding this argument. Firstly, thanks to the annotation by text type and individual text for each individual token, we can filter the data in a way that allows us to only compare the same text types. Such a comparison of filtered data still confirms the general change in ordering preference. For instance, comparable data derived from the Bible have a preference for *time-before-place* of 78%*** in OE, 58% in ME, and 32%** in EModE. More importantly, though, if we take a closer look at the changing preference, we can see that the change begins before we have access to more varied text types. Thus, we cannot draw a simple causal connection between text type and change in ordering preference.

In addition, the change in realization forms of the time adverbials may be linked to a broader development that English underwent with the loss of V2, as outlined by Los (2012). Los argues that English changed from a bounded to an unbounded system when it lost V2. This refers to a typological distinction that differentiates between different ways of macrostructural planning by speakers: in unbounded languages, the speakers mark sequences in narration explicitly with temporal markers. Such local anchors are, for instance, deictically used adverbs (e.g. *then*). By contrast, speakers of bounded languages only once explicitly anchor a narration in time, namely at the beginning. Subsequently, the temporal anchor is implicitly maintained throughout the text passage (cf. Los, 2012: 29ff). Assuming that OE was indeed an unbounded language, the change in the proportion of realization forms of the adverbials of time could be interpreted not only as a consequence of an increase in available text types but also as a consequence of the loss of local anchoring of narratives in time using deictic temporal adverbs.

Whether adverbials are realized as adverbs, noun phrases, prepositional phrases or clauses determines their position in clusters in two ways. For one, the different realization forms will in most cases differ in weight. Most adverb phrases will be lighter than most prepositional phrases, for instance. Thus, putting adverb phrases before prepositional phrases in a cluster is also a consequence of the weight principle, or the principle of end weight. It refers to the idea that phrases are put in an order of increasing weight (cf. e.g Biber et al., 2004: 812).

Secondly, these different realization forms reflect a difference in the givenness of the information they convey. As I have just mentioned, short adverbs are often used deictically. Such deictic adverbs refer to the preceding discourse and are therefore not discourse-new. Positioning them first in a cluster follows the principle of given-before-new. The principle given-before-new states that, in a clause, information which is new follows after information that is already known. This observation is prominently associated with Behaghel (1932, § 1426). Since the early 20th century, it has been confirmed in various studies (e.g. Prince, 1981; Gundel et al., 1993). Differentiating between given and new information in the sentence aims at the level of discourse organization that is widely referred to as information structure, which may be defined as "the formal expression of the pragmatic structuring of a proposition in a discourse" (Lambrecht, 1994: 5). Within this general concept, several distinct categories of information structure can be distinguished: presupposition and assertion (i.e. the speaker's assumptions about what the hearer knows or does not yet know), identifiability and activation (the speaker's assumptions about the awareness of the hearer regarding the discourse referents at the time of speaking), and topic and focus (the speaker's evaluation of the predictability of the propositions in the current discourse) (cf. Lambrecht, 1994: 6). An array of different terms have been introduced to capture the notions *new* and *given*, such as *discourse-new/-old* in opposition to *hearer-new/-old*, or a hierarchy of *in focus – activated – familiar – uniquely identifiable – referential – type identifiable* (cf. Taylor & Pintzuk, 2014: 55). When dealing with historical texts, most of these notions are inherently hard to identify. For the purpose of my argumentation here, I will therefore rely on the widely established basic definition of *given* as previously mentioned in the discourse (cf. Taylor & Pintzuk, 2014: 58). Adverbials whose interpretation depends on the context will fall into this category (unless, of course, when they are used cataphorically). Consider this OE example:

(15) *& Ocus, Persa cyning, þone mon oþere noman het*
And Ocus, Persians' king, who.$_{ACC}$ one another.$_{DAT}$ name.$_{DAT}$ called
Artecsersis, æfter þæm þe he Egyptum forhergede, he gefor
Artecsersis, after that.$_{DAT}$ that he Egypt.$_{DAT}$ plundered he went
siþþan on Iudana lond.
afterwards in Jews' land.$_{ACC}$
'And Ochus, king of the Persians, whom by another name they call Artaxerxes, after he had plundered Egypt, then went into the land of the Jews.'
(coorosiu,Or_3: 5.58.15.1120, Orosius)

Here, we have a cluster in clause-final position that is made up of an adverbial of time, which is realized as an adverb (*siþþan*), followed by an adverbial of place, which is realized as a prepositional phrase (*on Iudana lond*). In the preceding clause, we find the contextual information that the deictic time adverbial *siþþan* relates to: *æfter þæm þe he Egyptum forhergede* 'after he had plundered Egypt'. We can thus argue that *siþþan* does not give new information. By contrast, the adverbial of place *on Iudana lond* refers to a place that has not previously been mentioned. Against the backdrop of this example, I argue that the principle of given-before-new relates to the realization forms of the adverbials in this way: Short adverbs are more likely to be context-dependent deictic expressions than prepositional phrases. Thus, they are more likely to express given information, which tends to precede new information in the clause.

The factor realization form emerged as the second most important factor that influences the order of the adverbials of time and place in clusters. Above, I have shown that this factor is related to the more general principles of ordering the elements in the clause by their different weight and degree of givenness. How can the change from *time-before-place* to *place-before-time* be put in relation to the realization forms of the adverbials? The effect of this factor does not change diachronically, of course. However, we did attest a decrease in the proportion of time adverbials realized as short adverbs from OE to EModE, which boosts the ongoing change in ordering preference in the adverbial clusters. This support is twofold. On the one hand, fewer time adverbials realized as short adverbs will lead to a less clearly pronounced tendency of short adverbials of time preceding long adverbials of place (the weight principle). On the other hand, there will be a less clear association between given information (short deictic time adverbs) and new information (adverbials of place realized as prepositional phrases). These two aspects – alongside a continuous development towards a fixed position of the lexical verb and an increase of the number of clusters in end position – will contribute to a change in preference towards *place-before-time*.

6. Conclusion

In this study of the ordering preferences in clusters of time and place adverbials I have described a change from *time-before-place* to *place-before-time*. This process is gradual and steady, with the point of reversal towards the end of the ME period. It has been shown for the different periods how the preference in order is motivated by a number of factors which interact. Above all, the obligatoriness of the adverbials and their realization form emerged as the most influential factors. These factors capture the workings of more general principles: the proximity principle, the principle of end weight, and the principle of given-before-new.

The change in preference from time adverbials being put first in the cluster to place adverbials as the first element in the cluster can be accounted for when we consider that the position of the lexical verb as well as the position of the cluster in the clause become more and more fixed in the history of English. Eventually, this leads to the lexical verb preceding the cluster in the majority of cases. Consequently, the proximity principle will cause the complements to be placed in the front of the cluster, which is the position of greatest proximity to the verb they specify. For PDE, this tendency has been referred to as complements-first (cf. Pérez-Guerra, 2016: 104). As place adverbials make up the majority of complements, this means that adverbials of place will precede adverbials of time in clusters in the majority of cases.

Due to limitations of length, this paper does not discuss the role that a number of other factors may play in the change of this particular word order pattern. For instance, we may ask if and how language contact with Norman French helped establish the order of *place-before-time*. What is more, in a further study, we should consider those clusters that consist only of non-obligatory adverbials adjuncts, as these clusters are not subject to the main factor found to determine the order of elements in these cluster, i.e. obligatoriness. These issues deserve to be handled in a more detailed discussion in the future.

References

Akaike, Hirotugu (1974). A new look at the statistical model identification. *IEEE Transactions on Automatic Control* 22, 47–76.

Arnold, Jennifer, & Wasow, Thomas (2000). Heaviness vs. Newness: The Effects of Structural Complexity and Discourse Status on Constituent Ordering. *Language* 76(1), 28–55. https://doi.org/10.1353/lan.2000.0045

Bech, Kristin (2001). *Word Order Patterns in Old and Middle English: A Syntactic and Pragmatic Study*. Doctoral dissertation. University of Bergen.

Behaghel, Otto (1932). *Deutsche Syntax. Eine geschichtliche Darstellung. Band IV. Wortstellung. Periodenbau*. Heidelberg: Carl Winters.

Biber, Douglas, Johansson, Stig, Leech, Geoffrey, Conrad, Susan, & Finegan, Edward (2004). *Longman Grammar of Spoken and Written English*. 4th improved ed. Harlow: Longman.

BNC = The British National Corpus, version 3 (BNC XML Edition). 2007. Distributed by Oxford University Computing Services on behalf of the BNC Consortium. http://www.natcorp.ox.ac.uk/

Chrambach, Susanne (2013). Exploring historical corpora – The syntactic labels locative adverb and temporal adverb in the York-Toronto-Helsinki Parsed Corpus of Old English Prose. In Anja Hennemann, & Claudia Schlaak (Eds.), *Korpuslinguistische Untersuchungen: Analysen einzelsprachlicher Phänomene* (59–66). Berlin: Frank & Timme.

Chrambach, Susanne (2014). The order of adverbials of time and place in Old English. In Pfenninger et al. (Eds.), *Contact, Variation, and Change in the History of English*. [Studies in Language Companion Series 159] (39–60). Amsterdam/Philadelphia: John Benjamins.

Cinque, Guglielmo (2004). Issues in adverbial syntax. *Lingua: International Review of General Linguistics* 114(6), 683–710.

Daron, Carol F. (1974). *The Position of Adverbials in a Selected Corpus of Early Old English Prose*. Auburn Univ. Diss. Ann Arbor, Michigan: University Microfilms.

Ernst, Thomas (2002). *The Syntax of Adjuncts*. Cambridge: Cambridge University Press.

Givón, Talmy (1990). *Syntax. A functional-typological introduction*. Vol. II. Amsterdam/Philadelphia: John Benjamins.

Gries, Stefan Th. (2008). *Statistik für Sprachwissenschaftler*. Göttingen: Vandenhoeck & Ruprecht.

Gundel, Jeanette K., Hedberg, Nancy, & Zacharski, Ron (1993). Referring Expressions in Discourse. *Language* 69, 274–307. https://doi.org/10.2307/416535

Haider, Hubert (2000). Adverb placement - convergence of structure and licensing. *Theoretical Linguistics* 26, 95–134.

Haider, Hubert (2004). Pre- and postverbal adverbials in OV and VO. *Lingua: International Review of General Linguistics* 114(6), 779-807.

Hasselgård, Hilde (1992). Sequences of spatial and temporal adverbials in spoken and written English. In Gerhard Leitner (Ed.), *New Directions in English Language Corpora. Methodology, Results, Software Developments* (319–328). Berlin/New York: Mouton de Gruyter. https://doi.org/10.1515/9783110878202.319

Hasselgård, Hilde (1996). *Where and When? Positional and functional conventions for sequences of time and space adverbials in present-day English*. Oslo: Scandinavian University Press.

Hasselgård, Hilde (2010). *Adjunct Adverbials in English*. Cambridge: Cambridge University Press. https://doi.org/10.1017/CBO9780511676253

Hawkins, John A. (2000). The relative order of prepositional phrases in English: Going beyond Manner – Place – Time. *Language Variation and Change* 11, 231–266.

Heggelund, Øystein Imerslund (2010). *Word Order in Old English and Middle English Subordinate Clauses*. Doctoral dissertation. University of Bergen.

Hilpert, Martin (2013). *Constructional Change in English*. Cambridge: Cambridge University Press. https://doi.org/10.1017/CBO9781139004206

Hinterhölzl, Roland (2009). The role of information structure in word order variation and word order change. In Roland Hinterhölzl, & Svetlana Petrova (Eds.), *Information Structure and Language Change. New Approaches to Word Order Variation in Germanic* (45–66). Berlin and New York: Mouton de Gruyter.

Kroch, Anthony, & Taylor, Ann (2000). *The Penn-Helsinki Parsed Corpus of Middle English (PPCME2)*. Department of Linguistics, University of Pennsylvania. CD-ROM, second edition.

Kroch, Anthony, Santorini, Beatrice, & Delfs, Lauren (2004). *The Penn-Helsinki Parsed Corpus of Early Modern English (PPCEME)*. Department of Linguistics, University of Pennsylvania. CD-ROM, first edition.

Lambrecht, Knud (1994). *Information Structure and Sentence Form. Topic, focus and the mental representations of discourse referents*. Cambridge Studies in Linguistics 71. Cambridge: Cambridge University Press. https://doi.org/10.1017/CBO9780511620607

Lenker, Ursula (2010). *Argument and Rhetoric. Adverbial Connectors in the History of English*. Berlin/Boston: De Gruyter Mouton. https://doi.org/10.1515/9783110216066

Levin, Beth (1993). *English Verb Classes and Alternations. A Preliminary Investigation*. Chicago/London: The University of Chicago Press.

Los, Bettelou (2012). The Loss of Verb-Second and the Switch from Bounded to Unbounded Systems. In Anneli Meurman-Solin, María José López-Couso, & Bettelou Los (Eds.), *Information Structure and Syntactic Change in the History of English* (21–46). Oxford: Oxford University Press. https://doi.org/10.1093/acprof:oso/9780199860210.003.0002

Meurman-Solin, Anneli (2001). Genre as a Variable in Sociohistorical Linguistics. *European Journal of English Studies* 5(2), 241–256. https://doi.org/10.1076/ejes.5.2.241.7311

Pérez-Guerra, Javier (2016). Do you investigate word order in detail or do you investigate in detail word order? On word order and headedness in the recent history of English. *Corpus Linguistics and Linguistic Theory* 12(1), 103–128. https://doi.org/10.1515/cllt-2015-0063

Pittner, Karin (1995). Valenz und Relevanz – eine informationsstrukturelle Erklärung für "obligatorische" Adverbiale. In Robert J. Pittner, & Karin Pittner (Eds.), *Beiträge zu Sprache und Sprachen. Vorträge der 4. Münchner Linguistik-Tage der Gesellschaft für Sprache und Sprachen (GESUS) e.V.* (95–106). München: lincom europa.

Prince, Ellen (1981). Towards a taxonomy of given-new information. In Peter Cole (Ed.), *Radical Pragmatics* (223–256). New York: Academic Press.

Quirk, Randolph, Greenbaum, Sidney, Leech, Geoffrey, & Svartvik, Jan. (1985). *A Comprehensive Grammar of the English Language*. London: Longman.

R Development Core Team. (2008). *R: A language and environment for statistical computing*. R Foundation for Statistical Computing, Vienna, Austria. http://www.R-project.org.

Shannon, Thomas F., & Coffey, Michael P. (2004). The Janus-faced Order of Adverbials in Dutch and English. In Thomas F. Shannon, & Johan P. Snapper (Eds.), *Janus at the Millennium* (245–264). Lanham, MD: University Press of America.

Taylor, Ann, Warner, Anthony, Pintzuk, Susan, & Beths, Frank (2003). *The York-Toronto-Helsinki Parsed Corpus of Old English Prose*. available online at <http://www-users.york.ac.uk/~lang22/YCOE/YcoeHome.htm>

Taylor, Ann, & Pintzuk, Susan (2014). Testing the Theory. Information Structure in Old English. In Kristin Bech, & Kristine Gunn Eide, *Information Structure and Syntactic Change in Germanic and Romance Languages* (53–80). Amsterdam/Philadelphia: John Benjamins Publishing Company. https://doi.org/10.1075/la.213.03tay

Virtanen, Tuija (1992). *Discourse Functions of Adverbial Placement in English. Clause-Initial Adverbials of Time and Place in Narratives and Procedural Place Descriptions*. Åbo: Åbo Akademis Verlag.

Virtanen, Tuija (2010). Variation across texts and discourses: Theoretical and methodological perspectives on text type and genre. In Heidrun von Dorgeloh, & Anja Wanner (Eds.), *Topics in English Linguistics 70: Syntactic Variation and Genre* (53–84). Berlin: De Gruyter Mouton. https://doi.org/10.1515/9783110226485.1.53

Wårvik, Brita (2011). Connective or "disconnective" discourse marker? Old English þa, multifunctionality and narrative structuring. In Anneli Meurman-Solin, & Ursula Lenker (Eds.), *Varieng Vol. 8: Connectives in Synchrony and Diachrony in European Languages*. <http://www.helsinki.fi/varieng/journal/volumes/08/warvik/>.

Appendix

Table 2. Results of binary regression model for the Middle English data set that comprises only clusters made up of two elements (n = 929) after stepwise model selection ($R^2 = 0.92$)

Factor (level)	Estimate	Standard error	z-value	p-value	Odds ratio
realization form (advp pp)	4.807306017	0.7204345	6.672787076	2.51E-11	116.2820731
realization form (pp np)	−5.45543896	1.496008411	−3.646663296	0.000265668	0.00374586
obligatoriness (ac)	5.174821728	1.082509328	4.780394585	1.75E-06	174.6796519
obligatoriness (ca)	−6.18208298	1.227838922	−5.034929961	4.78E-07	0.001849596
clause pattern (XVS)	5.96989247	1.517205938	3.934793768	8.33E-05	456.3435976

Table 3. Results of binary regression model for the Early Modern English data set that comprises only clusters made up of two elements (n = 1015) after stepwise model selection ($R^2 = 0.89$)

Factor (level)	Estimate	Standard error	z-value	p-value	Odds ratio
realization form (advp pp)	1.848036047	0.698399256	2.646102543	0.008142513	6.347341396
realization form (np pp)	4.408681467	0.861016331	5.120322702	3.05E-07	82.16105998
complexity (more complex first)	−2.19471218	0.96957432	−2.263583241	0.02359976	0.111390617
obligatoriness (ac)	5.277913969	0.777986126	6.784072096	1.17E-11	195.9606686
obligatoriness (ca)	−5.02337068	0.732790159	−6.855128468	7.12E-12	0.006582302
position of the cluster regarding the verb (lexical verb – cluster)	−1.46764837	0.787623439	−1.863388394	0.062407642	0.23046682

Table 4. Examples from the EModE data for each subcategory of the adverbials of place and time, along with the corresponding elicitation question

Spatial location	Where?	*The weather detain'd me* **at home** *in the afternoon* (EVELYN-E3-H,932.380, The diary of John Evelyn. London)
Direction – Goal	Where to?	*I returned* **home** *after this sermon* (EVELYN-E3-H,905.194, The diary of John Evelyn. London)
Direction – Source	Where from?	**From Stamford** *the next day we rode to Huntington, where we lodged at the Post-masters house, at the signe of the Crowne* (JOTAYLOR-E2-H,1,140.C1.332, John Taylor: The pennyles pilgrimage)
Direction – Path	Along where?	*Why did not you go* **the same way** *upon the Tuesday that you went upon the Saturday?* (LISLE-E3-P1,4,111.375, Lisle state trial)
Distance	How far?	*thence I went home againe* **4 miles.** (FIENNES-E3-P1,168.342, The journeys of Celia Fiennes)
Time position	When?	*The weather detain'd me at home* **in the afternoone** (EVELYN-E3-H,932.380, The diary of John Evelyn. London)
Time duration – Source	Since when?	*Ne're was the like in Cambridge* **since my time** (MIDDLET-E2-P1,36.451, Thomas Middleton: A chaste maid in Cheapside)
Time duration – Goal	Until when?	*then I was busie in the kitchine and about the house* **till 6** (HOBY-E2-H,77.310, Diary of Lady Margaret Hoby)
Time duration – Span	For how long?	*After which I stayde in Bristoll* **about a weeke** (FOX-E3-H,154.243, The journal of George Fox)
Time frequency	How often?	*Upon Monday the 19th I saw him* **twice** *that day at my own House* (OATES-E3-H,4,82.C2.389, Oates state trial)
Time relationship	When?	*Whom Austin being* **already** *there before them, neither arose to meet, nor receiv'd in any brotherly sort* (MILTON-E3-H,X,148.60, John Milton: The history of Britain, that part especially now call'd England)

Variation and change at the interface of syntax and semantics

Concessive clauses in American English

Ole Schützler

Based on the *Corpus of Historical American English* (COHA), this chapter inspects diachronic changes of constructions involving the concessive conjunctions *although*, *though* and *even though* from the 1860s to the present day. Following a short summary of changes in semantics and clause structures, the main focus lies on factors that have an effect on the position of the subordinate clause relative to the matrix clause. A Bayesian logistic regression model is used to investigate in how far the position of a subordinate clause can be predicted from the semantics of the entire construction, the connective that is used, and the weight (or length) of the complement, and whether the preferred positions of subordinate clauses change over time.

Keywords: concessives, conjunctions, American English, syntax, Corpus Linguistics

1. Introduction

There is a vast body of research devoted to concessives in English. Most authors, however, concentrate on general semantic or theoretical aspects (e.g. König, 2006; Hermodsson, 1994; Azar, 1997; di Meola, 1998), while quantitative, corpus-based studies are the exception (but cf. Aarts, 1988; Hilpert, 2013 and Hoffmann, 2005). In particular, quantitative, diachronic studies of the syntax of concessives seem to be quite rare. This chapter addresses this gap in the research, focusing on the ordering of main clause and subordinate clause and how it is influenced by various factors.

There are several studies of clause ordering in English (e.g. Altenberg, 1986; Ramsay, 1987; Ford, 1993; Diessel, 2005, 2008; Wiechmann & Kerz, 2013). Altenberg (1986) looks at concessives along with other adverbials, while Wiechmann & Kerz (2013) focus explicitly on concessives constructed with *although* and *whereas*. Not primarily concerned with clause ordering, Aarts (1988) also presents some results

https://doi.org/10.1075/cilt.346.12sch

regarding the position of concessive subordinate clauses. The present study builds upon the background provided by previous research and expands our knowledge of clause ordering in several ways. For example, while providing a wealth of corpus-based description, Altenberg's (1986) study of spoken and written British English (BrE) is not multifactorial and thus might miss many possible explanatory factors and their interactions. Aarts (1988) is not primarily concerned with clause ordering and thus only provides very basic counts of subordinate clauses in different positions in BrE.

The present chapter is most strongly informed by Wiechmann & Kerz's (2013) methodologically advanced multifactorial approach. However, it makes additions to all three previous studies in that it inspects American English (AmE), includes a strong diachronic perspective, analyses concessive markers not considered in combination elsewhere, and uses semantic criteria that do not feature in previous quantitative research, with the exception of certain parts of Hilpert's (2013) study. In recent research, Schützler (2017) found that most concessive clauses in corpus data – at least if involving *although* and *though* – belong to the class of speech-act concessives (see 2.1 below), while most grammars of the language tend to present content concessives (also see below) as prototypical examples. One aim of the present chapter is to see whether this discrepancy is due to a relatively recent change, and to inspect, at the same time, what this might mean for concomitant syntactic developments. The focus on American English in this chapter will be followed by comparisons of both American and British English in future research.

The subordinating conjunctions *although*, *though* and *even though* are grammatically interchangeable under most circumstances and etymologically (and morphologically) related.[1] Substituting one for the other generally does not compromise the grammaticality of the sentence or result in any obvious change in meaning, as shown in (1), where the original corpus Example 1a is modified, using the alternative conjunctions. All three sentences are clearly possible and not obviously problematic in any way.

(1) a. *Although* Paul Taylor once studied painting, he is not a painter on canvas. (COHA, 1985, newspapers)
b. *Though* Paul Taylor once studied painting, he is not a painter on canvas.
c. *Even though* Paul Taylor once studied painting, he is not a painter on canvas.

1. According to the *Oxford English Dictionary Online*, the predecessors of *though* as a conjunction (OE *ðēah*, *þēah* or *þēh*) are first attested in the 9th and 10th centuries. A variant approximating the modern form (*þou*) is cited from the 14th century. It is around that time that *although* as a conjunction seems to have arisen, if of course in variant spellings. At least at the time of its introduction, it seems to have had emphatic value. Finally, *even though* is attested considerably later, in 1697. Like *although*, it is treated as a stronger variant derived from *though*.

Furthermore, all three conjunctions can express the semantic types of concession outlined in the next section. This is not true to the same extent of the conjunctions *whereas* and *while*, which may express concession but mostly function as markers of general contrast and were therefore excluded from the present study.

As shown in (2), *though* can also occur as what is called a "connective adjunct" by Huddleston & Pullum (2002: 736), a "linking adverbial" by Biber et al. (1999: 850–851), and a "conjunct" by Quirk et al. (1985: 632), namely a connective that functions between sentences, not intra-sententially.

(2) Fred Shepley said he hadn't ever paid any attention to the lions. He wished he had, *though*. (COHA, 1940, fiction)

The conjunct is a very interesting research object in itself. However, it is excluded from the study since it does not belong to the class of subordinating conjunctions, even if it is etymologically related to the three conjunctions treated in this chapter.

Clausal complements of *although*, *though* and *even though* may be finite, non-finite or verbless, as in Examples 3–5, respectively.[2] A clausal reading is possible in each case, and the different realisations do not appear to be fundamentally different in meaning. It has to be said, however, that in Examples 4 and 5 the subjects in both clauses (matrix and subordinate) are coreferential, and that it is only upon this condition that nonfinite/verbless clauses can easily be substituted for finite ones – cf. the construction type investigated by Hilpert (2013: 183), for example.

(3) … Clark was a good fellow, and a capable bookkeeper, *even though* he was a trifle slow. (COHA, 1899, fiction)

(4) Thus, *although* retreating, we were always ready to fight. (COHA, 1892, fiction)

(5) … [T]he local stations, *though* state-owned, were all under the control of locally elected management committees, … (COHA, 1973, non-fiction, commas added)

An interesting construction that is only possible in connection with *though* is shown in (6). Culicover (1976: 166) calls this "*though*-attraction", since within the subordinate clause, the complement (in this case an AdjP) is moved to the very front of the clause out of its default position after the verb. An alternative term for this construction is "*though*-movement" (Radford, 1981: 213; also cf. Aarts, 1988: 44–45; Quirk et al., 1985: 1097–1098). Although it only occurs in combination with

2. No difference was made between past participles and adjectives as complements, and indeed it is often difficult to keep them apart (e.g. *although parked in the driveway* … vs *although brand-new* …); along with present participles, both were treated as non-finite.

though, this particular syntactic variant was included in the analysis; its omission would have ignored one possible factor in the variation of clause ordering.

(6) His weakness lies chiefly in his strength, paradoxical *though* the statement may seem. (COHA, 1880, magazines)

Beyond the choice of different conjunctions and the selection of different clause structures (finite, nonfinite, verbless, *though*-attraction), variability exists at the level of clause ordering. Like most subordinate adverbial clauses, concessive clauses can be placed in initial, medial and final position relative to the matrix clause (cf. Altenberg, 1986: 20), as shown in Example 7, where (7b) and (7c) are constructed modifications of the original corpus example. This dimension of variation, too, seems to have no obvious effect on grammaticality or meaning.

(7) a. *Although* dazed by his astonishing discovery, the boy quickly recovered ... (COHA, 1903, fiction)
b. The boy, *although* dazed by his astonishing discovery, quickly recovered.
c. The boy quickly recovered, *although* dazed by his astonishing discovery.

Finally, subordinate clauses may vary considerably in length. Examples 8 and 9 show the shortest and the longest subordinate clause in the sample. The complement in (8) is exactly one word and one syllable in length, while in (9) it is an astounding 86 words and 128 syllables in length. Complements are underlined for emphasis.

(8) He is a very strict man, *even though* <u>kind</u>. (COHA, 1906, fiction)

(9) [...] I will concede him to be deeply learned [in astrology], *even though* <u>he has never yet proved to my entire satisfaction that the reason why my copy of Justinian has faded from a royal purple to a pale blue is, first, because the binding was renewed at the wane of the moon and when Sirius was in the ascendant, and, secondly, because (as Dr. O'Rell has discovered) my binder was born at a moment fifty-six years ago when Mercury was in the fourth house and Herschel and Saturn were aspected in conjunction, with Sol at his northern declination</u>. (COHA, 1896, fiction)

The four parameters described thus far – choice of subordinator, complement structure, position of subordinate clause, and complement length within the subordinate clause – are formal or syntactic in nature. While constructions involving *although, though* and *even though* are invariably classified as concessive, there are also more fine-grained semantic differences that will be outlined in the next part of the chapter.

The study as a whole is interested in how the syntactic parameters outlined above and the semantic parameters discussed below develop and interact in American English in the late modern and present-day period. In particular, the following questions are addressed: (i) Which semantic types of concessives do the three conjunctions preferably encode – in particular: Do they differ in this respect, and has this changed diachronically? (ii) Have there been any changes in the internal syntax and the length of subordinate clauses? (iii) Have there been any changes in the preferred position of subordinate clauses?

A hypothesis developed in the next section is that clause ordering will be affected by other formal parameters (choice of conjunction, clause structure, and length) as well as semantics. Question iii above is therefore best addressed in a multivariate approach, factoring in the other parameters. Only questions ii and iii are immediately syntax-related, but discussions of semantic aspects are clearly indispensable components of the present study.

The chapter is structured as follows: The second section discusses the three semantic types of concessives assumed to play a role in syntactic variation, as well as what Altenberg (1986) calls "contrastive sequencing", i.e. the arrangement of main and subordinate clauses, including previous accounts of how this syntactic arrangement may be conditioned. A separate section is dedicated to those two aspects since they require a somewhat more elaborate theoretical background. The third part outlines the methodologies that are used, discussing corpus data and introducing the Bayesian model used for the more complex multivariate analysis. The fourth part presents results, describing the individual parameters in diachrony before proceeding to the multivariate analysis of syntactic positions. The chapter concludes with a discussion and summary of findings and an outlook to future research needed on the topic.

2. Theoretical background and previous research

2.1 Three semantic types of concessives

Sweetser (1990: 76–77) describes three different semantic types of concessives, which she calls *content*, *epistemic* and *speech-act concessives*.[3] Content concessives are constructed and decoded based on so-called *topoi* (Azar, 1997: 306; Anscombre, 1989), which are sets of presuppositions based on world knowledge or other, more locally grounded (contextual) knowledge shared by the speaker (or writer) and the addressee (or reader). Very often, such presuppositions can be formalised as some kind of if-then relation (cf. König, 2006). For example, the topos "if you work hard, (then) you will (normally) succeed" enables concessives like (10):

3. See Crevels (2000: 315–317), Lang (2000) and Tsunoda (2012) for further categories of adverbial linking.

(10) *Although* I worked hard, I failed the test.

A corpus example of content concessives is shown in (11). The underlying topos is that, in the given context, a young man who comes of age will normally be given part of his inheritance. The topos employed in this late-19th-century example is no longer valid in western societies and thus demonstrates that topoi may well be restricted to a certain time or cultural context.

(11) George tells me that *although* he is long ago of age, he has as yet received no portion of his father's estates. (COHA, 1897, fiction)

Like content concessives, epistemic concessives are often based on topoi, but in this case the two propositions are not held together by a real-world relation of cause and effect but by an inference or conclusion based on the subordinate proposition. An example is shown in (12). Here, the observation that a rug is 5′7″ by 7′ in size (amounting to ca. 3.6 m^2) will trigger certain conclusions as to its functions, probably not including that of a prayer rug, since such rugs will prototypically be a good deal smaller. Thus, the conclusions and inferences that are prompted turn out to be false. The topos is once again not truly universal: It does not work in societies where large prayer rugs of this type are in fact used, and of course in communities that know nothing at all about prayer rugs and thus have no preconceptions concerning them.

(12) … *[A]lthough* five feet seven inches by seven feet in size, it is a prayer rug […]. (COHA, 1904, magazines)

A speech-act concessive is shown in (13). There is no link between the two propositions ("cellulose has no nutritional value" and "cellulose is useful as roughage") at either the content or the epistemic level. Rather, the construction as a whole presents two contrasting pragmatic perspectives. The matrix-clause proposition promotes a negative evaluation of cellulose, low nutritional value correlating with its uselessness as fodder. In contrast, the proposition in the subordinate clause indicates that cellulose does have some value (even if unrelated to nutritional value). The construction as a whole thus supplies negative and positive evaluative evidence, without recourse to any kind of if-then relation.

(13) [… C]ellulose has no nutritional value *although* it may serve a useful purpose as roughage. (COHA, 1982, non-fiction)

It could be argued that in speech-act concessives, rather than belonging to the same topos, the two propositions trigger two independent (and contrasting) topoi.

2.2 'Contrastive sequencing'

Most subordinate adverbial clauses can be placed in initial, medial and final position relative to the matrix clause, and concessive clauses are no exception (cf. Altenberg, 1986: 20). Some authors focus entirely on the difference between initial and final placement (e.g. Chafe, 1984: 437; Wiechmann & Kerz, 2013: 1, 7; Diessel, 2005: 452), either disregarding medial position, or categorising it as "non-final", together with initial position. The latter approach (of conflating initial and medial position into a single non-final category) is the one taken in this study (also see the section on methodology below).

An excellent discussion of competing motivations in clause placement is found in Diessel (2005), who does not treat concessive clauses in particular, however. The three factors Diessel discusses are related to (i) processing, (ii) discourse-pragmatics, and (iii) semantics.

Diessel's (2005: 455–458) approach to processing-based explanations strongly rests on Hawkins's (e.g. 1994, 1998) "performance theory of order and constituency", whereby successful parsing depends on two conditions: (i) the parser needs to realize that the sentence is complex, and (ii) the boundary between main and subordinate clause needs to be identified. If the subordinate clause is preposed, the complex structure of the sentence is recognised early, but the contents of the preposed subordinate clause need to be kept in working memory until the main-clause subject establishes the boundary between both clauses – the second condition for successful parsing. If, on the other hand, the subordinate clause follows the main clause, the complex sentence structure and the clause boundary are recognised at the same time, reducing the processing load. On this premise, Diessel (2005: 450–451) argues that sentence-final placement of adverbial clauses is cognitively ideal, and that alternative clause positions need to be motivated. Further, sentence-initial subordinate clauses would be expected to be relatively short.

"Discourse-pragmatic forces" may compete with processing-based constraints (Diessel, 2005: 459–461). Although not identical, discourse pragmatics and information structure (cf. Chafe, 1976, 1984: 440; Lambrecht, 1996; Krifka, 2008; Schützler, 2018a) seem closely related: In the words of Wiechmann & Kerz (2013: 3), "discourse-related" explanations concentrate "on variables such as the relative availability of the respective information and the discourse-organizing role of the adverbial clause". For example, a sentence-initial subordinate clause is of advantage if it refers to information given in the preceding discourse and, at the same time, has a grounding function for the following main clause, as shown in (11).

(14) He proposed bringing together [ten] experts on low-income housing, giving them a week to choose their best ideas and making a commitment to execute those ideas. *Although* several of the projects are sure to fail, Mr. Rouse said, "to fail is not wrong. To not take a chance is wrong." (COHA, 1987, newspapers)

The subordinate clause is clearly oriented forwards and backwards in discourse and thus makes an elegant transition between "the projects" discussed earlier in the example and what follows. It is not easy to establish whether or not the position of a subordinate clause has a discourse-pragmatic function, since a lot of context needs to be inspected to do so.

Diessel (2005: 461–465) also discusses semantic factors that impact upon the placement of subordinate clauses. For example, he argues that prototypical *if*-clauses are predominantly placed in sentence-initial position since this facilitates a smooth interpretation of the two contrasting consequences that it triggers (*if* … → *then* … → *otherwise* …), quite apart from the fact that the hypothetical truth value of either consequent will only be recognised on the basis of an earlier *if*-clause. The order *if* → *then* would also generally seem to be iconic of real-world sequentiality. With regard to concessives, subordinate clauses in constructions of the content and epistemic types prompt certain expectations or conclusions, respectively, which may have an effect on their position in the sentence. For example, the interpretations of the main-clause propositions in Examples 10 and 11 are clearly affected by the subordinate clauses that precede them. In those two cases, nuances of meaning resulting from the concessive can be added relatively effortlessly, since the concessive background is already given when the main clause is parsed. If the order of clauses was inverted, the semantics of the entire sentence would unfold less smoothly, since the initial main clause proposition would need to be partially reinterpreted. In speech-act concessives, this is less of a problem: The propositions that are involved could be said to be more loosely connected, since there is no clearly recognisable topos. The analyses presented below will therefore investigate whether specific semantic types of concessives prefer certain syntactic positions.

There is limited previous research on clause positioning in concessives. Aarts (1988: 43–44) finds that in written BrE *although* is non-final in 54.5% of all cases, while *though* (as a conjunction) is non-final 36.1% of the time. According to Biber et al. (1999: 834), concessive adverbial clauses are placed in sentence-final position in 60% of all cases, across different registers. And Altenberg (1986: 22–23) finds that in the written LOB Corpus, *although* occurs sentence-initially in 67% of cases, while *though* is in sentence-final position in 64% of cases. Clauses headed by *even though* are placed after the main cause in four out of the five cases Altenberg finds in the corpus. Altenberg argues that *although* is used more for grounding functions, i.e. providing a discourse-pragmatic or semantic canvas for the main clause. Finally, the study by Wiechmann & Kerz (2013) comes to the conclusion that discourse-pragmatic factors have the strongest effect on clause ordering – in their case, the presence of an anaphoric, discourse-deictic item in the subordinate clause correlates with non-final placement of the clause. The choice of subordinator is also highly relevant in their study; in this case, *although* and *whereas* are compared, the latter being considerably more likely to occur in final position. Other significant factors are length, clause-internal syntactic complexity and syntactic deranking (i.e. the use of nonfinite or verbless clauses). At least in the case of *although*, length and complexity correlate positively with final placement, while deranking increases the probability of non-final placement.

The present study adds to existing knowledge by (i) taking different intra-constructional relations into account, (ii) directly comparing a set of etymologically related markers (*although*, *though* and *even though*), and (iii) approaching syntactic variation and change from a diachronic perspective.

3. Methodology

Analyses in this chapter are based on data from the *Corpus of Historical American English* (COHA; Davies 2010-), which contains approximately 406 million words in four written genres (fiction, non-fiction, magazines, and newspapers) from the years 1810–2009. Only material dating from the 1860s to the 2000s was used for the present study, since there are no newspaper texts in the earlier decades of the 19th century. The selected part of the corpus is 352 million words in size, corresponding to between 17.1 and 29.5 million words per decade. The data were extracted from the corpus via the COHA online interface (http://corpus.byu.edu/coha/). Statistical analysis was conducted in R (R Development Core Team, 2016) and RStudio (RStudio Team, 2009–2016), for graphical displays the R-package *lattice* (Sarkar, 2014) was used.

For the diachronic syntactic and semantic analyses, two balanced subsamples were created, one representing the 1860s–1900s, the other one representing the 1960s–2000s. This approach reduced the workload involved in semantic and syntactic annotation, without compromising the aim of comparing Late Modern and Present-day English usage.[4] For each of the three conjunctions, random samples were drawn from each of the four genres in both time periods. Through further randomization it was ensured that occurrences within each subsample were no longer ordered by their date of publication. Within each of the resulting eight random

4. Alternatively, smaller samples from all decades of COHA could have been used, but results for each decade would have been considerably less robust.

samples per conjunction, the first forty cases that were analysable for syntax and semantics were used. If a case was fragmented or unclear, it was omitted. The total number of tokens that were semantically and syntactically analysed, and whose length was measured, was therefore $n = 2 \times 4 \times 3 \times 40 = 960$ (two periods, four genres, three conjunctions, and 40 tokens per cell). Following the semantic analysis, a total of nine items had to be excluded from the multivariate analysis: Their particular syntactic structure makes them immune to positional variation, since the concessive is embedded in the matrix clause below the clausal level. A typical example is shown in (15):

(15) Yet England, which more nearly escaped the devastation of war, suffered a genuine *though* more insensible crisis of order. (COHA, 1988, non-fiction)

Here, the concessive applies within an attributive AdjP, which prevents (or at least complicates dramatically) syntactic rearrangement. For the part of the analysis predicting final placement, the total number of tokens was therefore 951, not 960.[5]

The length of subordinate clauses was measured in words and syllables. Logged values of both measures are highly correlated (Pearson's r = .944; p = .000). In the regression model, length in syllables was preferred over length in words, since it was considered the more precise index. This simple approach was preferred to using additional or alternative measures of length (or complexity/weight), which do of course exist (see comment in concluding section)

The analysis proceeds from a descriptive perspective to an inferential one, first describing various formal and semantic parameters in diachrony and proceeding to a more complex regression model. The discussion of changes in the predictor variables (e.g. an increase in certain semantic types or clause structures over time) in combination with a multivariate analysis provides descriptive detail and shows factors in interaction.

In the multivariate analysis, Bayesian inference was used, modeling the data with the utilities in the *brms* package (Bürckner, 2016), which in turn uses Stan (Stan Development Team, 2016). Bayesian analysis was preferred over a standard mixed-effects model because it makes no assumptions as to sampling distributions, can be informed by tendencies found in previous research, and permits pooling (adjustment) against central tendencies, which makes the model somewhat more conservative (cf. Kruschke, 2015: 722–725). Following the strategy outlined in Gelman et al. (2013: 412–419), weakly informative priors (i.e. prior

5. While it seems to be possible for all three conjunctions to occur in combination with those phrasal concessives (as I have called them here), there are clear differences: Out of the nine instances detected in my data, six are headed by *though*, two are headed by *although*, and only one is headed by *even though*.

assumptions) were specified for all parameters based on the empirical evidence in the literature (Altenberg, 1986; Aarts, 1988; Schützler, 2018b), as listed in Table A2 in the appendix. Further model parameters used in the analysis are listed in the Appendix as well.

Independent variables used in the final model (and also discussed in the descriptive part) are VARIANT (i.e. the choice of subordinator, *although*, *though* or *even though*), TYPE (content, epistemic or speech-act), INTSYNT (finite, nonfinite/verbless and *though*-attraction), PERIOD (late 19th century vs late 20th century), LENGTH (length of subordinate clause in syllables, excluding the subordinator) and GENRE, as well as the interaction of VARIANT and TYPE.[6] The outcome variable is FINAL, i.e. the placement of subordinate clauses at the end of a sentence; initial and medial placement were pooled into a single category. Only LENGTH and PERIOD were included as fixed effects, all other effects were specified as random. Estimates for the levels of each random factor are partially pooled towards the overall intercept, which helps guard against overfitting (cf., e.g. Kruschke, 2015: 245; McElreath, 2016: 364–370). With regard to VARIANT and TYPE and their interaction, this seemed particularly important given the low number of cases for the epistemic type, which resulted in several sparsely populated cells. Candidate models were compared using the WAIC information criterion (Watanabe, 2010) and the LOOIC, its cross-validation-based correction (Vehtari, Gelman & Gabry, 2017), based on which Akaike weights were derived (cf. McElreath, 2016: 197–203).

4. Results

Results concerning developments in semantics, complement-internal syntax and complement length will be summarised relatively briefly, and only minimal discussion will be provided. The summary section at the end of the chapter will return to the results presented here.

4.1 Semantics

Proportions of the three semantic types of concessives (content, epistemic and speech-act) are shown in Figure 1, ordered by the three conjunctions and indicating differences between the two time periods within each panel.

6. The conflation of participial and verbless clauses into a single category rests on the fact that, in contrast to finite clauses, they are both reduced. Moreover, there is often but a fuzzy boundary between participles (in participial clauses) and adjectives (in verbless clauses), for example.

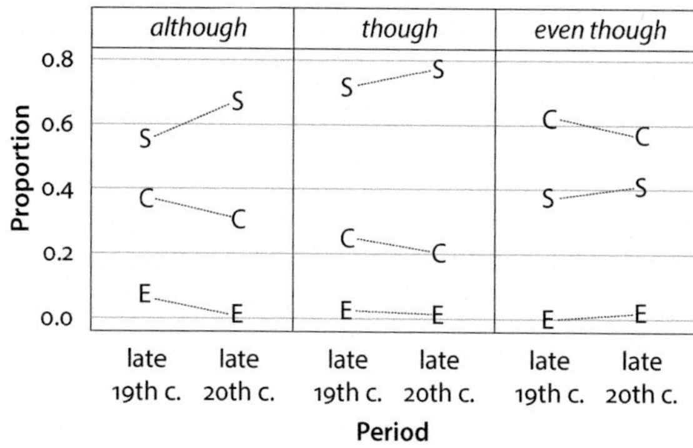

Figure 1. Changes in proportions of semantic types
(C = content; E = epistemic; S = speech-act)

There is a very clear difference between *although* and *though* on the one hand and *even though* on the other: The former predominantly encode speech-act concessives, while *even though* predominantly encodes content concessives. *Though* is somewhat more specialised towards the encoding of speech-act concessives than *although*. Epistemic concessives are quite low in frequency overall.[7]

For all three conjunctions, there is an increase in the relative number of speech-act concessives and a decrease in the relative number of content concessives. The change is statistically significant in the case of *although* (χ^2 (2) = 8.97; p = .011; φ = .167), while for *though* and *even though* it is not (*though*: χ^2 (2) = 1.51; p = .470; φ = .069; *even though*: χ^2 (2) = 3.71; p = .157; φ = .108). However, even for *although*, the effect size is rather modest.

4.2 Complement-internal syntax

Changes in the proportions of different syntactic realisations of subordinate clauses are shown in Figure 2, again ordered by the three conjunctions and indicating diachronic change within each panel. Finite and nonfinite (i.e. participial or verbless) clauses occur in combination with all three connectives, while the syntactic variant called *though*-attraction – illustrated in Example 6 above – is restricted to *though*. Nine cases were excluded from this particular analysis since they eluded clausal interpretation (see methodologies section above).

7. See Schützler (2017, 2018b) for further discussions and quantitative analyses of the semantics of concessive constructions.

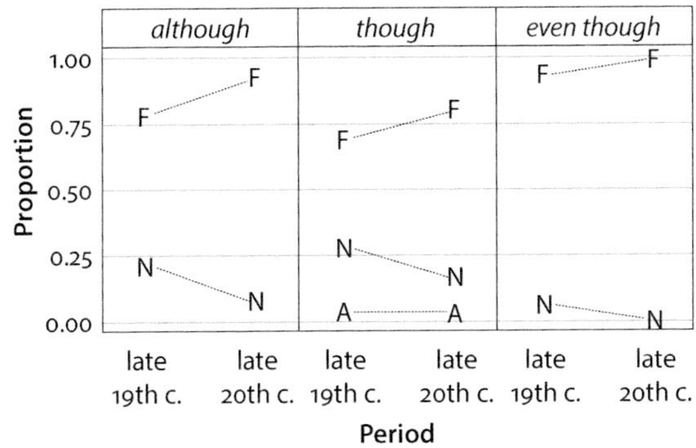

Figure 2. Changes in proportions of syntactic patterns within clauses (F = finite; N = nonfinite; A = *though*-attraction)

Finite clauses increase in relative frequency across all three conjunctions, while nonfinite clauses become less frequent; the (low) proportion of *though*-attraction remains constant ($n = 5$ in both subsamples). All three patterns are statistically significant. The effect is strongest for *although* (χ^2 (1) = 11.52; $p = .001$; $\varphi = .190$), followed by *though* (χ^2 (2) = 6.93; $p = .031$; $\varphi = .149$) and *even though* (χ^2 (1) = 6.08; $p = .014$; $\varphi = .138$).

4.3 Complement length

The lengths (in syllables) of clausal complements of *although*, *though* and *even though* are plotted in Figure 3. The boxplot indicates median and mean values.

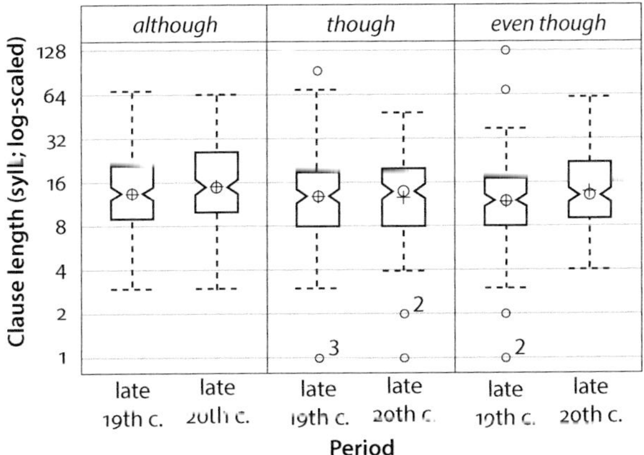

Figure 3. Diachronic comparison of clause length; symbols in box: Median (O), mean (+). Number of overplotted outliers indicated

In each panel, *t*-tests between the two time periods were performed on logged numbers of syllables. For *although*, the $\log_2$-mean increases from 3.73 in the late 20th century to 3.93 in the late 19th century, which corresponds to reconverted (non-logged) means of 13.3 and 15.2 syllables. The result of the *t*-test is not significant by a small margin ($p = .06$; Cohen's $d = .208$). For *though*, the $\log_2$-mean decreases from 3.67 to 3.62, which corresponds to reconverted means of 12.7 and 12.3 syllables, respectively. The difference is very clearly not significant and the effect extremely small ($p = .696$; $d = .044$). In contrast to the other two conjunctions, subordinate clauses headed by *even though* increase significantly in length between the two time periods that are investigated. The $\log_2$-mean changes from 3.55 to 3.79, which corresponds to non-logged means of 11.7 and 13.8 syllables, respectively ($p = .020$; $d = .262$). Changes in the distributions of complement lengths follow quite different patterns for all three conjunctions: The overall range of possible complement lengths remains quite stable for *although*, with only minor changes towards longer complements at the centre of the distribution (i.e. the box in the boxplot is elongated slightly towards higher numbers of syllables); for *though*, the distribution becomes more compact (i.e. dispersion is reduced), but particularly the mean value hardly changes; for *even though*, the outliers seen in the earlier period are no longer found in the later subsample, and at the same time the entire distribution undergoes a regular shift towards higher numbers of syllables.

4.4 Multifactorial analysis of contrastive sequencing

A technical summary of the Bayesian regression model is provided in Table A1 in the appendix. It lists the means and quantiles of the posterior distribution of the model parameters and also specifies the effective sample size and $\hat{R}$ ("R-hat"). The regression table is of limited value for interpretation, which is why it is relegated to the appendix, but readers familiar with logistic regression can refer back to it to confirm numerically what is shown in Figure 5 below.

Figure 4 summarizes the most important patterns in the data in the form of effect displays. Fitted values of the outcome (final position) across the levels or the range of each predictor are shown, controlling for other parameters. The error bars (and bands) indicate 50% and 95% credible intervals.

As can be seen in the left-hand panel of Figure 4, in comparison to *although*, the conjunction *though* is somewhat more likely to be placed in sentence-final position, which is a weak confirmation of Altenberg's (1986) and Aarts's (1988) findings. Relative to the other two connectives, *even though* clearly tends to prefer sentence-final position. This is in accordance with Altenberg's (1986) results, which, however, are based on very few data points for *even though*.

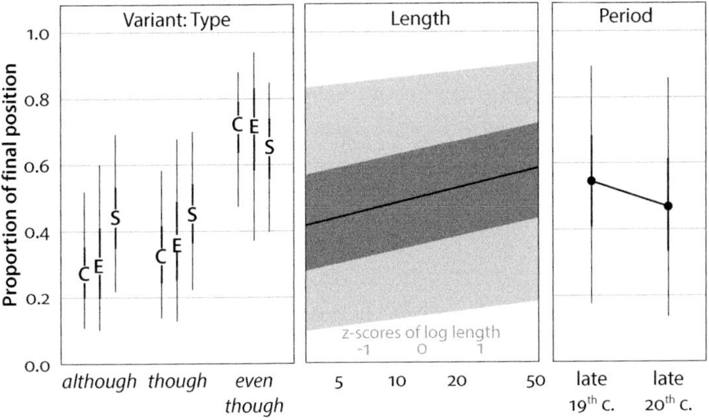

Figure 4. Effects plot for main effects

In combination with *although* and *though*, content and epistemic concessives are considerably more likely to be constructed using sentence-initial (or medial) subordinate clauses. The inverse pattern can be seen in connection with *even though*. However, due to the low number of epistemic concessives, the value for this semantic type may have been pooled towards the central tendency, so that epistemic and content concessives may in fact be more similar than would appear in Figure 4.

As expected, higher values of the predictor LENGTH correlate with a higher probability of sentence-final placement. The effect is relatively weak, which is evident if one inspects the relevant interval between the predictor's values at −1 and +1 standard deviation. There is also some general diachronic change, which is not particularly pronounced, however: Holding all other factors in the model constant, subordinate concessive clauses headed by the three conjunctions become somewhat more likely to be placed in non-final position in the sentence.

The impact of the four input variables (VARIANT, TYPE, LENGTH and PERIOD) on the probability of final position is compared in Figure 5. The plot shows predictive comparisons evaluated at hypothetical unit changes in each input variable. This makes it possible to appreciate the impact of each input variable, and, importantly, to compare effect magnitudes.

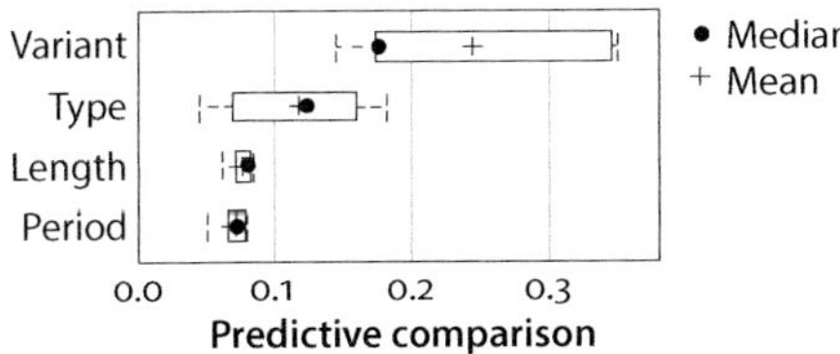

Figure 5. Predictive comparison of main effects

The value on the x-axis in Figure 5 indicates the change in the probability of final placement if the respective predictor category (on the y-axis) is changed by one unit. For instance, the effect of PERIOD was assessed by determining for all 951 cases the absolute change in probability had this case been sampled in the late 19th vs the late 20th century, all other things being equal. Assuming a one-unit change in the continuous predictor LENGTH is somewhat more problematic; instead of using true unit changes (e.g. ±1 syllable/log syllable), it was decided to re-define the one-unit change as a shift from the value at −1 standard deviations to the value at +1 standard deviations of the predictor. For the two nominal variables VARIANT and TYPE, the possible transitions (two in each case, e.g. from content to epistemic and from content to speech-act) were weighted in proportion to the probability of the respective pair in the distribution (cf. Gelman & Pardoe, 2007: 34). Clearly, VARIANT is the most important source of variation among the four variables considered, with a change between variants corresponding to a change of around 20% percentage points. The effect of TYPE is somewhat smaller (10–15% in absolute terms). Finally, LENGTH and PERIOD have only a rather minor impact of 5–10% on the position of subordinate clauses.

A very interesting effect not shown in Figure 5 is the random effect associated with the three different clause-internal structures found in subordinate clauses. This effect indicates that, if all other factors are held constant, the expected probability of final placement is 57% in finite clauses, 45% in nonfinite clauses (cf. similar results in Wiechmann & Kerz, 2013), and 44% in the construction type that was called *though*-attraction. Even though the length of clausal complements is controlled for, we can therefore say that finite clauses are more likely than nonfinite clauses to occur sentence-finally, and the special case of *though*-attraction – while technically finite – is very similar to nonfinite clauses in its effect on clause placement.

5. Discussion, conclusion and outlook

In the period under investigation, constructions involving the three conjunctions *although*, *though* and *even though* change in several ways, including their semantics, the length and syntactic structure of subordinate clauses, and the positions of matrix and subordinate clauses. In this final discussion, I will focus on these diachronic developments, although several general properties described in this chapter may also be of interest in their own right.

Semantic changes follow a relatively clear trajectory for all three conjunctions: Speech-act concessives increase in relative frequency, mainly at the cost of content concessives. In combination with *although* and *though*, speech-act concessives are the most frequent semantico-pragmatic variant even in the earlier data, and what we observe could therefore be interpreted as a focusing process, whereby semantic variability is reduced further. In the long term, this may result in a clearer form-to-function mapping. However, the increase in the relative frequency of speech-act concessives is also found in combination with *even though*, and in this case it leads to increased variability, i.e. a more serious competition between the two majority variants, content and speech-act concessives. A possible explanation that holds for all three conjunctions is an ongoing process of subjectification, characterised by a development away from purely content-oriented propositions towards expressions of a speaker's (or writer's) stance (cf. Finegan, 1995). For concessives, Crevels (2000) and Hilpert (2013: 165–167) assume that speech-act concessives are more subjective than content concessives, since in this case the contrast between propositions is not based on some real-world relation of cause and effect, but more obviously arises from some pragmatic goal of the speaker/writer. In this view, there is a general slow process of subjectification affecting concessives with all three conjunctions, and in combination with *although* and *though* this additionally results in a tidier, less variable situation.

Concerning the internal syntactic properties of subordinate clauses, two aspects play a role, clause structures (finite, nonfinite and *though*-attraction) and the length of the clausal complement. Concerning the former, it was found that all three conjunctions develop a significantly strengthened preference for finite clauses. From a construction-grammar perspective (cf. Goldberg, 2003), this development results in less schematic constructions characterised by reduced syntactic variation, since the majority variant (finite clauses) is strengthened even further.

With regard to clause length, changes are relatively modest: Only *even though* is complemented by significantly longer clauses in the late 20th century, but the effect is not large. Interestingly, this conjunction generally tends most strongly to sentence-final position, and the diachronic trend further strengthens this pattern. The development is in accordance with the information-structural principles of end-focus and end-weight (Quirk et al., 1985: 1356–1357, 1361), whereby material that is heavier (in information value, but also in structure) tends to be postponed. Conversely, we might argue, it is final positions that most strongly attract increasingly long structures.

Longer subordinate clauses are generally more likely placed in final position, but this is a relatively small effect compared to other factors that were discussed. The same is true for the difference between the two time periods investigated (late 19th and late 20th century). Seeing the general increase in factors that favour final placement (more speech-act concessives, somewhat longer clauses), the main effect of PERIOD to disfavour final placement will hardly be evident in a descriptive approach to the data, since it is counterbalanced by the other factors. However, if all factors are held constant, there remains a small diachronic effect whereby concessive subordinate clauses headed by the three conjunctions are more likely to be placed in non-final position in the late 20th century. One possible explanation is a subtle change in discourse strategies, as a consequence of which subordinate concessive clauses are coming to be used more in discourse-linking contexts as illustrated in Example 13. Although it does contribute positively to the model, this is a very minor effect.

Future research on the syntax of concessive clauses in English could make progress in several directions, five of which will be mentioned here. Firstly, there are of course alternative ways of operationalising the complexity and weight of subordinate clauses (cf. Wiechmann & Kerz, 2013, for example), and the methodology applied here does not claim to be the final word. Second, a wider range of predictors could be taken into consideration, particularly at the discourse-analytic level. Third, the difference between spoken and written English would be of great interest, as it is reasonable to assume that the mode of production will have an effect particularly on the syntactic arrangement of clauses. Fourth, other varieties of English need to be investigated in addition to American English – first and foremost British English, of course – in order to see whether the tendencies described in this chapter have more general validity. And, finally, the investigation can be expanded to earlier periods of English (e.g. Middle and Early Modern English), to find out more about the process whereby the present-day semantic and syntactic patterns have emerged.

References

Aarts, Bas (1988). Clauses of Concession in Written Present-Day British English. *Journal of English Linguistics* 21(1), 39–58. https://doi.org/10.1177/007542428802100104

Altenberg, Bengt (1986). Contrastive Linking in Spoken and Written English. In Gunnel Tottie, & Ingegerd Bäcklund (Eds.), *English in Speech and Writing. A Symposium* (13–40). Stockholm: Almqvist & Wiksell.

Anscombre, Jean-Claude (1989). Théorie de l'Argumentation,Topoï, et Structuration Discursive. *Revue Québécoise de Linguistique* 18(1), 13–55. https://doi.org/10.7202/602639ar

Azar, Moshe (1997). Concessive Relations as Argumentations. *Text* 17(3), 301–316. https://doi.org/10.1515/text.1.1997.17.3.301

Biber, Douglas, Johansson, Stig, Leech, Geoffrey, Conrad, Susan, & Finegan, Edward (1999). *Longman Grammar of Spoken and Written English*. London: Longman.

Bürckner, Paul-Christian (2016). *brms: Bayesian Regression Models using Stan*. R package version 1.3.0. Retrieved from http://cran.r-project.org/web/packages/brms/brms.pdf

Chafe, Wallace L. (1976). Givenness, Contrastiveness, Definiteness, Subjects, Topics, and Point of View. In Charles N. Li (Ed.), *Subject and Topic* (27–55). New York: Academic Press.

Chafe, Wallace L. (1984). How People Use Adverbial Clauses. *Proceedings of the Tenth Annual Meeting of the Berkeley Linguistics Society*, 437–449.

Crevels, Mily (2000). Concessives on Different Semantic Levels: A Typologocal Perspective. In Elisabeth Couper-Kuhlen, & Bernd Kortmann (Eds.), *Cause – Condition – Concession – Contrast. Cognitive and Discourse Perspectives* (313–339). Berlin: Mouton de Gruyter. https://doi.org/10.1515/9783110219043.4.313

Culicover, Peter W. (1976). *Syntax*. New York: Academic Press.
Davies, Mark (2010–). *The Corpus of Historical American English: 400 million words, 1810–2009*. Retrieved from http://corpus.byu.edu/coha/.
Diessel, Holger (2005). Competing Motivations for the Ordering of Main and Adverbial clauses. *Linguistics* 43(3), 449–470. https://doi.org/10.1515/ling.2005.43.3.449
Diessel, Holger (2008). Iconicity of Sequence. A Corpus-based Analysis of the Positioning of Temporal Adverbial Clauses in English. *Cognitive Linguistics* 19, 457–482. https://doi.org/10.1515/COGL.2008.018
Finegan, Edward (1995). Subjectivity and subjectivisation: an introduction. In Dieter Stein, & Susan Wright (Eds.), *Subjectivity and Subjectivisation. Linguistic Perspectives* (1–15). Cambridge: Cambridge University Press. https://doi.org/10.1017/CBO9780511554469.001
Ford, Cecilia E. (1993). *Grammar in Interaction. Adverbial Clauses in American English Conversations*. Cambridge: Cambridge University Press. https://doi.org/10.1017/CBO9780511554278
Gelman, Andrew, & Pardoe, Iain (2007). Average Predictive Comparisons for Models with Non-linearity, Interactions, and Variance Components. *Sociological Methodology* 37(1), 23–51. https://doi.org/10.1111/j.1467-9531.2007.00181.x
Gelman, Andrew, Carlin, John B., Stern, Hal S., Dunson, David B., Vehtari, Aki, & Rubin, Donald B. (2013). *Bayesian Data Analysis*. Boca Raton, Fla.: CRC Press.
Goldberg, Adele E. (2003). Constructions: a new theoretical approach to language. *Trends in Cognitive Sciences* 7(5), 219–224. https://doi.org/10.1016/S1364-6613(03)00080-9
Hawkins, John A. (1994). *A Performance Theory of Order and Constituency*. Cambridge: Cambridge University Press.
Hawkins, John A. (1998). Some Issues in a Performance Theory of Word Order. In Anna Siewierska (Ed.), *Constituent Order in the Languages of Europe* (729–780). Berlin: Mouton de Gruyter. https://doi.org/10.1515/9783110812206.729
Hermodsson, Lars (1994). Der Begriff 'konzessiv'. Terminologie und Analysen. *Studia Neophilologia* 66, 59–75. https://doi.org/10.1080/00393279408588131
Hilpert, Martin (2013). *Constructional Change in English: Developments in Allomorphy, Word Formation, and Syntax*. Cambridge: Cambridge University Press. https://doi.org/10.1017/CBO9781139004206
Hoffmann, Sebastian (2005). *Grammaticalization and English Complex Prepositions*. London: Routledge.
Huddleston, Rodney D., & Pullum, Geoffrey K. (2002). *The Cambridge Grammar of the English Language*. Cambridge: Cambridge University Press. https://doi.org/10.1017/9781316423530
König, Ekkehard (2006). Concessive Clauses. In Keith Brown (Ed.), *Encyclopedia of Language and Linguistics* (Vol. II, 820–824). Amsterdam: Elsevier. https://doi.org/10.1016/B0-08-044854-2/00277-7
Krifka, Manfred (2008). Basic Notions of Information Structure. *Acta Linguistica Hungarica* 55(3–4), 243–276. https://doi.org/10.1556/ALing.55.2008.3-4.2
Kruschke, John K. (2015). *Doing Bayesian Data Analysis. A Tutorial with R, JAGS, and Stan*. Amsterdam: Elsevier.
Lambrecht, Knud (1996). *Information Structure and Sentence Form*. Cambridge: Cambridge University Press.
Lang, Ewald (2000). Adversative Connectors on Distinct Levels of Discourse: A Re-examination of Eve Sweetser's Three-level Approach. In Elisabeth Couper-Kuhlen, & Bernd Kortmann (Eds.), *Cause – Condition – Concession – Contrast. Cognitive and Discourse Perspectives* (235–256). Berlin: Mouton de Gruyter. https://doi.org/10.1515/9783110219043.3.235

McElreath, Richard (2016). *Statistical Rethinking. A Bayesian Course with Examples in R and Stan*. Boca Raton, FL: CRC Press.
di Meola, Claudio (1998). Zur Definition einer logisch-semantischen Kategorie: Konzessivität als 'versteckte Kausalität'. *Linguistische Berichte* 175, 329–352.
Oxford English Dictionary Online. Oxford: Oxford University Press. http://www.oed.com/ [accessed 22/2/2017].
Quirk, Randolph, Greenbaum, Sidney, Leech, Geoffrey, & Svartvik, Jan (1985). *A Comprehensive Grammar of the English Language*. London: Arnold.
R Development Core Team. (2016). *R: A Language and Environment for Statistical Computing*. Version 3.2.4. [computer program] Retrieved from http://www.R-project.org
Radford, Andrew (1981). *Transformational Syntax: A Student's Guide to Chomsky's Extended Standard Theory*. Cambridge: Cambridge University Press.
Ramsay, Violetta (1987). The Functional Distribution of Preposed and Postposed 'if' and 'when' Clauses in Written Discourse. In Russell Tomlin (Ed.), *Coherence and Grounding in Discourse* (383–408). Amsterdam: John Benjamins. https://doi.org/10.1075/tsl.11.17ram
RStudio Team. (2009-2016). *RStudio: Integrated Development for R*. Version 1.0.136. Boston, MA: RStudio, Inc. Retrieved from http://www.rstudio.com/
Sarkar, Deepayan (2014). *lattice: Lattice graphics*. R-package version 0. 20–29. Retrieved from http://cran.r-project.org/web/packages/lattice/lattice.pdf
Schützler, Ole (2017). A corpus-based study of concessive conjunctions in three L1-varieties of English. In Isabelle Buchstaller, & Beat Siebenhaar (Eds.), *Language Variation – European Perspectives VI. Selected papers from the Eighth International Conference on Language Variation in Europe (ICLaVE 8), Leipzig, May 2015* (173–184). Amsterdam/Philadelphia: John Benjamins. https://doi.org/10.1075/silv.19.11sch
Schützler, Ole (2018a). Grammaticalization and information structure: Two perspectives on diachronic changes of *notwithstanding* in written *American English. English Language and Linguistics* 22(1), 101–122. https://doi.org/10.1017/S1360674316000411
Schützler, Ole (2018b). Concessive conjunctions in written American English: Diachronic and genre-related changes in frequency and semantics. In Richard J. Whitt (Ed.), *Diachronic Corpora, Genre, and Language Change* (195-218). Amsterdam/Philadelphia: John Benjamins. https://doi.org/10.1075/scl.85.09sch
Stan Development Team. (2016). *Stan Modeling Language Users Guide and Reference Manual*, Version 2.12.0. Retrieved from http://mc-stan.org
Sweetser, Eve E. (1990). *From Etymology to Pragmatics: Metaphorical and Cultural Aspects of Semantic Structure*. Cambridge: Cambridge University Press. https://doi.org/10.1017/CBO9780511620904
Tsunoda, Mie (2012). Five-level Classification of Clause Linkage in Japanese. *Studies in Language* 36(2), 382–429. https://doi.org/10.1075/sl.36.2.06tsu
Vehtari, Aki, Gelman, Andrew, & Gabry, Jonah. (2017). Practical Bayesian Model Evaluation Using Leave-one-out Cross-validation and WAIC. *Statistics and Computing*. 27(5), 1413–1432. https://doi.org/10.1007/s11222-016-9696-4
Watanabe, Sumio (2010). Asymptotic Equivalence of Bayes Cross Validation and Widely Applicable Information Criterion in Singular Learning Theory. *Journal of Machine Learning Research* 11, 3571–3594.
Wiechmann, Daniel, & Kerz, Elma (2013). The Positioning of Concessive Adverbial Clauses in English: Assessing the Importance of Discourse-pragmatic and Processing-based Constraints. *English Language and Linguistics* 17(1), 1–23. https://doi.org/10.1017/S1360674312000305

Appendix

Table A1. Regression table of Bayesian logistic regression predicting final position of subordinate clauses.

Coefficient	Mean	Quantiles			n_{eff}	$\hat{R}$
		.025	.5	.975		
Intercept	.04	−1.74	.03	1.93	23000	1
PERIOD	−.33	−.60	−.31	−.04	34000	1
LENGTH	.17	.02	.17	.32	36000	1
VARIANT: Varying intercepts						
Standard deviation	1.26	.19	1.06	3.44	28000	1
although		−2.36	−.54	.78		
though		−2.14	−.37	.98		
even though		−.83	.69	2.33		
TYPE: Varying intercepts						
Standard deviation	.60	.02	.39	2.42	7900	1
content	−.12	−1.33	−.05	.80		
epistemic	−.07	−1.31	−.02	.99		
speech-act	.07	−1.01	.04	1.12		
TYPE:VARIANT: Varying intercepts						
Standard deviation	.81	.16	.50	1.49	23000	1
Although						
content	−.31	−1.34	−.27	.57		
epistemic	−.25	−1.53	−.18	.67		
speech-act	.25	−.68	.24	1.18		
Though						
content	−.23	−1.23	−.19	.63		
epistemic	−.11	−1.31	−.07	.87		
speech-act	.13	−.78	.12	1.03		
Even though						
content	.31	−.63	.27	1.44		
epistemic	.30	−.73	.19	.87		
speech-act	−.19	−1.19	−.19	.87		
INTERNAL SYNTAX: Varying intercepts						
Standard deviation	.85	.10	.63	2.83	27000	1
though-attraction	−.30	−2.09	−.18	.90		
finite	.28	−.92	.26	1.49		
nonfinite	−.20	−1.50	−.17	.96		
GENRE: Varying intercepts						
Standard deviation	.68	.21	.55	1.99	24000	1
FIC	.34	−.49	.33	1.14		
MAG	−.45	−1.34	−.42	.30		
NEWS	.25	−.60	.25	1.04		
NF	−.25	−1.14	−.23	.51		

Table A2. Priors for the model parameters

Parameter	Distribution			Code
	Family	Location	Scale	
Intercept	Normal	0.5	1.5	normal(0.5, 1.5)
PERIOD, LENGTH	Cauchy	0	2.5	cauchy(0, 2.5)
VARIANT (SD)	Normal	0	2.5	normal(0, 2.5)
TYPE (SD)	Normal	0	2.5	normal(0, 2.5)
TYPE:VARIANT (SD)	Normal	0	2.5	normal(0, 2.5)
GENRE (SD)	Normal	0	2.5	normal(0, 2.5)
INTSYNT (SD)	Normal	0	2.5	normal(0, 2.5)

Further Specifications of the Bayesian Regression Model:
The model was run with three chains (30,000 iterations each; thinning: 2; warm-up: 2,000); The $\hat{R}$ diagnostics indicated convergence of the Markov chains. The Akaike weight for the final model was 0.67 (WAIC = 1201.1; LOOIC = 1201.2), the two closest contenders, dropping LENGTH and PERIOD, respectively, had Akaike weights of 0.17 and 0.14.

Further explorations in the grammar of intensifier marking in Modern English

Günter Rohdenburg

Picking up on earlier analyses, this paper explores a number of further issues bearing on the replacement of unmarked intensifiers by suffixed ones. While the evolutions of individual intensifiers may vary enormously, almost all grammatical constraints on intensifier marking can be accounted for in terms of a verbality cline: Structures displaying a high degree of verbality promote the establishment of suffixed intensifiers whereas less verbal structures tend to delay the process. The major findings supporting this generalization include the following:

- Past participles, which virtually always function as predicatives, represent one of the earliest categories to implement the change. In this respect, they contrast with present participles, which tend to behave like ordinary adjectives.
- Compared with predicative adjectives, attributive adjectives have been slow to replace unmarked intensifiers by suffixed ones.
- The establishment of the suffix is further advanced with complemented (non-attributive) adjectives than uncomplemented ones.

Keywords: unmarked/suffixed intensifiers, verbality, grammatical constraints, predicative/attributive/complemented adjectives, past/present participles, predicatively used prepositional phrases

1. Introduction

Let us begin by presenting a familiar quotation by John A. Hawkins in *A Comparative Typology of English and German*:

> The drift in the history of English has clearly been towards the more extensive use of more limited formal means, with the resulting complexity in the mapping between form and meaning. (Hawkins, 1986. 129)

Against this background, it is fascinating to find several clear-cut counter-tendencies in the recent history of Standard English (see e.g. Rohdenburg, 2018). One of them involves the persistent spread of the adverbial marker *-ly*, with most

https://doi.org/10.1075/cilt.346.13roh

adverbs derived from adjectives and in most functions. Supplementing a previous study (Rohdenburg, 2014), the present paper focuses on so-called intensifiers, and its purpose is to continue exploring the system-internal constraints bearing on the changeover from the zero variant as in (1) to the marked variant as in (2).

(1) …, he is extreame angry with his servants … (EEPF, 1635)

(2) The bear became extremely angry with the fly, … (wridom1, file G1A)

The notion of intensifier could be interpreted in more than one way. For our purposes, intensifiers are defined as degree adverbs scaling upwards from a presupposed norm. The definition covers the class of amplifiers as well as that of emphasizers like *really* to the extent that the latter have a scaling effect (Quirk *et al.*, 1972: 438-452). Downtoners (ibid., 452–458) such as *tolerable/tolerably*, *indifferent(ly)* and *passable/passably,* also functioning as qualifiers of the modified items in question, seem to show a similar behaviour to intensifiers. Accordingly, this paper devotes a brief analysis to *tolerable/tolerably* in Section 3.

My point of departure is provided by Nevalainen's (2008: 267) state-of-the-art assessment of the grammatical environments promoting or discouraging the advance of the marked alternative in EModE: "… zero intensifiers favour adverb and adjectival heads … intensifying *-ly* adverbs tend to occur with verbal and participial heads, …". This statement has been essentially corroborated by a series of corpus-based explorations covering the entire Modern English period and which involve a large number of intensifiers using both options. Consider, for instance, the analysis of *exceeding(ly)* in Table 1, which collapses all of the relevant data in the OED quotations between 1550 and 1849.

Table 1. The distribution of *exceeding(ly)* in the OED quotations between 1550 and 1849

		-ly	Ø	Total	% *-ly*
1	verbal heads (verb phrases)	80	–	80	100%
2	participles (past or present)	63	5	68	92.6%
3	adjectives (excluding past and present participles)	177	260	437	40.5%
4	adverbs	14	20	34	41.1%

Clearly, both categories 1 and 2 are in some sense more verbal than 3 and 4. After all, participles are derived from verbs, and they are usually associated with the auxiliary verb *be*. This suggests that it is the (intensified) category's degree of verbality that largely determines the degree of intensifier marking. To test the verbality hypothesis – previously invoked in a different context by Fischer (2001) – we will introduce a number of subcategories in the broad categories used in Table 1 and also include one or two novel ones.

Outside of verb phrases, the closest we come to verbal structures is with predicative uses of various grammatical categories. Henceforth, the designation predicative will be used as a cover term that in addition to explicit predicative structures such as (1) and (2) comprises a small number of closely related (or "implicit") ones without a copula, in particular object predicative and postnominal uses as in (3) and (4).

(3) …; I think him most excessive disagreeable! (NCF, 1782)

(4) Never anything happened so excessively provoking; … (NCF, 1782)

Now comparing predicative structures with attributives, we will always find that predicatives trigger distinctly higher proportions of marked intensifiers. In the spirit of De Smet (2012), it is hoped eventually to establish a network of contrastive and similarity relations between individual classes of intensifiable items, thus accounting for the general evolution of intensifier marking in the history of Standard English.

Concerning the corpus analyses conducted, a few methodological remarks may be in order: (a) The database available to me includes the *Oxford English Dictionary* (= OED), the fictional domain of the *British National Corpus* (= BNC) and a sizeable collection of historical fictional corpora provided by Chadwyck-Healey (see the bibliography for further details). Crucially, the fiction corpora lend themselves particularly well to the present study for two reasons: the involved and oral contexts of this text type can be expected to provide an especially high density of intensifiers (Biber, 1988), and the Chadwyck-Healey corpora are very much larger than any comparable databases available at present. (b) It has to be born in mind that the evolutions of individual intensifiers may differ enormously. The differences involve their frequency of occurrence, the speed at which they adopt and generalize the suffix and the extent to which they cover the whole range of intensifiable categories. In order to adequately determine the relative affinity of a specific grammatical category for the adoption of the associated intensifier's suffix, it has often been necessary to combine in one analysis more than one intensifier as well as use more than one database involving more or less extensive timespans. Needless to say, a lexically varied search ideally covering different periods or an extensive period may also serve the purpose of verifying the general validity of a single finding. In terms of size and text type, the datasets have been selected to suit the purpose in question as far as possible. (c) In the case of conjoined items modified by any intensifier, it is the first conjunct that is taken to determine the categorical status of the intensified phrase in question. (d) Based on the chi square test, three levels of statistical significance will be distinguished: significant ($p < 0.05$), highly significant ($p < 0.01$) and extremely significant ($p < 0.001$). With most sufficiently large samples, the figures compared reach significance levels ranging from $p < 0.01$ to $p < 0.001$. However, explicit mention of the significance levels in question will usually be made only for a few tables containing what might appear to be doubtful cases.

The rest of this paper is organized as follows: Section 2 distinguishes between the behaviour of past and present participles and also compares past participles with (mainly active) verb phrases. Section 3 distinguishes between predicative and attributive adjectives. Section 4 focuses on adverbs closely associated with predicative past participles. Section 5 deals with prepositional phrases occurring in predicative uses. Section 6 compares manner adverbs with predicative and attributive adjectives. The paper concludes in Section 7 by providing a summary and a brief discussion of these findings.

2. Past and present participles

In the literature concerned with intensifier marking, participles are generally treated as a homogeneous category (see Nevalainen, 1994, 2008; Peters, 1994: 284–285; Ungerer, 1988: 262–263). However, to account more precisely for the behaviour of intensified participles, we need to differentiate at least between two formal and two functional types, past and present participles on the one hand and predicative and attributive uses on the other. These subdivisions are illustrated in (5) and (6). The examples in (5) feature past participles, predicatives in (5a) and attributives in (5b). The examples in (6) illustrate present participles, predicatives in (6a) and attributives in (6b).

(5) a. The young lady was not mightily captivated with her lover: … (NCF, 1800)
b. "What was that?" cried my uncle, in a mighty changed voice. (NCF, 1886)

(6) a. Sir, you are extremely obliging. (EPD, 1732)
b. … I think Marriage an extream shocking thing. (EPD, 1735)

The vast majority of predicative past participle uses such as (5a) clearly derive from genuine *be*-passives as in (7).

(7) …, whilst Figg's blow was deliver'd so mightily that … (NCF, 1858)

As is well known, the borderline between genuine passives and predicative past participles is ill defined (see e.g. the "passive scale" in Quirk *et al.*, 1972: 808–811), and the two categories are often difficult if not impossible to tell apart. The general situation found with intensifiers resembles that described by De Smet (2012) for past participles in the *far from* construction: "only a handful could pass for genuine passives, … Of these, nearly all allow an adjectival reading, …" This is why, in the present paper, all examples instantiating the frame BE (…) + intensifier + past participle have been included in the category of predicative past participles.

Generally speaking, predicative past participles and (overwhelmingly active) verb phrases as in (8) tend to display similarly high rates of intensifier marking and with most intensifiers the use of the adverbial suffix is found to be virtually obligatory.

(8) The bright perspective mightily cheered one drooping soldier. (NCF, 1863)

The assumption that the establishment of marked intensifiers with predicative past participles followed in the wake of verb phrases seems to be supported by the analyses in Tables 2 and 3. In general, contrasts between the behaviour of verb phrases and predicative past participles are few and far between. This is what motivates the selection of most of the intensifiers in Table 2, which provide at least minimal differences between the two categories in the hypothesized direction. It is only *mighty/mightily* in Table 2 and *sore(ly)* dealt with in Table 3, which display robust contrasts between verb phrases and predicative past participles.

Table 2. Comparing verb phrases and predicative past participles modified by selected intensifiers in EModE and LModE databases (*exceeding(ly)*: EEPF (1518–1700), *excellent(ly)*: EEPF (1518–1700), *monstrous(ly)*: NCF (1782–1903) + EPD (18th and 19th c.), and *mighty/mightily*: NCF (1782–1903)*

	-ly	Ø	total	% -ly
1 (mostly active) verb phrases	405 (80/325)	–	405 (80/325)	100%
2 predicative past participles	262 (44/218)	9 (6/3)	271 (50/221)	96.7% (87.5%/ 98.7%)

* The bracketed figures distinguish between *mighty/mightily* and the remaining intensifiers.

Table 3. Comparing verb phrases and predicative past participles modified by *sore(ly)* in the EPD between 1680 and 1890

	-ly	Ø	total	% *-ly*
1 verb phrases	48	12	60	80%
2 predicative past participles	27	46	46	58.7%

Considered as a whole, the predicative past participles in Table 2 are seen to be lagging behind (mostly active) verb phrases (at $p < 0.001$). However, of the four intensifiers analyzed, the contrast is, at $p < 0.01$, only significant for *mighty/mightily*, which was relatively slow to adopt marked intensifiers. Table 3 displays a similar contrast with *sore(ly)* (at < 0.05) in the EPD between the late 17th and the late 19th century. If anything, the general displacement of the zero form *sore* by the suffixed variant *sorely* in Standard English has been much slower than that of *mighty* by *mightily*. In fact, the zero form can even today be found modifying predicative past participles as in (9).

(9) …; the MacIans might just try it (i.e. food), though they were sore hurt themselves. (wridom1, file APW)

Admittedly, the use of *sore* has for some time been characteristic of non-standard speech, and it is not clear to what extent this may have distorted the results in Table 3. For the time being, therefore, they should be treated with due caution.

Even though past participles may represent various stages of adjectivalization, they still retain much of the morphology, syntax and semantics of their immediate source construction.

By contrast, present participles as in (6) (which tend to be vastly outnumbered by past participles) are less clearly related to any intensified verbal construction. In the EModE and LModE data analyzed – they have not yet been found in examples of the frame BE (…) + intensifier + present participle where they might be given a progressive interpretation along with an adjectival one. In addition, the type of paraphrase for both the predicative and attributive examples in (6a)–(6b) by means of (10a)–(10b) shows the extent to which intensified *-ing* forms have diverged from intensified verbal constructions.

(10) a. … obliges extreme(ly).
b. … a thing that shocks extreme(ly).

Unlike intensified past participles, whose morphology is identical with that of its presumed verbal source, there are at least three formal features contrasting intensified adjectival *-ing* forms and their presumed verbal paraphrases: (a) (10a)–(10b) employ a different verb form from (6a)–(6b), (b) preposed intensifiers in (6a)–(6b) tend to be replaced by postposed ones in (10a)–(10b), and (c) in the case of basically transitive source verbs – and unlike (10a)–(10b) – the paraphrases in question usually need to be augmented by a direct object of some sort. What is more, unlike past participles, they regularly occur in attributive uses, which can be taken to constitute a further stage of adjectivalization.

There is no doubt, then, that intensified past participles should be assigned a higher degree of verbality than present participles. Thus, we would expect past participles to trigger higher rates of marked intensifiers than present participles. Extracting the relevant data from Table 1, we find the initial hypothesis confirmed (at $p < 0.001$) in the data of Table 4 (covering a time span of 300 years).

Table 4. Comparing past and present participles modified by *exceeding(ly)* in the OED quotations between 1550 and 1849

		-ly	Ø	total	% *-ly*
1	past participles	53	–	53	100%
2	present participles	10	5	15	66.7%

Two further analyses exhibiting similar contrasts between past and present participles are presented in Tables 5 and 6 dealing with *monstrous(ly)* and *mighty/mightily*. Both tables also display the relevant figures for ordinary adjectives, which indicate that present participles usually show a similar behaviour to ordinary adjectives. This is why in later analyses present participles are tacitly included in the category of adjectives.

Table 5. Comparing past and present participles modified by *monstrous(ly)* in the EPD (18th and 19th c.)

		-ly	Ø	total	% *-ly*
1	past participles	10	1	11	90.9%
2	present participles	4	9	13	33.3%
3	remaining adjectives	18	116	134	13.4%

Admittedly, due to the general infrequency of attributive past and present participles, Tables 4–6 do not yet distinguish between predicative and attributive uses. Since predicatives resemble verbal structures more closely than attributives, we would of course expect them to be further advanced than attributives in the adoption of marked intensifiers. Let us begin by taking a look at present participles. In order to achieve statistically reliable results for a single intensifier it has again been necessary to collapse several databases covering an extended period. Consider now the evidence given for *exceeding(ly)* and *extreme(ly)* in Tables 7 and 8, which clearly confirms the initial hypothesis.

Table 6. Comparing past and present participles modified by *mighty/mighti(ly)* in EModE and LModE narrative databases (EEPF: 1518–1700, ECF: 1705–1780, NCF1: 1782–1840)

		-ly	Ø	total	% *-ly*
1	past participles	131	1 (creazed)	132	99.2%
2	present participles	–	12	12	0%
3	remaining adjectives	2	304	306	0.7%

Table 7. Comparing predicative and attributive uses of present participles modified by *exceeding(ly)* in the OED quotations, the EEPF, the EPD, and the ECF between 1550 and 1759

		-ly	Ø	total	% *-ly*
1	predicative present participles	10	7	17	58.8%
2	attributive present participles	8	–	8	0%

Table 8. Comparing predicative and attributive present participles modified by *extreme(ly)* in the OED quotations, the EEPF, the EPD, and the ECF between 1550 and 1759

		-ly	Ø	total	% *-ly*
1	predicative present participles	68	3	71	95.8%
2	attributive present participles	3	5	8	37.5%

This brings us to past participles. Here, the chance of coming across an attributive example is remote, and in the data presented in Table 1 we do not find a single one. Thus it will be necessary to collapse the data comprising a large number of intensifiers over a period of almost four centuries. Consider now the evidence in Table 9, which provides the expected result: Unlike predicatives, where intensifier marking is near-categorical, attributives display only a fairly low percentage of suffixed intensifiers.

Table 9. Comparing predicative and attributive uses of past participles modified by selected intensifiers in EModE and LModE databases (*exceeding(ly)*: EEPF (1518–1700), *excellent(ly)*: EEPF (1518–1700), *desperate(ly)*: EEPF (17th c.) + ECF1 (1705–1756), *monstrous(ly)*: NCF (1782–1903) + EPD (18th and 19th c.), *perfect(ly)*: EEPF (1518–1599), *tolerable/y*: ECF (1705–1780), and *mighty/mightily*: NCF (1782–1903)

		-ly	Ø	total	% *-ly*
1	predicative past participles (*mighty*/rest)	335 (44/291)	10 (6/4)	345 (50/295)	97.1% (88%/98.6%)
2	attributive past participles (*mighty*/rest)	2 (0/2)	6 (2/4)	8 (2/6)	25%/ (0%/33.3%)

3. Predicative and attributive adjectives

This returns us to the category of adjectives, which were already dealt with in a previous article (Rohdenburg, 2014). Again, we will have to distinguish between four subcategories, predicative adjectives vs attributive ones, and – within the predicatives – between complemented and uncomplemented uses. These subdivisions are illustrated by Examples (11a)–(11b) and (12a)–(12b).

(11) a. … the idea that she was marvellously sly, – – –; … (ECF,1751)
b. …, or drawing out flax into marvellous coarse thread, … (NCF, 1830)

(12) a. …. The workmen … were mightily proud of him. (NCF,1857)
b. …, he looked mighty conspicuous; … (NCF, 1893)

We are assuming, of course, that attributive adjectives are not usually associated with complements. While the combination may occur with a peripheral class of adjectives (Rohdenburg, 1998), it is not found in the corpora investigated. On the basis of the observations made in Section 3 and the earlier paper, we can advance the following predictions:

1. Predicative adjectives, which resemble predicative past participles more closely than attributive ones, can be expected to be further evolved in the introduction of suffixed intensifiers.
2. Those predicative adjectives that – just like most verbs – are associated with a complement – can be assumed to trigger higher rates of intensifier marking than uncomplemented ones.

Both assumptions have been borne out in a series of analyses. The overall contrast between predicative and attributive adjectives is documented in Tables 10–11 devoted to *exceeding(ly)* and *monstrous(ly)* and that between adjectives with or without complements is evidenced in Tables 12–13, which deal with *exceeding(ly)* and *mighty/mightily*.

Table 10. Comparing predicative and attributive adjectives modified by *exceeding(ly)* in the OED quotations between 1550 and 1849

		-ly	Ø	total	% *-ly*
1	predicative adjectives	154	169	323	47.7%
2	attributive adjectives	33	96	129	25.6%

Table 11. Comparing predicative and attributive adjectives modified by *monstrous(ly)* in the NCF (1782–1903)*

		-ly	Ø	total	% *-ly*
1	predicative adjectives	23 (8/15)	48 (37/11)	71 (45/26)	32.4% (17.8%/57.7%)
2	attributive adjectives	85 (1/4)	33 (15/18)	38 (16/22)	13.2% (6.3%/18.2%)

* The bracketed figures distinguish between authors born in the 18th or the 19th century.

Table 12. Comparing complemented and uncomplemented predicative adjectives modified by *exceeding(ly)* in the OED quotations between 1550 and 1849

		-ly	Ø	total	% *-ly*
1	presence of complement	31	14	45	68.9%
2	absence of complement	123	155	278	44.2%

Table 13. Comparing complemented and uncomplemented predicative adjectives modified by *mighty/mighti(ly)* in NFC2 (1826–1903)

		-ly	Ø	total	% *-ly*
1	presence of complement	11	–	11	100%
2	absence of complement	7	7	14	50%

Notice that the contrast between predicative and attributive adjectives is only partially due to the presence of complements in the former category. Crucially, the comparison of Tables 10 and 12 shows that the adjective category involves a threefold division in terms of intensifier marking: Complemented predicatives trigger more suffixed intensifiers than uncomplemented ones, and, in turn, even uncomplemented predicatives induce a higher share of suffixed intensifiers than attributives. In this connection, it should be pointed out that the contrast between predicative and attributive adjectives and that between complemented and uncomplemented predicatives also play a decisive role in adjective comparison, and that in a perfectly parallel manner (Mondorf, 2009; Rohdenburg, 2014). This certainly is an intriguing grammatical parallel which would deserve to be examined in greater detail.

While the focus of this paper is not on the comparison of individual intensifiers as to their evolutionary pathways, it will become apparent that, as a class, intensifiers may differ strikingly in their bias towards the generalization of the affix. Furthermore, the speed at which a given intensifier adopts the suffixed variant is not just dependent on the syntactic category of the intensified item, but seems also to be affected, within a given class, by individual characteristics of the intensified items themselves. Concerning attributive adjectives after *extreme(ly),* it was observed in Rohdenburg (2014, 137, 145) that shorter adjectives retain the zero form much better than longer ones. A similar observation can be made in the case of *tolerable/tolerably* in Table 14. To begin with, there is the pervasive contrast between predicative and attributive adjectives. Crucially, the evidence in Table 14 leaves no doubt that, within the category of attributive uses, the high frequency adjective *good* as in Example (13) helps to preserve the outgoing variant *tolerable* much longer than the complementary set of attributive adjectives.

Table 14. Comparing predicative and attributive adjectives modified by *tolerable/tolerably* in the ECF and NCF1 (1703–1824)

		-ly	Ø	total	% *-ly*
1	predicative adjectives	154	1	155	99.4%
2	attributive adjectives				
	a) all examples	60	22	82	73.2%
	b) *good*	12	17	29	41.4%
	c) remaining adjectives	48	5	53	90.6%

(13) "He occasionally gives some tolerable good rules for preserving health, however," replied Travers; … (NCF1, 1800)

Assuming that, due to its frequency, *good* is cognitively more accessible in this environment than most other adjectives, this means that, in line with the Complexity Principle (see e.g. Rohdenburg, 1998: 73–75; 2016; Vosberg & Rohdenburg, this volume), more easily processed adjectives tend to trigger a smaller percentage of the more explicit (and bulky) variant than the remaining more complex ones.

4. Two kinds of adverbs

As yet I have not made much progress in accounting for the behaviour of intensified adverbs. However, I noticed early on that adverbs like *well* and *ill* occurring in common collocations with predicative past participles as in (14)–(15), tended to promote the use of the marked intensifier.

(14) These two being excellently well vers'd in the Trade, … (EEPF,1683)

(15) The king of Thrace …, was exceedingly well affected towards him: … (EEPF, 1598)

By contrast, when used as manner adverbs as in (16) and (17), the same items were far less likely to trigger suffixed intensifiers.

(16) …; methought their beating of hemp became them excellent well; … (EEPF, 1665)

(17) This inuention pleased the King exceeding well, … (EEPF, 1608)

Evidence supporting the contrast is found in Tables 15 and 16, which also include the figures for (simple) past participles, those not forming a close collocation with an adverb as in (14)–(15).

Table 15. Comparing the type *well* + past participle and manner adverbs modified by *excellent(ly)* in the EEPF (1518–1700)

		-ly	Ø	total	% *-ly*
1	*well* etc. + predicative past participle	10	–	10	100%
2	manner adverbs	7	5	12	58.3%
3	(simple) predicative past participle	30	–	30	100%

Table 16. Comparing the type *well* + past participle and manner adverbs modified by *exceeding(ly)* in the EEPF (1518–1700)

		-ly	Ø	total	% *-ly*
1	*well* + predicative past participle	12	1	13	92.3%
2	manner adverb	11	11	22	50%
3	(simple) predicative past participle	165	1 *(troubled)*	166	99.4%

It is apparent that the collocation *well* + past participle shows similar rates of suffixed intensifiers to simple past participles. Tentatively, I would interpret this high degree of similarity as being due to the influence exerted by simple past participles on the complex *well* + past participle. It should be pointed out, however, that the contrast between *well* + past participle and manner adverbs seems to have levelled out after the Early Modern English period.

5. Prepositional phrases and NPs

In the preceding sections, we have seen in several domains that arguably more verbal categories are definitely more likely to establish marked intensifiers than paradigmatically related ones. This section takes a brief look at intensified predicative prepositional phrases denoting a variety of properties. The prepositional phrases searched for contain the initial prepositions *against, at, for, in, on, out of* and *to*. In addition to (22b) below using a *to*-phrase, illustrative examples featuring the three more commonly occurring prepositions *in, at* and *out of* are given in (18)–(20).

(18) … a Woman, who is extreamly in Anger. (EEPF, 1683)

(19) … I am, (*sic*) extremely at your service. (NCF, 1792)

(20) I am exceedingly out of humour with Mr. Lovelace: … (ECF, 1748)

Unlike the predicative structures considered so far, these uses do not have any immediately comparable syntactic rivals. Considering their categorical occurrence in predicative function, such prepositional phrases could also be expected to induce comparatively high proportions of suffixed intensifiers. Even so, it may come as a bit of a surprise to find that they regularly equal the shares of intensifier marking found with predicative past participles. Compare, for instance, the evidence in Tables 17, 18 and 19, where prepositional phrases and past participles on the one hand contrast with adjectives on the other. Even the weakest contrast between prepositional phrases and (predicative) adjectives in Table 19 reaches the basic significance level set at $p < 0.05$.

Table 17. Comparing predicative uses of prepositional phrases, past participles and adjectives modified by *extreme(ly)* in the EEPF (1518–1700)

		-ly	Ø	total	% *-ly*
1	prepositional phrases	11	–	11	100%
2	past participles	58	–	58	100%
3	adjectives	72	34	106	67.9%

Table 18. Comparing predicative uses of prepositional phrases, past participles and adjectives modified by *exceeding(ly)* in the EEPF (1518–1700) and the ECF1 (1705–1756)

		-ly	Ø	total	% *-ly*
1	prepositional phrases	7	–	7	100%
2	past participles	203	1	204	99.5%
3	adjectives	100	332	432	23.2%

Table 19. Comparing predicative uses of prepositional phrases, past participles and adjectives modified by *desperate(ly)* in the 17th century data of the EEPF and the ECF1 (1705–1756)

		-ly	Ø	total	% *-ly*
1	prepositional phrases*	25	–	25	100%
2	past participles	23	–	23	100%
3	adjectives	17	4	21	81.0%

* All of the relevant examples involve the phrase *in love (with).*

Thus, in the case of prepositional phrases, we may have to reckon with additional factors responsible for the unexpectedly high proportion of marked intensifiers.

Furthermore, we have come across a small number of property-denoting predicative NPs in LModE, which are also invariably associated with suffixed intensifiers. In some cases, these NPs appear to be derived from existing prepositional phrases. Compare, for instance:

(21) a. This fancy of the men, which is extremely the mode, makes an agreeable circulation of inamoratos, … (ECF, 1769)

b. We drink, we game, we whore, we run in Debt; and in all Sorts of Extravagances are perfectly in the mode. (EPD, 1754)

(22) a. …; for without vanity, I have been extremely the taste of the men. (ECF, 1769)

b. The White Slave has been found to be greatly to the taste of American audiences. (AD, 1874)

6. Manner adverbs and adjectives

This brings us finally to a comparison of intensified manner adverbs and adjectives, whose uses are illustrated again for the benefit of the reader:

(23) a. manner adverb: Your Ladyship, … speaks exceedingly well. (ECF, 1741)
b. predicative adjective: Thus exceedingly happy are we at present. (ECF, 1748)
c. attributive adjective: You are an exceeding good girl! (ECF, 1754)

The corresponding functions of the intensified expressions are sketched in (24a)–(24c).

(24) a. manner adv: modifier of (prototypical) VP
b. predicative adj: head of (peripheral) VP
c. attributive adj: modifier of NP and closely related paradigmatically to predicative adj

The relationship holding between predicative and attributive adjectives in (24b)–(24c) is in accordance with the verbality concept as described in Section 3. However, manner adverbs would presumably be classed as less verbal than predicative adjectives and more verbal than attributive adjectives. If so, we would expect the percentage of suffixed intensifiers modifying manner adverbs (a) to be higher than that of attributive adjectives and (b) to be lower than that of predicative adjectives. Crucially, the two analyses in Tables 20 and 21 available to me do not agree with these predictions.

Table 20. Comparing manner adverbs and adjectives modified by *excellent(ly)* in the EEPF (1518–1700)

		-ly	Ø	total	% *-ly*
1	manner adverbs	5	7	12	41.7%
2	predicative adjective	15	13	28	30%
3	attributive adjective	4	31	35	11.4%

Table 21. Comparing manner adverbs and adjectives modified by *exceeding(ly)* in the EEPF (1518–1700)

		-ly	Ø	total	% *-ly*
1	manner adverbs	11	11	22	50%
2	predicative adjective	215	51	266	19.2%
3	attributive adjectives	1	98	99	1.0%

Table 22. Classification of intensified items according to their relative proportions of the *-ly* suffix

	high	intermediate	low
1	verb phrases	pred adj/*-ing* [+/–complem.]	attributive adj/*-ing*
2	predicatives a. past participles b. the type *well pleased* c. prepositional phrases	manner adv	attributives a. past participles b. the type *well pleased*

While prediction (a) turns out to be correct in both cases, prediction (b) is clearly false. At this stage, we have to concede, then, that the relationship between manner adverbs and adjectives defies a straightforward interpretation in terms of different degrees of verbality as hypothesized above. In this connection, it should be pointed out that the majority of the items classed as manner adverbs are represented by *well*. Thus we cannot exclude the possibility that future research taking the cognitive accessibility of the three kinds of intensified expressions into account may be more successful in making sense of their mutual relationships.

7. Concluding remarks

On the basis of the data presented so far and other explorations not detailed here, it is possible to classify the intensified categories into three broad classes ranging from high to low proportions of adverbial marking:

We can interpret these groups as representing successive stages of a diffusional change, with group I being the earliest to establish the suffix and group III being the least far advanced. In addition, we have been able to explain most contrasts between and within the three groups in terms of the gradable notion of verbality. The major contrasts are represented in (25) by four "greater than" relations:

(25) a. VP > predicative past participle
b. past participle > adj/*-ing*
c. predicative > attributive
d. [+ Complement] > [– Complement]

However, several important issues have not been dealt with conclusively. Most important, the behaviour of manner adverbs does not fit in with the concept of verbality used so far. In addition, the fact that both individual intensifiers and intensified items may have specific biases interacting with those of the syntactic categories involved remains to be explored more systematically. Other intriguing questions concern parallel tendencies in two domains involving related manifestations of grading, *far from* structures as in (26) and adjective comparison.

(26) Her remarks were far from (being) out of place.

Thus, the categorical use of marked intensifiers with predicative prepositional phrases as described in Section 5 is paralleled – at a surprisingly early stage – by *far from* structures as in (26). Here, predicative prepositional phrases are also associated with relatively high degrees of grammatical explicitness, which in this case involves a frequently added copula (Vosberg & Rohdenburg, this volume).

References

Biber, Douglas (1988). *Variation across Speech and Writing*. Cambridge: Cambridge University Press. https://doi.org/10.1017/CBO9780511621024

Fischer, Olga (2001). The Position of the Adjective in (Old) English from an Iconic Perspective. In Olga Fischer, & Max Nänny (Eds.), *The Motivated Sign (= Iconicity in Language and Literature* 2) (249–276). Amsterdam: John Benjamins.

Hawkins, John A. (1986). *A Comparative Typology of English and German: Unifying the Contrasts*. London: Croom Helm.

Mondorf, Britta (2009). *More Support for* more-*Support: The Role of Processing Constraints on the Choice between Synthetic and Analytic Comparative Forms*. Amsterdam & New York: John Benjamins. https://doi.org/10.1075/silv.4

Nevalainen, Terttu (1994). Aspects of Adverbial Change in Early Modern English. In Dieter Kastovsky (Ed.), *Studies in Early Modern English* (243–259). Berlin: Mouton de Gruyter. https://doi.org/10.1515/9783110879599.243

Nevalainen, Terttu (2008). Social Variation in Intensifier Use: Constraint on *-ly* Adverbialization in the Past? *English Language and Linguistics* 12, 289–315. https://doi.org/10.1017/S1360674308002633

Peters, Hans (1994). Degree Adverbs in Early Modern English. In Dieter Kastovsky (Ed.), *Studies in Early Modern English* (269–288). Berlin: Mouton de Gruyter. https://doi.org/10.1515/9783110879599.269

Quirk, Randolph, Greenbaum, Sidney, Leech, Geoffrey, & Svartvik, Jan (1972). *A Grammar of Contemporary English*. London: Longman.

Rohdenburg, Günter (1998). Attributive Adjectives like *similar* and *different* Involving Prepositional Complements. In Wolfgang Kühlwein (Ed.), *Language as Structure and Language as Process. In Honour of Gerhard Nickel on the Occasion of his 70th Birthday* (63–79). Trier: Wissenschaftlicher Verlag.

Rohdenburg, Günter (2014). Syntactic Constraints on the Use of Dual Form Intensifiers in Modern English. In Kristin Davidse, Caroline Gentens, Lobke Ghesquière, & Lieven Vandelanotte (Eds.), *Corpus Interrogation and Grammatical Patterns* (132–149). Amsterdam & Philadelphia: John Benjamins.

Rohdenburg, Günter (2016). Testing two Processing Principles with Respect to the Extraction of Elements out of Complement Clauses. *English Language and Linguistics* 20, 463–486. https://doi.org/10.1017/S1360674316000307
Rohdenburg, Günter (2018). On the Differential Evolution of Simple and Complex Object Constructions in English. In Hubert Cuyckens, Hendrik De Smet, Liesbeth Heyvaert, & Charlotte Maekelberghe (Eds.), *Explorations in English Historical Syntax* (77–104). Amsterdam: John Benjamins.
De Smet, Hendrik (2012). The Course of Actualization. *Language* 88, 801–833. https://doi.org/10.1353/lan.2012.0056
Ungerer, Friedrich (1988). *Syntax der englischen Adverbien*. Tübingen: Niemeyer. https://doi.org/10.1515/9783111354538
Vosberg, Uwe & Rohdenburg, Günter. The Rivalry between *far from being* + Predicative Item and its Counterpart Omitting the Copula in Modern English. In this volume.

Electronic sources

BNC	British National Corpus 1995. Version 1.0. BNC Consortium/Oxford University Computing Services. (100,000,000 words)
ECF	Eighteenth-Century Fiction 1996. Chadwyck-Healey. (9,702,696 words, omitting duplicates)
ECF1	First part of the ECT containing only those authors born in the 17th century (5,130,162 words)
EEPF	Early English Prose Fiction 1997–2000. Chadwyck-Healey. In *association with the Salzburg Centre for Research on the English Novel SCREEN*. (9,562,865 words)
EPD	English Prose Drama 1996-1997. Chadwyck-Healey. (26,454,639words)
NCF	Nineteenth-Century Fiction 1999–2000. Chadwyck-Healey. (37,589,837 words)
NCF1	First part of the NCF containing only those authors born in the 18th century (11,373,834 words)
OED	The Oxford English Dictionary (Second Edition) on CD-ROM 1992 (Version 1.10). Edited by John A. Simpson & Edmund S. C. Weiner. Oxford: Oxford University Press.
wridom1	imaginative component of the BNC (= narrative fiction). (18,863,529 words)

The rivalry between *far from being* + predicative item and its counterpart omitting the copula in Modern English

Uwe Vosberg and Günter Rohdenburg

Distinguishing between several subtypes of the frame *far from* + optional and recessive *being* + predicative phrase, this paper charts the evolution of the rivalling variants in British and American English over the last few centuries. The paper reports on two major findings. First, in line with the Complexity Principle, there is a tendency for more complex predicatives to help preserve the more explicit *being* variant better than simpler ones. In particular, morphologically complex adjectives and syntactically complex noun phrases in the predicative slot are shown to retain the *being* variant longer than less complex ones. Second, as regards the establishment of the less explicit zero variant, the relation between British and American English corresponds to the so-called lag and overtake scenario. While initially trailing behind British English, American English has – in more recent times – adopted the zero variant much faster than British English.

Keywords: optional function word, complex predicatives, complexity/morphological/syntactic constraints, British-American contrasts, the lag and overtake scenario, contrasts between OED quotations and narrative textbases

1. Setting the scene

Modern English possesses a number of spatial adjectives and prepositions that may refer to both physical and metaphorical distance. They include the items in (1)–(3), which are here used in metaphorically transferred senses.

(1) a. The practice of writing was close to being sacred.
    b. … the quaint notion that the practice of writing was close to Ø sacred. (*Los Angeles Times*, 1993)

(2) a. The news blaring from the radio was beyond being bad.
    b. The news blaring from the radio was beyond Ø bad. It was sinister, spooky, … (*Los Angeles Times*, 1995)

https://doi.org/10.1075/cilt.346.14vos

(3) a. The current situation is far from being exceptional.
b. The current situation is far from Ø exceptional.

(4) a. Sussex is far from being the driest part of the country, however.
b. Sussex is far from Ø the driest part of the country, however.
(*Daily Telegraph,* 2004)

We are concerned with a prominent feature shared by *close to, beyond* and *far from*: In examples like (1)–(4), the gerund form *being* has become optional. Thus we can distinguish between a (recessive) plus variant containing an explicit marker of the predicative function and the equivalent (progressive) zero variant.

The present paper deals exclusively with *far from*, where, unlike *close to* and *beyond*, the rivalry between the more or less explicit variants can be traced as far back as the middle of the 17th century. In fact, in some of its uses, the *being* variant has been largely phased out by now. While we realize that the metaphorically used *far from* has evolved a number of further syntactic uses (De Smet, 2012), we will – with the exception of type D mentioned in (11), (20) and Tables 1 and 17 below – confine ourselves to those corresponding to gerundial *being* as in (3) and (4). Of course, this rules out the literal physical reading of Example 4b and cases such as (5a), which do not correspond to paraphrases like (5b).[1]

(5) a. He was still far from Ø an explanation as to why this was the case.
b. *He was still far from being an explanation as to why this was the case.

Even within these limits, we find a bewildering array of phenomena and widely differing affinities for predicative marking by means of *being*. This makes it necessary to establish a number of distinctive syntactic categories. To begin with, this paper distinguishes three types of predicative expressions: adjective phrases (AdjPs [including participles]) as in (3) and (6), noun phrases (NPs) as in (4) and (7) and prepositional phrases (PPs) as in (8).

1. There is a further range of expressions modified by *far from* that have been excluded from consideration. Among them are the following:

a) attributive adjectives
b) manner adverbs
c) *far from* associated with other finite and non-finite verb forms
d) *far from* associated with *having been* rather than *being*
e) postnominal adjectives or NPs
f) object predicatives
g) conjunction-headed subjectless and verbless clauses introduced by *(al)though, while, whether* and *if.*

All of these uses are relatively infrequent. While the first four altogether lack an alternative including *being* (cases a–c) or a semantically equivalent zero variant (case d), the *being* variant is rarely met with in cases e–g.

(6) a. She was far from (being) calm. (+ AdjP)
b. She was far from (being) inarticulate.
c. She was far from (being) annoyed.

(7) a. He was far from (being) a loner. (+ NP)
b. He is far from (being) the youngest English midfielder.

(8) I was far from (being) at ease. (+ PP)

With adjectives representing the prototypical predicative category, we will find that *being* is dispensed with more commonly than with NPs and PPs.

Furthermore, apart from evolutionary changes in the direction of the zero variant, we recognise several types of constraint that may potentially influence the rivalry between the two variants:

a. text types and stylistic levels (see Sections 2 and 3)
b. sociolinguistic factors including regional differences (see Section 4)
c. two types of complexity constraints including prior context and frequency of occurrence on the one hand (see Section 3.1) and system-internal complexity on the other (see Sections 3.2 and 4.2)

As regards (a) and (b), we will focus on the contrast between the *Oxford English Dictionary* (= OED) and fiction databases as well as differences between British English (= BrE) and American English (= AmE). As to system-internal complexity in (c), we will be mostly concerned with morphological and syntactic contrasts with adjectives and NPs, respectively. Here, our analyses are inspired by the Complexity Principle, which runs as follows:

In the case of more or less explicit grammatical options, the more explicit one(s) will tend to be favoured in cognitively more complex environments (see e.g. Rohdenburg, 1996, 2016; Schlüter, 2005; Vosberg, 2006; Mondorf, 2009; Berlage, 2014).

Specifically, we hypothesize that the ratio of explicit predicative marking by means of *being* may be correlated with the presumed morphological and syntactic complexity of the predicative item. In other words, we expect adjectives like *inarticulate* and NPs like *the youngest English midfielder* as in (6b) and (7b) to help retain *being* more frequently than items like *calm* or *a loner* as in (6a) and (7a).

A further locus of categorization concerns *far from* itself and its clausal integration. Here, we will focus on the following three cases. Type A, illustrated by Examples 3, 4 and 6–8, clearly represents the most prominent type. In these cases, *far from* occurs within a finite copula clause featuring its own subject.[2] In the other

2. Although they are not very common, corresponding constructions featuring other copular verbs (*appear, become, feel, look, prove, remain, seem* and *sound*) have also been assigned to this category. In addition, examples involving an ellipted form of the verb *be* in a second conjunct as in Example i, where the first conjunct contains the combination of subject + copular verb + predicative item, have also been included in type A.

(i) In disposition he was sociable, and far from being proud; … (NCF, 1848)

two types represented by (9) and (10), *far from* + associated phrase is not integrated in this way. Rather, the sequence functions as an adverbial modifying a (typically finite) clause with its own subject.

(9) Type B: Far from (being) satisfied with this reply, she began to make her own inquiries.

(10) Type C: The Head Master, far from (being) happy with the decision, decided to implement it after all.

In B, illustrated by (9), the modified clause follows the *far from* phrase, and in C, exemplified by (10), subject and (finite) verb of the modified clause enclose the *far from* structure. In both B and C, the implicit subject of the gerund or its truncated counterpart is only made explicit in a separate clause. This is why, according to the Complexity Principle, we would predict that examples of types B and C should be harder to process than those of type A. Indeed, types B and C have as yet hardly begun to drop the predicative marker *being* (see Tables 4, 13–16).

In addition, we also find gerunds possessing their own notional subjects as in (11), which makes the gerund form an obligatory feature.

(11) Type D: Far from it(s) being improbable, it is virtually certain.

Strictly speaking, therefore, the analysis of type D would be beyond the scope of the present paper. We only include the type in order to point out in Section 4.2 a striking contrast between BrE and AmE. An overview of the cross-classification of the four types of clause structures and three types of predicative expressions adopted here is given in Table 1.

Table 1. Overview of clause types and types of predicative phrases

	adjective phrase	**noun phrase**	**prepositional phrase**
Type A (explicit copula)	Peter was far from (being) happy.	… the best referee.	… at ease.
Type B	Far from (being) happy, Peter went home.	… the best referee, …	… at ease, …
Type C	Peter, far from (being) happy, went home.	… the best referee, …	… at ease, …
Type D	Far from Peter/Peter's/ him/his being happy, …	… the best referee …	… at ease, …

The following are some remarks on the methodology of the corpus analyses conducted. The evidence presented in this paper is drawn from the quotations in the OED, the *British National Corpus* (= BNC), the historical fictional database provided by Chadwyck-Healey as well as the Gutenberg Project and a large number of full-text British and American newspapers from the 1990s and early 2000s (see the bibliography for further details). Unfortunately, concerning the publication dates of the historical narratives used and their authors' years of birth, our knowledge is far from complete. With several corpora, we often lack the relevant publication dates while with others the authors' years of birth may not always be available to us. Here, our policy has usually been to give preference to the authors' years of birth. Thus, the asterisk may be used to indicate an unacceptable structure or the year(s) of birth of the author(s) in question. In the case of conjoined items in the predicative phrase dependent on *far from*, it is the first conjunct that is taken to determine the categorical status of the phrase in question. We have attempted to back up most theoretical pronouncements by statistically significant analyses based on the chi square test. Accordingly, the datasets have been selected – in terms of size and text type – to suit the purpose in question as far as possible. However, explicit mention of the significance levels in question will usually be made only for a few tables containing what might appear to be doubtful cases.

The rest of this paper is organized as follows: Section 2.1 compares the evolution of type A involving adjectives in a series of fictional corpora and the OED between the 17th century and the 1990s. Section 2.2 presents further historical data concerning the remaining categories. Section 3 explores some of the complexity constraints affecting type A adjectives and NPs. Sections 4.1 and 4.2 document some important contrasts between BrE and AmE from both a diachronic and synchronic perspective. Finally, the conclusion in Section 5 provides a summary of the major findings made in this paper.

2. Historical developments

2.1 Clausal type A involving adjectives in the narrative database and the OED

Based on Tables 2 and 3, Figure 1 charts the evolutionary pathways of the rivalling variants with adjectives involving type A structures for two kinds of databases, a series of British narrative corpora and the quotations in the OED. What is most striking about the fiction data is the dramatic decline of the *being* variant between the early and mid-18th century and later periods. By contrast, the corresponding decline in the OED quotations is less abrupt and more evenly spaced out. Significantly, this observation is in line with several others made in earlier work (Rohdenburg, 2013). One possible explanation for this divergence is the fact that the OED quotations of any Modern English period have been contributed by a very much larger and – in terms of genres – far less homogeneous set of authors than that of contemporary fictional sources.

Table 2. The incidence of type A adjectives including (those derived from) past participles in a series of historical narrative databases of BrE*

	being	Ø	total	% *being*
EEPF (1606–1693)	40	2	42	95.2%
ECF1 (*1660–1697 = 1705–1756)	115	9	124	92.7%
ECF2 (*1703–1752 = 1749–1780)	95	14	109	87.2%
NCF1 (*1740–1759 = 1782–1814)	12	39	51	23.5%
NCF1 (*1760–1799 = 1790–1837)	22	42	64	34.4%
NCF2 (*1800–1829 = 1826–1891)	55	117	172	32.0%
MNC/B (*1800–1829)	25	75	100	25.0%
NCF2 (*1830–1869 = 1858–1903)	11	58	69	15.9%
LNC/B (*1830–1869)	25	101	126	19.8%
ETC/B (*1870–1894)	7	23	30	23.3%
wridom1(1960–1993)	6	146	152	3.9%

* Here and in Table 10, the date ranges following the equal sign specify the publication dates.

Table 3. The incidence of type A adjectives including (those derived from) past participles in the quotations of the OED

	being	Ø	total	% *being*
1650–1699	8	3	11	72.3%
1700–1749	7	3	10	70.0%
1750–1799	9	6	15	60.0%
1800–1849	6	7	13	46.2%
1850–1899	9	25	34	26.5%
1900–1949	6	15	21	28.6%
1950–1988	9	19	28	32.1%

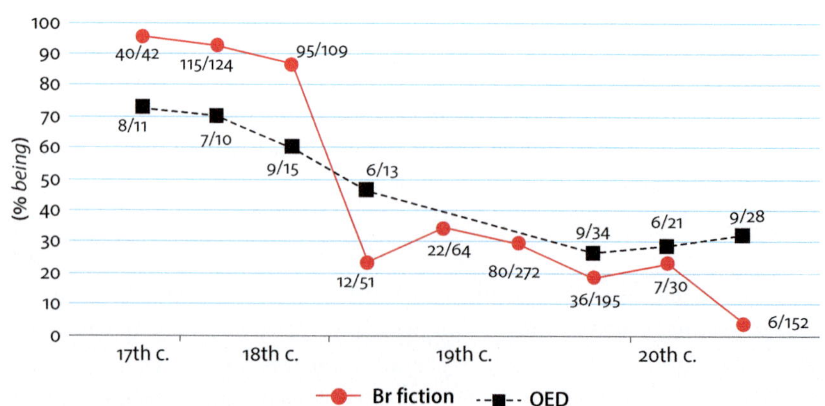

Figure 1. Comparing the evolutionary pathways of type A adjectives in British narrative fiction and the OED quotations

2.2 Other environments

On the basis of the OED quotations between 1650 and 1988, Table 4 adds up the relevant occurrences for all of the types introduced in Section 1. The data suggest two things:

- In addition to explicit predicative adjectives of type A, it is type A NPs where the (older and more explicit) *being* variant has lost some ground.
- Elsewhere, the *being* variant does not seem to have declined at all.

Table 4. The incidence of three kinds of predicative slot fillers in the clausal types A, B, C and D in the OED quotations between 1650 and 1988

type		*being*	Ø	total	*being* (%)
A	1 adjectives	54	78	132	40.9%
	2 NPs	35	8	43	81.4%
	3 PPs	7	–	7	100%
B	4 adj + NPs	16	–	16	100%
C	5 adj + NPs + PPs	17	–	17	100%
D	6 adj + NPs	5	–	5	100%

In view of these findings, we will usually concentrate in this paper on documenting type A examples featuring adjectives and NPs. It is only in contrastive analyses involving present-day British and American newspapers that other clause types may also be taken into consideration.

3. Complexity constraints

In Section 3.1, we will briefly touch on two aspects of cognitive accessibility before moving on in Section 3.2 to a central morphological constraint. Section 3.2 documents the role played by different morphological types of adjectives in influencing the distribution of the two variants in question. Subsequently, in Section 3.3, we present three syntactic constraints involving type A adjectives and NPs.

3.1 Cognitive accessibility

In an earlier paper by Rohdenburg & Schlüter (2000: 452, 454–456), it was observed that the tendency to omit *being* in the novels by Daniel Defoe is particularly striking in the case of previously mentioned or invoked items. A typical environment for the use of zero is illustrated in Example 12:

(12) …, Are you willing I should go? No says she very affectionately, I am far from willing: … (ECF, 1719)

Admittedly, we cannot completely rule out the possibility that in (12) we are dealing with another constraint, the *horror aequi* Principle, which involves the cross-linguistic tendency to avoid the (near-)adjacency of (near-)homophonous grammatical items (like "being willing") (see e.g. Berlage, 2014: 218–230).

In addition, the cognitive accessibility of a given adjective may also be enhanced by its textual frequency. Consider, for instance, the analysis presented in Table 5, which compares the use of the *being* variant with high frequency past participles like *pleased* and *satisfied* and all others. The contrast is illustrated in Examples 13a–b and 14a–b.

(13) a. …; on the contrary, I am far from pleased with my own want of fortitude. (NCF, 1792)

b. But the incident was far from being closed. (LNC\B, *1859)

(14) a. Yet am I far from satisfied with myself. (NCF, 1792)

b. …, her kindness towards him was so far from being exhausted, that … (NCF, 1793)

In Table 5, a distinction is drawn between the high frequency items *pleased* and *satisfied* on the one hand and the remaining ones on the other. Of the remaining items, only two, *ashamed* and *exhausted*, are found to occur twice. It is apparent that increased syllable length is not a significant factor accounting for the presence of *being*. However, the frequency contrast neatly explains the use of the two variants: While *pleased* and *satisfied* are typically associated with the zero variant, the remaining participles largely retain the *being* variant. At $p < 0.001$, the contrast is particularly clear in row 4, which collapses the data for all of the syllabic types in question.

Table 5. Comparing word length in terms of syllables in examples of type A with (adjectives derived from) past participles ending in *-ed/'d* in the NCF and LNC/B corpora (*1740–*1869)

		being	zero	total	% *being*
1 mono- syllabic	*pleased*	–	5	5	0.0%
	remaining cases	5	2	7	71.4%
2 disyllabic		12	5	17	70.6%
3 trisyllabic and longer	*satisfied*	2	16	18	11.1%
	remaining cases	11	10	21	52.4%
4 total	*pleased + satisfied*	2	21	23	8.7%
	remaining cases	28	17	45	62.2%

3.2 The relevance of morphologically-based categories

Several observations had indicated to us that there are many cases where it is the morphological make-up of the adjective category rather than syllable length that influences the choice between the two variants. We noticed, for instance, that morphologically simple – though bisyllabic – items as in (15) promote the choice of the zero variant just like most other monomorphemic but monosyllabic items.

(15) able, barren, clever, cruel, evil, feeble, level, narrow, noble, sober, tender, quiet, simple

Moreover, the bimorphemic past participles in Table 5 above – whether monosyllabic as in (16) or more complex prosodically – generally behave the same as far as the retention of *being* is concerned.

(16) closed, cured, duped, grudged, grieved

It was decided, therefore, to subdivide the class of adjectives into two basic sets, morphologically complex and morphologically simple ones. The division follows the definition given in Huddleston & Pullum (2008: 1628): "A complex word is one that is analysable into a sequence of smaller units, while a word that is not so analysable is simple." The units recognized by Huddleston & Pullum include free and bound bases, affixes and combining forms.

Within the category of complex items, a further distinction was drawn between three subcategories hypothesized to generally represent ascending degrees of processing difficulty:

a. items ending in the suffix *-y* as in *easy* and *happy*
b. remaining adjectives not derived from past participles and
c. (adjectives derived from) past participles

These distinctions are motivated by earlier observations concerning suffixed adjectives. First, items ending in *-y* have been classed as constituting the most frequent and most easily processed type (Huddleston & Pullum, 2008: 1712; Mondorf, 2009: 128–131). Second, adjectives derived from past participles have been found to possess the following properties: (a) As a morphological type, they almost invariably disallow the use as synthetic comparatives (Mondorf, 2009), and (b) predicatively used past participles have always tended to trigger exceptionally high rates of intensifier marking (Rohdenburg, 2014, this volume). Since *far from* in the types of constructions under consideration generally functions as a downtoner (De Smet, 2012), we can expect it to display similar constraints to the two other manifestations of grading.

In line with the Complexity Principle (see Section 1), it was assumed that the degrees of processing difficulty should be largely reflected in the proportions of the more explicit *being* variant. The results of our explorations are presented in Figure 2, which specifies part of the historical data for the British narrative database on the one hand and the OED quotations on the other. The evidence in the narrative corpora essentially confirms our expectations: The percentage of the *being* variant is lowest for the simple adjectives and highest for the presumably most complex past participles. The remaining complex adjectives represent a transitional category. In addition, the items ending in the suffix *-y* are seen to parallel the behaviour of simple adjectives. In the OED, however, it is only the contrast between past participles and other adjectives that proves to be significant. Surprisingly, the simple items and the remaining complex ones minus the past participles display approximately the same percentage of the *being* variant.

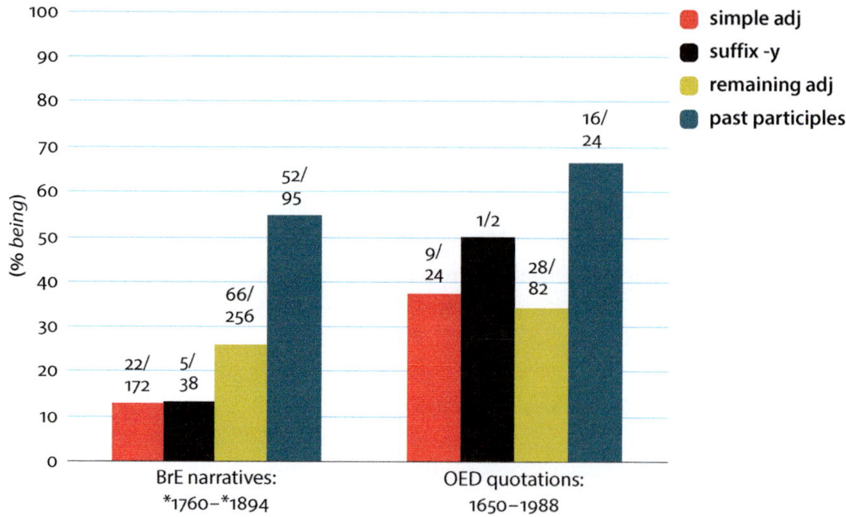

Figure 2. The effect of complexity contrasts on the choice of *being* after *far from* with type A adjectives

Intriguingly, however, the contrast between the narrative corpora and the OED coincides with another contrast between the two types of databases. This is shown in Table 6: While the share of simple adjectives is comparatively high in the narratives (30.7%), it is very much lower in the OED data (18.2%).[3]

3. In this respect, the situation in the narrative corpora is paralleled by that in the British *Early Prose Drama* (EPD) corpus (not detailed here).

Table 6. Comparing the proportions of *being* with the (absolute) proportions of simple and complex adjectives in historical databases of BrE

	proportion of *being* within the total of *being* + zero variants	**proportion of (simple and complex) examples within the total of adjectives**
1 BrE narratives *1760–1894		
a. simple adjectives	12.8%	30.7%
b. complex adjectives	31.6%	69.3%
2 OED 1650–1988		
a. simple adjectives	37.5%	18.2%
b. complex adjectives	41.7%	81.8%

3.3 Syntactic constraints in the language of present-day British newspapers

So far, syntactic constraints involving type A adjectives and NPs have only been discovered in the large newspaper databases of the 1990s and early 2000s. In the present paper, we will have to confine ourselves to simply outlining three specific factors responsible for either delaying or speeding up the advance of the zero variant.

The first phenomenon concerns the modification of adjectival phrases. Here, we focus on equative comparatives as in (17a–b).

(17) a. … and, as far as his jaw is concerned, it is far from being as delicate as Murray makes out. (t96)

b. Ipswich were far from as negative as on their last visit, … (t93)

Examples like (17a)–(17b) may be hypothesized to be much more complex to process than the usual run of unmodified adjectives. As shown in Table 7, the equative type substantially delays the decline of the *being* variant.

Table 7. Comparing equative comparatives involving type A adjectives (*as* adj *as* NP/S) with all other adjectival uses in British newspapers from the early 1990s*

	being	Ø	total	% *being*
1 equative comparatives	14	4	18	77.8%
2 other adjectival uses	22	355	377	5.8%

* Database for 1: t90–00, g90–00, d91–00, i93–94, m93–00
Database for 2: first quarters of t90, g90, d91, i93

In the area of type A NPs, we have come across two specific kinds of environments that display the opposite behaviour. Here, it is the rarer and simpler type of structure that is especially attracted to the zero variant. In the first case, we compare *a/an*-initial NPs ending in the pro-form *one* as in (18a-b) with all others featuring a lexical head as in (18c), which may be assumed to be more complex.

(18) a. But the problem is far from being a new one, and … (g98)
b. The cheating scandal at Virginia is far from an isolated one. (g01)
c. … the village is far from being a heritage site. (t00)

In the second case, we are dealing with NPs beginning with the phrase *one of*. Here, we single out examples like (19a), where the anaphorically used pro-form *one* stands in for the preceding subject noun. The relationship is made explicit in Example (19b), a type that – with or without *being* – can be assumed to be extremely rare.

(19) a. …– the mood was far from one of hopelessness.
(d98) [anaphoric proform *one*]
b. The mood was far from a mood of hopelessness.

Examples like (19a) are compared with all remaining NPs beginning with *one of*, as, for instance, in (19c).

(19) c. This was far from being one of Brown's tactical triumphs.
(t96) [cataphoric *one*]

Examples like (19c), which contain cataphorically used pro-forms, may be hypothesized to be more complex than those of type (19a). Moreover, the contrast is further sharpened by the fact that the NPs following *one of* in type (19a) typically consist of only one word. In both cases, the arguably less complex types represented by (18a–b) and (19a) have indeed been found to significantly speed up the advance of the zero variant. Consider the evidence in Tables 8 and 9.

Table 8. Comparing *a*/*an*-initial and *one*-final NPs of type A with all other *a*/*an*-initial NPs in selected British newspapers from the 1990s and early 2000s*

	being	Ø	total	% *being*
1 *a*/*an* … *one* (anaphoric use)	6	32	38	15.8%
2 *a*/*an* … lexical head	212	292	504	42.1%

* Database used for 1: t90–04, g90–05, d91–00, d02, d04–05, i93–94, i02–05, m93–00
Database used for 2: t90–91, g90–91, d91–92, m93–95, t04 (first two quarters), g05 (first two quarters), d05, i05

Table 9. Comparing type A NPs of the type *one of hopelessness* with all others beginning with *one of* in British newspapers from the 1990s and early 2000s (t90–04, g90–05, d91–00, d02, d04–05, i93–94, i02–05, m93–00)*

	being	Ø	total	% *being*
1 the type *one of hopelessness* (anaphoric use)	1 (3)	9 (1.6)	10 (1.7)	10.0%
2 all other NPs (cataphoric use)	20 (4.9)	10 (5)	30 (4.5)	66.7%

* The bracketed figures specify the average number of words following *one of*.

4. Comparing British and American English

This brings us to a comparison of contrasts and similarities between BrE and AmE. We will begin by comparing the general trajectories of change in the domain of type A adjectives in Section 4.1. In Section 4.2, we will explore present-day regional contrasts whose investigation was initiated in a pilot study by Rohdenburg & Schlüter (2009: 405–406).

4.1 Historical contrasts: The lag and overtake scenario

We turn now to a consideration of Figure 3, which is based on the data in Table 10 as well as Table 2 in Section 2.1. Assuming that in the 17th and early 18th centuries BrE and AmE displayed fairly similar proportions of the *being* variant, its subsequent decline must have been far less abrupt in AmE than BrE. Interestingly, closer analysis (not detailed here) has shown that the delayed decline of the *being* variant in AmE is paralleled by a similarly delayed decline of the textual frequency of the two variants. Comparing the authors born between 1760 and 1829, we find that AmE lags behind BrE concerning the adoption of the zero variant. However, AmE equals the British ratios by the middle and end of the 19th century and begins to overtake BrE in the following period between the 1890s and the 1920s ($p < 0.10$). Thus the evolutionary pathways of the *being* variant in the two regional varieties illustrate the so-called lag and overtake scenario introduced by Hundt (2009). In present-day English, the proportions of the *being* variant in both BrE and AmE are close to zero, with AmE retaining a slight advance over BrE in terms of the zero variant (see further Section 4.2: Tables 13–14).

How does AmE fare concerning the contrasts between the four morphological categories distinguished in British narrative fiction? Compare the presentation of the data in Figure 4, which, for the sake of convenience, repeats the information contained in Figure 2. First of all, we note again that, overall, there is a big difference in narrative fiction between BrE and AmE in the periods under comparison ranging

Table 10. The incidence of type A adjectives including (those derived from) past participles in a series of historical narrative databases of AmE

	being	Ø	total	% *being*
EAF1 (*1760–1799 = 1789–1850)	120	110	230	52.2%
EAF2 (*1800–1829 = 1828–1850)	77	67	144	53.5%
MNC/A (*1800–1829)	19	21	40	47.5%
LNC/A (*1830–1869)	34	119	153	22.2%
ETC/A (*1870–1894)	9	65	74	12.2%

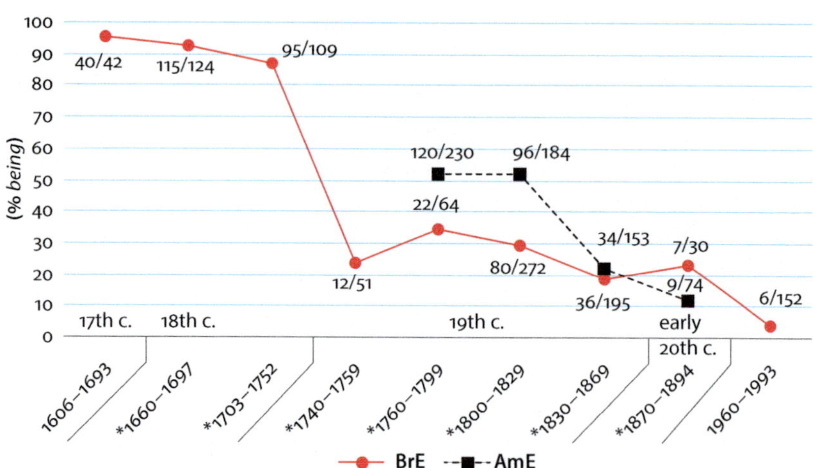

Figure 3. Comparing the evolutionary pathways of type A adjectives in British and American narrative fiction

from the 1790s to the 1920s. In parallel with the OED data, the contrast between simple and complex items in AmE is relatively weak and mainly due to the striking retention of *being* with past participles (see Table 11). Moreover, as in the case of the OED, the remaining complex cases show almost the same behaviour as simple ones in AmE (see Figure 4).

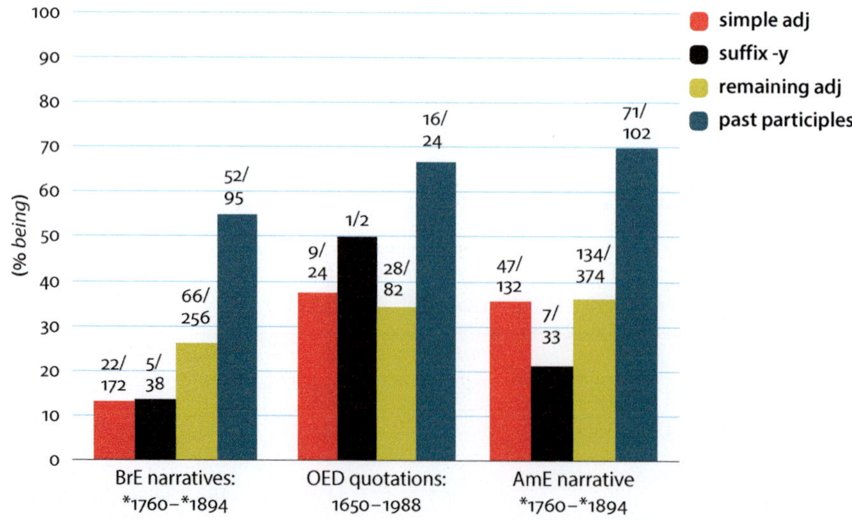

Figure 4. The effect of complexity contrasts on the choice of *being* after *far from* with type A adjectives

Thus, the greatest contrast between British and American narratives is found in the area of simple adjectives. Here, too, we note that both findings correlate with a relatively low overall percentage of simple adjectives in AmE (30.7% in BrE, 20.6% in AmE, see Table 11). It is as though the low share of simple adjectives aligns them to the very much larger category of complex adjectives.

Table 11. Comparing the proportions of *being* with the (absolute) proportions of simple and complex adjectives in historical databases of BrE and AmE

	proportion of *being* within the total of *being* + zero variants	**proportion of (simple and complex) examples within the total of adjectives**
1 BrE narratives *1760–1894		
a) simple adjectives	12.8%	30.7%
b) complex adjectives	31.6%	69.3%
2 OED 1650–1988		
a) simple adjectives	37.5%	18.2%
b) complex adjectives	41.7%	81.8%
3 AmE narratives *1760–1894		
a) simple adjectives	35.6%	20.6%
b) complex adjectives	41.7%	79.4%

We have seen, then, that, in the case of type A adjectives, the trend towards the zero variant must have been slowed down in AmE during the 18th century and part of the 19th century.

As far as NPs in type A are concerned, it is only the most common use beginning with *a/an* that provides a statistically sufficient database for a similar comparison. The evidence in Table 12, whose figures are significant at $p < 0.05$, shows that the results of the earlier analysis involving adjectives are essentially paralleled by that dealing with *a/an*-initial NPs. However, there are two differences between the two: (a) Unlike adjectives, the regional contrast is not particularly strong with *a/an*-initial NPs and (b) closer analysis of *a/an*-initial NPs (not detailed here) suggests that the American overtake phase does not appear to have been reached before the early 1900s.

Table 12. Comparing BrE and AmE in a series of fictional databases (authors born between 1740 and 1894) with respect to clausal type A involving *a/an*-initial NPs

	being	Ø	total	% *being*
BrE	35	19	54	64.8%
AmE	65	16	81	80.2%

4.2 Some remaining contrasts: The present-day situation as reflected in large collections of British and American newspapers

Comparing the behaviour of adjectives in British and American papers from the early 1990s, we can make two observations on the basis of Tables 13 and 14: As regards type A, the use of *being* in both regional varieties is close to zero, with BrE retaining a slightly higher ratio of the more explicit variant (at $p < 0.05$). Also, in both regional varieties, past participles are clearly more strongly attached to the *being* variant than all others. While the contrast, at $p < 0.001$, is extremely significant in the American data, it is not significant in BrE ($p < 0.10$). Concerning the more complex type B, AmE is found to use the zero variant in roughly a quarter of all examples, whereas BrE still uses the *being* variant in all cases. However, with type C, there is no statistically significant contrast between the two regional varieties.

Table 13. Comparing three clausal types involving adjectives in British newspapers from the early 1990s (first quarters of t90, g90, d91, i93)*

	being	Ø	total	% *being*
1 type A	22 (14/8)	355 (283/72)	377 (297/80)	5.8% (4.7%/10%)
2 type B	64 (32/32)	–	64 (32/32)	100%
3 type C	16 (10/6)	3 (2/1)	19 (12/7)	84.2% (83.3/85.7%)

* The bracketed figures distinguish between ordinary adjectives and (those derived from) past participles.

Table 14. Comparing three clausal types involving adjectives in American periodicals from the early 1990s (W90, D92, L93, L92: A sample of 75 instances, TAL89–94)*

	being	Ø	total	% *being*
1 type A	25 (9/16)	746 (601/145)	771 (610/161)	3.2% (1.5%/9.9%)
2 type B	46 (22/24)	16 (10/6)	62 (32/30)	74.2% (68.8%/80%)
3 type C	16 (10/6)	–	16 (12/7)	100% (83.3%/85.7%)

* The bracketed figures distinguish between ordinary adjectives and (those derived from) past participles.

A similar picture emerges in the area of *a/an*-initial NPs in Tables 15 and 16. While BrE retains the *being* variant in half of all relevant examples of type A, the corresponding share in AmE is down to a fifth of the total. And again, with type B, there is a clear-cut difference between the two varieties: BrE retains over 90% of the *being* variant, while in AmE the figure is down to 75%. In the corresponding data from the entire BNC (not detailed here), covering the period from the 1960s to 1993, the proportion of the *being* variant with *a/an*-initial NPs of type A amounts to 69.0% (N = 87). This suggests that even in BrE these uses have undergone considerable change in the late 20th century. Again, concerning type C, there is no statistically significant contrast between BrE and AmE. Moreover, it comes as a surprise to find that even in AmE, the proportion of the *being* variant tends to hover round the 100% mark. Future investigations will have to examine more closely to what extent this situation is due to an increased processing load produced by the overall sentence structure alone, the complexity of the slot fillers in question or a combination of both factors.

Table 15. Comparing three clausal types involving *a/an*-initial NPs in British newspapers from the early 1990s (t90–91, g90–91, d91–92 m93–95)

	being	Ø	total	% *being*
1 type A	163	164	327	49.8%
2 type B	221	16	237	93.2%
2 type C	80	5	85	94.1%

Table 16. Comparing three clausal types involving *a/an*-initial NPs in American newspapers from the early 1990s (W90, D92–95, L92)

	being	Ø	total	% *being*
1 type A	46	181	227	20.3%
2 type B	64	21	85	75.3%
3 type C	15	–	15	100.0%

Finally, this brings us to type D as in Examples (11) and (20).

(20) ... a footnote revealed that far from the Aristotle File being the work of Soren Berdichev, ..., it had in fact been compiled and authored by the boy himself. (wridom1, file g04)

Clearly, such cases do not allow the gerund form *being* to be omitted. In present-day English, type D is, however, extremely interesting from the contrastive perspective. Consider the evidence in Table 17.

Table 17. The incidence of type D, involving a notional subject of the gerund form *being*, in British and American newspapers from the early 1990s and the early 2000s

	number of examples	word count	frequency per million words
1 BrE early 1990s (t90–95, g90–95, d91–95, i93–94, m93–00)	222	711,595,976	0.312
2 BrE early 2000s (t01–04, g01–05, i02–05, d02, d04–05)	211	788,883,762	0.267
3 AmE early 1990s (D92–95, W90–92, L92–99, N01)	3	844,534,633	0.004

While the type is reasonably common in BrE, it is virtually absent in AmE. However, comparing the incidence of type D from the early 1990s with that from the early 2000s we notice that BrE has been moving in the direction of AmE by reducing slightly its frequency of occurrence. Evidently, examples like 20 have corresponding uses with gerunds of many other verbs, and informal observations suggest that similar contrasts exist between the two regional varieties with respect to larger or even unrestricted sets of verbs.

5. Conclusion

In conclusion, we have surveyed the evolution of a neglected phenomenon where a more explicit variant is, over time, replaced by a simpler one. In English, this is a general type of change, which is familiar from a number of parallel developments resulting in the increasing omission of various function words. Some well-known processes of a similar kind have affected the following items:

- the infinitive marker following *help* (see e.g. Berlage, 2014)
- the complementizer *that*
- relative clause markers
- reflexive pronouns.

As in the case of *far from*, most of these changes have for some time been spearheaded by AmE. We have shown, however, that during the 18th and much of the 19th century the advance of the zero variant in AmE was trailing behind that of BrE. This means that, properly speaking, we are dealing with a typical lag and overtake phenomenon. Regarding the specific environments favouring or disfavouring the changeover from the *being* variant to zero, we have focused on a number of morpho-syntactic complexity constraints. In particular, we have found that, in line with the Complexity Principle, more complex items and structures tend to delay the replacement of *being* by zero. Thus, there is an instructive parallel between intensifier marking (Rohdenburg, this volume) and comparative formation (Mondorf, 2009) on the one hand and the variable use of *being* in *far from* constructions on the other. With all three phenomena, and in contrast to simple adjectives, past participles have always displayed a striking affinity for the more explicit variants in question: the adverbial suffix *-ly*, the analytic comparative using *more* or the inclusion of *being*. In this connection, we have also noticed that – compared with British historical narratives – both the (predominantly British oriented) OED and American historical narratives share a diminished sensitivity to specific complexity contrasts. Beyond that, we have isolated – though far from explored in depth – two general factors facilitating the use of the zero variant with a given lexical item, namely high frequency and previous mention.

There are many avenues for further research opened up by the present paper. Above all, it is the vast area of NPs and prepositional phrases associated with *far from* which, so far, has not received the attention it deserves. In addition, the analysis of spatial adjectives and adverbs like *close to* and *beyond* (see Section 1), which have only in more recent times begun to replace the gerundial use of *being* by zero, could be expected to provide several rewarding research topics. Finally, the comparatively greater avoidance of simple adjectives characteristic of the American narratives and the OED quotations should be considered in more detail. Our preliminary hypothesis is that, in actual fact, both databases are only showing a relative aversion to a spectrum of more frequent and informal items.

References

Berlage, Eva (2014). *Noun Phrase Complexity in English*. Cambridge: Cambridge University Press. https://doi.org/10.1017/CBO9781139057684

Huddleston, Rodney, & Pullum, Geoffrey K. (2008). *The Cambridge Grammar of the English Language*. Cambridge: Cambridge University Press.

Hundt, Marianne (2009). Colonial lag, colonial innovation or simply language change. In Günter Rohdenburg, & Julia Schlüter (Eds.), *One Language, Two Grammars? Differences between British and American English* (13–37). Cambridge: Cambridge University Press. https://doi.org/10.1017/CBO9780511551970.002

Mondorf, Britta (2009). *More Support for More-Support: The Role of Processing Constraints on the Choice between Synthetic and Analytic Comparative Forms*. Amsterdam & Philadelphia: John Benjamins. https://doi.org/10.1075/silv.4

Rohdenburg, Günter (1996). Cognitive complexity and increased grammatical explicitness in English. *Cognitive Lingustics* 7, 149–182. https://doi.org/10.1515/cogl.1996.7.2.149

Rohdenburg, Günter (2013). Using the OED quotations database as a diachronic corpus. In Manfred Krug, & Julia Schlüter (Eds.), *Research Methods in Language Variation and Change* (136–157). Cambridge: Cambridge University Press. https://doi.org/10.1017/CBO9780511792519.010

Rohdenburg, Günter (2014). Syntactic constraints on the use of dual form intensifiers in Modern English. In Kristin Davidse, Caroline Gentens, Lobke Ghesquiere, & Lieven Vandelanotte (Eds.), *Corpus Interrogation and Grammatical Patterns* (131–149). Amsterdam/New York: John Benjamins.

Rohdenburg. Günter (2016). Testing two processing principles with respect to the extraction of elements out of complement clauses. *English Language and Linguistics*, 463–486.

Rohdenburg, Günter (2019). Further explorations in the grammar of intensifier marking in Modern English. In Claudia Claridge & Birte Bös (Eds.), *Developments in English Historical Morpho-Syntax* (269-285). Amsterdam/Philadelphia: John Benjamins.

Rohdenburg, Günter, & Schlüter, Julia (2000). Determinanten grammatischer Variation im Früh- und Spätneuenglischen. *Sprachwissenschaft* 4(25), 443–496.

Rohdenburg, Günter, & Schlüter, Julia (2009). New departures. In Günter Rohdenburg & Julia Schlüter (Eds.), *One Language, Two Grammars? Differences between British and American English* (364–423). Cambridge: Cambridge University Press. https://doi.org/10.1017/CBO9780511551970.020

Schlüter, Julia (2005). *Rhythmic Grammar: The Influence of Rhythm on Grammatical Variation and Change in English*. Berlin & New York: Mouton de Gruyter. https://doi.org/10.1515/9783110219265

De Smet, Hendrik (2012). The course of actualization. *Language* 88(3), 601–633. https://doi.org/10.1353/lan.2012.0056

Vosberg, Uwe (2006). *Die große Komplementverschiebung. Außersemantische Einflüsse auf die Entwicklung satzwertiger Ergänzungen im Neuenglischen*. Tübingen: Narr.

Electronic corpora

BNC	*British National Corpus* (1995). Version 1.0. BNC Consortium/Oxford University Computing Services. (100,000,000 words)
d91-00, 02, 04–05	*Daily Telegraph and Sunday Telegraph* on CD-ROM (1991–2000), (2002), (2004–5). Chadwyck-Healey/ProQuest. (478,837,273 words)
D92-95	*Detroit Free Press* on CD-ROM (1992–1995). Knight Ridder Information Inc. (102,989,512 words)
EAF	*Early American Fiction* (2000). Chadwyck-Healey. (34,634,666 words)
EAF1	First part of EAF containing only those authors born in the eighteenth century (*1744–*1799). (15,891,451 words)
EAF2	Second part of the EAF containing only those authors born in the nineteenth century (*1801–*1827). (18,743,215 words)
ECF	*Eighteenth-Century Fiction* (1996). Chadwyck-Healey. (9,702,696 words, omitting duplicates)
EEPF	*Early English Prose Fiction* (1997–2000). Chadwyck-Healey. In association with the Salzburg Centre for Research on the English Novel SCREEN. (9,562,865 words)
EPD	*English Prose Drama* (1996–1997). Chadwyck-Healey. (26,454,639 words)
ETC	*Early Twentieth Century Corpus* – a selection of British and American writings by authors born between 1870 and 1894. Source: Project Gutenberg. Compiled in the Research Project 'Determinants of Grammatical Variation in English', University of Paderborn (16,351,681 words)

ETC/A	American writings in the ETC. (11,550,273 words)
ETC/B	British writings in the ETC. (4,801,408 words)
g90-05	*Guardian* (including *The Observer* 1994–2005) on CD-ROM (1990–2005). Chadwyck-Healey/ProQuest. (645,817,821 words)
i93-94, 02–05	*Independent and Independent on Sunday* on CD-ROM (1993–94), (2002–5). ProQuest. (242,608,117 words)
L92-95	*Los Angeles Times* on CD-ROM (1992–5) Knight Ridder Information Inc. (320,016,164 words)
L96-99	*Los Angeles Times* (1996–9) (courtesy of The Los Angeles Times Editorial Library). (275,506,490 words)
LNC	*Late-Nineteenth-Century Corpus* – a selection of British and American writings (complementary to the EAF and NCF) by authors born between 1830 and 1869. Source: Project Gutenberg. Compiled in the Research Project 'Determinants of Grammatical Variation in English', University of Paderborn. (47,677,728 words)
LNC/A	American writings in the LNC. (26,859,926 words)
LNC/B	British writings in the LNC. (20,817,802 words)
m93-00	*Daily Mail and Mail on Sunday* on CD-ROM (1993–2000). Chadwyck-Healey. (206,762,410 words)
MNC	*Mid-Nineteenth-Century Corpus* – a selection of British and American writings (complementary to the EAF and the NCF) by authors born between 1803 and 1829. Source: Project Gutenberg. Compiled in the Research Project 'Determinants of Grammatical Variation in English', University of Paderborn. (17,347,730 words)
MNC/A	American writings in the MNC. (7,264,854 words)
MNC/B	British writings in the MNC. (10,082,876 words)
N01	*New York Times* on CD-ROM (2001). ProQuest. (52,132,979 words)
NCF	*Nineteenth-Century Fiction* (1999-2000). Chadwyck-Healey. (37,589,837 words)
NCF1	First part of the NCF containing only those authors born in the eighteenth century (*1728–*1799). (11,373,834 words)
NCF2	Second part of the NCF containing only those authors born in the nineteenth century (*1800–*1869). (26,041,862 words)
OED	*The Oxford English Dictionary* (Second Edition) on CD-ROM (1992) (Version 1.10). Edited by John A. Simpson and Edmund S. C. Weiner. Oxford: Oxford University Press.
t90-04	*The Times and The Sunday Times* on CD-ROM (1990–2004). Chadwyck-Healey/ProQuest. (729,848,339 words)
TAL89-94	*Time Magazine* on CD-ROM (1989–1994). (12,123,886 words)
W90-92	*Washington Times* (including *Insight on the News* 1990–1992) on CD-ROM (1990–1992). Wayzata Technology. (93,889,488 words)
wridom1	imaginative component of the BNC (=narrative fiction). (18,863,529 words)

Index

W

Y